GENETIC ALGORITHMS IN APPLICATIONS

Edited by **Rustem Popa**

Genetic Algorithms in Applications
Edited by Rustem Popa

Published by InTech

Janeza Trdine 9, 51000 Rijeka, Croatia

Publishing Process Manager Marina Jozipovic

Technical Editor Teodora Smiljanic

Cover Designer InTech Design Team

Additional hard copies can be obtained from orders@intechopen.com

Genetic Algorithms in Applications, Edited by Rustem Popa
p. cm.
ISBN 978-953-51-0400-1

For EU product safety concerns:
IN TECH d.o.o., Prolaz Marije Krucifikse Kozulić 3, 51000 Rijeka, Croatia,
info@intechopen.com or visit our website at intechopen.com.

Meet the editor

Rustem Popa was born in Galati, Romania, in 1960. He received his masters degree from the Politehnica University, Bucharest, Romania, in 1984. In 1999, he obtained his PhD degree from the Dunarea de Jos University, Galati, Romania. He worked as a design engineer and then as a scientific researcher at the Research and Design Institute for Shipbuilding in Galati. Since 1990 he has been with the Dunarea de Jos University in Galaþi and, since 2002, he has been an associate professor at the Department of Electronics and Telecommunications. Dr Popa has more than 20 years' teaching experience in the area of digital electronics, medical electronics and soft computing. He is the author and co-author of four books and over 50 journal and conference papers. His research interests include computational intelligence, evolvable hardware, digital signal processing and medical electronics. He was editor-in-chief of the Annals of Dunarea de Jos University of Galati, fascicle III – ISSN 1221-454X in 2006 and 2007. He was also an IPC member and reviewer for many international conferences.

Contents

Preface

Genetic Algorithms (GAs) are global optimization techniques used in many real-life applications. They are one of several techniques in the family of Evolutionary Algorithms – algorithms that search for solutions to optimization problems by "evolving" better and better solutions.

A Genetic Algorithm starts with a population of possible solutions for the desired application. The best ones are selected to become parents and then, using genetic operators like crossover and mutation, offspring are generated. The new solutions are evaluated and added to the population and low-quality solutions are deleted from the population to make room for new solutions. The members of the population tend to get better with the increasing number of generations. When the algorithm is halted, the best member of the existing population is taken as the solution to the problem.

Genetic Algorithms have been applied in science, engineering, business and social sciences. A number of scientists have already solved many real-life problems using Genetic Algorithms. This book consists of 16 chapters organized in five sections.

The first section contains five chapters in the field of automatic control. Chapter 1 presents a laser tracking system for measuring a robot arm's tip with high accuracy using a GA to optimize the number of measurement points. Chapter 2 presents a model predictive controller that uses GAs for the optimization of cost function in a simulation example of industrial furnace control. Chapter 3 describes a design method to determine PID controller parameters using GAs. Finite-thrust trajectory optimization using a combination between Gauss Pseudospectral Method and a GA is proposed in Chapter 4. Chapter 5 describes the optimization of an above-knee prosthesis physical parameters using GAs.

The next section of the book deals with scheduling of resources and contains two chapters in this field. Chapter 6 analyzes the Unit Commitment Problem, that is the problem of selecting electrical power systems to be in service during a scheduling period and determining the length of that period. Chapter 7 deals with several typical applications of GAs to solving optimization problems arising from railway management information system design, transportation resources allocation and traffic control for railway operation.

The third section contains four chapters in the field of electrical and electronics engineering. Chapter 8 proposes a new VLSI architecture which is able to implement Memetic Algorithms (which can be viewed as the hybrid GAs) in hardware. Chapter 9 describes a distributed estimation technique that uses GA to optimize frequency and time division multiple access which is employed in several wireless sensor networks systems. Chapter 10 deals with the problem of direction of arrival estimation through a uniform circular array interferometer. GAs have been compared with other optimization tools and they have confirmed a more robust behavior when low computing power is available. The last chapter in this section, Chapter 11, presents the GA application in three functions commonly executed in power control centers: power flow, system restoration and unit commitment.

The fourth section of the book has three chapters that illustrate two applications of character recognition and a multi-criteria classification. Chapter 12 applies a GA for offline handwriting character recognition. Chapter 13 deals with writer identification by integrating GAs with several other known techniques from pattern recognition. Chapter 14 proposes an early diagnosis of Alzheimer's disease by combining a multi-criteria classification model with a GA engine, with better results than those offered by other existing methods.

Finally, the last section contains two chapters dealing with trading systems. Chapter 15 discusses the development of artificial trading systems for portfolio optimization using a multi-modular evolutionary heuristic capable of dealing efficiently with the zero investment strategy. Chapter 16 provides some insight into overfitting in the environment of trading in market and proposes a GA application for trading in market toward a stable profitable method.

These evolutionary techniques may be useful to engineers and scientists from various fields of specialization who need some optimization techniques in their work and who are using Genetic Algorithms for the first time in their applications. I hope that these applications will be useful to many other people who may be familiarizing themselves with the subject of Genetic Algorithms.

Rustem Popa
Department of Electronics and Telecommunications
"Dunarea de Jos" University of Galati
Romania

Part 1

GAs in Automatic Control

1

Selection of Optimal Measuring Points Using Genetic Algorithm in the Process to Calibrate Robot Kinematic Parameters

Seiji Aoyagi
Kansai University,
Japan

1. Introduction

At present state, almost the industrial robot tasks are performed by the teaching playback method, in which the robot repeats positioning its joint angles, which are taught manually in advance using a teaching pendant, etc. This method is based on comparatively high repeatability of a robot arm. The problem here is that the laborious and time-consuming online manual teaching is inevitable whenever the specification of the product is changed. It is desirable to teach the task easily and quickly to the robot manipulator when the production line and the production goods are changed.

Considering these circumstances, the offline teaching based on the high positioning accuracy of the robot arm is desired to take the place of the online manual teaching (Mooring et al., 1991). In the offline teaching, the joint angles to achieve the given Cartesian position of the arm's tip are calculated using a kinematic model of the robot arm. However, a nominal geometrically model according to a specification sheet does not include the errors arising in manufacturing or assembly. Moreover, it also does not include the non-geometric errors, such as gear transmission errors, gear backlashes, arm compliance, etc., which are difficult to geometrically consider in the kinematic model. Under this situation, the joint angles obtained based on the non-accurate nominal kinematic model cannot realize the desired arm's tip position satisfactorily, making the offline teaching unfeasible.

Therefore, some method of calibrating precisely the geometric and non-geometric parameters in a kinematic model is required, in which the three dimensional (3-D) absolute position referring to a world coordinate system should be measured (Mooring & Padavala, 1989; Whitney et al., 1986; Judd & Knasinski, 1990; Stone, 1987; Komai & Aoyagi, 2007). The parameters are obtained so as that the errors between the measured positions and the predicted positions based on the kinematic model are minimized by a computer calculation using a nonlinear least square method.

In this study, a laser tracking system was employed for measuring the 3-D position. This system can measure the 3-D position with high accuracy of several tens micrometer order (Koseki et al., 1998; Fujioka et al., 2001a; Fujioka et al., 2001b). As an arm to calibrate, an articulated robot with seven degrees of freedom (DOF) was employed. After the geometric parameters were calibrated, the residual errors caused by non-geometric parameters were further reduced by using neural networks (abbreviated to NN hereinafter), which is one of the originalities of this study.

Several researches have used NN for robot calibration. For example, it was used for interpolating the relationship between joint angles and their errors due to joint compliance (Jang et al., 2001). Two joints liable to suffer from gravitational torques were dealt with, and the interpolated relationships were finally incorporated into the forward kinematic model. So the role of NN was supplemental for modeling non-geometric errors. It is reported that the relationship between Cartesian coordinates and positioning errors arising there was interpolated using NN (Maekawa, 1995). Joint angles themselves in forward kinematic model, however, were not compensated, and experimental result was limited to a relative (not absolute) measurement using a calibration block in a rather narrow space. Compared with these researches, in the method proposed in this study, the joint angles in the forward kinematic model are precisely compensated using NN so that the robot accuracy would be fairly improved in a comparatively wide area in the robot work space. As instrumentation for non-contact absolute coordinate measurement in 3-D wide space, which is inevitable for calibration of the robot model and estimation of the robot accuracy, a laser tracking system is employed in this study.

To speed up the calibration process, the smaller number of measuring points is preferable, while maintaining the satisfactory accuracy. As for a parallel mechanism, methods of reducing the measurement cost were reported (Tanaka et al., 2005; Imoto et al., 2008; Daney et al., 2005). As one of the methods of selecting optimal measurement poses, the possibility of using genetic algorithm (GA) was introduced (Daney et al., 2005): however, it was still on the idea stage, i.e., it was not experimentally applied to a practical parallel mechanism. As for a serial type articulated robot, it was reported that the sensitivities of parameters affecting on the accuracy are desired to be averaged, i.e., not varied widely, for achieving the good accuracy (Borm & Menq, 1991; Ishii et al., 1988). As the index of showing the extent how the sensitivities are averaged, observability index (OI) was introduced in (Borm & Menq, 1991), and the relationship between OI and realized accuracy was experimentally investigated: however, a method of selecting optimal measurement points to maximize OI under the limitation of point number has not been investigated in detail, especially for an articulated type robot having more than 6-DOF. In this paper, optimal spatial selection of measuring points realizing the largest OI was investigated using GA, and it was practically applied to a 7-DOF robot, which is also the originality of this study.

2. Measurement apparatus featuring laser tracking system

2.1 Robot arm and position measurement system

An articulated robot with 7-DOF (Mitsubishi Heavy Industries, PA10) was employed as a calibration object. A laser tracking system (Leica Co. Ltd., SMART310) was used as a position measuring instrument. The outline of experimental setup using these apparatuses is shown in Fig. 1

The basic measuring principle of laser tracking system is based on that proposed by Lau (Lau, 1986). A laser beam is emitted and reflected by a tracking mirror, which is installed in the reference point and is rotated around two axes. Then, this beam is projected to a retroreflector called Cat's-eye, which is fixed at the robot arm's tip as a target (see Figs. 2 and 3). The Cat's-eye consists of two hemispheres of glasses, which have the same center and have different radiuses. A laser beam is reflected by the Cat's-eye and returns to the tracking mirror, following the same path as the incidence.

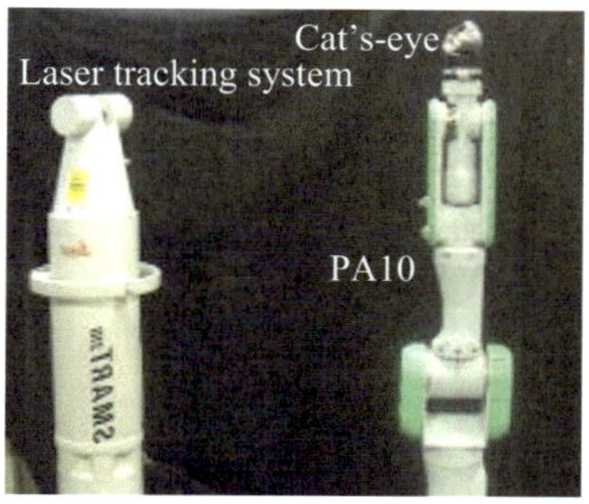

Fig. 1. Experimental setup for measuring position of robot arm's tip

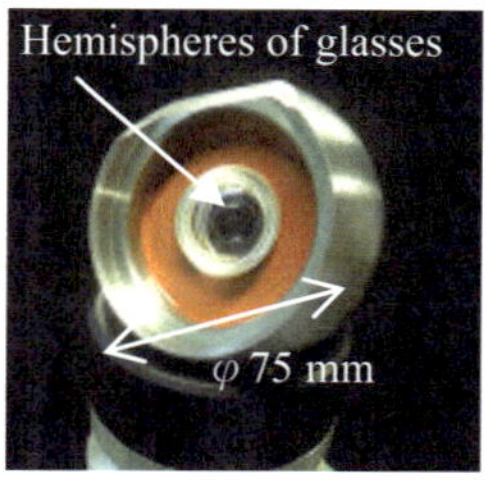

Fig. 2. Cat's-eye

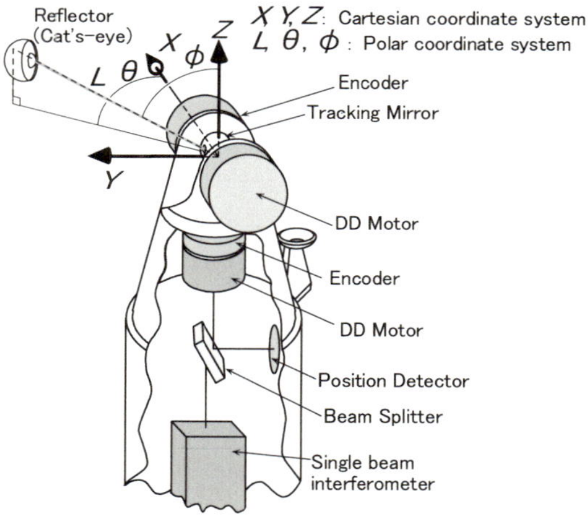

Fig. 3. Principle of measurement of SMART310

The horizontal and azimuth angle information of laser direction is obtained by optical encoders, which are attached to the two axes of the tracking mirror. The distance information of laser path is obtained by an interferometer. Using the measured angles and distance, the position of the center of Cat's-eye, i.e., the position of robot arm's tip, can be calculated with considerably high accuracy (the detail is explained in the following subsection).

2.2 Estimation of measuring performance

According to the specification sheet, the laser tracking system can measure 3-D coordinates with repeatability of ±5 ppm (μm/m) and accuracy of ±10 ppm (μm/m). In this subsection, these performances are experimentally checked.

First, Cat's-eye was fixed, and static position measurement was carried out to verify the repeatability of the laser tracking system. Figures 4, 5, and 6 show the results of transition of measured x, y, and z coordinate, respectively. Looking at these figures, it is proven that the repeatability is within ±4μm, which does not contradict the above-mentioned specification which the manufacturer claims.

Second, the known distance between two points was measured to verify the accuracy of the laser tracking system. Strictly speaking, the performance estimated here is not the accuracy, but is to be the equivalence. The scale bar, to both ends of which the Cat's-eye be fixed, was used as shown in Fig. 7. The distance between two ends is precisely guaranteed to be 800.20 mm. The positions of Cat's-eye fixed at both ends were measured by the laser tracking system, and the distance between two ends was calculated by using the measured data. The results are shown in Fig. 8. Concretely, the measurement was done for each end, and the difference between corresponding data in these ends was calculated off-line after the measurement. Looking at this figure, it is proven that the data are within the range of ±10 μm; however, the maximal absolute error from 800.2 mm is 25 μm, which is somewhat degraded compared with the specification. The error is supposedly due to some uncalibrated mechanical errors of the laser tracking system itself.

In the following sections, although the robot accuracy is improved by calibration process, the positioning error still be in sub-millimeter order, i.e., several hundreds micrometer order, at the least. Therefore, the used laser tracking system, whose error is several tens micrometer order at the most, is much effective for the application of robot calibration.

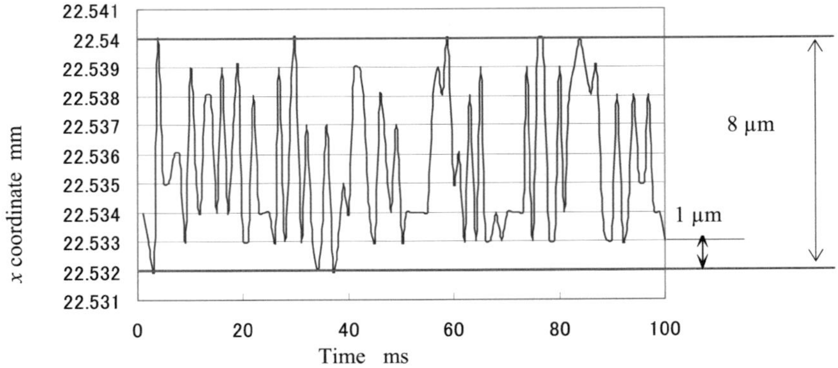

Fig. 4. Result of transition of x coordinate

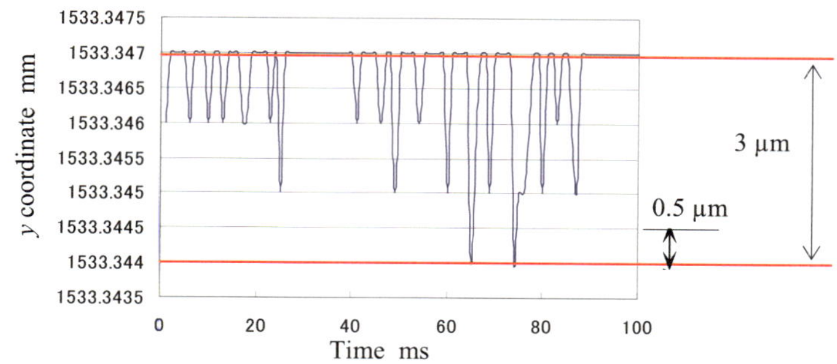

Fig. 5. Result of transition of *y* coordinate

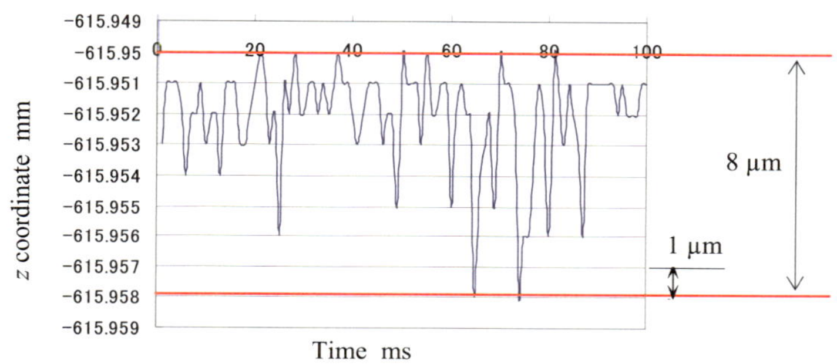

Fig. 6. Result of transition of *z* coordinate

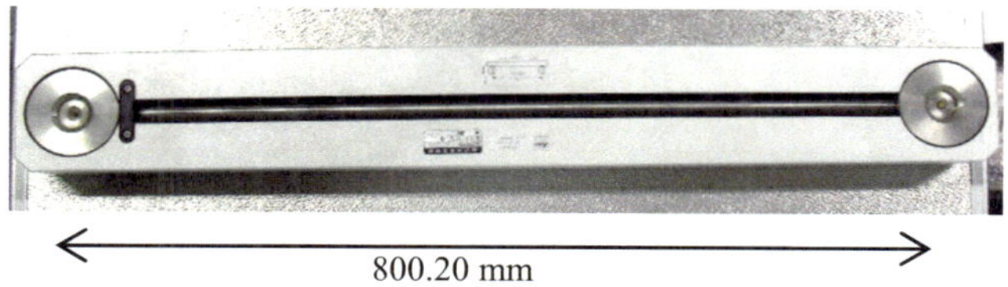

Fig. 7. Scale bar

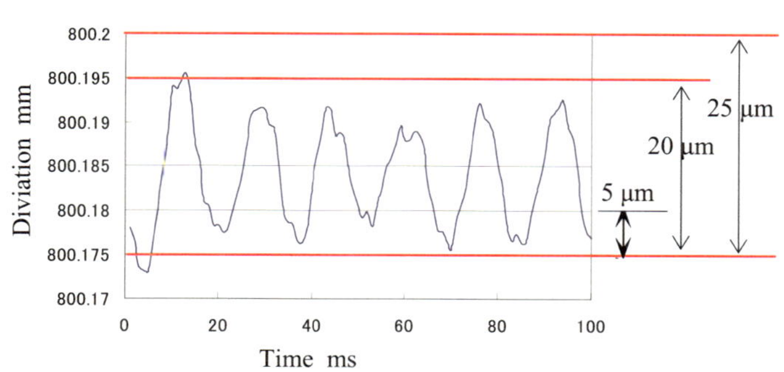

Fig. 8. Result of measurement of scale bar

3. Calibration of kinematic parameters

3.1 Kinematic model using DH parameter

In this research, the kinematic model of the robot is constructed by using Denabit-Hartenberg (DH) parameters (Denavit & Hartenberg, 1955). The schematic outline of the DH notation is shown in Fig. 9. In this modeling method, each axis is defined as Z axis and two common perpendiculars are drawn from Z_{i-1} to Z_i and from Z_i to Z_{i+1}, respectively. The distance and the angle between these two perpendiculars are defined as d_i and θ_i, respectively. The torsional angle between Z_i and Z_{i+1} around X_{i+1} is defined as α_i. The length of the perpendicular between Z_i and Z_{i+1} is defined as a_i. Using these four parameters, the rotational and translational relationship between adjacent two links is defined. The relationship between two adjacent links can be expressed by a homogeneous coordinate transformation matrix, the components of which include above-mentioned four parameters.

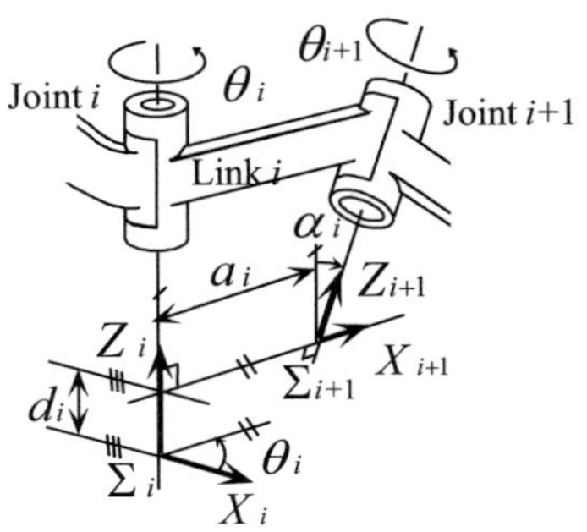

Fig. 9. DH notation

The nominal values of DH parameters of PA10 robot on the basis of its specification sheet are shown in Table I. The deviations between the calibrated values (see the next subsection) and the nominal ones are also shown in this table.

The kinematic model of the relationship between the measurement coordinate system (i.e., SMART310 coordinate system) and the 1st axis coordinate system of the robot is expressed by a homogeneous transformation matrix using 6 parameters (not 4 parameters of DH notation), which are 3 parameters of $\theta_r, \theta_p, \theta_y$ for expressing the rotation, and 3 parameters of x_0, y_0, z_0 for expressing the translation.

The kinematic model from the robot base coordinate system to the 7th joint coordinate system is calculated by the product of homogeneous coordinate transformation matrices, which includes 4×7 = 28 DH parameters.

As for the relationship between the 7th joint coordinate system and the center position of Cat's-eye, it can be expressed by using translational 3 parameters x_8, y_8, z_8.

Thus, as the result, the kinematic model of the robot is expressed by using 6+28+3 = 37 parameters in total, which is as follows:

$$\mathbf{P} = (x_0, y_0, z_0, \theta_r, \theta_p, \theta_y, a_1, d_1, \alpha_1, \theta_1, \cdots, a_7, d_7, \alpha_7, \theta_7, x_8, y_8, z_8)^T \quad (1)$$

Joint	θ [deg]		d [mm]		a [mm]		α [deg]	
	Nominal value	Deviation	Nominal value	Deviation	Nominal value	Deviation	Nominal value	Deviation
1	0.0	-0.44	315.0	1.24	0.0	-0.56	-90.0	0.10
2	0.0	0.04	0.0	0.39	0.0	0.34	90.0	-0.16
3	0.0	0.57	450.0	0.96	0.0	0.32	-90.0	0.01
4	0.0	-0.15	0.0	0.35	0.0	-0.14	90.0	-0.32
5	0.0	2.12	500.0	-0.33	0.0	-0.17	-90.0	-0.52
6	0.0	0.21	0.0	0.32	0.0	0.61	90.0	-0.17
7	0.0	-1.29	80.0	-0.82	0.0	1.02	0.0	-1.25

Table 1. DH Parameters of PA10 Robot

3.2 Nonlinear least square method for calibrating geometric parameters

The Cat's-eye is attached to the tip of PA10 robot, and it is positioned to various points by the robot, then the 3-D position of the robot arm's tip is measured by the laser tracking system. The parameters are obtained so that the errors between the measured positions and the predicted positions based on the kinematic model are minimized by a computer calculation.

The concrete procedure of calibration is described as follows (also see Fig. 10): Let the joint angles be $\mathbf{\Theta} = (\theta_1, \theta_2, \cdots, \theta_7)$, designated Cartesian 3-D position of robot arm's tip be $\mathbf{X}_r = (X_r, Y_r, Z_r)$, measured that be $\mathbf{X} = (X, Y, Z)$, nominal kinematic parameters based on DH notation be $\mathbf{P}_n$ (see (1)). Then, the nominal forward kinematic model based on the specification sheet is expressed as $\mathbf{X} = \mathbf{f}(\mathbf{\Theta}, \mathbf{P}_n)$.

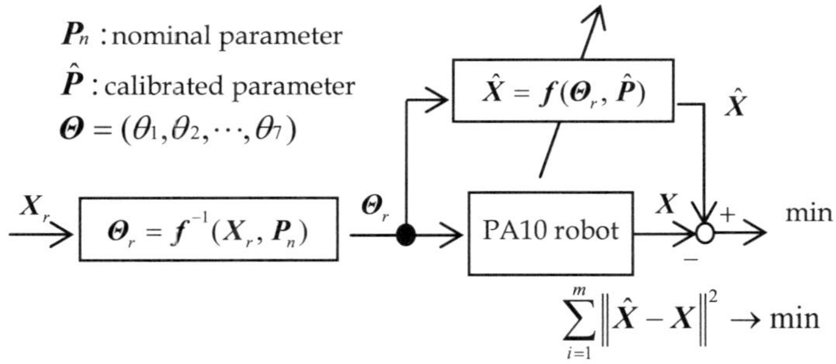

Fig. 10. Calibration procedure using nonlinear least square method

By using the nominal kinematic model, the joint angle $\mathbf{\Theta}_r$ to realize $\mathbf{X}_r$ are calculated, i.e., the inverse kinematic is solved, which is expressed in the mathematical form as $\mathbf{\Theta}_r = \mathbf{f}^{-1}(\mathbf{X}_r, \mathbf{P}_n)$.

The joint angles are positioned to $\mathbf{\Theta}_r$, then, the 3-D position of robot arm's tip is measured as $\mathbf{X}$. Let the calibrated parameters be $\hat{\mathbf{P}}$, and the predicted position based on the calibrated model be $\hat{\mathbf{X}}$, then the forward kinematic model using them is expressed as $\hat{\mathbf{X}} = \mathbf{f}(\mathbf{\Theta}_r, \hat{\mathbf{P}})$. The $\hat{\mathbf{P}}$ is obtained so that the sum of errors between the measured positions $\mathbf{X}$ and the predicted positions $\hat{\mathbf{X}}$ is minimized by using a nonlinear least square method.

3.3 Modeling of non-geometric errors (Method 1)

Referring to other researches (Whitney et al., 1986; Judd et al., 1990), the typical non-geometric errors of gear transmission errors and joint compliances are modeled herein, for the comparison with the method using NN proposed in this study, the detail of which is explained in the next subsection 3.4.

It is considered that the gear transmission error of θ^{gt} arises from the eccentricity of each reduction gear. This error is expressed by summation of sinusoidal curve with one period and that with n periods as follows:

$$\Delta\theta_i^{gt} = P_{i1}{}^{gt}\sin(\alpha_i + \phi_{i1}) + P_{i2}{}^{gt}\sin(n_i\alpha_i + \phi_{i2}), \tag{2}$$

where i is joint number ($1 \le i \le 7$), α_i is the joint angle detected by a rotary encoder sensor, n_i is the reduction ratio of the gear, $P_{i1}{}^{gt}, P_{i2}{}^{gt}, \phi_{i1}, \phi_{i2}$ are parameters to be calibrated.

As for the joint no. 2 and no. 4, which largely suffer from torques caused by arm weights, the joint angle errors of $\Delta\theta_2{}^{com}$ and $\Delta\theta_4{}^{com}$ due to joint compliances are expressed as follows:

$$\Delta\theta_2{}^{com} = P_1{}^{com}\sin\alpha_2 + P_2{}^{com}\sin(\alpha_2 + \alpha_4), \tag{3}$$

$$\Delta\theta_4{}^{com} = P_3{}^{com}\sin(\alpha_2 + \alpha_4), \tag{4}$$

where $P_1{}^{com}, P_2{}^{com}, P_3{}^{com}$ are parameters to be calibrated.

In the forward kinematic model, θ_i is dealt with as: $\theta_i = \alpha_i + \Delta\theta_i^{gt}$ $(i = 1, 3, 5, 6, 7)$, $\theta_i = \alpha_i + \Delta\theta_i^{gt} + \Delta\theta_i^{com}$ $(i = 2, 4)$. As the parameters, $P_{i1}{}^{gt}, P_{i2}{}^{gt}, \phi_{i1}, \phi_{i2}$ $(1 \le i \le 7)$, $P_1{}^{com}, P_2{}^{com}, P_3{}^{com}$ are added to $\boldsymbol{P}$ in (1), forming 68 parameters in total.

3.4 Using neural networks for compensating non-geometric errors (Method 2)

Non-geometric errors have severely nonlinear characteristics as shown in (2)-(4). Therefore, a method is proposed herein as follows: after the geometric parameters were calibrated, the residual errors caused by non-geometric parameters were further reduced by using NN, considering that NN gives an appropriate solution for a nonlinear problem.

The concrete procedure using NN is described as follows (also see Fig. 11): Typical three layered forward type NN was applied. The input layer is composed of 3 units, which correspond to Cartesian coordinates of X, Y, and Z. The hidden layer is composed of 100 units. The output layer is composed of 7 units, which correspond to compensation values of 7 joint angles, which are expressed as $\mathbf{\Delta\hat{\Theta}}_p = (\Delta\hat{\theta}_1, \Delta\hat{\theta}_2, \cdots, \Delta\hat{\theta}_7)$ and is added to the $\mathbf{\Theta}$ parameter in DH model.

In the learning of NN, measured data of robot arm's tip $\mathbf{X} = (X, Y, Z)$ is adopted as the input data to NN. Then, the parameter $\Delta\hat{\mathbf{\Theta}}_P$ to satisfy $\mathbf{X} = \mathbf{f}(\hat{\mathbf{\Theta}}_r, \hat{\mathbf{P}} + \Delta\hat{\mathbf{\Theta}}_P)$ is calculated numerically by a nonlinear least square method, where $\hat{\mathbf{\Theta}}_r = \mathbf{f}^{-1}(\mathbf{X}_r, \hat{\mathbf{P}})$ are the joint angles to realize $\mathbf{X}_r$ based on the kinematic model using the calibrated parameters $\hat{\mathbf{P}}$ (see the previous subsection 3.2).

Then, the obtained many of pairs of $(\mathbf{X}, \Delta\hat{\mathbf{\Theta}}_p)$ are used as the teaching data for NN learning, in which the connecting weights between units, i.e., neurons, are calculated. For this numerical calculation, RPROP algorithm (Riedmiller & Braun, 1993), which modifies the conventional back-propagation method, is employed.

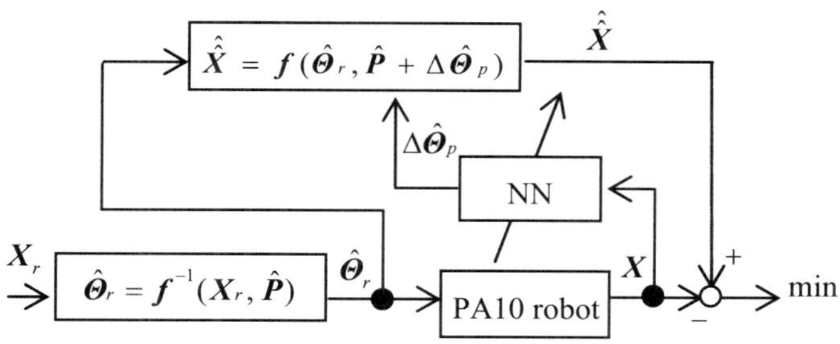

Fig. 11. Learning procedure of NN

3.5 Implementation of neural networks for practical robot positioning

Figure 12 shows the implementation of NN for practical robot positioning. When $\mathbf{X}_r$ is given, the compensation parameter $\Delta\hat{\mathbf{\Theta}}_P$ is obtained by using the NN, then, the accurate kinematic model including $\Delta\hat{\mathbf{\Theta}}_P$ is constructed. Using this model, the joint angle $\hat{\hat{\mathbf{\Theta}}}_r = \mathbf{f}^{-1}(\mathbf{X}_r, \hat{\mathbf{P}} + \Delta\hat{\mathbf{\Theta}}_P)$ is calculated numerically, and it is positioned by a robot controller. Then, $\mathbf{X}_r$ is ideally realized.

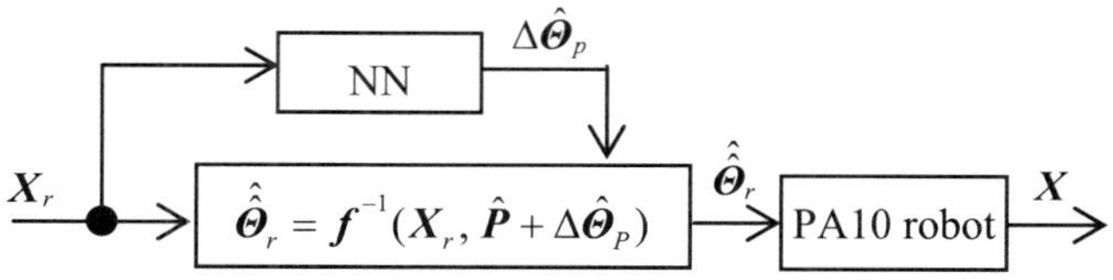

Fig. 12. Implementation of NN

4. Experimental results of calibration

4.1 Measurement points for teaching and verification

Measurement area of 400×400×300 mm was set, as shown in Fig. 13. This area was divided at intervals of 100 mm for x, y, and z coordinates, respectively. As the result, 5×5×4 = 100 grid points were generated. The group of the grid points was used for teaching set for calibration.

On the other hand, the group of 100 points was taken as shown in Fig. 14. Points were located at regular intervals on a circular path, of which radius is 100 mm and center is (500, 100, 600) mm. They were used for verification set for the calibration result.

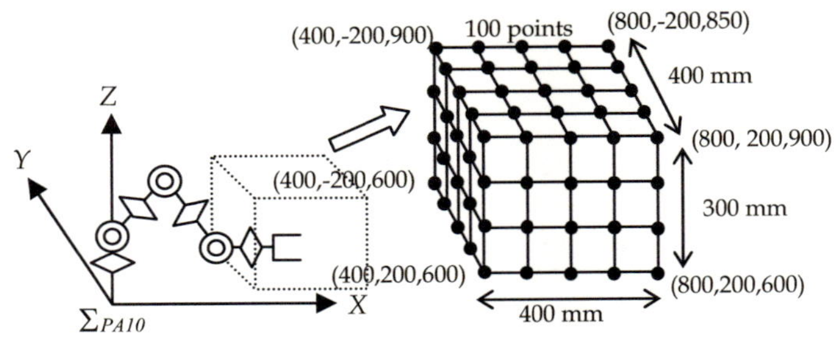

Fig. 13. Measurement points for teaching data

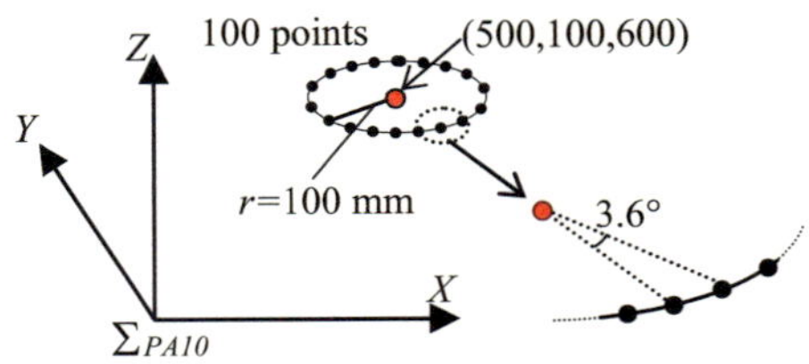

Fig. 14. Measurement points for verification data

4.2 Estimation of effect of calibrated model

The joint angles to realize the verification set were calculated based on the calibrated model, and they were positioned by a robot controller. Note that, this calculation of inverse kinematics is not solved analytically, so it should be numerically solved, since the adjacent joint axes in the calibrated model are no longer accurately parallel or perpendicular to each other.

Then, the Cartesian 3-D positions of the robot arm's tip, i.e., the verification set, were measured by the laser tracking system. By comparing the measured data with the designated data, the validity of the calibrated kinematic model was estimated.

Figure 15 and Table 2 show the results in the first trial (called Trial 1). In this figure, error means the norm of $\sqrt{(X-X_r)^2+(Y-Y_r)^2+(Z-Z_r)^2}$. This definition is used for the following of this article.

4.3 Discussion

It was proven that the error was drastically reduced from 5.2 mm to 0.29 mm by calibrating geometric parameters using a nonlinear least square method. It was proven that the error was further reduced to 0.19 mm by compensating non-geometric parameters using NN, indicating effectiveness of Method 2.

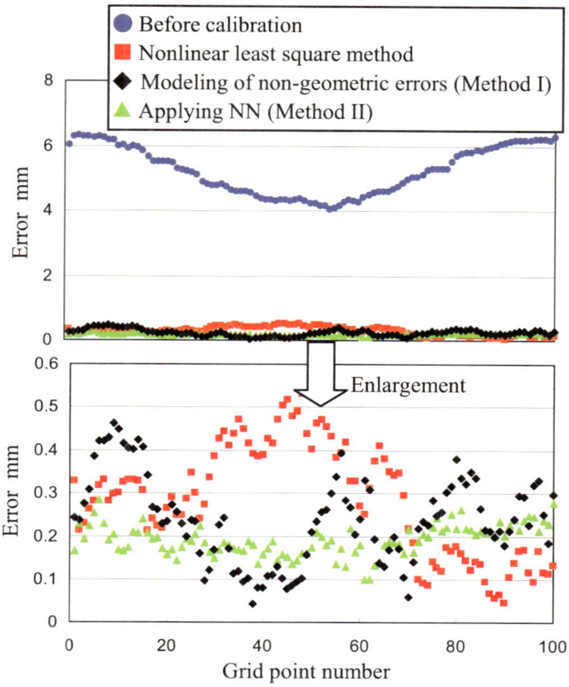

Fig. 15. Result at verification points

	Trial 1	Trial 2	Trial 3
Before calibration	5.23	8.37	7.86
Nonlinear least square method	0.29	0.35	0.33
Modeling of non-geometric errors (Method 1)	0.24	0.26	0.27
Applying NN (Method 2)	0.19	0.17	0.15

Table 2. Average of errors in points for verification (unit; mm)

The error was reduced by calibrating both geometric and non-geometric parameters using a nonlinear least square method, i.e., by applying Method 1. The improvement from calibrating only the geometric parameters (not non-geometric parameters) using a nonlinear least square method, however, was subtle and incremental, which was from 0.29 to 0.24 mm.

To verify that the experimental result is repeatable, the calibration process was carried out again for the same verification data set on the same circular path, called Trial 2. And it was carried out for a data set on another circular path, of which z coordinate is shifted from original 600 to 700 mm, called Trial 3. The results are added and shown in Table 2. Compared Trial 2 and 3 with Trial 1, it is proven that the experimental trend of average errors is repeatable.

Eventually, it was proven that Method 2 of first calibrating the geometric parameters and next further compensating the non-geometric parameters using NN is the best among these procedures. The reason of superiority of Method 2 is thought to be as follows: there are many unexpected non-geometric errors besides the gear transmission errors and joint compliances. Therefore, Method 1 of only considering these two type non-geometric errors did not work so well. On the other hand, NN can compensate all types of non-geometric errors by imposing the resultant errors in its learning process appropriately to the variety of connecting-weights of neurons.

Even in case of using NN, there remain still positioning errors of approximately 0.2 mm. They supposedly arise from the limitation of generalization ability of NN, since the points for verification are considerably apart from those for teaching.

5. Selection of optimal measuring points using Genetic Algorithm (GA)

5.1 Meaning of reducing number of measuring points

For shortening the time required for the calibration process, reducing the number of measuring points while maintaining the accuracy is effective. For increasing the calibration accuracy, it is important that the sensitivity of (tip position displacement)/(parameter fluctuation) is uniform for all the parameters in the kinematic model. As the index of showing the extent how the sensitivity is uniform among the parameters, observability index (OI) was reported (Borm & Menq, 1991). The larger OI means the higher uniformity. In this section, under the limitation of point number, optimal spatial selection of measuring points achieving the largest OI is investigated using genetic algorithm (GA).

The procedure of obtaining OI is described hereinafter. Let the forward kinematic model be $\mathbf{X} = \mathbf{f}(\mathbf{\Theta}, \mathbf{P})$, as already explained in subsection 3.2. Then, the error of robot arm's tip $\mathbf{\Delta X}$ with respect to the error of geometric parameters $\mathbf{\Delta P}$ is expressed as follows:

$$\mathbf{\Delta X} = \frac{\partial \mathbf{X}}{\partial \mathbf{P}} \mathbf{\Delta P} = \mathbf{J} \mathbf{\Delta P}, \tag{5}$$

where $\boldsymbol{J}(3 \times n)$ is the Jacobian matrix, n is the number of geometric parameters. Assuming the number of measuring points be m, equation (5) is extended as follows:

$$\mathbf{\Delta Y} = \mathbf{B \Delta P}, \tag{6}$$

where $\mathbf{\Delta Y} = \left[\mathbf{\Delta X}_1{}^T, \mathbf{\Delta X}_2{}^T, \ldots, \mathbf{\Delta X}_m{}^T \right]^T$ $(3m \times 1)$, and $\mathbf{B} = \left[\mathbf{J}_1{}^T, \mathbf{J}_2{}^T, \ldots, \mathbf{J}_m{}^T \right]^T$ $(3m \times n)$. By applying singular value decomposition to the extended Jacobian matrix $\boldsymbol{B}$, singular values $\sigma_1 \sim \sigma_n$ are obtained, which are equivalent to the sensitivities of geometric parameters $p_1 \sim p_n$, respectively. By using $\sigma_1 \sim \sigma_n$, OI is defined as follows:

$$\mathrm{OI} = \frac{\sqrt[n]{\sigma_1 \, \sigma_2 \ldots \sigma_n}}{\sqrt{m}}. \tag{7}$$

5.2 Selection of measuring points using GA

It is impossible to analytically define the optimal measuring points that maximize OI. Therefore, GA is applied in this study, which is known as an effective method for searching an optimal (or nearly optimal) solution of a severely nonlinear problem.

The procedure of pursuing the optimal spatial selection of measuring points is described hereinafter. Let us assume that the number of measuring points is limited to 8, for example. Then, a chromosome is provided, which consists of *X*, *Y*, and *Z* coordinates of 8 points. As 8 bit is assigned to each coordinate, the chromosome consists of totally 8 points×3 coordinates×8 bit = 192 bit, as shown in Fig. 16.

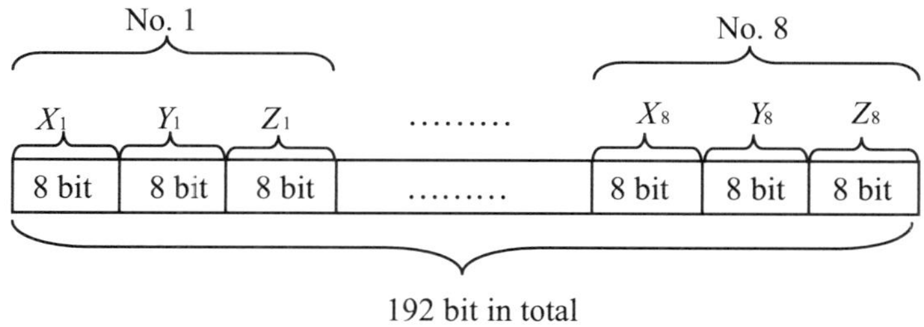

Fig. 16. Chromosome of GA

Since 14 singular values were almost zero, the effective number of singular values is 37-14=23 (Ishii et al., 1988). Three equations are obtained for *X*, *Y*, and *Z* coordinates at each point measurement, so the practical minimum number of measurement points is 8, since 23/3=7.67. Note that these 14 parameters are independent in a strict meaning; therefore they are uniquely obtained in the previous section. By contrast, in this section, the practical small measurement number is focused on; so they are regarded as approximately redundant (dependent) and omitted.

Six chromosomes are randomly employed at first. By repeating crossover and mutation at each generation with referring to the fitness function of OI, they are finally converged to such a chromosome that realizes the largest OI.

5.3 Experimental results of GA search

At several numbers of generations, GA search was stopped, and the resultant 8 measuring points and corresponding OI were checked. At these 8 points, the robot arm's tip was measured by the laser tracking system. Using the measured data, the kinematic model was calibrated by a nonlinear least square method. Then, based on the calibrated kinematic model, the robot arm's tip was positioned to 100 points for verification, where the absolute error was estimated again by the laser tracking system. These procedures were repeated during the progress of GA search.

The resultant relationship between OI and the positioning error is shown in Fig. 17. At first, the 8 points were selected at random, then, the GA search progresses, finally it is truncated when the number of generation reaches 1,000. From this figure, it is proven that OI is increased and the resultant error is reduced as the GA search progresses.

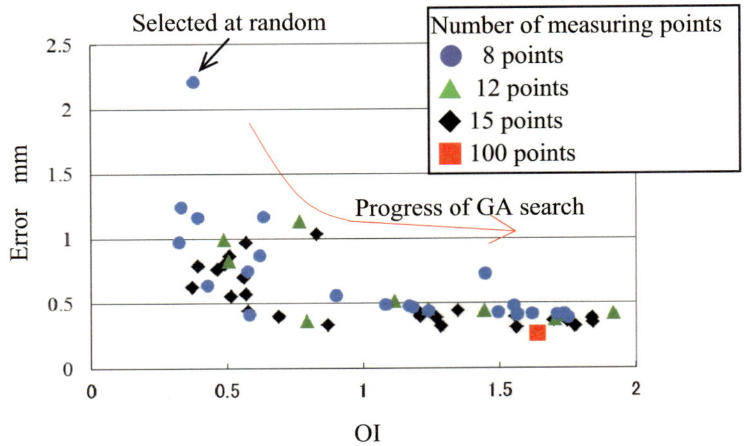

Fig. 17. Relationship between OI and positioning error

The data in cases that the number of measuring points is 12 and 15 are also shown in this figure. Looking at the figure, in these cases, the resultant error is less dependent on OI value. It is supposedly because the number of measuring points is enough compared with minimum 8 points. For reference, OI of 100 points in teaching points shown in Fig. 13, and the resultant error using these points, are also depicted in this figure of Fig.17. It indicates that 100 points are not necessary. As the result, even 8 minimal measuring points are enough for achieving good accuracy better than 0.5 mm in this example case, provided that they are optimally selected in advance using GA computational search.

Figure 18 shows an example of 8 measuring points, which were selected by the GA search. The resultant OI for these 8 points was 1.75. For the reference, randomly selected 8 points at the beginning of the GA search are also shown in this figure, the OI for which is 0.3. Looking at this figure, measuring points with larger OI are distributed widely in the 3-D space, whereas those with smaller OI are gathered in a comparatively small area.

6. Conclusions

We employed a laser tracking system for measuring robot arm's tip with high accuracy. By using the measured data, the kinematic model of a 7-DOF articulated robot arm was calibrated. Using the calibrated model, high positioning accuracy within 0.3 mm was realized.

To briefly summarize the achievements of this article, 1) the geometric parameters were calibrated by minimizing errors between the measured positions and the predicted ones based on the kinematic model. 2) The residual errors mainly caused by non-geometric parameters were further reduced using neural networks. 3) Optimal measuring points, which realize high positioning accuracy with small point number, were selected using genetic algorithm (GA).

If the orientation of robot arm's tip could be precisely measured using some sensor such as a gyroscope (Fujioka et al., 2011b), the robot kinematic model of realizing both position and orientation can be calibrated, which is planned to do in a future projected work.

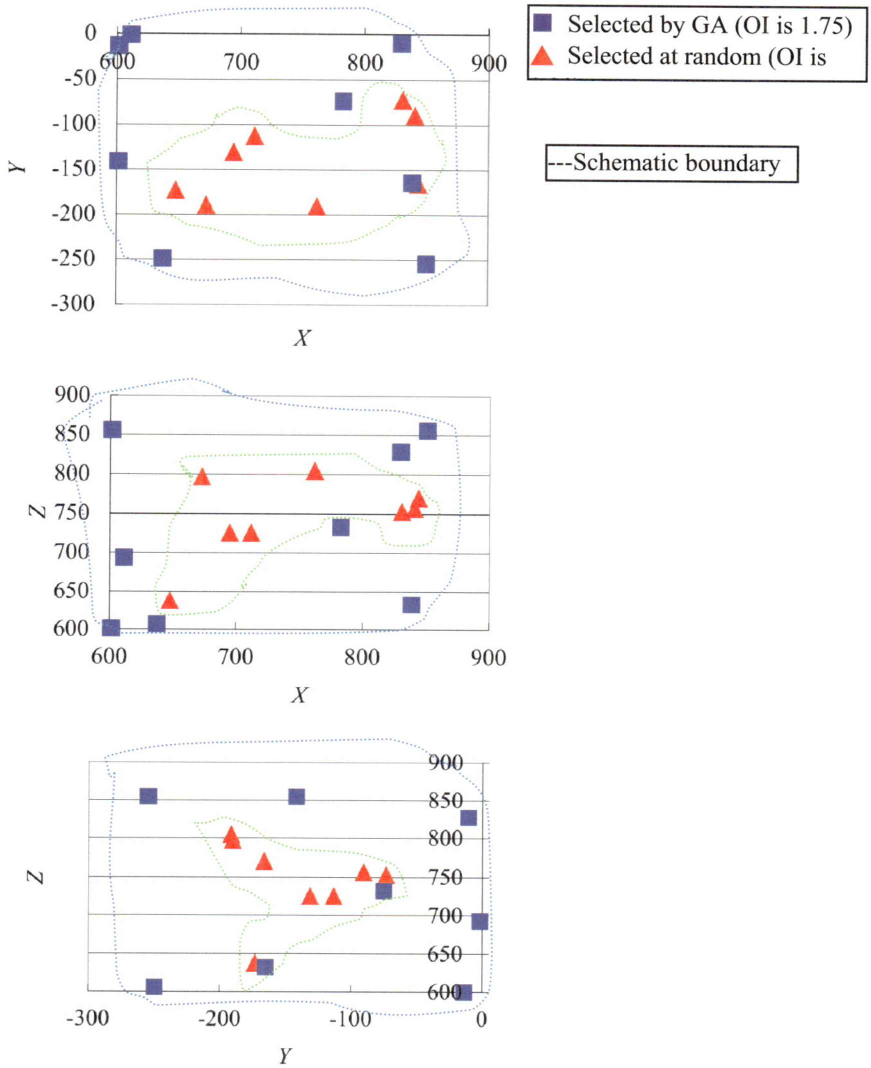

Fig. 18. Distribution of selected measuring points

7. References

Borm, J. & Menq, C. (1991). Determination of Optimal Measurement Configurations for Robot Calibration Based on Observability Measure. *The Int. J. Robotics Research,* Vol. 10, No. 1, pp. 51-63.

Denavit, J. & Hartenberg, R. S. (1955). A Kinematic Notation for Lower Pair Mechanism Based on Matrices, *ASME J. Applied Mechanics,* pp. 215-212.

Daney, D.; Papegay, Y. & Madeline, B. (2005). Choosing Measurement Poses for Robot Calibration with the Local Convergence Method and Tabu Search. *The Int. J. Robotics Research,* Vol. 24, No. 6, pp. 501-518.

Fujioka, J.; Aoyagi, S.; Ishii, K.; Seki, K. & Kamiya, Y. (2001a). Study on Robot Calibration Using a Laser Tracking System (2nd Report) -Discussion on How to Select Parameters, Number of Measurement and Pose of Measurement in Multiple Positioning Method-. *J. The Japan Society for Precision Engineering,* Vol. 67, No. 4, pp. 676-682 (in Japanese).

Fujioka, J.; Aoyagi, S.; Seki, H. & Kamiya, Y. (2001b). Development of Orientation Measuring System of a Robot Using a Gyroscope (2nd Report) -Proposal of Position and Orientation Calibration Method of a Robot Using Both Laser Tracking System and Gyroscope-. *J. The Japan Society for Precision Engineering,* Vol. 67, No. 10, pp. 1657-1663 (in Japanese).

Imoto, J.; Takeda, Y.; Saito, H. & Ichiryu, K. (2008). Optimal Kinematic Calibration of Robots Based on the Maximum Positioning-Error Estimation. *J. The Japan Society of Mechanical Engineers,* Vol. 74, No. 748, pp. 243-250 (in Japanese).

Ishii, M.; Sakane, S.; Kakikura, M. & Mikami, Y. (1988). Robot Manipulator Calibration for 3D Model Based Robot systems. *J. Robotics Society of Japan,* Vol. 7, No. 2, pp. 74-83 (in Japanese).

Jang, J. H.; Kim, S. H. & Kwak, Y. K. (2001). Calibration of Geometric and Non-Geometric Errors of an Industrial Robot. *Robotica,* Vol. 19, pp. 311-321.

Judd. R. P. & Knasinski, Al. B. (1990). A Technique to Calibrate Industrial Robots with Experimental Verification. *IEEE Trans. Robotics and Automation,* Vol. 6, No. 1, pp. 20-30.

Komai, S. & Aoyagi, S. (2007). Calibration of Kinematic Parameters of a Robot Using Neural Networks by a Motion Capture System. *Proc. Annual Spring Meeting The JSPE,* pp. 1151-1152, Tokyo, Japan, March 2007 (in Japanese).

Koseki, Y.; Arai, T.; Sugimoto, K.; Takatsuji, T. & Goto, M. (1998). Accuracy Evaluation of Parallel Mechanism Using Laser Tracking Coordinate Measuring System. *J. Society of Instrument and Control Engineers,* Vol. 34, No. 7, pp. 726-733 (in Japanese).

Lau, K.; Hocken, R. J. & Haight, W. C. (1986). Automatic Laser Tracking Interferometer System for Robot Metrology. *Precision Engineering,* Vol. 8, No. 1, pp. 3-8.

Maekawa, K. (1995). Calibration for High accuracy of Positioning by Neural Networks. *J. Robotics Society of Japan,* Vol. 13, No. 7, pp. 35-36 (in Japanese).

Mooring, B. W. & Padavala, S. S. (1989). The Effect of Kinematic Model Complexity on Manipulator Accuracy. *Proc. IEEE Int. Conf. Robotics and Automation,* pp. 593-598, Scottsdale, AZ, USA, May, 1989.

Mooring, B. W.; Roth, Z. S. & Driels, M. R. (1991). *Fundamentals of Manipulator Calibration,* Wiley & Sons, ISBN 0-471-50864-0, New York, USA.

Riedmiller, M. & Braun, H. (1993). A Direct Adaptive Method for Faster Backpropagation Learning: The RPROP Algorithm. *Proc. IEEE Int. Conf. Neural Networks,* pp. 586-591.

Stone, H. W. (1987). *Kinematic Modeling, Identification, and Control of Robotic Manipulators,* Kluwer Academic Publishers, ISBN-13:978-0898382372, Norwell, MA, USA.

Tanaka, W.; Arai, T.; Inoue, K.; Mae,Y. & Koseki, Y. (2005). Calibration Method with Simplified Measurement for Parallel Mechanism. *J. The Japan Society of Mechanical Engineers,* Vol. 71, No. 701, pp. 206-213 (in Japanese).

Whitney, D. E.; Lozinski, C. A. & Rourke, J. M. (1986). Industrial Robot Forward Calibration Method and Results. *J. Dyn. Syst. Meas. Contr.,* Vol. 108, No. 1, pp. 1-8.

2

Model Predictive Controller Employing Genetic Algorithm Optimization of Thermal Processes with Non-Convex Constraints

Goran Stojanovski and Mile Stankovski
Ss Cyril and Methodius University, Skopje, Faculty of Electrical Engineering and Information Technologies, Institute of Automation and System Engineering Republic of Macedonia

1. Introduction

In every aspect of professional life, improving the work conditions, reducing the costs and increasing the productivity are the goals that managers try to achieve. Nevertheless, one must have in mind that compromises has to be made along the way. The process where we chose what is most important usually is called optimization.

No mater the field of optimization, the problem must be transfered to a problem of mathematical optimization. The mathematical optimization refers to the selection of a best element from some defined domain. Depending on the type of the problem it can be solved by one of the many techniques for mathematical programming. Here we give a list of commonly used mathematical programming techniques:

- Linear programming;
- Second order cone programming;
- Quadratic programming;
- Convex programming;
- Nonlinear programming;
- Stochastic programming;
- Robust programming, etc.

As many as there are, the standard techniques are usually designed to solve some specific type of problem. On the other hand, in industry we deal with specific problems in different plants, and for some of them, we cannot find a solution to the optimization problem easily. That is why the engineers around the world work hard to improve these techniques and to make them more general.

Optimization in industry is very important since it directly affects the cost of the production, hence the cost of the product itself. One of the most used algorithms for optimal control in the industry is the Model Predictive Control or MPC.

In this paper we will present a model predictive controller that uses genetic algorithms for the optimization of the cost function. At the begining in the next section we will explain the general idea behind MPC in details. In section 3 we will present the considered plant, and we will give some details about the modeling and identification of the industrial furnace. Also we will present the constraints that should be considered in order to match the physical conditions on the plant. Later, in section 4 the basic idea for GA-based MPC will be presented, along with an overview of the development of this algorithm in the recent years. In section 5 we will present the proposed technique for implementing GA-based optimization that allows straightforward implementation of non convex constraints and we will illustrate the effectiveness of this method through one simulation example of industrial furnace control. At the end we will give final remarks and propose the possibilities for future research in this area.

2. Model Predictive Control - basic concept and structure

Process industries need an easy to setup predictive controller that costs low and maintains an adaptive behavior which accounts for time-varying dynamics as well as potential plant miss-modeling. Accounting these requirements, the MPC has evolved into one of the most popular techniques for control of complex processes.

The essence of model predictive control lies in optimization of the future process behavior with respect to the future values of the executive (or manipulated) process variables Camacho & Bordons (2004). The general idea behind MPC is very simple. If we have a reliable model of the system, represented as in equation (1) or similar, we can use it for predicting the future system outputs. At each consecutive time of sampling k the controls inputs are calculated according to equation (2).

$$\begin{aligned} x(k+1) &= Ax(k) \; + \; Bu(k); \; x(0) = x_0 \\ y(k+1) &= Cx(k) \; + \; Du(k) \; + \; \theta \end{aligned} \tag{1}$$

$$u(k) = [u(k|k), u(k+1|k), \;...,\; u(k+N_c-2|k),\; u(k+N_c-1|k)] \tag{2}$$

In equation (2), A, B, C, D are the system matrices, and θ is the vector of output disturbances; N_c represents the control horizon and the notation $u(k+p|k)$ means the prediction of the control input value for the future time $k+p$ calculated at time k. These control inputs are calculated in such a way as to minimize the difference between the predicted controlled outputs $y(k+p|k)$ and foreseen set points $r(k+p|k)$ for these outputs, over the prediction horizon N_p, $(p = 1, 2, \dots, N_p)$. Then only the first element from the calculated control inputs is applied to the process, i.e. $u(k) = u(k|k)$. At the next sample time $(k+1)$, we have a new measurement of the process outputs and the whole procedure is repeated. In every step of this algorithm, the length of the control and prediction horizons is kept same, but is shifted for one value forward (the principle of receding horizon).

One of the early conceptualizations of MPC is presented on figure 1. The control input trajectory over the control horizon is determined in the predictive algorithms on the basis of the model, by minimizing a cost function. A basic structure of MPC is presented in figure 2. In order to obtain proper results, we must to incorporate constraints to the system that we want to control.

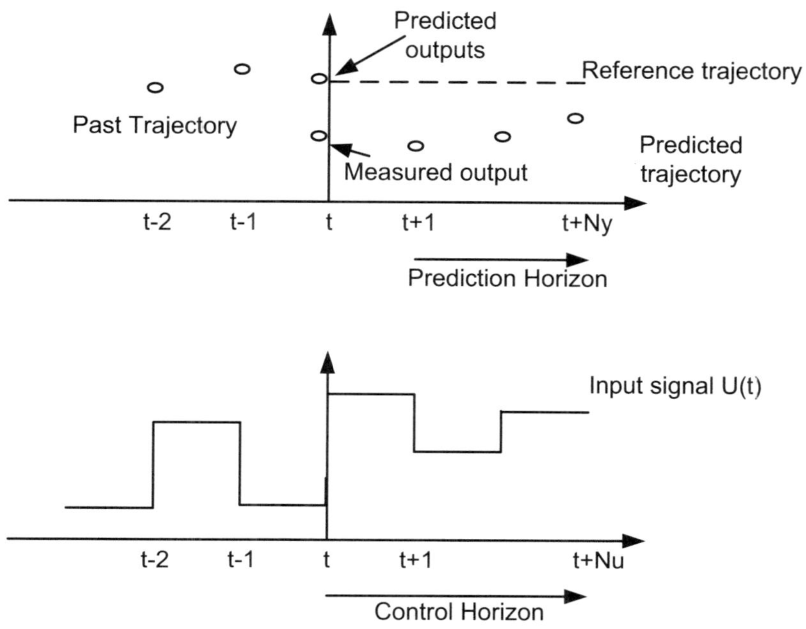

Fig. 1. Conceptualization of model predictive control algorithms

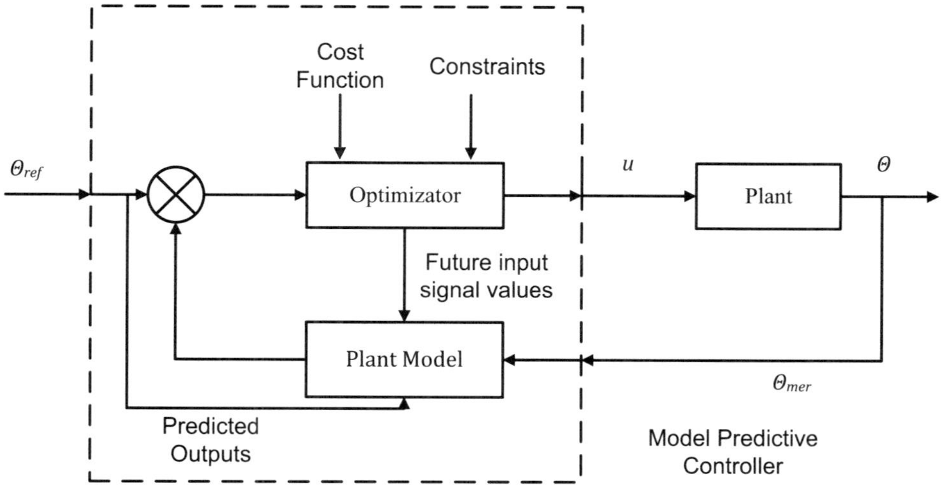

Fig. 2. The basic structure of a MPC

This cost function in general consists of two parts. The first one represents the differences between the set points and the predicted outputs and is known as the cost of predicted control errors. The second part represents the penalties for the changes of the control value. The most common used cost function is the quadratic, and it can be formulated as in equation (3).

$$J(k) = \sum_{p=N_1}^{N_p} \|w(k+p|k) - y(k+p|k)\|^2 + \lambda \sum_{p=0}^{N_c} \|\Delta u(k+p|k)\|^2 \tag{3}$$

The idea is to use one function not only to minimize the output errors, but in a way to keep the changes of the control value at the minimum. The notation in equation 3 is obvious, and the control horizon must satisfy the constraints $0 < N_c \leq N_p$. In order to get decreased dimensionality of the optimization problem which will lead to a smaller computational load, we usually assume that $N_c < N_p$. The value of λ differs depending on the process that we want to control and determines how big control change we will allow to be performed at one step of the algorithm. The predicted control values are obtained with minimizing the cost function.

What is crucial for the MPC is the plant-model mismatch. In case of precise simulation model, the algorithm guarantees optimal behavior of the plant, but in case of significant plant-model mismatch that can occur due to linearization in the point that is different from the working point of the plant, or mistake in the modeling of the plant, a robust approach must be considered when designing the control.

In this direction, improved modeling and identification methods are required for use in MPC design. The use of linear, non-linear, hybrid and time-delay models in model-based predictive control is motivated by the drive to improve the quality of the prediction of inputs and outputs Allgöwer et al. (1999); Dimirovski et al. (2004; 2001); Jing & Dimirovski (2006); Zhao (2001).

Model-based predictive control algorithms have been successfully applied to industrial processes, since the operational and economical criteria may be incorporated using an objective function to calculate the control action. The main advantages of MPC (Keyser (1991); Prada & Valentin (1996)) can be summarized as pointed out below.

- Multi-variable cases can be fairly easily dealt with;
- Feed-forward control is naturally introduced to compensate measured disturbances;
- Dynamical processes featuring large time-delays or with non-minimum phase or even instability phenomena can be successfully controlled;
- Constraints can be readily included.

Based on the characteristics, the thermal systems suites best for control process in MPC algorithms (Dimirovski et al. (2004; 2001)). In thermal systems such as high-power, multi-zone furnaces the complexity of energy conversion and transfer processes it seems to be ideally suited to the quest for an improved control and supervision strategies. Additionally, if we consider that the biggest part form the expences of the industry is the price of the energy resources, it is logical for the scientists to push towards designing and implementing intelligent control algorithms such as MPC. These algorithms trend to reduce the cost and improve the quality of the final product of the companies.

Although commonly used, MPC algorithms still have difficulties dealing with non convex constraints. In order to overcome these difficulties, scientists throughout the world work on developing new nonlinear and soft-computing based MPC algorithms.

3. The 20 MW industrial furnace in FZC 11 Oktomvri

As a test plant we use a MIMO system representation with three inputs and three outputs. This system represents a model of a high consumption 20 MW gas-fried industrial furnace, and it has been previously identified in Stankovski (1997). Structural, non-parametric and parameter identification has been carried out using step and PRBS response techniques in the operational environment of the plant as well as the derivation of equivalent state realization. With regard to heating regulation, furnace process is represented by its 3x3 system model. The families of 3x3 models have 9 controlled and 9 disturbing transfer paths in the steady and transient states Stankovski (1997). The structural model of the furnace is depicted in figure 3.

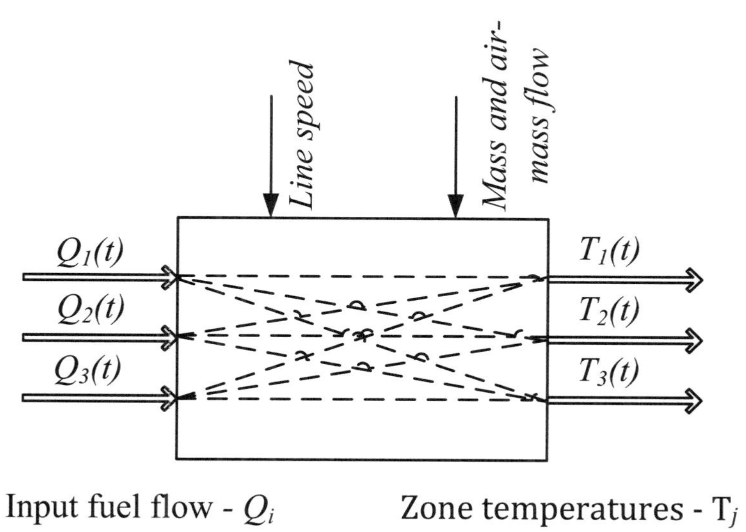

Fig. 3. Input/Output Diagram of the conceptual MIMO system model for gas-fired furnace in FZC "11 Oktomvri"

Experiments involved the recorded outputs (special thermocouples): temperature changes in the three zones in response to input signal change solely in one of the zones. Firstly, only the burners at the first zone were excited and data for the temperatures in all three zones is collected; the temperature T_j and the corresponding fuel flow Q_i for each input-output process channel (transfer path) were recorded.

After collecting the data, the parameter modeling of the furnace was conducted and the system's state space model presented in equation 4 was derived.

$$\begin{aligned} \dot{x} &= Ax + Bu \\ y &= Cx + Du \end{aligned} \tag{4}$$

Where the values od matrix A are defined in equation (5), the values od matrix B are defined in equation (6), and the values od matrices C and D are defined in equation (7).

$$A = diag(P_i), i = 1,2,...9; P_{ij} = \begin{bmatrix} -1/T_1 & -1/T_1 \\ 0 & -1/T_2 \end{bmatrix} \quad (5)$$

$$B = [S, S, S], S = \begin{bmatrix} 0 & 1.93 & 0 & 0 & 0 & 0 \\ 0 & 0 & 0 & 1.29 & 0 & 0 \\ 0 & 0 & 0 & 0 & 0 & 0.2 \end{bmatrix} \quad (6)$$

$$C = \begin{bmatrix} V & \bar{0} & \bar{0} \\ \bar{0} & V & \bar{0} \\ \bar{0} & \bar{0} & V \end{bmatrix}$$

$$V = [1,0,1,0,1,0]\,,\ \bar{0} = [0,0,0,0,0,0] \quad (7)$$

$$D = 0$$

The time constants are $T_1 = 6.22\ min$ and $T_2 = 0.7\ min$.

The plant we are dealing with is powered by two fuel lines each with capacity of 160 units per sampling period. Each of the three control valves can supply (if the control algorithm needs to) up to 100 fuel units per sampling period. For the three valves that is maximum 300 fuel units per sampling period used, which is covered by the 320 units power of the fuel lines. Nevertheless, it is usual to use only one of the fuel lines and to keep the second line as a backup in case of malfunctioning of the first. In that kind of situation we need to consider the additional constraints on the systems that has been produced by the defect. Although it can implement standard constraints as in equation (8), the standard MPC algorithm, with some improvments, can implement the constraints in the form of equation (9).

$$0 <= u_i \leq 100, i = 1,2,3 \quad (8)$$

$$u_1 + u_2 + u_3 \leq 160 \quad (9)$$

What is usual for such plant is that when the process is starting, additional power supply line is started that allows the plant to produce more than 160 fuel units. Nevertheless, this power supply line cannot be used for a long time and must be turned off during steady state regime of the plant. It supplies additional 20 fuel units, that can be used in the sampling period, and 10 more that can be used in the next sampling period. By adding this constraint to our system we derive equation (10).

$$\begin{array}{c} u_1(k) + u_2(k) + u_3(k) \leq 180 \\ u_1(k+1) + u_2(k+1) + u_3(k+1) \leq 170 \\ u_1(k+i) + u_2(k+i) + u_3(k+i) \leq 160,\ i = 2,3,...,\ N_c. \end{array} \quad (10)$$

This mathematical formulation defines a non convex constraint over the optimization problem. Through the literature there can be found only few algorithms that can successfully solve an optimization problem with non convex constraints. One of these algorithms uses an genetic algorithm optimization search in order to optimize the cost function. Using this type of algorithm the designer can easily solve optimization problems over nonlinear plant models and plants with non convex constraints. For further reading of optimization problems subject to non convex constraints, the reader may refer to Raber (1999)

4. Presentation of algorithm employing GA in MPC

4.1 MPC optimization using genetic algorithms

Genetic algorithms (GA) inspired by Darwinian theory, represent powerful non-deterministic iterative search heuristic Al-Duwaish & Naeem (2001). Genetic algorithms operate on a population consisted of encoded strings, where each string represents a solution. This algorithm uses the crossover operator in order to obtain the new solutions. Like in humans, the new generation of the solution inherits properties from its parent solutions, both good and bad properties. Each solution from the set has its own fitness value. This value represents a merit that defines the likeliness for surviving in the next generation. It is essential for these algorithms to produce new properties in the next generation. For that purpose the mutation operator is used. This procedure is iteratively repeated until it derives a solution that satisfies some norm or the run time exceeds to some threshold.

To apply this idea to an optimization problem, a first generation is composed of a set of points in the optimization domain. After that a chromosome is defined for each of these points. When the algorithm start to work iteratively in order to obtain new (and better) population, a genetic operator is applied to the chromosomes. Usually, when optimization is the problem, the algorithm chooses the chromosomes with the best evaluation function. These chromosomes have more probabilities to be selected from the chromosomes of the current population. The selected elements are part of the mating, crossover and mutation processes. For detailed reading on genetic algorithms the reader may refer to Goldberg (1989). Also we would like to recommend some other texts for further reading such as Mitchell (2008), Konak et al. (2006), Poli et al. (2008) and Weise (2009) that are considering optimization using genetic algoritms form different aspects.

One of the first papers about the genetic algorithms for optimization of MPC were presented by Onnen et al. (1997) and Blasco et al. (1998). In Onnen et al. (1997) the authors present an algorithm that is a combination of GA and MPC and explore its behaviour in controlling non-linear processes with model uncertainties. In Blasco et al. (1998) the authors also investigate the use of GAs for optimization in nonlinear model-based predictive control but focus on dealing with real-time constraints. Besides the good results showed in the start, there are only few more papers about applications with GA-MPC and algorithm improvements. Most of these papers exploit GA based MPC for nonlinear process control like the ones presented in Al-Duwaish & Naeem (2001) and Potocnik & Grabec (2000). Nevertheless the potential, the algorithm for GA based MPC is rarely used.

The basic flow diagram of genetic algorithm optimization that is used in this work is presented in figure 4.

The GA-MPC controller allows a very flexible cost function, and there are no limitations in the model or the index type used to minimize it. These characteristics enable application to non-linear processes and could therefore solve many industrial processes control problems. It is necessary to mention that this control type has the inconvenience of a noticeable computational burden, and this could affect its application to processes that need to consider real-time control. Nevertheless, this controller is very useful for dealing with slow dynamics processes and for implementing complex cost functions. These aspects of GA-MPC are studied below.

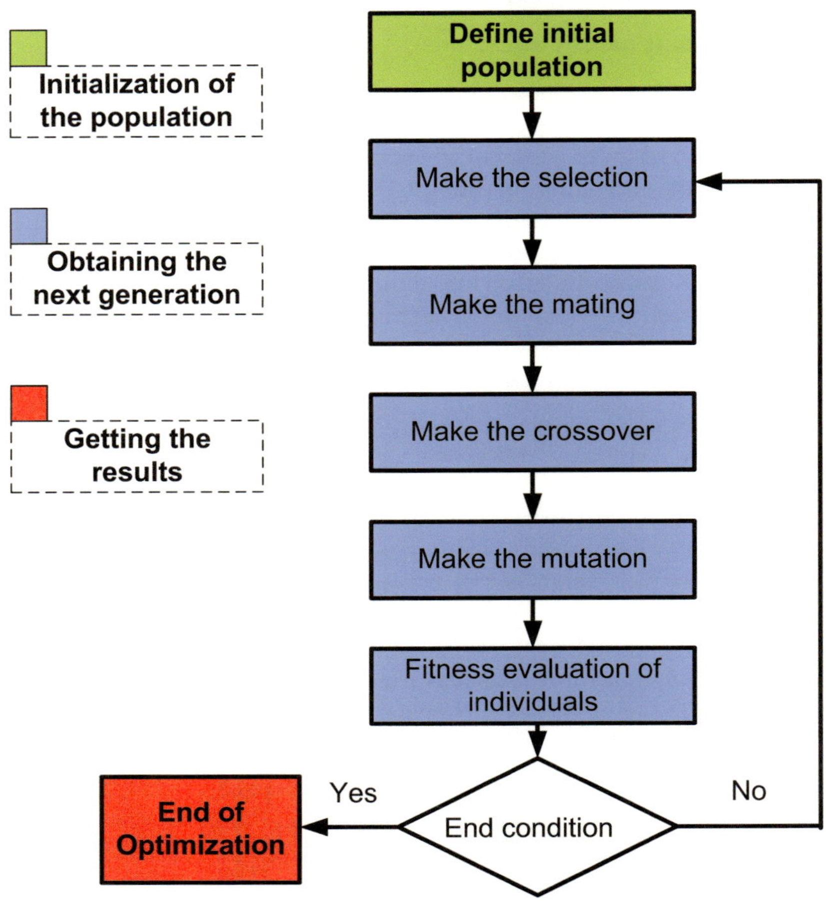

Fig. 4. Basic flow diagram of genetic algorithm

4.2 Non convex constraints

Model predictive control algorithms are usually implemented on models with linear or fixed constraints of the process and control variables. Although sufficient for most of the controllers and processes, in some particular cases, complex constraints can not be neglected. In this work we present an easy to go method for incorporating non convex constraints in model predictive controllers using genetic algorithm optimization of the cost function.

5. GA-MPC algorithm for easy implementation of non convex constraints

In this subsection we will present an effective algorithm for GA-MPC for dealing with non convex and/or nonlinear constraints. The basic structure of an GA-MPC algorithm is presented in figure 5.

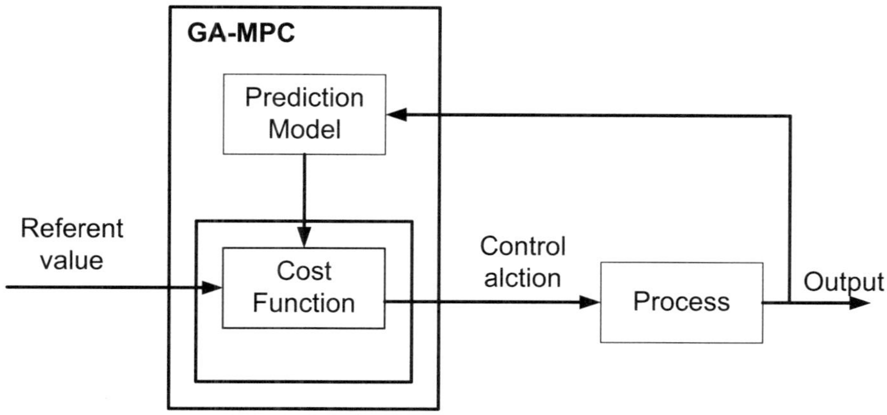

Fig. 5. Predictive control loop with GA

As said before, the optimizer used in the GA-MPC is a genetic algorithm. Genetic algorithms are optimization techniques based on the laws of species evolution. With each generation, a species evolves spreading to adapt better to their environment Blasco et al. (1998). In order to make the optimization, we need to define a cost function that will serve as a criteria for evaluation of the chromosomes.

The main advantage of GA based MPC algorithms are that they have no restrictions regarding the model of the system that needs to be optimized. That is why this type of algorithms is suitable for use in nonlinear control processes and respectively they can be very useful for solving many industrial processes control problems. One of the downsides of this algorithm is the big computational burden that it introduces. In order to compute the optimal solution of a problem, this algorithm may take up to few seconds, depending of the population and the other settings of the GA, which makes it unsuitable for use in processes that have fast dynamics. On the other hand, the complex thermal processes that exist almost in every industrial plant, usually have very large time constants, and a sampling period that is measured in seconds or even in minutes. That is why we decided to test this algorithm on a complex thermal plant, specifically, for controlling the process of a high consumption industrial furnace.

The proposed genetic-based control algorithm is shown in figure 5. This controller uses the model obtained with identification of the industrial furnace in FZC 11 Oktomvri factory in Kumanovo to search for the optimal control signals. In the same time this algorithm must comply with the constraints of the system, and optimize the cost function as given in the previous section. At every step time k the algorithm executes the following operations in the listed order.

1. Evaluate the outputs of the system, using the identified model.
2. Use genetic algorithm optimization search to find the optimal control moves for the cost function that satisfy the constraints. This can be accomplished as follows:
   (a) generate a set of random possible control moves.

(b) find the corresponding process outputs for all possible control moves using the identified models.

(c) evaluate the fitness of each solution using the cost function and the process constraints.

(d) apply the genetic operators (selection, mating, crossover and mutation) to produce new generation of possible solutions.

(e) repeat this procedure until predefined number of generations is reached and thus the optimal control moves are determined.

3. Apply the optimal control moves generated in step 2 to the process.
4. Repeat steps 1 to 3 for time step $k + 1$

This algorithm was originally proposed in Al-Duwaish & Naeem (2001), we have used it with some adoptation as it can be seen from the text.

The practical implementation of the GA based MPC is performed in MATLAB software package, using the Genetic Algorithm Toolbox. This package also lets you specify:

- Population size
- Number of elite children
- Crossover fraction
- Migration among subpopulations (using ring topology)
- Bounds, linear, and nonlinear constraints for an optimization problem

The constraint can be implemented using a constraint property of the toolbox in the following format:

$$\begin{aligned}
c = [&u_{pc}(1) + u_{pc}(2) + u_{pc}(3) - 180;\\
&u_{pc}(4) + u_{pc}(5) + u_{pc}(6) - 170;\\
&u_{pc}(7) + u_{pc}(8) + u_{pc}(9) - 160;\\
&u_{pc}(10) + u_{pc}(11) + u_{pc}(12) - 160;\\
&u_{pc}(13) + u_{pc}(14) + u_{pc}(15) - 160;];
\end{aligned}$$

Here $u_{pc}(1), u_{pc}(2), u_{pc}(3)$ are the control actions for the three valves in the following sampling period and these values need to be calculated in a way to optimize the control of the furnace. Respectively $u_{pc}(4), u_{pc}(5), u_{pc}(6)$; $u_{pc}(7), u_{pc}(8), u_{pc}(9)$; $u_{pc}(10), u_{pc}(11), u_{pc}(12)$ and $u_{pc}(13), u_{pc}(14), u_{pc}(15)$ are the control actions for the three valves in the second, third forth and fifth sampling period. The presented constraint is in the case of control horizon of 5 sampling period.

6. Simulation results

The control goal is to keep the temperature in the three zones of the furnace at the referent temperature, with minimum possible fuel consumption. The simulation experiment will be conducted in conditions of malfunctioning of one of the power lines, so the maximum fuel units that can be supplied to the process is 160 (without the additional power supply line that can provide 20 fuel units for limited period of time). According to our previous research we have chosen the most appropriate values for the prediction and control horizon Stojanovski et al. (2009). In this paper we will compare the result obtained form the GA-MPC algorithm witn and without imlementation of the non convex constraints to the model. In this experiment we are changing the referent temperature in the furnace to three different values, and the controller is trying to minimize the error during the simulation. The temperature in the three zones of the industrial furnace is presented on figure 6, figure 7 and figure 8 respectively.

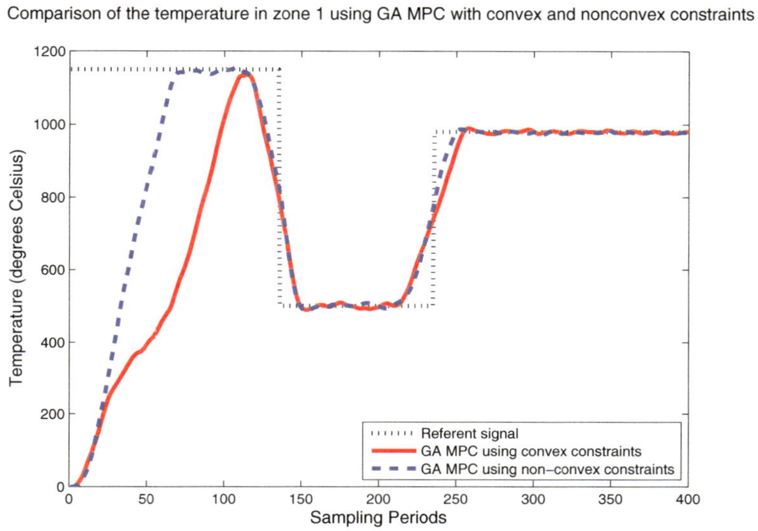

Fig. 6. Temperature in the first zone of the furnace

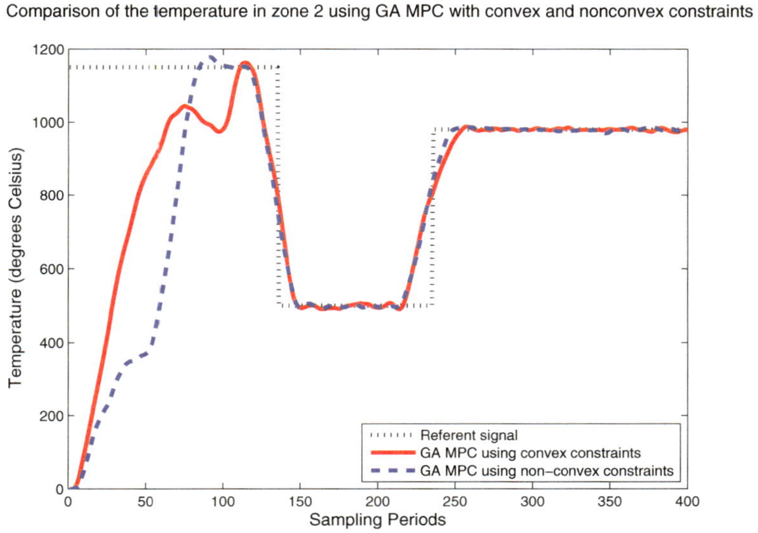

Fig. 7. Temperature in the second zone of the furnace

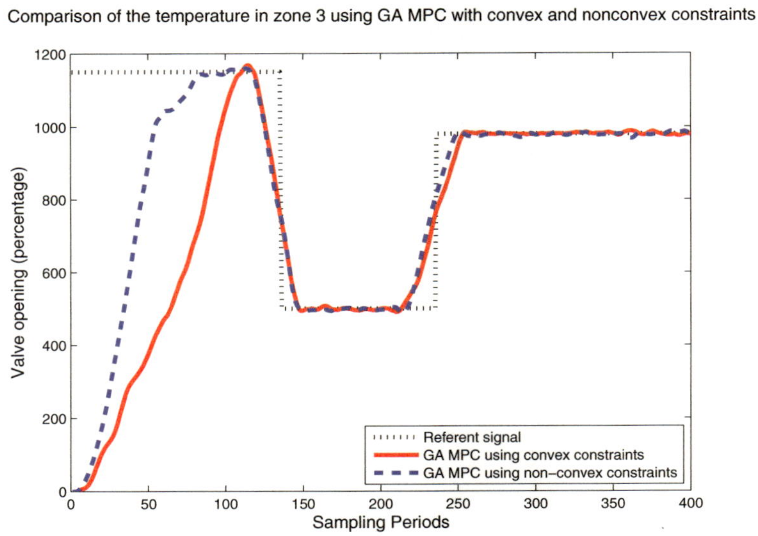

Fig. 8. Temperature in the third zone of the furnace

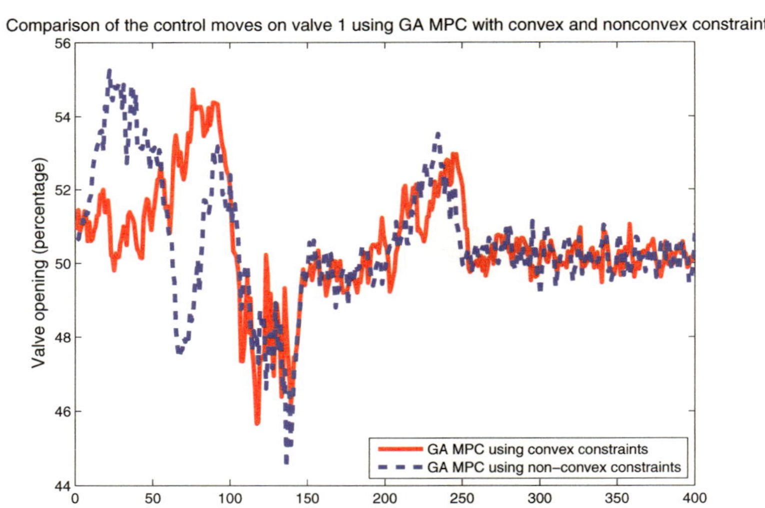

Fig. 9. Comparison of the calculated control moves for control valve 1 (convex vs. non-convex GA-MPC)

The sum of the control signals, that is subject to the nonstandard constraint is presented on figure 12. We can notice that the control signal, calculated using the genetic optimization based MPC algorithm, never violate the constraints. On the other hand, when using the GA algorithm that consideres the non convex constraints we have small constraint violations during the optimization. From the pictures depicted it is obvious that the second control method, that consideres non convex constraints, is slightly better. The values for the first zone of the furnace, both for GA based MPC that are and are not considering non convex constraints are depicted on figure 9. For the second and third control valve the results are depicted on figures 10 and 11 respectively.

It is obvious that both control algorithms have satisfactory behaviour and are reaching the referent temperatures. Anyway, one must point out that the GA-MPC algorithm that has not

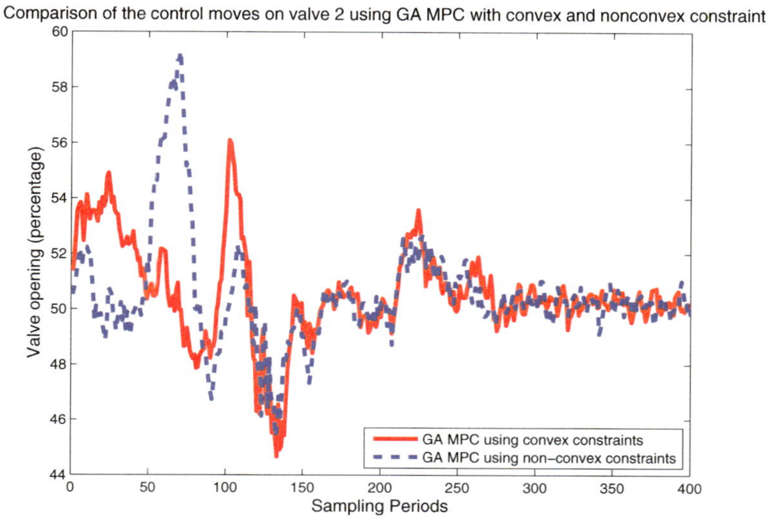

Fig. 10. Comparison of the calculated control moves for control valve 2 (convex vs. non-convex GA-MPC)

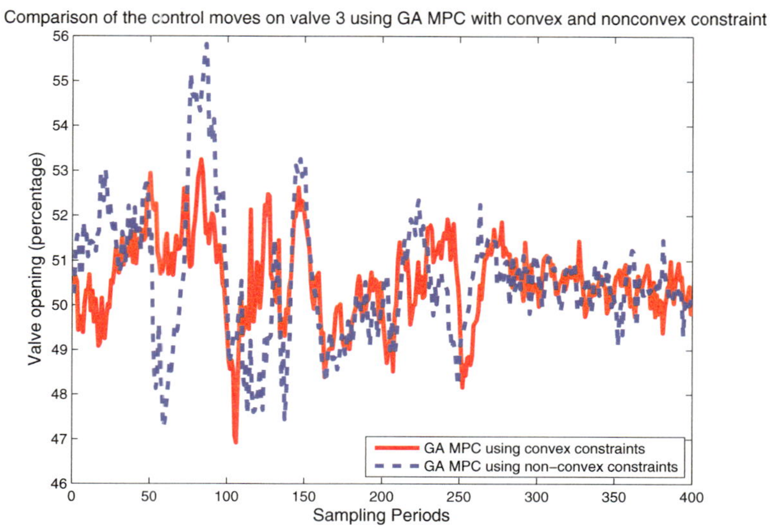

Fig. 11. Comparison of the calculated control moves for control valve 3 (convex vs. non-convex GA-MPC)

implemented non convex constraints on the cost function has worse performance than the one that has implemented non convex constraints. The difference in the calculation of the control signal is obvious if we look at figure 12, where the algorithm with convex constraints can not include the additional power supply line into the calculation of the optimal control moves.

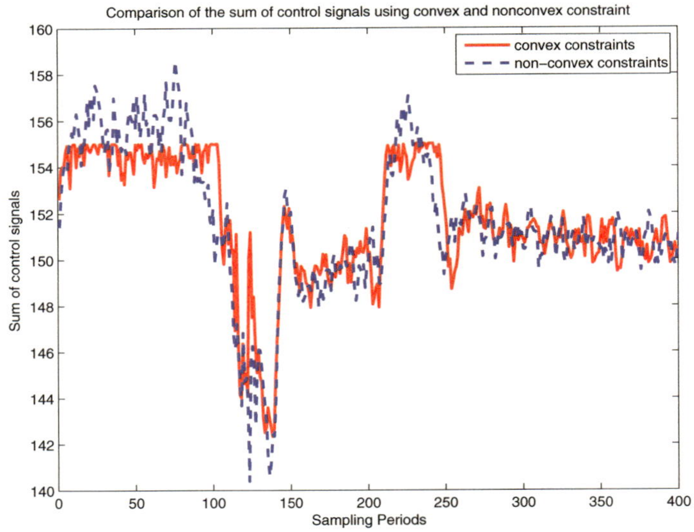

Fig. 12. Comparison of the calculated control actions regarding the energy consumption constraint (convex vs. non-convex)

7. Conclusion

The simulations of the proposed MPC with genetic algorithm optimization can track the referent temperature reasonably good under the defined constraints. We have presented an easy solution for implementing nonstandard constraints in MPC algorithms that improves the results of the standard MPC algorithms while slightly increasing the processing power.

We have shown that the use of GA-MPC can significantly improve industrial control of complex processes through implementing complex cost functions, but the engineers must have in mind that this algorithm still cannot be implemented on a fast dynamics processes. Besides GA-MPC's great potential for industry application, this technique is rarely used in industry.

8. References

Al-Duwaish, H. & Naeem, W. (2001). Nonlinear model predictive control of hammerstein and wiener models using genetic algorithms, *Control Applications, 2001. (CCA '01). Proceedings of the 2001 IEEE International Conference on*, pp. 465 –469.

Allgöwer, F., Badgwell, T., Qin, S., Rawlings, J. & Wright, S. (1999). Nonlinear predictive control and moving horizon estimation - and introductory overview, *in* P. Frank (ed.), *Advances in Control, Highlights of ECC-99*, Springer, pp. 391–449.

Blasco, X., Martinez, M., Senent, J. & Sanchis, J. (1998). Generalized predictive control using genetic algorithms (gagpc). an application to control of a non-linear process with model uncertainty, *Engineering Applications of Artificial Intelligence* 11: 355–367.

Camacho, E. & Bordons, C. (2004). *Model Predictive Control*, Springer-Verlag, London.

Dimirovski, G., Dinibutun, A. T., Vukobratovic, M. & Zhao, J. (2004). Optimizing supervision and control for industrial furnaces: Predictive control based design (invited plenary lecture), *in* V. Sgurev, G. Dimirovski & M. Hadjiski (eds), *Automatic Systems for Building the Infrastructure in Developing Countries - Global and Regional Aspects DECOM-04*, Union for Automation & Informatics of Bulgaria and the IFAC, pp. 17–28.

Dimirovski, G., Dourado, A., Ikonen, E., Kortela, U., Pico, J., Ribeiro, B., Stankovski, M. J. & Tulunay, E. (2001). Learning control of thermal systems, Springer-Verlag, London, pp. 317–337.

Goldberg, D. (1989). *Genetic Algorithms in Search Optimization and Machine Learning*, Addison Wesley Publishing Co.Inc.

Jing, Y. & Dimirovski, G. (2006). Decentralized stabilization control for composite systems with time-varying delays and uncertainties, *Information and Communication Technologies*, Vol. 1, pp. 1404–1409.

Keyser, R. D. (1991). Basic principles of model based predictive control, *European Control Conference, Proceedings of*, pp. 1753–1758.

Konak, A., Coit, D. W. & Smith, A. E. (2006). Multi-objective optimization using genetic algorithms: A tutorial, *Reliability Engineering and System Safety* (91): 992 – 1007.

Mitchell, M. (2008). *An Introduction to Genetic Algorithms (Complex Adaptive Systems)*, A Bradford Book; Third Printing edition.

Onnen, C., Babuska, R., Kaymak, U., Sousa, J. M., Verbruggen, H. B. & Isermann, R. (1997). Genetic algorithms for optimization in predictive control, *Control Engineering Practice* 5(10): 1363 – 1372.

Poli, R., Langdon, W. B. & McPhee, N. F. (2008). *A Field Guide to Genetic Programming*, Lulu Enterprises, UK Ltd.

Potocnik, P. & Grabec, I. (2000). Model predictive control using neural networks and genetic algorithms, *in* M. Dville & R. Owens (eds), *Proceedings of the 16th IMACS World Congress 2000 on Scientific Computation, Applied Mathematics and Simulation*, pp. 1–6.

Prada, C. D. & Valentin, A. (1996). Set point optimization in multivariable constrained predictive control, *13th World Congress of the International Federation of Automatic Control, Proceedings of the*, Oxford, UK: Pergamon Press, pp. 351–356.

Raber, U. (1999). *Nonconvex All-Quadratic Global Optimization Problems: Solution Methods, Application and Related Topics*, PhD thesis, zur Erlangung des akademischen Grades eines Dr. rer. nat.

Stankovski, M. (1997). *Non-conventional control of industrial energy processes in large heating furnaces*, PhD thesis, Ss Cyril and Methodius University - Skopje.

Stojanovski, G., Stankovski, M. & Kolemisevska-Gugulovska, T. (2009). Performance analysis on mpc of industrial furnace depending on the control and prediction horizon, *Proceedings of the 9th ETAI Conference*, pp. A2–2.

Weise, T. (2009). *Global Optimization Algorithms - Theory and Application -*.

Zhao, J. (2001). Hybrid control for global stabilization of a class of systems, *in* T. Leung & H. Qin (eds), *Advanced topics in nonlinear control systems*, Vol. 40, World Scientific, (Singapore, River Edge, NJ), chapter 4, pp. 129–160.

3

Enhancing Control Systems Response Using Genetic PID Controllers

Osama Y. Mahmood Al-Rawi
Electrical and Electronic Engineering Department, Gulf University, Kingdom of Bahrain

1. Introduction

The acronym PID stands for Proportion-Integral-Differential control. Each of these, the P, the I and the D are terms in a control algorithm, and each has a special purpose. Conventional PID controller has a simple structure and can provide satisfactory performance for many control problems. For process control systems, in particular, more than 95% of the controllers used are of PID type (Ogata, 2002). This is because it is easily applicable to field use, and also easily adjustable. The process of stabilization or improving the performance of the system is achieved by attaching a controller or compensator to the closed loop system. There are different types and structures of controllers. However, the controller cannot deal fully with nonlinear and/or time varying systems. In the design of a PID controller, the main difficulty has been how the control gains should be selected for good control performance, especially where the process to be controlled is of high order with complex nonlinear dynamics. This problem is made more difficult by the need to keep these gains tuned, during operations, to ensure robust performance in the face of plant parameter variations, load or environment disturbances and measurement noise. Genetic algorithms (GAs) are one of the efficient tools that are employed in solving optimization problems (Rothlauf, 2006). Because of the simplicity and robustness, PID controllers are frequently the used controllers in industries (Almeida et al., 2005). Parameters adjustment of PID controllers is an old challenge in the field of control system design. Some of methods have been proposed to select the PID coefficients, but they are not completely systematic methods and result in a poorly tuned controller that needs some trail and error. So far, finding new methods to automatically select PID parameters was interest of researches (Ho, 2003), (Almeida et al., 2005), (Nasri et al., 2007), and (Mansour, 2011). However in this chapter, the selection of optimal PID controller coefficients are introduced and applied based on genetic algorithms technique. Therefore it is possible to find genetically the optimal controller coefficients, K_p, K_i, and K_d with the constraint of minimizing absolute or square error signal to achieve system stability and to enhance system performance. However in feedback control systems the most important requirement is the stability of the whole system (Bartoszewicz, 2011). Another requirement is the speed, i.e. in the case of a changing reference value or a disturbance; the control error should be eliminated as soon as possible. Finally, simulation results will be implemented using MATLAB/SIMULINK to test system performance and stability. Due to the fact that in the last two decades MATLAB became the standard computing environment for engineers from different fields of science, a number of researchers addressed the issue of control system toolbox in MATLAB/SIMULINK.

2. Feedback control systems

Feedback is a powerful idea, which is used extensively in natural and technical systems. The principle of feedback is very simple; base correcting actions on the difference between desired and actual performance. In engineering feedback has been rediscovered and patented many times in many different contexts (Rodić, 2009) and (Bartoszewicz, 2011). Different types of controllers are used to improve the output of feedback control system. Figure 1 shows one of the main types of cascade or series controller, which are used in many different control system applications. In general there are three major types of continuous-time controllers (Ogata, 2002):

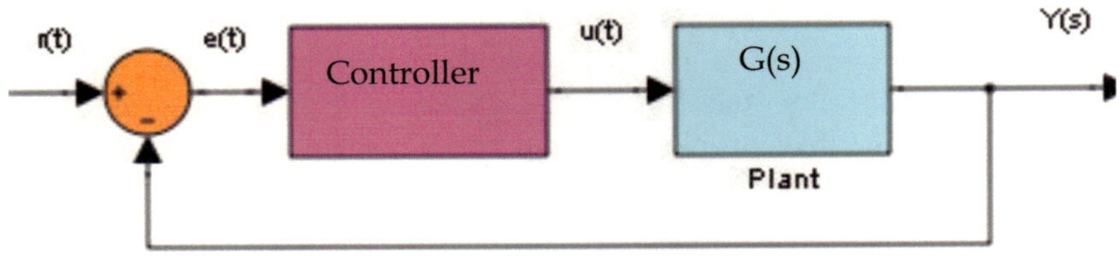

Fig. 1. Block diagram of feedback control system with cascade controller.

2.1 Proportional control action

This is the simplest type of continuous control law. The controller output *u(t)* is made proportional to the actuating error signal *e(t)*. The proportionality constant is called the proportional gain, K_p, and the control law can be written as:

$$u(t) = K_p e(t) \tag{1}$$

where $e(t) = r(t) - y(t)$ for unity feedback system, *e(t)* is the error signal, *r(t)* is the reference input of the system, and *y(t)* is the output of the system. Taking Laplace-transform of equation (1) yield,

$$\frac{U(s)}{E(s)} = K_p \tag{2}$$

One important thing to be noted about proportional control is that is incapable of maintaining the output steady state value at the desired value. This is clear from the equation above, note that as long as a non-zero actuation is required to maintain the system at the desired value, the error cannot be zero. Mathematically, *u(t)*= 0, therefore *e(t)* = *u(t)*/ K_p = 0. As the value of the gain increased, the steady state error will be decreased. However, K_p is limited by the dynamics of the system. Therefore the value of K_p will have to be arrived at by compromising between the steady state error and the dynamic stability of the system.

2.2 Integral control action

In a controller with integral control action, the value of the controller output is changed at a rate proportional to the actuating error signal. If zero steady state error is desirable, this means a control mode that is a function of the history of error will be accumulation. The longer the error persists, the stronger the control action should be to cancel it. The mathematical operation of integration is a means of implementing this action as:

$$\frac{du(t)}{dt} = K_i e(t) \tag{3}$$

or

$$u(t) = K_i \int_0^t e(t)dt \tag{4}$$

where K_i is an integral gain constant. In Laplace-transformed quantities, the transfer function of the integral controller is

$$\frac{U(s)}{E(s)} = \frac{K_i}{s} \tag{5}$$

It can be seen that the integral action is capable of reducing the steady state to zero. This is because even though the steady state error is reduced to zero, the integral controller is still capable of maintaining some actuation (i.e $u(t) = 0$) because of the past history of error values. Note that integral control is usually combined with proportional control to give a PI controller, and the control law will be written as:

$$u(t) = K_p e(t) + K_i \int_0^t e(t)dt \tag{6}$$

where $K_i = \frac{K_p}{T_i}$, and T_i is the integral time. In Laplace-transformed quantities, the transfer function of the PI controller is

$$\frac{U(s)}{E(s)} = K_p + \frac{K_i}{s} \tag{7}$$

The PI controller has two tuning parameters, namely K_p and K_i. It should be noted that the integral action has a de-stabilizing influence on the system and therefore it may be necessary to reduce the proportional gain somewhat if the integral action causes too much oscillation (Ogata, 2002).

2.3 Derivative control action

The use of integral action is sufficient to reduce the steady state error to zero. However, the dynamic or the transient response may still be poor because of large oscillations, overshoots etc. The derivative control action, sometimes called rate control, is where the magnitude of the controller output is proportional to the rate of change of the actuating error signal. Derivative control can be used in such cases to stabilize the dynamic behavior of the system. Mathematically the derivative control law can be written as

$$u(t) = K_d \frac{de(t)}{dt} \tag{8}$$

where K_d is the derivative gain constant. Taking Laplace-transform of equation (8) yield,

$$\frac{U(s)}{E(s)} = K_d s \tag{9}$$

Thus the derivative action can be used to create damping in a dynamic system and thus stabilize its behavior. It must however be noted that derivative action slows down the initial response to the system. While derivative control action has the advantage of being anticipatory, it has the disadvantages that it amplifies noise signals and may cause a saturation effect in the actuator. However the derivative control action can never be used alone because this control action is effective only during transient periods. However derivative control is usually combined with proportional control to give a PD controller (Ogata, 2002), and the control law can be written as:

$$u(t) = K_p e(t) + K_d \frac{de(t)}{dt} \tag{10}$$

Substituting for $K_d = K_p\, T_d$ and taking Laplace-transform of equation (10) yields,

$$\frac{U(s)}{E(s)} = K_p(1 + T_d s) \tag{11}$$

where T_d is the derivative time. In addition the combination of proportional control action, integral control action, and derivative control action is termed as Proportional-plus-Integral-plus-Derivative control action. This combined action has the advantages of each of the three individual control actions. The equation of a controller with this combined action is given by

$$u(t) = K_p e(t) + \frac{K_p}{T_i}\int_0^t e(t)dt + K_p T_d \frac{de(t)}{dt} \tag{12}$$

Taking Laplace-transform of equation (12), yield the transfer function of PID controller

$$\frac{U(s)}{E(s)} = K_p(1 + \frac{1}{T_i s} + T_d s) \tag{13}$$

or

$$\frac{U(s)}{E(s)} = K_p + \frac{Ki}{s} + K_d s \tag{14}$$

3. Design and tuning rules of PID controllers

In general, the Design Procedure for determining parameters of the PID controller is a trail and error approach. After obtaining a mathematical model of the control system and adjust the parameters of a compensator to improve system performance. The most time consuming part of such work is the checking of the system performance by analysis with each adjustment of the parameters. The designer should make use of a digital computer to avoid much of the numerical drudgery necessary for this checking (Ogata, 2002). Once a satisfactory mathematical model has been obtained, the designer must construct a prototype and test the open loop system. If the absolute stability of the closed loop is assured, the designer closes the loop and tests the performance of the resulting closed loop system. Because of the neglected loading effects among the components, nonlinearities, distributed parameters, and so on, which were not taken into consideration in the original design work (Mansour, 2011), the actual performance of the prototype system will probably differ from the theoretical predictions (Rodić, 2009). Thus the first design may not satisfy all the requirements on performance. By trail and error, the designer must make changes in the prototype until the system meets the desired specifications. However the process of selecting the controller parameters to meet given performance specifications is known as controller tuning. The controller tuning greatly affects the control system properties, such as robustness to disturbances and noise, performance and robustness to delays (Mansour, 2011). For example, figure 2 shows a block diagram of a simple cascade PID control of a plant. If a mathematical model of a plant can be derived, then it is possible to apply various design techniques for determining parameters of the controller that will meet the transient and steady-state specifications of the closed-loop system. However, if the plant is so complicated that its mathematical model cannot be easily obtained, then analytical approach to the design of PID controller is not possible (Ogata, 2002). Then we must resort to experimental approaches to tuning of PID controllers.

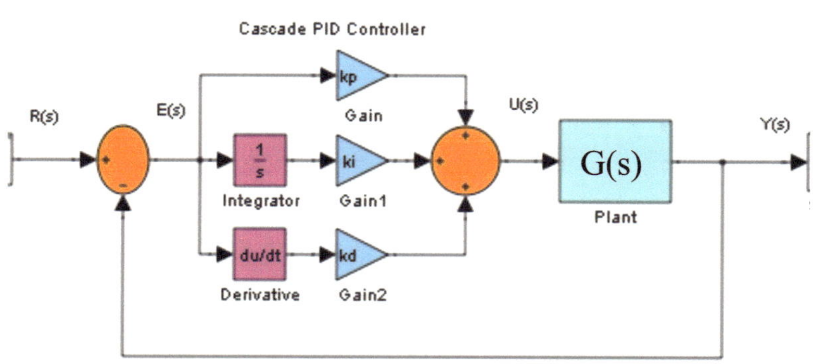

Fig. 2. Closed-loop control system with cascade PID controller.

Therefore, an alternative approaches in designing control systems by using graphical methods such as root-locus, Bode plot or by using frequency response methods. It is important to note that using such graphical methods the final results is not unique, because the best or optimal solution may not be precisely defined if the time-domain specifications or frequency-domain specifications are given. Thereafter, many different rules are suggested for tuning PID controllers, such as Ziegler and Nichols rules. However Ziegler and Nichols suggested rules when mathematical models of plants are not known (Ogata, 2002). In addition these rules can, of course, be applied to the design of systems with known mathematical models.

3.1 Controller performance evaluations

In order to evaluate the performance of a closed-loop control system, a cost criterion must be set. The most common ones are in PID controller design methods, the most common performance criteria are J_{IAE} (Integral of Absolute Error), J_{ISE} (Integral of Square Error), J_{ITAE} (Integral of Time-Weighted Absolute Error), and J_{ITSE} (Integral of Time-Weighted Square Error). They are given, respectively, in (15) - (18)

$$J_{IAE} = \int_0^{\infty} |e(t)|\, dt \tag{15}$$

$$J_{ISE} = \int_0^{\infty} (e(t))^2\, dt \tag{16}$$

$$J_{ITAE} = \int_0^{\infty} t|e(t)|\, dt \tag{17}$$

$$J_{ITSE} = \int_0^{\infty} t(e(t))^2\, dt \tag{18}$$

These four integral performance criteria in the frequency domain have their own advantage and disadvantages. For example, disadvantage of the J_{IAE} and J_{ISE} criteria is that its minimization can result in a response with relatively small overshoot but a long settling time because the J_{ISE} performance criterion weights all errors equally independent of time. Furthermore by using the J_{ITSE} performance criterion this tends to overcome the disadvantages of the J_{ISE} criterion.

4. Genetic algorithms

4.1 Introduction

In the early 1960s Rechenburg (1965) conducted studies at the technical university of Berlin in the use of an evolutionary strategy to minimize drag on a steel plate (Goldberg, 2002). Genetic algorithms were used by Holland (1975) and his students at the University of Michigan in the late 1970s and early 1980s to analyse a range of engineering problems (Goldberg, 2002) and (Franz, 2006). In particular, Goldberg (1983) used genetic algorithms to optimize the design of gas pipeline systems. Genetic algorithms are one of the efficient tools that are employed in solving optimization problems (Rothlauf, 2006). The basic idea of genetic algorithm is as follow (Goldberg, 2002), the genetic pool of a given population potentially contains many solutions, or candidate solutions. These solutions are not active because the genetic combination on which it relies is split between several subjects. Only the association of different genomes can lead to the solution. Optimization in genetic algorithm is based on optimization of a fitness function which is a function of environment individuals or genes (Rothlauf, 2006). Each new generation is generated by applying reproduction, crossover and mutation operand on old generation. Then in new generation good genes that lead to better fitness function have more chance to survive. Finally after some generations the optimal solution will be attained.

4.2 Genetic operators

In such algorithms, the fittest among a group of genetic algorithms creatures can survive and constitute a new generation (Rothlauf, 2006). In every new generation, a new offspring is created using features of the fittest individuals of the current population. A fitness value is assigned to each solution representing the ability of an individual to 'compete'. By combining information from the chromosomes, selective breeding of individuals is utilized to produce offspring better than the parents. The goal is to produce an individual with the fitness value close to the optimal. The basic genetic operators are (Goldberg, 2002):

4.2.1 Selection

The selection mechanism favors the individuals with high fitness values. It allows these individuals better chance for reproduction into the next generation while reducing the reproduction ability of least fitted members of population. Fitness of an individual is usually determined by an objective function. However, there are many different types of selection methods, such as Roulette wheel and tournament selection which are widely used in different genetic algorithms applications (Goldberg, 2002).

4.2.2 Crossover

The crossover operator divides a population into the pairs of individuals and performs recombination of their genes with a certain probability. If one-point crossover is performed, one position in the individual genetic code is chosen (Goldberg, 2002). All gene entries after that position are exchanged among individuals. The newly formed offspring created from this mating are put into the next generation. Recombination can be done at many points, so that multiple portions of good individuals are recombined, this process is likely to create even better individuals.

4.2.3 Mutation

When using mutation operator a portion of the new individuals will have some of their bits flipped with a predefined probability. The purpose of mutation is to maintain diversity within the population and prevent premature convergence. The usage of this operator allows the Individuals in genetic algorithms are usually in the form of character strings that are analogous to the chromosome found in DNA (Rothlauf, 2006). Each individual represents a possible solution within a search space. A number of individuals constitute a population. The individuals in the population are then made to go through a process of evolution, in order to produce a new generation of individuals that is closer to the optimal solution (Goldberg, 2002). The process of evolution is based on the following principles:

- Individuals in a population compete for resources and mates.
- The most successful individuals in each generation will have a chance to produce more offspring than those individuals that perform poorly.
- Genes from good individuals propagate throughout the population so that two good parents will sometimes produce offspring that are better than either parent. Thus each successive generation will become more suited to their environment.

4.3 Genetic algorithms applications to control system design

Because of the simplicity and robustness, PID controllers are frequently used controllers in industries (Mansour, 2011). Parameter adjustment of PID controllers is an old challenge in the field of control system design. Some of methods have been proposed to select the PID coefficients, but they are not completely systematic methods and result in a poorly tuned controller that needs some trail and error. So far, finding new methods to automatically select PID parameters was interest of researches (Almeida et al., 2005). In this chapter the idea of designing optimal PID controller based on genetic algorithms is defined and applied. According to the controller type and location in closed loop control system. Then this idea can be verified and tested by simulation results (see section 5).

4.3.1 Genetic controller algorithm

It is possible to introduce and explain the following computing procedure based on genetic algorithm for optimal selection of controller parameters. This algorithm is clearly shown in Figure 3 and can be explained with the following steps:

1. Specify the controller type and location.
2. Start with a randomly generated population of size ($M_P \times N_P$). (i.e. population of controller parameters (gains) is randomly generated according to a specified parameters range).
3. Calculate the fitness $f(x)$ of each chromosome x in the population.
4. Apply elitism technique to retain one or more best solutions from the population.
5. Apply genetic algorithms operators to generate a new population:
   a. Select a pair of parent chromosomes from the probability of selection being an increasing function of fitness. Selection is done with replacement, which means the same chromosome can be selected more than once to become a parent.
   b. With probability P_C, crossover the pair at a randomly chosen point (chosen with uniform probability) to form two offspring.
   c. Mutate the two offspring at each locus with probability P_m, and place the resulting chromosomes in the new population.
6. Replace the current population with the new population.
7. If stopping criterion is not met then go to step 3 (repeat steps 3-7).
8. Display results and stop program.

To understand this algorithm, we should define the overall system transfer function according to the type and location of the controller. In addition, it is important to determine the following parameters:

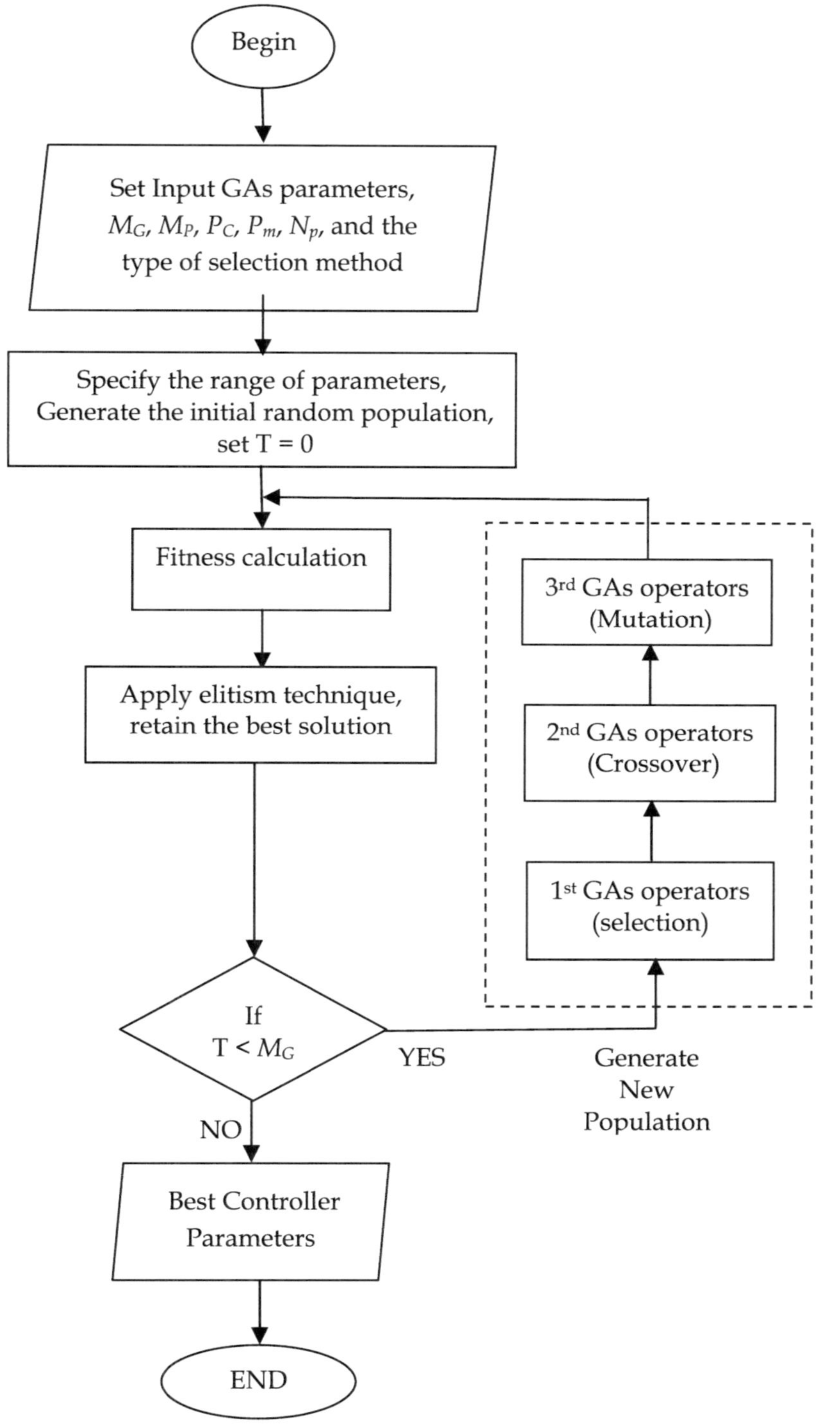

Fig. 3. Flowchart of Genetic PID Controller Algorithm

M_P: Maximum population size.
M_G: Maximum number of generations.
N_P: Number of controller parameters.
R: Range of controller parameters.
P_C: Probability of crossover.
P_m: Probability of mutation.
$f(x)$: The type of fitness function.

The stop criterion may be, for example, maximum number of generations. However, this iterative process leads to the improved performance of candidate set of PID gains. Note that, it is preferable to apply the elitism technique, which is first introduced by Kenneth De Jong in 1975 (Rothlauf, 2006), to forces the genetic algorithms to retain some number of the best individuals at each generation as shown in Fig. 3. Such individuals can be lost if they are not selected to reproduce or if they are destroyed by crossover or mutation. Many researchers have found that elitism significantly improves the genetic algorithms performance (Burns, 2001). Genetic algorithms are typically iterated for anywhere maybe less than 100 or higher. However, each iteration of the process is called a *generation*. The entire set of generations is called *run*. At the end of a run there are often one or more highly fit chromosomes in the population. Since randomness plays a large role in each run, two runs with different random-number seeds will generally produce different detailed behaviors. There are a number of details to fill in, such as the size of the population and the probabilities of crossover and mutation, and the success of the algorithm often depends greatly on these details. In addition the type of selection method used, as well as the type of the fitness function, this is an important issue to achieve optimal solution (Rothlauf, 2006) and (Goldberg, 2002). In control systems the design of PID controllers is difficult and time consuming (Ho, 2003). In this chapter a powerful design method based on real-coded genetic algorithms to solve the minimization of the J_{ITSE} criterion is described. Genetic algorithms provide a much simpler approach to off-line tuning of such controllers than the rather complicated non-genetic optimization algorithms (Burns, 2001). However, in particular PID controllers have many types and different structures, depending on the location of the proportional, integral and derivative control, which can be placed in forward path in cascade with the plant, or in the feedback path.

4.3.2 Tuning genetic PID controller

Figure 4 represent a block diagram of the feedback control system based on genetic PID controller. The controller parameters are tuned by genetic algorithms starting from initial population (Almeida et al., 2005), which is generated randomly and now it is important to calculate the fitness of each chromosome in the population (save best fit individual from the initial population). This is achieved by setting these values to the PID controller, to test the system output response by using unit step input signal as shown in Fig. 4.

4.3.3 Fitness function

Fitness is a numeric value assigned to each member of a population to provide a measure of the appropriateness of each candidate solution (Goldberg, 2002). Fitness functions used in genetic PID controllers are generally based upon the error between the actual and predicted solutions. However, better solutions are achieved according to decreasing the error signal.

The overall operation of a genetic PID controller can be better explained through the flowchart shown in Figure 2. A successful tuning of genetic PID controller can be achieved by choosing a successful fitness function (Rothlauf, 2006). According to Fig. 4 it is possible to collect error signal data to calculate the J_{ITSE} criterion of equation (18), which is desired to be minimized. Whereas this criterion is used to calculate the fitness function, knowing that this function is a maximization function and can take one of the following two forms:

$$f(x) = L_V - J_{ITSE}(x) \tag{19}$$

or

$$f(x) = \frac{L_V}{1 + J_{ITSE}(x)} \tag{20}$$

Where L_V is a very large value more than 100. The fitness function defined in Equation (20) is much preferable and gives best results; therefore it will be used through the simulation results of this chapter. After that the same procedure will be applied to the next generation. When genetic operators are used to produce offspring better than the parents, continuous improvement of average fitness value from generation to generation is achieved by using the genetic operators. To see the effectiveness of the proposed procedure in this chapter, let us take the following examples.

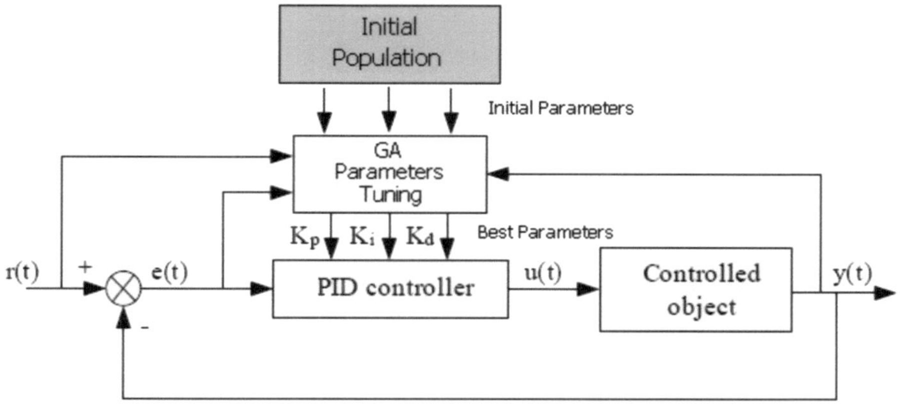

Fig. 4. Tuning genetic PID Controller.

5. Simulation results

5.1 Example 1

Consider the altitude rate control system shown in figure 5 below (Ogata, 2002).

The unit step response of the uncompensated closed loop system is shown in Fig. 6. The response shows high frequency oscillation at the beginning of the response due to the complex poles at -0.0417±j2.4489. The response is dominated by the pole at s=-0.0167, the settling time is at 210 sec. It is desired to speed up the response and also eliminate the oscillatory mode at the beginning of the response.

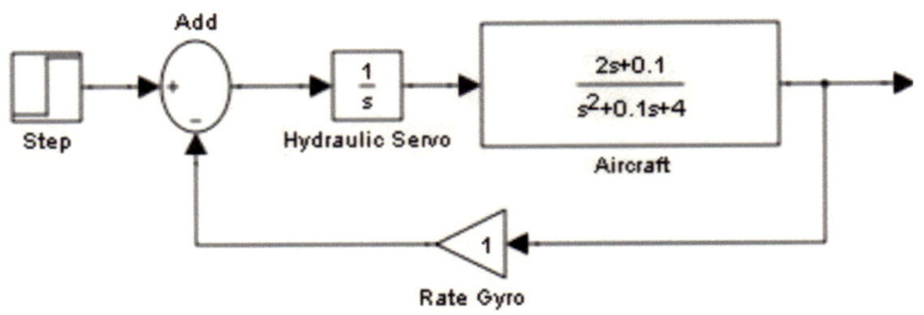

Fig. 5. Block diagram of altitude rate control system

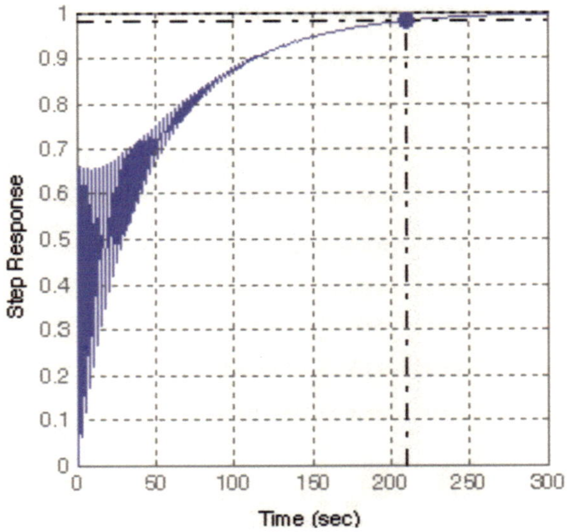

Fig. 6. Step Response of the uncompensated closed loop system, example 1.

Therefore it is desired to improve the system response by using genetic PD controller to enhance the transient response, or using PID controller to enhance both transient and steady state closed loop system response. Let us try to apply the algorithm in section (4.3) step by step to show you the activity of the proposed algorithm. In addition the genetic algorithms which are introduced in this chapter uses roulette wheel selection method and the fitness function defined before (20). In example 1 it is desired to find genetically the parameters of the PD controller, but this need to define first the following genetic input parameters in Table 1.

Genetic Input Parameters						Genetic Output Results	
M_P	M_G	N_P	R	P_C	P_m	K_p	K_d
200	50	2	-500 to 500	0.7	0.09	199.93	67.82

Table 1. Genetic input parameters and results of example 1.

The simulation results of example 1 are shown in Fig. 7 and 8. Figure 7 shows the best and average fitness during generations. Note that an optimal solution is achieved after the 10th generation as it is clear in Fig. 7 (a). Furthermore Fig. 8(a) shows the closed loop step response with genetic PD controller of the system defined in example 1. it is clear that the system response is improved and achieved better performance by using genetic PD controller. Figure 8(b) shows the control signal of the system. Finally Fig. 8(c) and (d) illustrate the variations of the best values of the controller gains K_d, and K_p respectively in each generation.

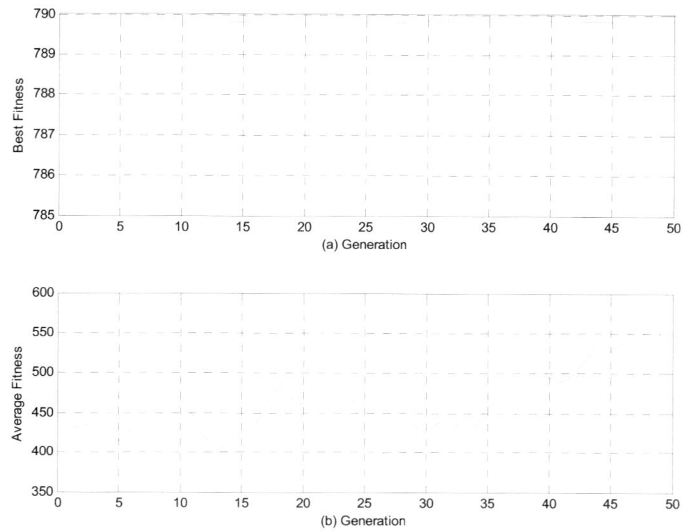

Fig. 7. Variation of fitness during generations. (a) Best fitness, (b) Average fitness.

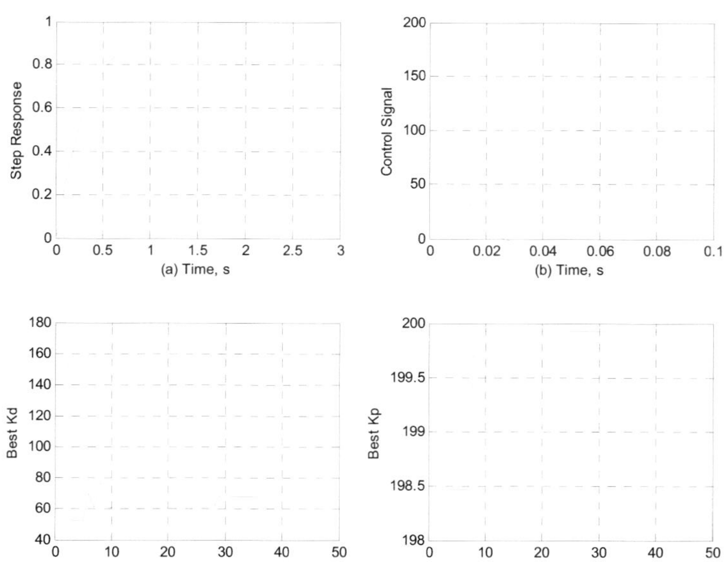

Fig. 8. Simulation results of example 1. (a) Step response of closed loop system with genetic PD controller, (b) Control input, *u(t)*, (c) variation of best value K_d in each generation, (d) variation of best value K_p in each generation.

5.2 Mathematical model of DC motor

Consider the separately excited DC motor system with armature control (Namazov and Basturk , 2010) and (Nasri et al., 2007), the voltage applied to the armature of the motor is adjusted without changing the voltage applied to the field. Figure 9 shows a separately excited DC motor equivalent model. This model is then built in using MATLAB/Simulink as illustrated in Fig. 10.

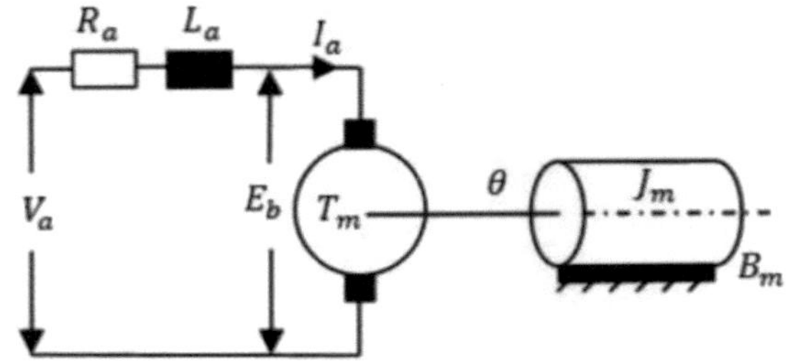

Fig. 9. Separately excited DC motor.

$$V_a(t) = R_a.i_a(t) + L_a.\frac{di_a(t)}{dt} + e_b(t) \tag{21}$$

$$e_b(t) = K_b.\omega(t) \tag{22}$$

$$T_m(t) = K_m.i_a(t) \tag{23}$$

$$T_m(t) = J_m.\frac{d\omega(t)}{dt} + B_m.\omega(t) \tag{24}$$

where
$V_a(t)$ = armature voltage (V)
R_a = armature resistance (Ω)
L_a = armature inductance (H)
I_a = armature current (A)
E_b = back emf (V)
w = angular speed (rad/s)
T_m = motor torque (N m)
θ = angular position of rotor shaft (rad)
J_m = rotor inertia (kg m2)
B_m = viscous friction coefficient (Nm s/rad)
K_m = motor torque constant (Nm/A)
K_b = back emf constant (V s/rad)

Let us combine the upper equations (21) to (24) together and taking the Laplace transforms yields,

$$V_a(s) = \omega(s).\frac{1}{K_m}.[L_a.J_m.s^2 + (R_a.J_m + L_a.B_m).s + (R_a.B_m + K_b.K_m)] \tag{25}$$

Then the relation between rotor shaft speed and applied armature voltage is represented by transfer function:

$$\frac{\omega(s)}{V_a(s)} = \frac{K_m}{L_a.J_m.s^2 + (R_a.J_m + L_a.B_m).s + (R_a.B_m + K_b.K_T)}. \tag{26}$$

And the transfer functions between shaft position and armature voltage at no-load are:

$$\frac{\theta(s)}{V_a(s)} = \frac{K_m}{L_a.J_m.s^3 + (R_a.J_m + L_a.B_m).s^2 + (R_a.B_m + K_b.K_T).s}. \tag{27}$$

where

$$\theta(s) = \frac{1}{s}\omega(s) \tag{28}$$

Therefore, now it is possible to build the Simulink DC motor model, using the transfer functions (25) to (28) as shown in Fig. 10 below. Motor model was converted to a 2-in 4-out subsystem. Input ports are armature voltage and load torque (T_{load}) and the output ports are armature current, motor torque, angular shaft speed and position.

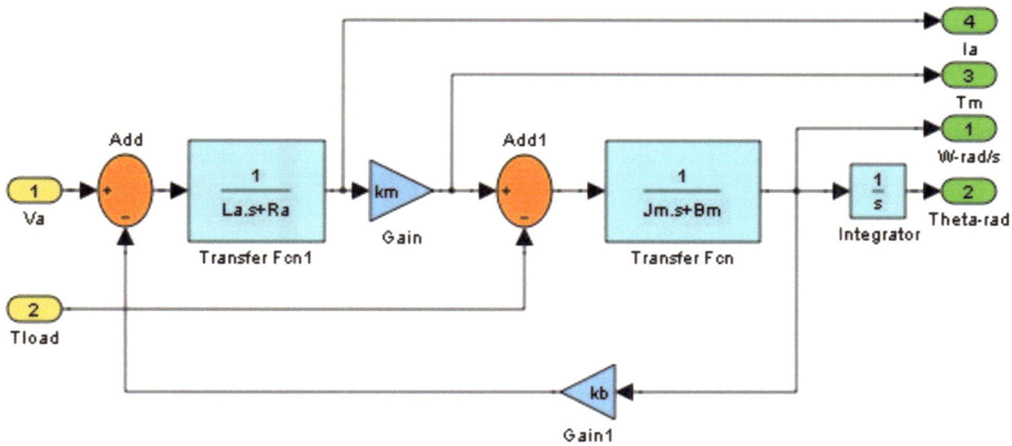

Fig. 10. DC motor Simulink model.

5.2.1 Example 2

Consider A 3.70 kW, 240V, 1750 rpm DC motor with the following parameters in Table 2 (Namazov and Basturk , 2010):

Ra (Ω)	*La* (H)	J_m (kg m2)	B_m (Nms/rad)	K_m (Nm / A)	K_b (Vs/rad)
11.2	0.1215	0.02215	0.002953	1.28	1.28

Table 2. DC motor parameters.

The closed loop output response of the uncompensated DC motor speed control system is shown in Fig. 11. However it is clear that the system is stable but it has a large steady state error.

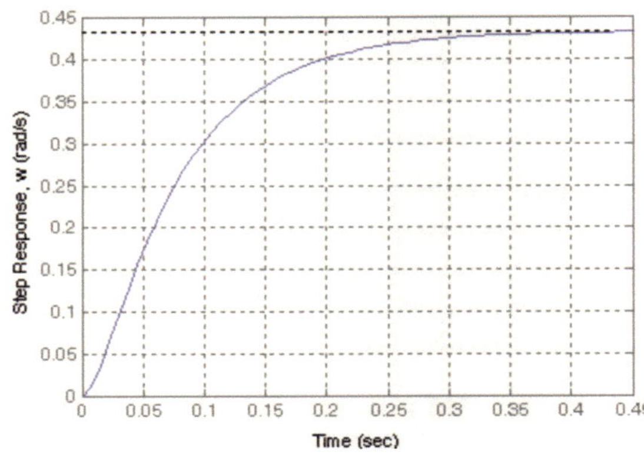

Fig. 11. The closed loop output response of the uncompensated DC motor speed control system.

Genetic PID controller

To improve the closed loop output response of the DC motor speed control system. It is desired to use the genetic PID controller as shown in Fig. 12. With the following genetic parameters in Table 3

Genetic Input Parameters						Genetic Output Results		
M_P	M_G	N_P	R	P_C	P_m	K_p	K_d	K_i
500	20	3	-500 to 500	0.75	0.09	3.8087	0.0203	9.93

Table 3. Genetic input parameters and results of example 2.

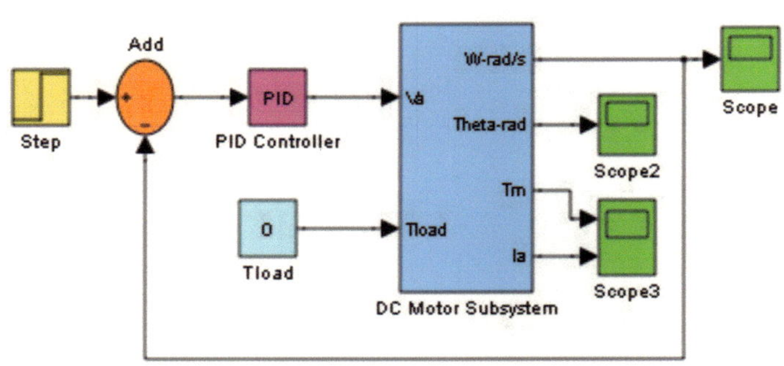

Fig. 12. Speed Control of DC Motor System with PID Controller.

The simulation results of example 2 are shown in Fig. 13 to 15. Figure 13 shows the best and average fitness during generations. Note that an optimal solution is achieved around the 10th generation as it is clear in Fig. 13 (a). Furthermore Fig. 13(a) shows the closed loop step response with genetic PID controller of the speed control system. It is clear that the system response is improved and achieved better performance by using the proposed genetic PID controller. Figures 14(b) to (d) illustrates the variations of the best values of the controller gains K_d, K_p and K_i respectively in each generation. In addition Fig. 15 shows the Root locus plot and Bode plot of the open loop system of example 2 with PID controller.

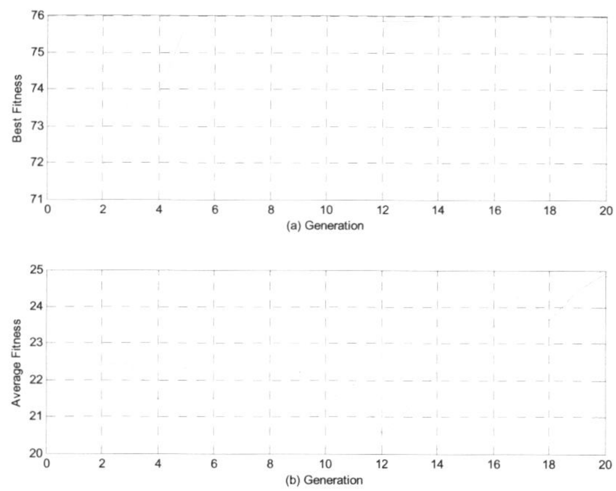

Fig. 13. Variation of fitness during generations of example 2. (a) Best fitness, (b) Average fitness.

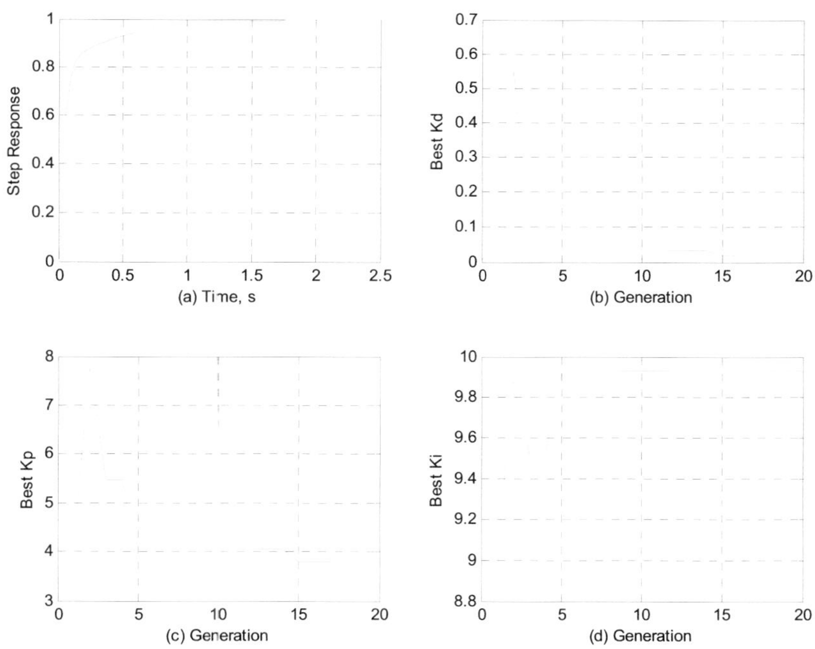

Fig. 14. Simulation results of example 2 at no-load condition. (a) Step response of speed control system with genetic PID controller, (b) variation of best value K_d in each generation, (c) variation of best value K_p in each generation, (d) variation of best value K_i in each generation.

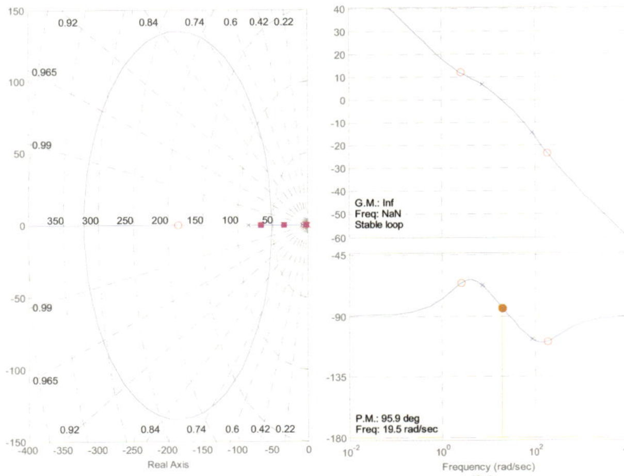

(a) (b)

Fig. 15. Open loop test of example 2 with PID controller (a) Root locus plot, (b) Bode plot.

From table 3, it is clear that the derivative gain Kd has a small value. This is because we need to improve the transient response of the system or to reduce the steady state error. Therefore we can use PI controller to improve such system response. Moreover, to test the system of example 2 under load condition, with the same results obtained previously in Table 3. A constant load torque of 5 N.m at time 2 second is applied to the closed loop system as shown in Fig. 16. The simulation results show the step response of speed control system with genetic PID controller under load test condition. In addition the motor torque and Armature current of the motor are illustrated in Fig. 16 (b) and (c) respectively.

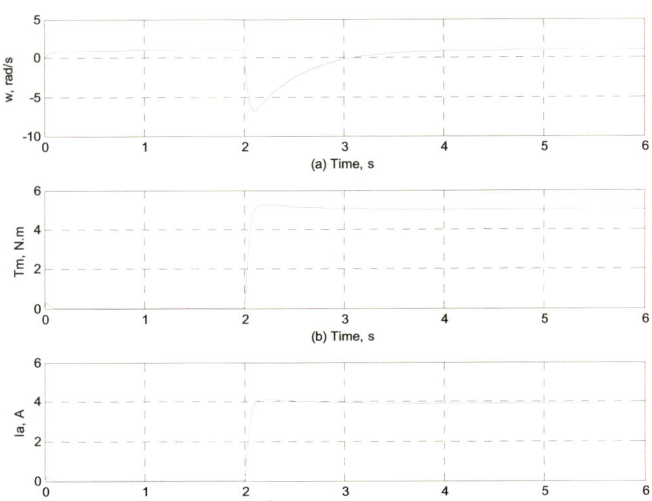

Fig. 16. Simulation results of example 2 with constant T_{load} of 5 N.m at time 2 sec.
(a) Step response of speed control system with genetic PID controller, (b) Motor Torque,
(c) Armature current of the motor.

5.2.2 Example 3

For the Position control shown in Fig. 17 below. It is desired to achieve optimal output response by applying the algorithm proposed in this chapter. The genetic PID controller shown in Fig. 12 is used to improve the output system response with the following genetic parameters in Table 4.

Genetic Input Parameters						Genetic Output Results		
M_P	M_G	N_P	R	P_C	P_m	K_p	K_d	K_i
500	20	3	-500 to 500	0.75	0.09	9.7058	4.0305	0.050714

Table 4. Genetic input parameters and results of example 3 with PID controller.

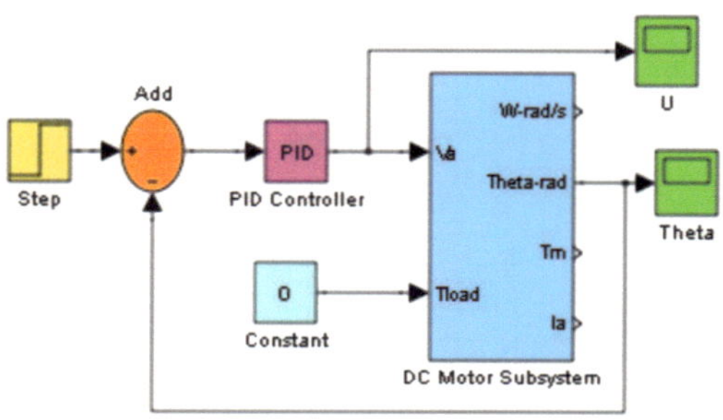

Fig. 17. DC motor position control system with genetic PID controller.

The simulation results of example 3 at no-load condition with genetic PID controller are shown in Fig. 18 below.

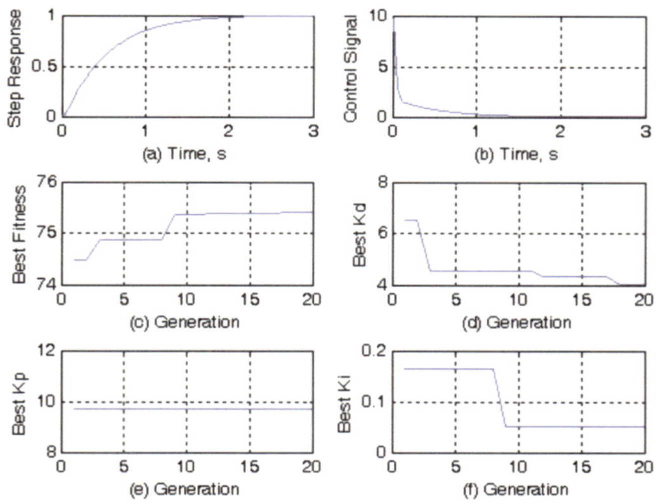

Fig. 18. Simulation results of example 3 at no-load condition with genetic PID controller. (a) Step response of position control system, (b) Control input, (c) Variation of best fitness during generations, (d) variation of best value K_d in each generation, (e) variation of best value K_p in each generation, (f) variation of best value K_i in each generation.

Note that the value of the integral gain is very small, so it can be neglected. In addition it is possible to achieve system stability by using only PD controller as shown in Fig. 19 below. Table 5 represents the genetic input parameters and output results of example 3 with PD controller.

Genetic Input Parameters						Genetic Output Results	
M_P	M_G	N_P	R	P_C	P_m	K_p	K_d
200	50	2	-500 to 500	0.8	0.05	19.91	6.52

Table 5. Genetic parameters and results of example 3 with PD controller.

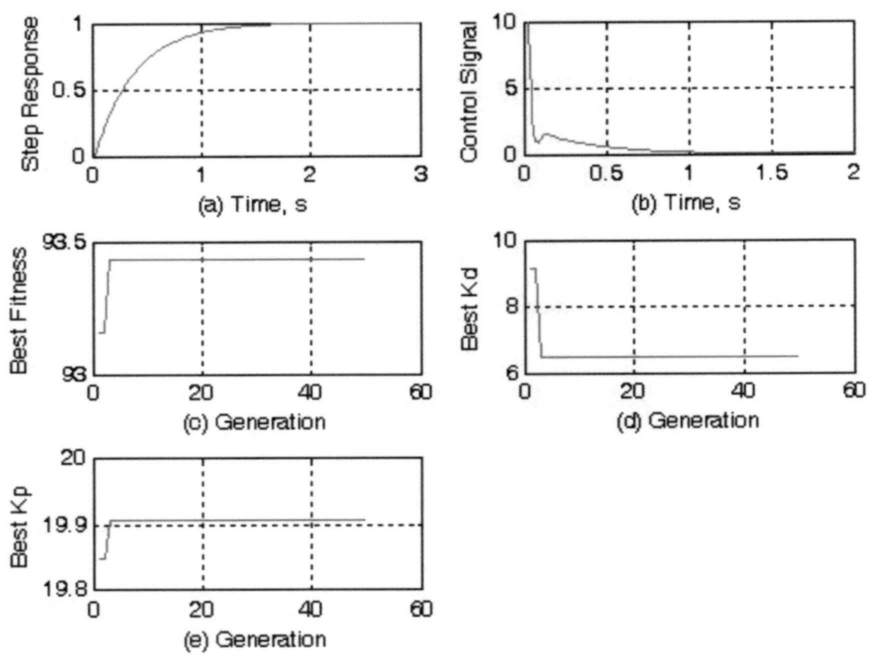

Fig. 19. Simulation results of example 3 at no-load condition with genetic PD controller. (a) Step response of position control system, (b) Control input, (c) Variation of best fitness during generations, (d) variation of best value K_d in each generation, (e) variation of best value K_p in each generation.

6. Robust stability using genetic PID controller

The principal objective of control engineering is to design control systems which are robust with respect to external disturbances and modelling uncertainty. The attenuation of disturbances will be discussed in this section clearly. This is done by adding two types of disturbances in order to show you the activity of genetic controllers against disturbances. Figure 20 represents the closed loop system with genetic controller, which is designed according to the algorithm proposed in this chapter.

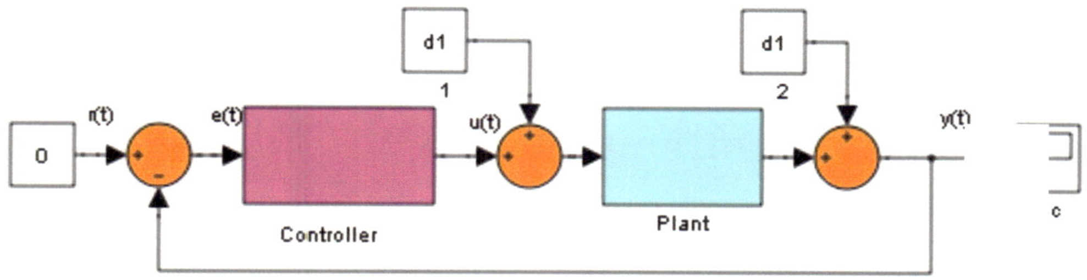

Fig. 20. Closed loop system test against input and output disturbances.

The disturbance can affect plants and no countermeasure can be applied, as the controller can only counteract after the changes at the system output (Bartoszewicz, 2011) and (Mansour, 2011).

Referring to example 1 (section 5.1), by using the same results of genetic controller obtained before. In order to test the system performance against input and output disturbances, this is achieved by assuming zero reference input and taking the effects of each disturbance alone input disturbance (d1) and output disturbance (d2), which are assumed to be a constant value applied to the system. Figure 21 and 22 shows the closed loop output response subjected to input disturbance and output disturbance respectively. The results show the viability of the system against disturbances. In addition this means that the genetic controller give an optimal results that achieve robust stability.

The same procedure is applied to example 2 for different load cases and for the two types of disturbances as shown in figures 23 to 25. The results are clearly seam to be effective against disturbances rejection.

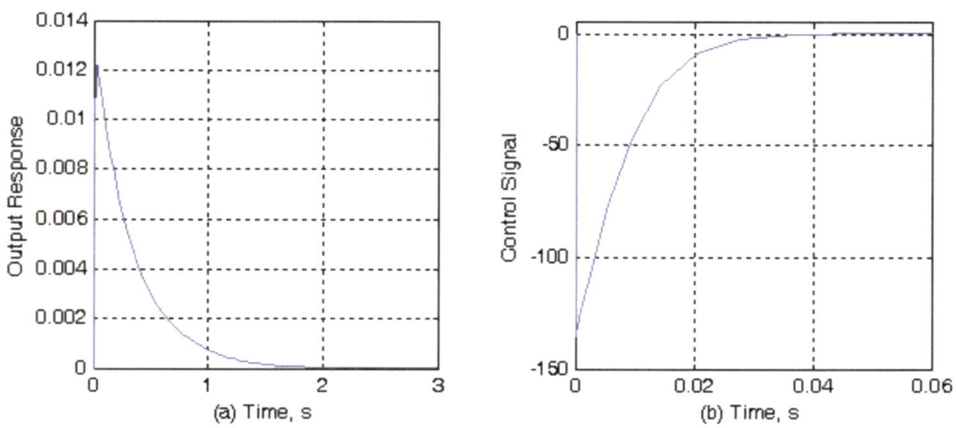

Fig. 21. Output response of closed-loop system of example 1against unit step load disturbance (at the plant input). (a) System output response, (b) Control input.

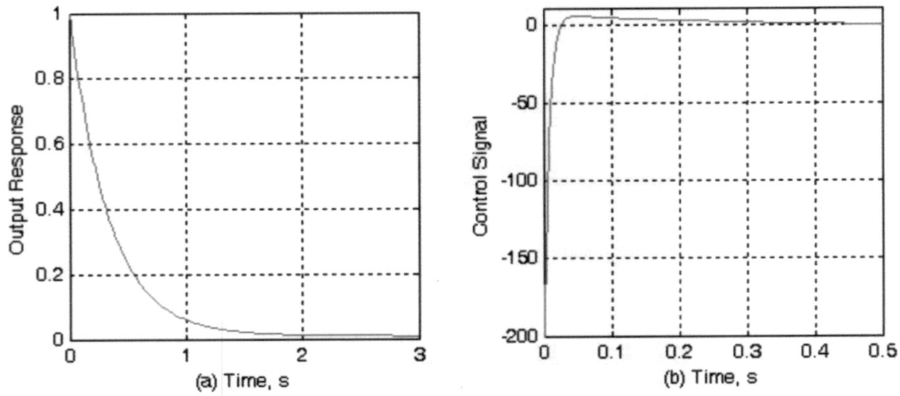

Fig. 22. Output response of closed-loop system of example 1against unit step output disturbance. (a) System output response, (b) Control input.

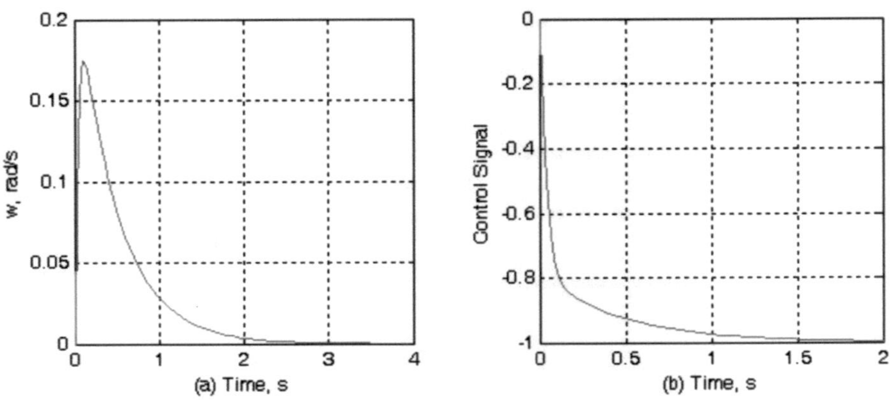

Fig. 23. Output response of closed-loop system of example 2 at no-load against unit step load disturbance. (a) System output response, (b) Control input.

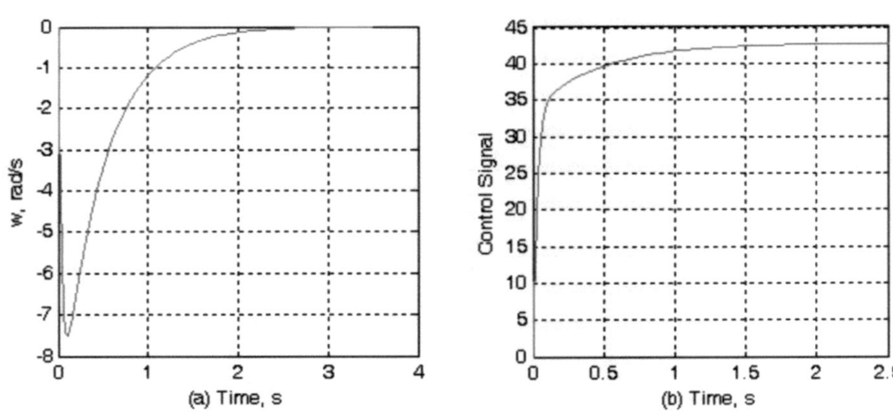

Fig. 24. Output response of closed-loop system of example 2, T_{load}= 5 N.m against unit step load disturbance. (a) System output response, (b) Control input.

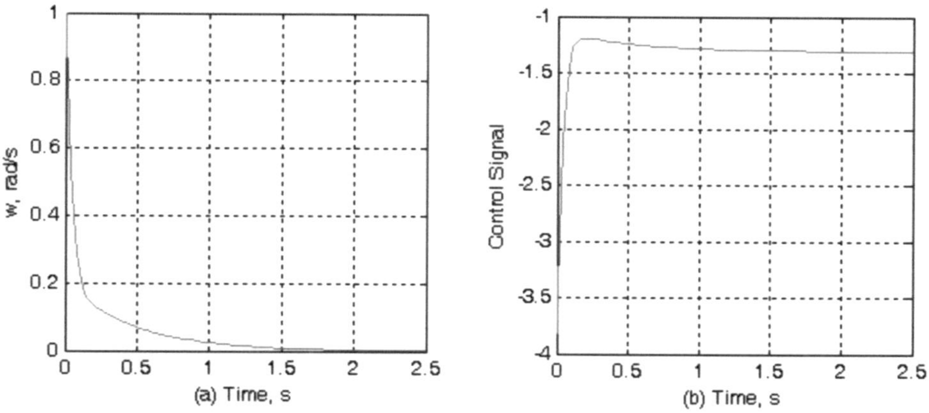

Fig. 25. Output response of closed-loop system of example 2 at no-load against unit step output disturbance. (a) System output response, (b) Control input.

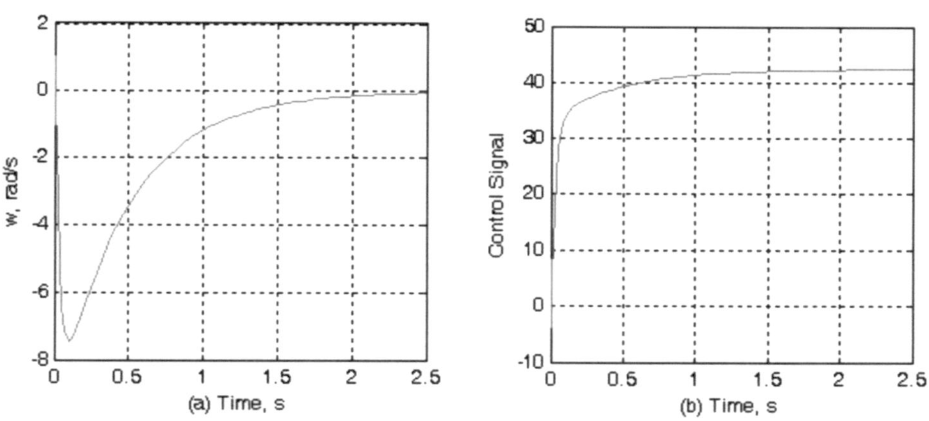

Fig. 26. Output response of closed-loop system of example 2, with T_{load} = 5 N.m against unit step output disturbance. (a) System output response, (b) Control input.

7. Conclusions

PID controllers are widely used in industrial control applications due to their simple structures, comprehensible control algorithms and low costs. In this chapter a new design method to determine PID controller parameters using genetic algorithms is presented. The aim of this chapter is to achieve parameters tuning of a PID controller using genetic algorithms. To reach that goal a fitness function in terms of system error signal which are functions of performance criteria is introduced. This is an important factor to achieve optimal controller parameters which give satisfied results. Maximization of such a fitness function by genetic algorithms causes a satisfactory steady state error and maximum over shoot as well as less control energy in comparison with conventional control methods.

In this work different control systems are tested through simulation results by using MATLAB/SIMULINK program to show that the proposed controller can perform an efficient search for the optimal PID controller, which tend to improve the dynamic performance of the system in a better and simple way. In addition the control system is tested against external disturbances. However robustness is a significant property that allows for the control system to maintain its function despite of external disturbances. For future work, it is possible to apply the algorithm proposed in this chapter to many different types of controllers for both SISO and MIMO systems. Also it can be applied efficiently to discrete types PID controllers.

8. Acknowledgements

First of all, the author would like to thank the government of Bahrain by the Ministry of Education for their continued support for scientific research and to attain the highest levels of the academic field. Furthermore, my deepest gratitude goes to my parents, wife and sons for their unconditional support, understanding, patience and encouragement. It is to them that this work is dedicated.

9. References

A. D. Rodić (2009) *Automation and Control Theory and Practice*, Published by InTech.

Andrzej Bartoszewicz (2011) *Robust Control Theory and Applications*, Published by InTech

David E. Goldberg (2002) *Genetic Algorithms in search, Optimization, and Machine learning* 5th edition Pearson Education Asia.

Franz Rothlauf (2006) *Representations for Genetic and Evolutionary Algorithms*, Springer-Verlag Berlin Heidelberg.

Gustavo Maia de Almeida, Valceres Vieira Rocha e Silva, Erivelton Geraldo Nepomuceno, and Ryuichi Yokoyama (2005), Application of Genetic Programming for Fine Tuning PID Controller Parameters Designed Through Ziegler-Nichols Technique, ICNC 2005, LNCS 3612, pages 313–322, *Springer*-Verlag Berlin Heidelberg.

Katsuhiko Ogata (2002) *Modern Control Engineering* 4th edition Prentice Hall.

Manafeddin Namazov and Onur Basturk (2010) DC motor position control using fuzzy proportional-derivative controllers with different defuzzification methods An Official Journal of Turkish Fuzzy Systems Association Vol.1, No.1, pages 36-54, 2010.

Mehdi Nasri, Hossein Nezamabadi-pour, and Malihe Maghfoori (2007) A PSO-Based Optimum Design of PID Controller for a Linear Brushless DC Motor, *World Academy of Science, Engineering and Technology* 26, pages 211-215.

Ming-Tzu Ho (2003) Synthesis of H^{∞} PID controllers: A parametric approach, Available online at www.sciencedirect.com, PERGAMON, *Automatica*, Vol. 39, pages 1069 – 1075.

Roland S. Burns (2001) *Advanced Control Engineering*, Butterworth-Heinemann, Linacre House, Jordan Hill, Oxford.

Tamer Mansour (2011) *PID Control, Implementation and Tuning* Published by InTech

4

Finite-Thrust Trajectory Optimization Using a Combination of Gauss Pseudospectral Method and Genetic Algorithm

Qibo Peng

College of Aerospace and Material Engineering, National University of Defense Technology, Changsha, China

1. Introduction

Finite-thrust propulsion is now widely used in space missions, such as lunar or mars descent, interplanetary transfer, spacecraft rendezvous, etc.. The finite-thrust optimal control problem is qualitatively different from the impulsive case as there are now no integrable arcs and the control itself, must be modeled and determined. Optimizing finite-thrust trajectory is a challenging problem due to the existence of long powered arcs. Therefore, obtaining optimal trajectory is sometimes tedious and time consuming.

Finite-thrust trajectory optimization has been studied by many researchers. Traditional optimization method for this problem is indirect optimization method, which rely on solving the necessary conditions derived from the Pontryagin et al. minimum principle. For example, the Pontryagin maximum principle is applied to the problem of optimal thrust programming for the least fuel consumption of the lunar soft landing in Ref. [1]. But with the increasing of the applicable extension, the model complicate, the various uncertainties and the strict requirement to the system, the indirect optimization method is faced with the more and more challenge. In recent years, direct solution methods have been used extensively in a variety of trajectory optimization problems, such as shooting methods and collocation methods. Cho [2] applied shooting method to the lunar soft-landing problem; Huang [3] proposed a hybrid strategy combining genetic algorithms (GA) and SQP to optimize the lunar landing trajectory; Pourtakdoust [4] used direct collocation method to solve the three-dimensional optimal orbital transfer for thrust-limited spacecraft. Luo [5] proposed a hybrid strategy to optimize the rendezvous phasing trajectory, and the discrete variables are solved by integer-coded GA.

To solve the problem, an optimization method combined a collocation method-Gauss Pseudospectral Method (GPM) and Genetic Algorithm (GA) is proposed in this chapter. Firstly, both the control and state variables are discretized at the nodes of discretization. Different from the traditional collocation schemes, piecewise-continuous polynomials such as linear or cubic splines are used as the interpolating polynomials over each time segment, the Lagrange interpolating polynomials are used to approximate the state and control in GPM. By using GPM, the continuous time optimal control problem is converted into a nonlinear programming problem (NLP). Then GA is employed to solve this NLP. The results of a numerical simulation verified the validity of the proposed optimization method. Results also indicate that the method has good performance on accuracy and fast convergence.

2. Problem statement for finite-thrust trajectory optimization

A general problem statement for finite-thrust trajectory optimization can be stated as follows [6]: determine the optimal transfer time t_f and optimal control variable $\mathbf{u}(t)$, $0 < t < t_f$, that minimize the performance index

$$J = \Phi\left(\mathbf{x}(t_0), t_0, \mathbf{x}(t_f), t_f\right) + \int_{t_0}^{t_f} L(\mathbf{x}(t), \mathbf{u}(t), t)dt \tag{1}$$

subject to the dynamic equations

$$\dot{\mathbf{x}}(t) = \mathbf{f}(\mathbf{x}(t), \mathbf{u}(t), t) \quad t \in [t_0, t_f] \tag{2}$$

where $\mathbf{x}(t)$ is the state variables, $\mathbf{x}(t) \in \mathbb{R}^n$, t_0 and t_f are the initial and terminal time. The boundary conditions

$$\phi(\mathbf{x}(t_0), t_0, \mathbf{x}(t_f), t_f) = 0 \tag{3}$$

and the path constraints

$$\mathbf{C}(\mathbf{x}(t), \mathbf{u}(t), t) \le 0 \tag{4}$$

3. Optimization method

To solve the complex finite-thrust optimization problem with strict constraints, an optimization method is proposed in this section. It is a combination of a collocation method-GPM and GA. Here the GPM is used to transforming the optimal control problem to a NLP, and then GA is employed to solving the resulting NLP. The detailed optimization method is given as follows [7].

3.1 NLP construction by GPM

We will give the detailed method how to transforming the finite-thrust optimal control problem to a NLP. The problem formulation will be presented in this section.

The Gauss pseudospectral method, like Legendre and Chebyshev methods, is based on approximating the state and control trajectories using interpolating polynomials. In the case of the GPM, the Lagrange interpolating polynomials are used to approximate the state and control. By using GPM, the continuous-time optimal control problem is converted into a NLP. The GPM for the powered descent control problem is summarized as follows [8][9].

First, the original time interval $t \in \left[t_0, t_f\right]$ is transformed in the time interval $t \in [-1, 1]$ via the affine transformation:

$$t = \frac{t_f - t_0}{2}\bar{\tau} + \frac{t_f + t_0}{2} \tag{5}$$

The cost function, constraints, and boundary conditions can be given in terms of $\bar{\tau}$. Then the state is approximated using a basis of *N+1* Lagrange interpolating polynomials L,

$$\mathbf{x}(\bar{\tau}) \approx \mathbf{X}(\bar{\tau}) = \sum_{i=0}^{N} L_i(\bar{\tau})\mathbf{X}(\bar{\tau}_i) \tag{6}$$

where $L_i(\bar{\tau})\ (i = 0,\cdots,N)$ are defined as

$$L_i(\bar{\tau}) = \prod_{j=0,j\neq i}^{N} \frac{\bar{\tau} - \bar{\tau}_j}{\bar{\tau}_i - \bar{\tau}_j} \tag{7}$$

Additionally, the control is approximated using a basis of N Lagrange interpolating polynomials $\tilde{L}_i(\bar{\tau}),(i = 1,\cdots,N)$ as

$$\mathbf{u}(\bar{\tau}) \approx \mathbf{U}(\bar{\tau}) = \sum_{i=1}^{N} \tilde{L}_i(\bar{\tau})\mathbf{U}(\bar{\tau}_i) \tag{8}$$

where

$$\tilde{L}_i(\bar{\tau}) = \prod_{j=1,j\neq i}^{N} \frac{\bar{\tau} - \bar{\tau}_j}{\bar{\tau}_i - \bar{\tau}_j} \tag{9}$$

Differentiating Eq. (6), we obtain

$$\dot{\mathbf{x}}(\bar{\tau}_k) \approx \dot{\mathbf{X}}(\bar{\tau}_k) = \sum_{i=0}^{N} \dot{L}_i(\bar{\tau}_k)\mathbf{X}(\bar{\tau}_i) = \sum_{i=0}^{N} D_{ki}(\bar{\tau}_k)\mathbf{X}(\bar{\tau}_i) \tag{10}$$

where D_{ki} ($D \in \mathbb{R}^{N\times(N+1)}$) is known as differentiation matrix. In the GPM, the dynamics are collocated at the N Legendre-Gauss (LG) points $\bar{\tau}_k (k = 1,\cdots,N)$. The derivative of each Lagrange polynomial at the LG points can be represented in a differential approximation matrix $D \in \mathbb{R}^{N\times(N+1)}$. The elements of the differential approximation matrix are determined offline as follows:

$$D_{ki} = \dot{L}_i(\bar{\tau}_k) = \begin{cases} \dfrac{(1+\bar{\tau}_k)\dot{P}_N(\bar{\tau}_k) + P_N(\bar{\tau}_k)}{(\bar{\tau}_k - \bar{\tau}_i)\left[(1+\bar{\tau}_i)\dot{P}_N(\bar{\tau}_i) + P_N(\bar{\tau}_i)\right]}, & i \neq k \\ \dfrac{(1+\bar{\tau}_i)\ddot{P}_N(\bar{\tau}_i) + 2\dot{P}_N(\bar{\tau}_i)}{2\left[(1+\bar{\tau}_i)\dot{P}_N(\bar{\tau}_i) + P_N(\bar{\tau}_i)\right]}, & i = k \end{cases} \tag{11}$$

where $k = 1,\cdots,N$ and $i = 0,\cdots,N$. The dynamic constraint equation $\dot{\mathbf{X}}(\bar{\tau}) = \mathbf{f}\left(\mathbf{X}(\bar{\tau}),\mathbf{U}(\bar{\tau});t_0,t_f\right)$ is transcribed into an algebraic constraint using the differential approximation matrix as follows:

$$\sum_{i=0}^{N} D_{ki}\mathbf{X}(\overline{\tau}_i)-\frac{t_f-t_0}{2}\mathbf{f}\left(\mathbf{X}(\overline{\tau}_k),\mathbf{U}(\overline{\tau}_k),\overline{\tau}_k;t_0,t_f\right)=0 \tag{12}$$

In addition, $X_0 \equiv X(-1)$ and X_f is defined using the Gauss quadrature given by

$$\mathbf{X}(\overline{\tau}_f)\equiv\mathbf{X}(\overline{\tau}_0)+\frac{t_f-t_0}{2}\sum_{k=1}^{N} w_k\mathbf{f}(\mathbf{X}(\overline{\tau}_k),\mathbf{U}(\overline{\tau}_k),\overline{\tau},t_0,t_f) \tag{13}$$

where w_k are the Gauss weights.

The continuous cost function $J=\Phi\left(\mathbf{X}_0,t_0,\mathbf{X}_f,t_f\right)+\int_{t_0}^{t_f} g(\mathbf{X},\mathbf{U})dt$ is approximated as

$$J=\Phi\left(\mathbf{X}_0,t_0,\mathbf{X}_f,t_f\right)+\frac{t_f-t_0}{2}\sum_{k=1}^{N} w_k g\left(\mathbf{X}_k,\mathbf{U}_k,\overline{\tau}_k;t_0,t_f\right) \tag{14}$$

The boundary constraints are also discretized at the LG points as

$$\phi\left(\mathbf{X}_0,t_0,\mathbf{X}_f,t_f\right)=0 \tag{15}$$

Furthermore, the path constraints are evaluated at the LG points as

$$C\left(\mathbf{X}_k,\mathbf{U}_k,\overline{\tau}_k;t_0,t_f\right)\le 0 \ \ (k=1,\cdots,N) \tag{16}$$

The cost function in Eq. (14) and the algebraic constraints in Eqs. (12), (13), (15) and (16) define an NLP whose solution is an approximate solution to the continuous Mayer problem. Finally, it is noted that discontinuities in the state or control can be handled efficiently by dividing the trajectory into phases, where the dynamics are transcribed within each phase and then connected together by additional phase interface constraints.

3.2 NLP solution by GA

Many methods can be used to solve the NLP, such as the steepest descent algorithm, hill-climbing algorithm, evolution algorithm and so on. Here genetic algorithm is employed to solve the optimization problem due to its excellent performance on global searching and the convenience to realize by computer.

Genetic algorithms are search procedures based on the mechanics of natural genetics. All natural species survive by adapting themselves to the environment. Genetic algorithm search combines a Darwinian survival-of-the-fittest concept to eliminate unfit characteristics and utilizes random information exchange, with exploitation of knowledge contained in old solutions, to effect a search mechanism with power and speed. In using genetic algorithms, the usual goal is to find solutions that are closer to the globally optimal point. This technique has gained popularity in the recent years as a robust optimization tool for variety of problems in engineering, science, economics, finance, etc.

A simple genetic algorithm is composed of three operators: (1) selection, (2) crossover, and (3) mutation. Selection is a process where an old string is carried through into a new population J depending on the performance index values. Due to this move, strings with better fitness values get larger numbers of copies in the next generation. Selecting good strings for this operation can be implemented in many different ways. In conjunction with the selection procedures, the good strings can either be allowed to change (pure selection) or retained in to the next evolution (elite selection). A simple crossover follows selection in three steps. First, the newly selected strings are paired together at random. Second, an integer position "n" along every pair of strings is selected uniformly at random. Finally, based on a probability of crossover, the paired strings undergo crossing over at the integer position "n" along the string. This results in new pairs of strings that are created by swapping all the characters between characters 1 and "n" inclusively. Although the crossover operation is a randomized event, when combined with selection it becomes an effective means of exchanging information and combining portions of good quality solutions. Selection and crossover give GA most of their search power. The third operator, mutation, is simply an occasional random alteration of a string position (based on probability of mutation). In a binary code, this involves changing a 1 to a 0 and vice versa. The mutation operator helps in avoiding the possibility of mistaking a local minimum for a global minimum. When mutation is used sparingly (about one mutation per thousand bit transfers) with selection and crossover, it improves the global nature of the genetic algorithm search. [10]

By using GPM, the optimal control problem was transcribed to a NLP by parameterizing the state and control using global polynomials and collocating the differential-algebraic equations using nodes obtained from a Gaussian quadrature. The dispersed state and control variables at LG points should be optimized using a parameter optimization technique. Here GA can be easily used as a parameter optimization technique for solving the problem.

4. Numerical examples: Lunar powered descent trajectory optimization

In this section, a trajectory optimization problem for lunar powered descent is presented to verify the validity of the proposed optimization method.

To make the optimization problem easier to solve, the dynamical system considered in most of previous studies on lunar powered descent is a two dimensional dynamics [7][11]. The descent trajectory of the lunar lander is assumed to remain in a vertical plane without any provision for possible lateral movements. However, for standard trajectory design or simulation before launching the rocket, the error can not be ignored. To obtain more accurate results and demonstrate the validity of this method to solve complex optimization problem, a three dimensional descent dynamics with high precision is established in this paper, and many strict constraints is given.

Here, we give the simple formulation of the optimization.

4.1 Problem formulation

4.1.1 Dynamics equations

The lunar lander is in a circular orbit with an initial altitude H_0. A Hohmann transfer orbit is used to decrease the altitude from H_0 to the pericynthion (altitude 15km). From here the powered descent begins. The powered-descent phase of the lunar-landing mission is initiated at or near the pericynthion of the free descent orbit and finishes near the lunar surface (about altitude 2km). It is a continuous thrust maneuver of the duration of several minutes. The largest part of fuel is consumed during this phase [12].

The following frame of reference is established to describe the powered descent maneuver.

1. Moon Centred Inertial (MCI) coordinate system $O-X_1Y_1Z_1$
   The Origin is at the center of the moon; OX_1 axis is along the direction of the Moon's revolution, and OY_1 axis is pointing at the ascending node of the Moon's orbit relative to the equator.
2. Moon Centred Fixed (MCF) coordinate system $O-XYZ$
   The Origin is at the center of the moon; OX axis is along the direction of the Moon's revolution, and OY axis is in the Moon's equator plane, pointing at the Sinus-Medii.
3. Orbit coordinate system $o-xyz$
   The Origin is at the center of gravity of the lunar lander; ox axis is along the radial direction, oy axis is along the direction of the horizontal velocity at initial state of powered-descent.

It is assumed that the moon has a homogeneous gravity field and a constant rotation angular velocity. The coordinate systems and defined parameters are shown in Fig. 1.

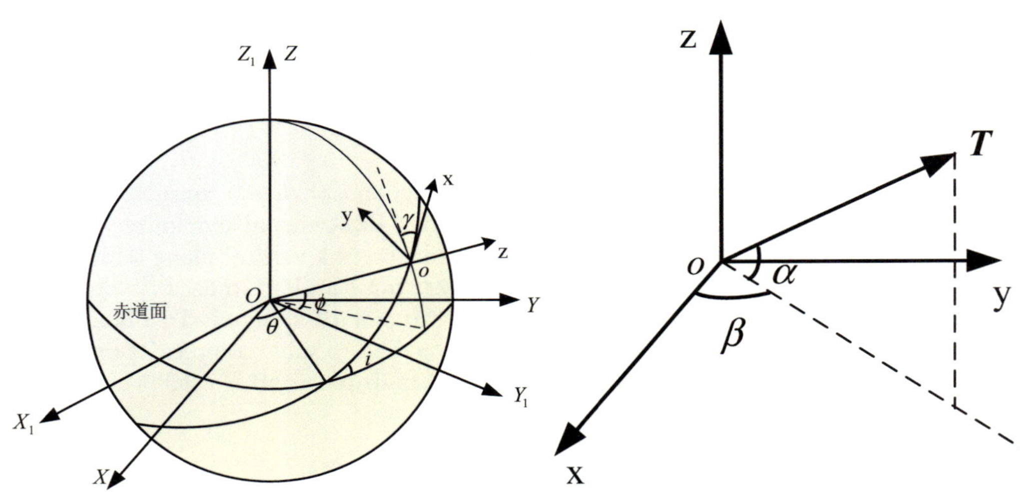

Fig. 1. Coordinate systems

The dynamics equations for lunar powered descent can be denoted as follow.

$$\begin{cases} \dot{r} = w \\ \dot{\theta} = \dfrac{u\sin\gamma - v\cos\gamma}{r\cos\phi} \\ \dot{\phi} = \dfrac{u\cos\gamma + v\sin\gamma}{r} \\ \dot{u} = \dfrac{T\cos\alpha\cos\beta}{m} - \dfrac{uw}{r} + \dfrac{uv}{r}\tan\phi\sin\gamma - \dfrac{v^2}{r}\tan\phi\cos\gamma \\ \quad -2w\omega\cos\phi\sin\gamma + 2v\omega\sin\phi - r\omega^2\sin\phi\cos\phi\cos\gamma \\ \dot{v} = \dfrac{T\cos\alpha\sin\beta}{m} - \dfrac{vw}{r} + \dfrac{uv}{r}\tan\phi\cos\gamma - \dfrac{u^2}{r}\tan\phi\sin\gamma \\ \quad +2w\omega\cos\phi\cos\gamma - 2u\omega\cos\phi - r\omega^2\sin\phi\cos\phi\sin\gamma \\ \dot{w} = \dfrac{T\sin\alpha}{m} - \dfrac{\mu_L}{r^2} + \dfrac{u^2+v^2}{r} - 2v\omega\cos\phi\cos\gamma + 2u\omega\cos\phi\sin\gamma + r\omega^2\cos^2\phi \\ \dot{m} = \dfrac{T}{I_{sp}g_0} \end{cases} \tag{17}$$

where thrust size T and thrust direction angle α,β are control variables for the dynamics. Other parameters nomenclature is given in appendix.

4.1.2 Objectives

The aim of optimal trajectory design is to minimize the amount of fuel required to perform a free end-time descent from the given initial state to the given terminal state. The objective function is:

$$\tilde{J} = \int_0^{t_f} \dot{m}dt = \int_0^{t_f} \frac{T}{I_{sp}g_0}dt = \frac{T}{I_{sp}g_0}t_f \tag{18}$$

The magnitude of thrust T is defined as a constant here, so the objective is to minimize the total powered descent time. The objective function can therefore be expressed as

$$J = t_f \tag{19}$$

4.1.3 Constraints

Firstly the boundary conditions including position and velocity constraints of lunar lander at initial time t_0 and final time t_f are considered.

The constraints at the initial time are

$$\theta(\tau_0) = \theta_0,\ \ \phi(\tau_0) = \phi_0,\ \ r(\tau_0) = R_L + h_0 \tag{20}$$

$$u(\tau_0) = V_0 - (R_L + h_0)\omega\cos\phi\sin\gamma,\ \ v(\tau_0) = (R_L + h_0)\omega\cos\phi\cos\gamma,\ \ w(\tau_0) = 0 \tag{21}$$

The constraints at the final time are

$$\theta(\tau_f)=\theta_f,\ \phi(\tau_f)=\phi_f,\ r(\tau_f)=R_L+h_f \tag{22}$$

$$u(\tau_f)=0,\ v(\tau_f)=0,\ w(\tau_f)=0 \tag{23}$$

Then constrained by the propulsion system, the thrust direction angle should be subject to

$$\alpha\in[\alpha_{\min},\alpha_{\max}],\ \beta\in[\beta_{\min},\beta_{\max}] \tag{24}$$

where $\alpha_{\min}$, $\alpha_{\max}$, $\beta_{\min}$ and $\beta_{\max}$ are the boundary of thrust direction angle.

4.2 Simulation example

Here a test case scenario is given to validate the optimization method.

The initial and final conditions - treated as boundary conditions by the optimization algorithm - are given by Equation (25)

$$\begin{cases} h_0=15km \\ \theta_0=0^\circ \\ \phi_0=90^\circ \\ u_0=1.6943km/s \\ v_0=0 \\ w_0=0 \end{cases} \qquad \begin{cases} h_f=2km \\ \theta_f=5^\circ \\ \phi_f=76^\circ \\ u_f=0 \\ v_f=0 \\ w_f=0 \end{cases} \tag{25}$$

The constraints of thrust direction angle are set as follows:

$$\alpha\in[-50^\circ,50^\circ],\ \beta\in[150^\circ,220^\circ] \tag{26}$$

The values of the other parameters used in this scenario are summarized here:

$$\begin{array}{ll} T=45kN, & m_0=15t \\ R_L=1738km, & i_0=90^\circ \\ I_{sp}=365s, & \omega=2.6617\times10^{-6}rad/s \end{array} \tag{27}$$

Here taking the LG points N=50, and GPM-GA is employed to solve the optimization problem. The results show that the optimal flight time for lunar landing is 472.74s, and require a fuel mass of 5947.2kg. The trajectory of lunar lander is shown in Fig. 2, where the result of methodology outlined in this paper, are compared to the indirect method (Pontryagin's maximum principle). As can be see, the two methods yield practically the same results.

The velocity of lunar lander in the orbit coordinate system $o-xyz$ is shown in Fig. 3, while the time history of thrust direction angle during landing is shown in Fig. 4.

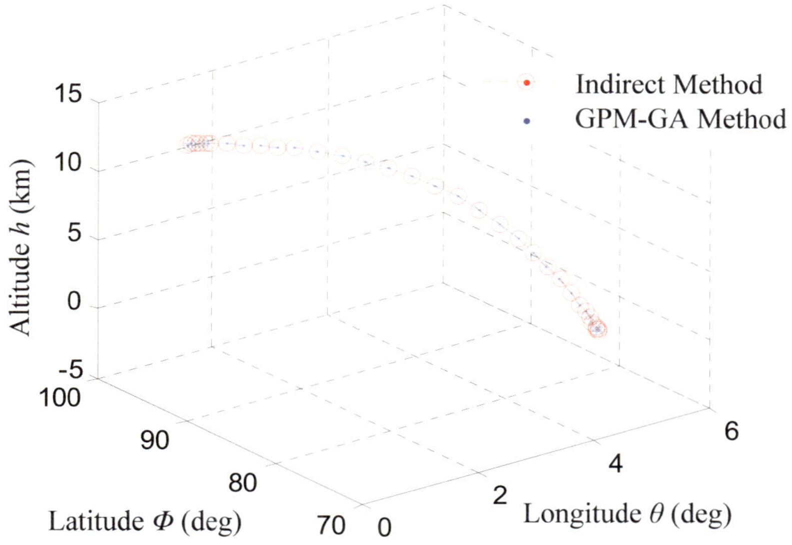

Fig. 2. The descent trajectory of lunar lander

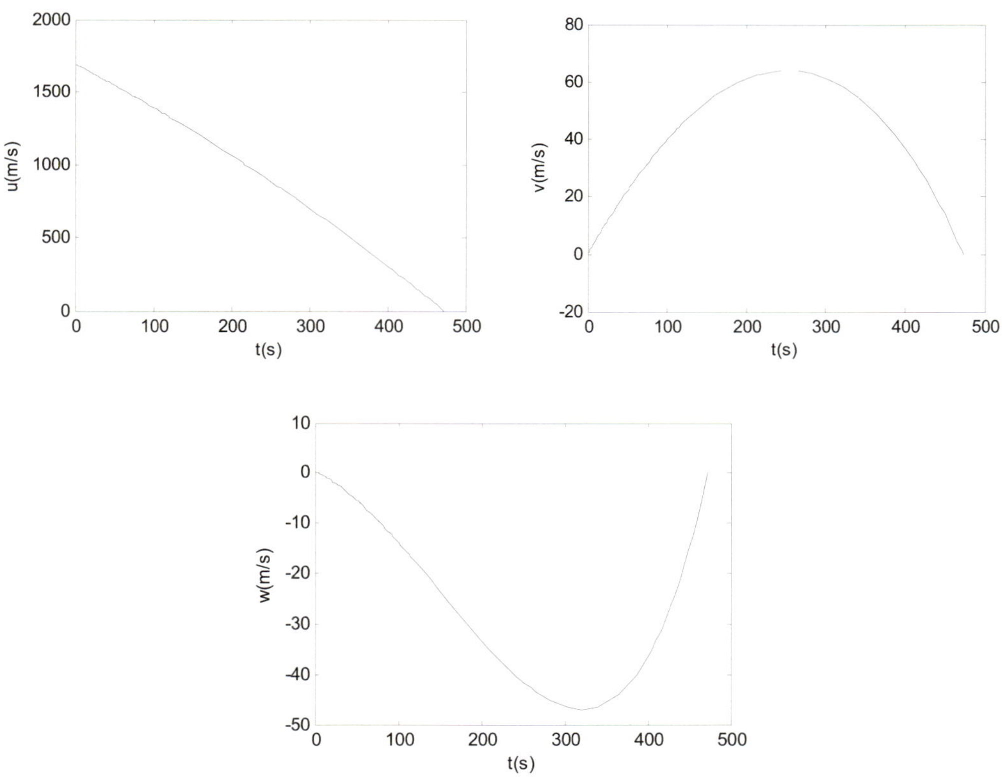

Fig. 3. Time history of velocity

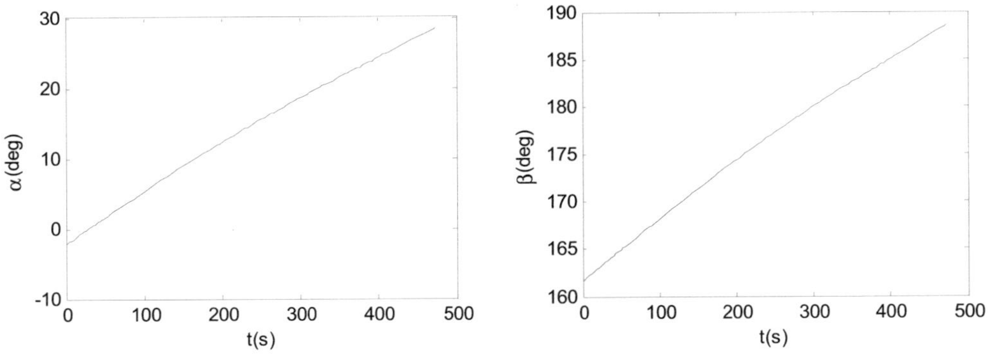

Fig. 4. Time history of thrust direction angle

The simulation results indicate that the GPM-GA optimization algorithm has high accuracy, and the error with results solved by indirect method is very small. What's more, the calculation will converge rapidly even when the initial values for GPM are chosen at random in the bound. Less than 2 minutes are needed for a result to be obtained on a PC with a 3.0GHz/Pentium 4 CPU. However, if using the traditional method such as direct shooting method to solve the optimal descent trajectory, the program can only be converged when the initial guess is closed to optimal values, and the calculation time is longer. For example, more than 20 minutes are needed for calculation with the method in reference [3].

4.3 Results analysis

4.3.1 Demonstration of computational feasibility

The feasibility of the computational solution can be validated by comparing the results to the propagated states via a separate ODE Runge-Kutta propagator. By interpolating the values of the control function, $\mathbf{u}(t_i)$, at the discretization time points and then integrating the differential dynamical equations 17, via MATLAB's ode45 solver, a comparison of error norms can be made with the results of methodology outlined in this paper. Results showed that powered descent trajectory dose satisfy the end-point conditions within an input constraint.

4.3.2 Demonstration of computational optimality

To demonstrate the necessary conditions needed for optimality the first step requires the formulation of the Hamiltonian [13]

$$H(\lambda,x,u,t)=L(x,u,t)+\lambda^T f(x,u,t) \tag{28}$$

where $L(\cdot)$ is the Lagrange cost, and $f(\cdot)$ is the vector field for the right hand side of the differential dynamical equations.

The objective function is defined as

$$J(x,u,t)=-m(t_f) \tag{29}$$

therefore

$$L(\cdot)=0 \tag{30}$$

and

$$H(\cdot)=\lambda^T f(x,u) \tag{31}$$

It can be shown that $H(\cdot)$ is constant with respect to time, with boundary conditions

$$H(t_f)=-\frac{\partial\Phi(x_f,t_f)}{\partial t_f} \tag{32}$$

To determine the final value of the Hamiltonian, the Endpoint Lagrangian, given as,

$$\begin{aligned}\Phi(x_f,t_f)=&-m(t_f)+\mu_1(r_f-r(t_f))+\mu_2(\theta_f-\theta(t_f))\\&+\mu_3(\phi_f-\phi(t_f))+\mu_4(u_f-u(t_f))\\&+\mu_5(v_f-v(t_f))+\mu_6(w_f-w(t_f))\end{aligned} \tag{33}$$

is substituted into the Hamiltonian Value Condition:

$$H(t_f)=0 \tag{34}$$

where, $\mu_i, i=1,\ldots 6$ is Lagrange multipliers.

This indicates that the Hamiltonian should be 0 for all the time in this problem. The Hamiltonian from the optimization solution in this paper is almost 0 with respect to time, and it can be used to verify that the numerical results satisfy the necessary Karush-Kuhn-Tuhker (KKT) conditions for optimality.

5. Conclusion

An optimization algorithm GPM-GA method is presented to solve the optimal finite-thrust trajectory with an input constraint in the paper. The results of a numerical simulation verified the validity of the proposed optimization method. The results indicate that the method can provide good performance on accuracy and fast convergence. It is expected that this novel optimization algorithm can be used to solve the similar optimization problems.

6. Appendix

Nomenclature

m	mass of lunar lander	**r**	position vector of lunar lander
m_0	initial mass of lunar lander	t	flight time
I_{sp}	propulsion system's specific impulse	u , v , w	velocity of lunar lander in the orbit

g_0	gravitational acceleration on the Earth surface ($9.81m/s^2$)	γ	angle between axis oy and north direction of the moon
μ_L	gravity constant of the moon	θ , ϕ	longitude and latitude
$\boldsymbol{\omega}$	rotation angular velocity of the moon	**T**	thrust
h	altitude from lunar surface of lunar lander	α , β	thrust direction angle

7. References

[1] Meditch J. S. On the Problem of Optimal Thrust Programming for a Lunar Soft Landing, IEEE Transaction Automatic Control, 1964, pp.477-484.

[2] Cho D. H., Jeong B., Lee D., et al. Optimal Perilune Altitude of Lunar Landing Trajectory, Int'l Journal of Aeronautical & Space Sciences, 10 (2009), pp.67-74.

[3] Huang W. D., Wang W. and Xi X. N. Overall Mission Trajectory Optimization for Manned Lunar Landing Mission Using a Hybrid Algorithm, the 2nd Information Engineering and Computer Science (ICIECS), Wuhan, China, December 2010.

[4] Pourtakdoust S. H., Jalali M. A. Thrust-Limited Optimal Three-Dimensional Spacecraft Trajectory, AIAA-95-3325-CP, 1995, pp.1395-1404.

[5] Luo Y. Z., Li H. Y., Tang G. J. Hybrid approach to optimize a rendezvous phasing strategy, Journal of Guidance, Control and Dynamics, 30 (1) (2007), pp.185-191.

[6] Fahroo F., Ross I. M. Direct Trajectory Optimization by a Chebyshev Pseudospectral Method, Journal of Guidance, Control and Dynamics, 25 (1) (2002), pp.160-166.

[7] Peng Q. B., Li H. Y., Shen H. X. Rapid Lunar Exact-Landing Trajectory Optimization Via Gauss Pseudospectral method, Journal of Astronautics (in Chinese), 31 (4) (2010), pp.1012-1016.

[8] Houacine M. and Khardi S. Gauss Pseudospectral Method for Less Noise and Fuel Consumption from Aircraft Operations, Journal of Aircraft, 47 (2010), pp.2152-2159.

[9] Huntington G. T. Optimal Reconfiguration of Spacecraft Formations Using the Gauss Pseudospectral Method, Journal of Guidance, Control, and Dynamics, 31 (2008), pp.689-698.

[10] KrishnaKumar K. Genetic Algorithms - A Robust Optimization Tool, the 31st Aerospace Sciences Meeting & Exhibit, Reno, Nevada, January 1993.

[11] Tu L. H., Yuan J. P., Luo J. J., et al. Lunar Soft Landing Rapid Trajectory Optimization Using Direct Collocation Method and Nonlinear Programming, the 2nd International Conference on Space Information Technology, 2007.

[12] Uchiyama K.: Guidance Law for Lunar Lander with Input Constraint, AIAA Guidance, Navigation and Control Conference and Exhibit, Hilton Head, South Carolina, USA, August 2007.

[13] Doman D. B., Bollino K. P., Ross I. M. Nonlinear Feedback Control for Rapid, On-Line Trajectory Optimization of Reentry Vehicles, AFRL-VA-WP-TP-2006-307, December 2005.

5

Genetic Algorithm Application in Swing Phase Optimization of AK Prosthesis with Passive Dynamics and Biomechanics Considerations

Ghasem Karimi and Omid Jahanian
Young Researchers Club, Mashhad Branch, Islamic Azad University, Mashhad, Iran

1. Introduction

A long standing common goal for engineers and physiologists has been to exploit the unique designs of the body to develop anthropomorphic artificial limbs that exhibit human-like stability, strength and speed in a variety of natural environments and also have similar mechanical behaviours and strength. Although tremendous technological progress has been made in rehabilitation technology, orthotic and prosthetic (O&P) limbs cannot yet perform as well as their biological counterparts.

Study on biomechanics and new models of walking have led to establish frameworks for making improvements in prostheses performance. As electromyography muscle signals (EMG) (Basmajian & Tuttle, 1973) showed a low level of muscular activity in human and gorilla legs during walking, ideas on biped mechanisms, able to walk without any joint actuations or active controllers were formed. Modelling the ballistic motion assumption of human swing leg during normal walking was proposed by (Mochon & McMahon, 1980) and since then it has been improved by others. Afterwards, the term Passive-dynamic walking was devised. Passive-dynamic walking machines that walk on shallow slopes were first designed, simulated and built by Tad McGeer (McGeer, 1990a, 1990b). These machines consist of hinged rigid bodies that make collisional and rolling contact with a slope, rigid ground surface. They are powered by gravity and have no active control (Lotfi et al, 2006).

One main advantage of passive dynamic bipeds is their simplicity which makes them easier to understand, build and modify. Although they are the most energy efficient ones, they are not able to support multi-behaviours, and this is because of their dependency on gravity as source of energy and their rigid structure. In order to have multi-behaviour systems some basic changes like adding active elements (actuators) or considering compliant elements (joints and links) are necessary (Baines, 2005).

Either the swing phase motion assumed as a passive motion or not, the importance of multi behaviour function of an above knee (AK) prosthesis is obvious, as the published results by Zahedi represents that changing walking speed happens considerable times during a day, and also other behaviours like stop, standing, ascending or descending ramps and stairs. So some controlling parameters are needed to alter the function of prosthesis. As prosthetic knee joints with different types of controlling parameters can be considered as an intelligent robot, so it has made necessary the combination of biomechanics and robotics results in the electronically controlled knee joint. In this way the basic principle is detection of the current state of amputee gait by integrated sensors and real-time adaptation of the flexion and extension resistances of the prosthetic knee (Zahedi, 2004). In this way Zarrugh and Radclif simulated the swing phase dynamics of an amputee wearing an above-knee prosthesis with a four-bar knee mechanism using a pneumatic swing control unit, which provides an analysis process in evaluating prosthetic devices at design stage (Zarrugh & Radclif, 1976). Tsai and Mansour compared hydraulic and mechanical knee swing phase simulation and design of above knee prostheses (Tsai & Mansour, 1986). Blumentritt studied a rotary hydraulic prosthetic knee mechanism for a transfemural amputee (Blumentritt et al., 1998). Kim and Oh developed an above knee prosthesis using magnetorheological damper (Kim & Oh, 2001). A comparison between a magnetorheological controlling prosthetic knee and a conventional model was done in (Herr & Wilkenfeld, 2003). Kapti and Yucenur also worked on design and control of an active artificial knee joint (Kapti & Yucenur, 2006). A biomimetic variable-impedance kneed prosthesis was proposed by Vilalpando and Herr in order to improve gait and metabolic energy consumption of above-knee amputees on variant terrain conditions (Vilalpando & Herr, 2009). Joshi and Anand studied on smart and adaptive lower limb prosthesis and discussed about electrorheological and magnetorheological fluids actuators. Vilalpando and Herr continued their design in their variable-impedance kneed prosthesis so called the agonist-antagonist active knee, which comprises an active powered knee with two series-elastic actuators positioned in parallel in an agonist-antagonist arrangement which were optimized to minimize level-ground walking electrical energy cost (Vilalpando & Herr, 2009).

As previously mentioned changing the stance on prosthetics form passive systems to active ones implies energy consumption in prostheses. That is why optimization in the imbedded controlling parameter in order to reduce energy consumption and form a more natural gait is necessary (Karimi, 2010; Tahani & Karimi, 2010). In this study genetic algorithm is applied as an evolutionary method in order to optimize the involved parameters in a way that the deviation of the prosthesis shank angle from its natural pattern is reduced and also optimize the variation pattern of a controlling parameter (SEP) for the best performance of the prosthesis.

2. A new prosthesis

One of the recent applications of robotics is in newly devised prostheses which can improve amputee's gait and safety beside its multi-behaviour function on various terrains. These benefits are acquired by energy consumption and using different controlling parameters. The prosthesis which is the subject of this study comprises SEP controlling parameter in knee joint.

2.1 SEP

SEP is a controlling parameter which has direct effect on AK prosthesis acceleration and generally motion of the leg during swing phase. In modelling of this phase of human walking in an above knee prosthetic leg, Figure 1, the shank angular position pattern varies according to different knee torsion Spring End Position (SEP). SEP parameter, adjusts the jam/elongation of spring and consequently the initial acceleration in the prosthesis knee.

This idea led us to optimize a variation pattern for this parameter in order to obtain a normal swing motion for the prosthesis. Figure 1 represents the SEP controlling parameter.

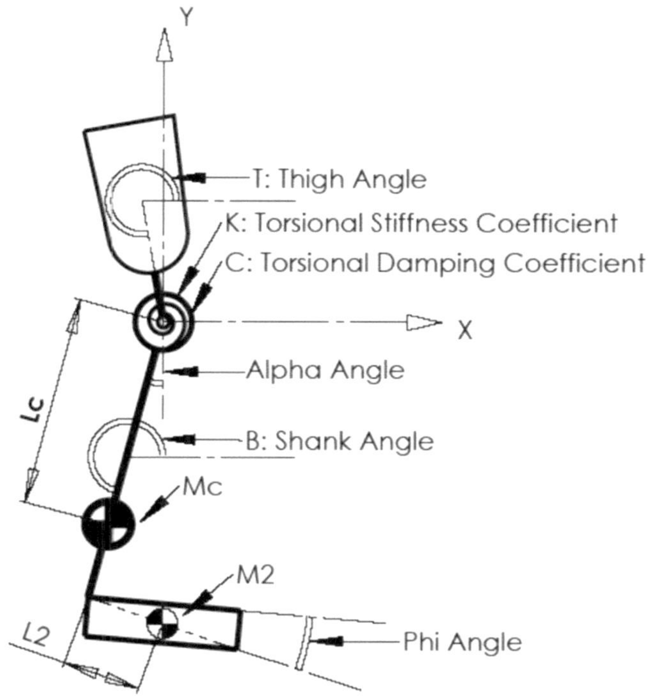

Fig. 1. Represents the SEP controlling parameter. Alpha angle is the SEP.

The most important advantage of the variable impedance controlling parameter is its ability to adapt the motion on variant terrain conditions. The SEP, acts as a variable-impedance controlling parameter which has no limitations in adaption to polycentric knee mechanisms or large flexion angles in comparison to other variable-impedance ones.

2.2 Dynamic equation

The dynamic modelling of an AK prosthesis is according to Lagrange dynamic equation method which is based on variation of kinetic and potential energy of the system. This system is assumed to act as a 2D open kinematical chain in sagittal plane which its ankle joint moves according to the natural pattern.

$$F(\dot{x}_B, \ddot{x}_B, \dot{y}_B, \ddot{y}_B, l_1, T, \dot{T}, B, \dot{B}, \ddot{B}, A, \dot{A}, \ddot{A}, m_1, k, c, SEP) = 0 \quad (1)$$

In (1) x_B is the horizontal motion of support, y_B is the vertical motion of support, l_1 is the distance between the prosthesis shank link centre of mass and knee joint, T is the thigh angle, B is the shank angle, A is the ankle joint angle, m_1 is the prosthetic shank mass, k is the stiffness coefficient, c is the damping coefficient and SEP is the spring end position. In passive modelling SEP is not a variable and is set in a specific amount.

2.3 Modelling considerations

In modelling the prosthesis after deriving governing equation, geometrical, initial and boundary conditions should be determined. In order to achieve an anthropomorphic prosthesis the geometrical data should be in accordance with anthropometry. On the other hand initial and boundary conditions have to be driven from natural gait and anthropometric data combination through a dynamic simulation.

2.3.1 Anthropometry

In prosthetic limb design, there have to be an exact similarity between the physical and geometric dimensions of prosthesis and it's sound limb. So the amputee's lost limb dimensions have to be obtained from anthropometric data references in order to be applied in the design of such devices.

No.	Segment	Formula	Amount (mm) for H=1770
1	Thigh length	0.245 H	433.65
2	Shank length	0.246 H	435.42
3	Foot length	0.152 H	269.04
4	Foot height	0.039 H	69.03
5	Pelvic width	0.191 H	338.07
6	Torso length	0.288 H	509.76

Table 1. Body segment lengths expressed as a fraction of body height H.

In this paper, the segmental dimensions are gathered in Table1 from the study of Yeadon and Morlock (Yeadon & Morlock, 1989) which is in adaption to (Winter, 2009) anthropometric data. More information about segments dimensions are included in Figure 2.

The item numbers 2, 3 and 4 in Table1 are directly presented in dynamic equation but all the items in the fourth column of this table are the geometric data considered in simulation.

2.3.2 Natural gait

Gait is a functional task requiring complex interactions and coordination among most of the major joints of the body particularly of the lower extremity. This fundamental task has been the subject of study by scientists for several centuries, both with description of typical body movements and of pathological conditions and therapeutic interventions (Nordin & Frankel, 2001). In brief, a gait refers to a particular sequence of lifting and placing the feet during legged locomotion. Gait analysis is useful for evaluating the effectiveness of prosthetic limbs, including their alignment, design, and performance, and for assessing orthotic designs and modifications (Gage et al., 2008).

According to the natural gait the following requirements for prosthetic knee function can be considered during level walking. At heel strike the prosthetic knee must be stabilized as the foot begins plantar flexion. During this Load Bearing period, the prosthesis has two major functions: body weight support and reduction in the impact of heel strike. This is achieved by a yielding flexion of the knee joint, which requires high flexion resistance. During the single support phase, the body moves over the stabilized leg like an inverse pendulum.

During this phase, the ground reaction force vector changes its position from heel to forefoot. This means that the flexed knee tends to extend rapidly so an appropriate extension resistance is necessary to prevent abrupt extension of the knee. This resistance should adapt to different gait speeds. As it is represented in Figure 3, swing phase starts with the knee already flexed 30 degrees; the maximum knee angle is 55 to 65 degrees and time for achieving this range of knee motion is very short. The prosthetic knee should start with minimal flexion resistance and adapt automatically to a wide range of gait speeds. At mid-swing the shank changes the direction of rotation due to mass reaction forces and the knee starts to extend. Terminal swing phase starts when the shank is in vertical position and ends when the extended leg hits the ground again. It is important that the knee joint extends quickly so that the leg is fully extended, yet the terminal impact should be minimal. So we can conclude that the important approach in stance phase is the system strength and components elasticity and in swing phase is the transition and dynamics.

The final conditions of the swing phase is the initial condition of double limb support and stance phase in human walking which is represented in Fig.2. Many tries have been made to improve the swing phase. The importance of pendulum motion of swing leg during the inverse pendulum behavior of stance leg in swing phase is, that in specific time it has to get to the exact position in order to make the heel strike and bear the ground reaction forces to avoid falling down and make a continuous cyclic motion. Beside the mentioned necessity in order to obtain the continuous human like walking motion, the trajectories of prosthesis motion have to be similar to natural limbs trajectories which are one of the gait analysis results. The trajectories conformity is much more important in prosthesis design than biped robots.

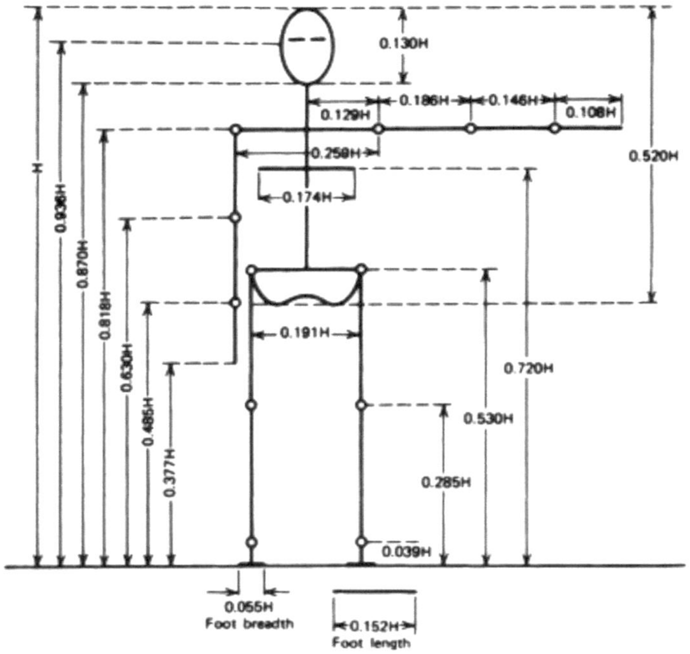

Fig. 2. Anthropometric segment length of human body as a function of body height (Winter, 2009).

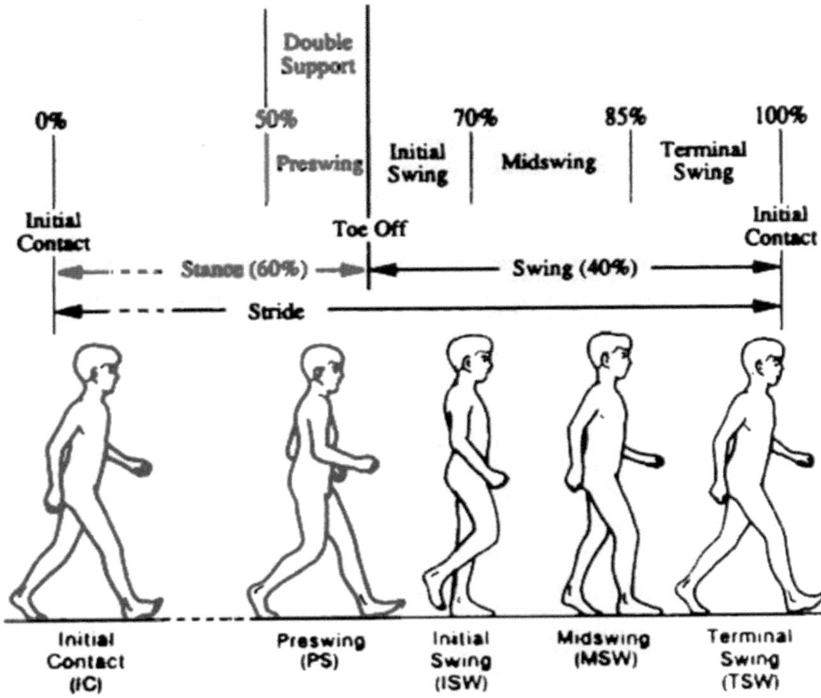

Fig. 3. Sequential representation of swing phase in a stride (Gage et al., 2008).

The gait analysis data that is used as natural pattern in composition and optimization of the model are gathered from a study results (Anderson & Pandy, 2001) in which the data have been obtained from five healthy adult males with the average age of 26 ± 3 years. The subject's mass average was 70.1 ± 7.8 kilograms and the average of their height was 177 ± 3 centimetres. The subjects walked at an average speed of 81 meters per minute, which is very close to the optimal speed. The standard data is included in Table2 in which the natural joint angles in sagittal plane are presented at 43 time steps.

Time (s)	Stance Ankle (Rad)	Swing Ankle (Rad)	Knee Stance (Rad)	Knee Swing (Rad)	Hip Stance (Rad)	Hip Swing (Rad)
0	-0.14266	-0.17031	-0.35879	-0.95979	0.480028	-0.12193
0.0112	0.157054	0.158689	0.349567	0.926263	-0.49235	0.144231
0.0224	0.171445	0.147064	0.34034	0.892733	-0.50468	0.16653
0.0336	0.185835	0.135439	0.331113	0.859203	-0.517	0.188829
0.0448	0.200225	0.123814	0.321886	0.825672	-0.52933	0.211128
0.056	0.214615	0.112189	0.312659	0.792142	-0.54166	0.233427
0.0672	0.229005	0.100565	0.303432	0.758612	-0.55398	0.255726
0.0784	0.243396	0.08894	0.294205	0.725082	-0.56631	0.278025
0.0896	0.257786	0.077315	0.284978	0.691552	-0.57863	0.300324
0.1008	0.272176	0.06569	0.275751	0.658021	-0.59096	0.322623

Time (s)	Stance Ankle (Rad)	Swing Ankle (Rad)	Knee Stance (Rad)	Knee Swing (Rad)	Hip Stance (Rad)	Hip Swing (Rad)
0.112	0.286566	0.054065	0.266524	0.624491	-0.60328	0.344923
0.1232	0.300956	0.04244	0.257297	0.590961	-0.61561	0.367222
0.1344	0.315347	0.030816	0.24807	0.557431	-0.62794	0.389521
0.1456	0.329737	0.019191	0.238843	0.523901	-0.64026	0.41182
0.1568	0.344127	0.007566	0.229615	0.49037	-0.65259	0.434119
0.168	0.358517	-0.00406	0.220388	0.45684	-0.66491	0.456418
0.1792	0.372907	-0.01568	0.211161	0.42331	-0.67724	0.478717
0.1904	0.387298	-0.02731	0.201934	0.38978	-0.68956	0.501016
0.2016	0.401688	-0.03893	0.192707	0.35625	-0.70189	0.523316
0.2128	0.416078	-0.05056	0.18348	0.322719	-0.71421	0.545615
0.224	0.430468	-0.06218	0.174253	0.289189	-0.72654	0.567914
0.2352	0.444858	-0.07381	0.165026	0.255659	-0.73887	0.590213
0.2464	0.459249	-0.08543	0.155799	0.222129	-0.75119	0.612512
0.2576	0.473639	-0.09706	0.146572	0.188598	-0.76352	0.634811
0.2688	0.488029	-0.10868	0.137345	0.155068	-0.77584	0.65711
0.28	0.502419	-0.12031	0.128118	0.121538	-0.78817	0.679409
0.2912	0.516809	-0.13193	0.118891	0.088008	-0.80049	0.701708
0.3024	0.5312	-0.14356	0.109664	0.054478	-0.81282	0.724008
0.3136	0.54559	-0.15518	0.100437	0.020947	-0.82515	0.746307
0.3248	0.55998	-0.16681	0.09121	-0.01258	-0.83747	0.768606
0.336	0.57437	-0.17843	0.081983	-0.04611	-0.8498	0.790905
0.3472	0.58876	-0.19006	0.072756	-0.07964	-0.86212	0.813204
0.3584	0.603151	-0.20168	0.063529	-0.11317	-0.87445	0.835503
0.3696	0.617541	-0.21331	0.054302	-0.1467	-0.88677	0.857802
0.3808	0.631931	-0.22493	0.045075	-0.18023	-0.8991	0.880101
0.392	0.646321	-0.23656	0.035848	-0.21376	-0.91142	0.902401
0.4032	0.660711	-0.24818	0.026621	-0.24729	-0.92375	0.9247
0.4144	0.675102	-0.25981	0.017394	-0.28082	-0.93608	0.946999
0.4256	0.689492	-0.27143	0.008167	-0.31435	-0.9484	0.969298
0.4368	0.703882	-0.28306	-0.00106	-0.34788	-0.96073	0.991597
0.448	0.718272	-0.29468	-0.01029	-0.38142	-0.97305	1.013896
0.4592	0.732662	-0.3063	-0.01951	-0.41495	-0.98538	1.036195
0.4704	0.747053	-0.31793	-0.02874	-0.44848	-0.9977	1.058494
0.4816	0.761443	-0.32955	-0.03797	-0.48201	-1.01003	1.080793

Table 2. Natural joint angles during swing phase of level walking.

2.3.3 Simulation

In order to form initial and boundary condition compatible for the dynamic equation, the anthropometric and natural gait data have to be combined. Table3 represents the output of the simulation including the initial and boundary conditions required for solving and optimization of this prosthesis. In addition to getting the required data, this simulation enables checking whether the natural gait and anthropometric data are well-matched. As there is no scuffing in the period of simulation during swing phase the gait data seem to be perfectly compatible with the anthropometric data. Figure 4 shows the sequences of swing phase in simulation.

Time Steps	Natural Shank Angle	Natural Thigh Angle	Natural Thigh Angular Velocity	Support Horizontal Velocity	Support Vertical Velocity	Support Horizontal Acceleration	Support Vertical Acceleration
0	0.578775	1.450997	-0.0926	2.085763	-0.19384	2407532	2081169
0.0112	0.520547	1.445103	-0.18379	2.155146	-0.20347	15.29589	4.334005
0.0224	0.488704	1.483037	-0.26886	2.313525	-0.13476	11.1319	10.03051
0.0336	0.474554	1.521221	-0.3143	2.520254	-0.04515	17.46207	5.405915
0.0448	0.461398	1.560398	-0.32279	2.718959	0.052183	5.51442	7.527583
0.056	0.464864	1.598753	-0.2805	2.827531	0.140593	9.136001	6.316703
0.0672	0.468643	1.637421	-0.34595	2.890862	0.207024	-0.3457	3.987605
0.0784	0.473223	1.67689	-0.42096	2.878061	0.2561	-1.23726	3.256767
0.0896	0.478435	1.716991	-0.43914	2.814379	0.296222	-2.81393	3.138184
0.1008	0.500215	1.756215	-0.23267	2.6675	0.323789	-10.6329	1.87989
0.112	0.518477	1.791921	0.127042	2.482889	0.331519	10.43345	2.782719
0.1232	0.550558	1.824002	0.380297	2.387977	0.335759	0.663911	0.737596
0.1344	0.562869	1.853758	0.616458	2.292245	0.32502	3.2396	1.332002
0.1456	0.607319	1.880763	0.821164	2.216995	0.308783	-2.14831	-0.14356
0.1568	0.634139	1.907583	0.638073	2.246379	0.328349	-12.3028	-3.59487
0.168	0.68123	1.93723	0.406127	2.227345	0.365575	1.324267	-0.9684
0.1792	0.730495	1.969051	0.276325	2.134311	0.40457	1.473616	-1.33174
0.1904	0.78045	2.001561	0.332699	2.037523	0.420251	6.799638	4.344001
0.2016	0.846032	2.032254	0.667514	1.928631	0.379645	8.805118	8.865213
0.2128	0.889531	2.058309	0.965982	1.804976	0.31419	15.65576	11.25232
0.224	0.96445	2.080895	1.402308	1.652249	0.244795	17.90474	10.1825
0.2352	1.017734	2.09929	1.733438	1.48242	0.176105	25.17289	12.20293
0.2464	1.085859	2.115081	1.879596	1.370442	0.158352	6.909545	-0.24444
0.2576	1.169233	2.128678	2.241855	1.264396	0.085641	2.885545	4.885733
0.2688	1.231371	2.138483	2.321678	0.956186	0.045551	-47.8642	3.756828
0.28	1.324206	2.144095	3.547173	1.30599	-0.20625	87.58613	-40.0517

Time Steps	Natural Shank Angle	Natural Thigh Angle	Natural Thigh Angular Velocity	Support Horizontal Velocity	Support Vertical Velocity	Support Horizontal Acceleration	Support Vertical Acceleration
0.2912	1.396087	2.128753	4.826859	1.705063	-0.50548	-29.3813	6.513214
0.3024	1.465127	2.110571	4.902961	1.511375	-0.57037	14.02588	-18.9013
0.3136	1.549296	2.090074	4.6823	1.226518	-0.55152	-68.4011	24.75477
0.3248	1.623709	2.077264	4.154421	0.888195	-0.43596	9.231962	-6.38834
0.336	1.698494	2.064828	4.316685	0.945869	-0.47979	0.559802	-1.01714
0.3472	1.774242	2.053353	3.892167	0.821086	-0.38779	-22.0264	17.22422
0.3584	1.835164	2.044497	4.493227	1.270116	-0.56788	105.8443	-54.7064
0.3696	1.872827	2.029827	3.330411	0.942208	-0.29592	-155.35	103.6241
0.3808	1.914513	2.036624	3.142915	1.095494	-0.27335	195.5028	-111.897
0.392	1.942482	2.029704	2.900612	1.196359	-0.24747	-179.97	127.7413
0.4032	1.974327	2.044105	2.074551	1.039283	-0.01456	152.7027	-91.4537
0.4144	1.976393	2.046171	2.998227	1.638025	-0.31366	-47.2443	44.00475
0.4256	1.966797	2.054019	2.109768	1.392019	0.009798	4.846665	11.20596
0.4368	1.960762	2.065429	2.334231	1.647849	-0.03519	39.633	5.38277
0.448	1.951722	2.073833	2.175698	1.6916	0.06316	-32.2434	38.56185
0.4592	1.92932	2.08632	2.255567	1.836874	0.055971	62.44801	-46.2666
0.4704	1.897135	2.089024	3.509053	2.416419	-0.43095	39.93598	-39.5263
0.4816	1.853654	2.080432	5.122795	2.649166	-1.08193	72.46124	-2116.42

Table 3. Natural, initial and boundary conditions required for solving and optimization

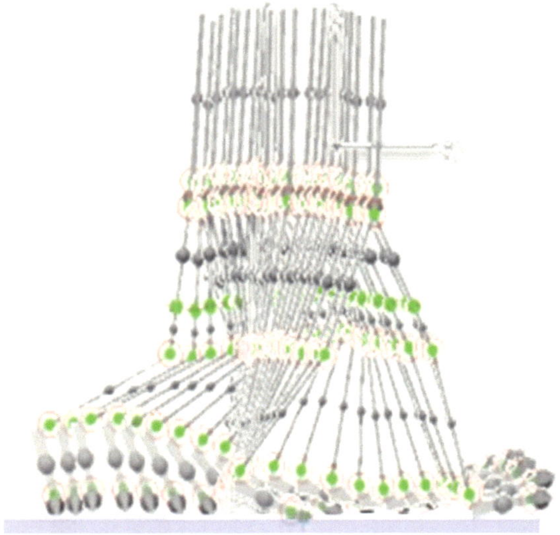

Fig. 4. The sequences of simulation during swing phase.

2.4 Solving method

Second order Taylor series is a numerical method in solution of such equations. The period of swing motion is divided into 43 time steps.

$$h = \frac{t_{final} - t_{initial}}{n} = 0.0112 \qquad \text{(The step period)} \tag{2}$$

$$\ddot{B}_i = \acute{F}\left(\dot{x}_{B_i}, \ddot{x}_{B_i}, \dot{y}_{B_i}, \ddot{y}_{B_i}, l_1, T_i, \dot{T}_i, B_i, \dot{B}_i, A_i, \dot{A}_i, \ddot{A}_i, m_1, k, c, SEP\right)$$

Derived from the dynamic equation at the i $_{th}$ time step (3)

$$\dot{B}_{i+1} = \dot{B}_i + h\ddot{B}_i \tag{4}$$

$$B_{i+1} = B_i + h\dot{B}_i + \frac{h^2}{2}\ddot{B}_i \tag{5}$$

Equations (2), (3), (4), and (5) represent the principle of the cyclic numerical solution process.

The shank orientation, B, is planned to be optimized by means of genetic algorithm. It is obvious that B_1 and $\dot{B}_1$ are comprised by initial condition.

3. Optimization

The prosthesis optimization can be performed according to different approaches, generally, minimizing energy expenditure, and minimizing the kinematical deviation from a standard pattern. The optimizing parameters are stiffness and damping coefficient of knee joint and inertial properties of the shank link. Fixed and moving ankle assumptions are two different states in the design of prosthesis which are compared according to the obtained results.

In order to design and fabricate prosthetic legs able to perform efficient multi behaviours the same as their natural counterparts considering physical parameters such as mass amount mass distribution, joints stiffness and damping as controlling parameters is necessary.

3.1 Optimization procedure

There are two distinct approaches in optimization of this problem which relates to considering only physical properties or both physical properties and SEP controlling parameter.

3.1.1 Passive prosthesis optimization

In this approach only physical parameters are applied to optimize the performance of prosthesis and as previously mentioned physical parameters are the shank mass amount (m_1), the shank centre of mass (l_1), knee joint damping and knee joint stiffness coefficients (c and k). After adding initial and boundary condition and other constant values like foot mass to the dynamic equation, the optimizing program guesses the physical properties. Afterwards the mentioned solving method will determine the resulted shank angle. Using an evolutionary algorithm to find the best gesture for physical properties in order to form the most similar pattern of walking to the natural one is the rest of optimization procedure.

3.1.2 SEP prosthesis optimization

In this approach in addition to the input data the SEP pattern is also needed as a variable in the dynamic equation. So initially there should be a procedure to determine the SEP pattern. SEP pattern is obtained from the dynamic equation to which natural shank angle, initial and boundary condition are added by using an evolutionary program in which it is tried to minimize the domain of resulted SEP pattern variation during swing phase.

Adding all the provided data to the dynamic equation and again using an evolutionary program to optimize the physical properties are similar to the passive optimization. In this way the best physical properties are determined for the best SEP pattern. In this study the evolutionary program which is applied in the optimization procedure is genetic algorithm.

3.2 Genetic algorithm

Evolutionary algorithms are optimization procedures that search for the solution that optimize a given function in a prescribed search space. Each solution (individual) is represented by the integer or real values of a finite number of variables, which can vary in prescribed intervals. The optimization procedure is usually started by generating the initial population of individuals in a random way (the first generation). Each algorithm is characterized by its own rules that force the evolution of the population to favor the improvement of the function to be optimized. Some parameters, typical of each algorithm, control the evolution and determine the algorithm capability of finding the optimal solution (Sentinella & Casalino, 2009).

Genetic algorithms as an evolutionary method are stochastic iterative processes that are not guaranteed to converge; the termination condition may be specified as some fixed maximal number of generations or as the attainment of an acceptable fitness level (Baydal et al.). Figure5 represents the genetic algorithm proceeding.

In this algorithm the optimizing parameters are the shank mass (m_1), shank centre of mass position (l_1), knee torsion stiffness (k), and damping coefficient (c) which are obtained by decoding each 48 character length chromosomes of a generation. Chromosomes population of each generation is 1500. The first generation is randomly produced. In this study the fitness function is based on the difference between the calculated angle of shank and the natural pattern and it tries to minimize the amount of fitness value.

After solving the dynamic equation according to the mentioned optimization procedure for each chromosome fitness value is determined. If none of the fitness values of the generation attain the termination condition (0.001), the cyclic function of this program will compose a new generation by familiar processes including selection, crossover and mutation. In this study the maximum number of generations can reach to 6000. Afterwards the lowest amount of fitness value ever in all generation specifies the result of optimization.

The selection process is designed according to roulette wheel, which selects the individuals according to the inverse of the amount of fitness value. In crossover; each parent chromosome is divided into four parts to compose an offspring. The possibility rate of crossover is defined 0.9. Mutation process is also another function which its possibility rate is 0.3. These functions produce at last 0.995 of population of a generation. The rest of generation are the elite members of previous generation which are directly brought over.

The search space of parameters and penalty coefficients can be defined according to fabrication and application considerations.

In this optimization algorithm both termination conditions; the attainment of an acceptable fitness level and a fixed maximal number of generations are defined somehow that if the first one doesn't occur the other one will terminate the program.

The following pseudo codes in Figure6 and Figure7 are the genetic algorithm optimizing programs of SEP pattern and the physical parameters in this study respectively which can be followed in every programming environment.

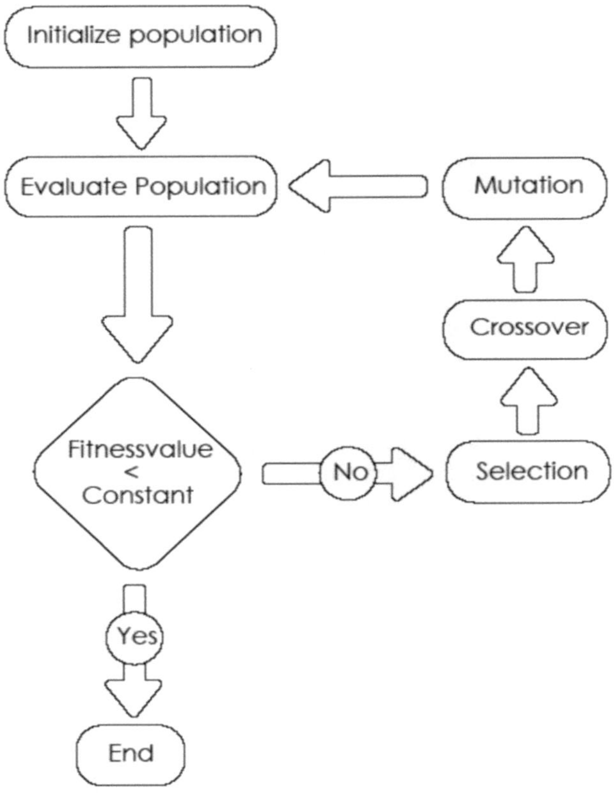

Fig. 5. The genetic algorithm procedure.

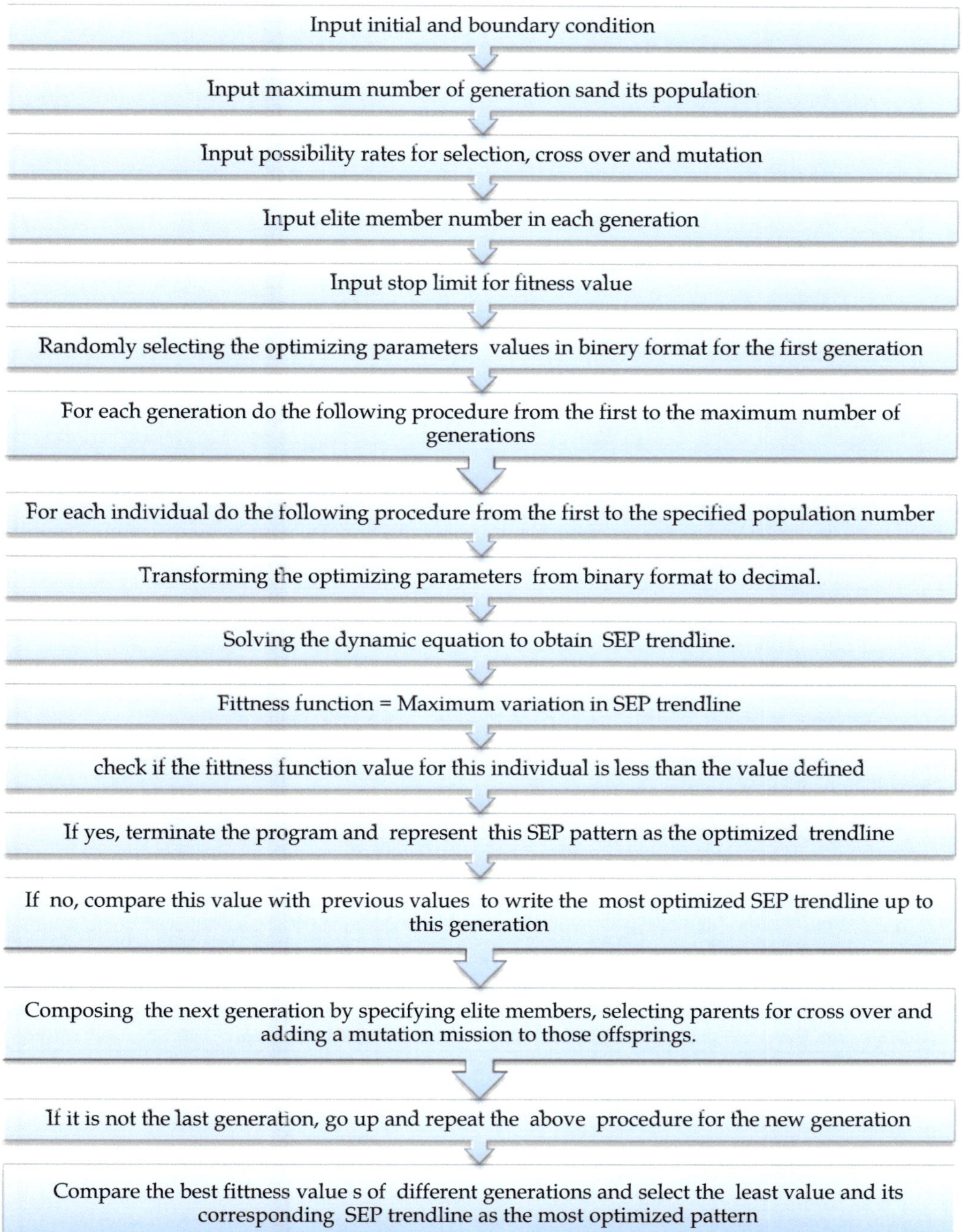

Fig. 6. SEP pattern optimization program code.

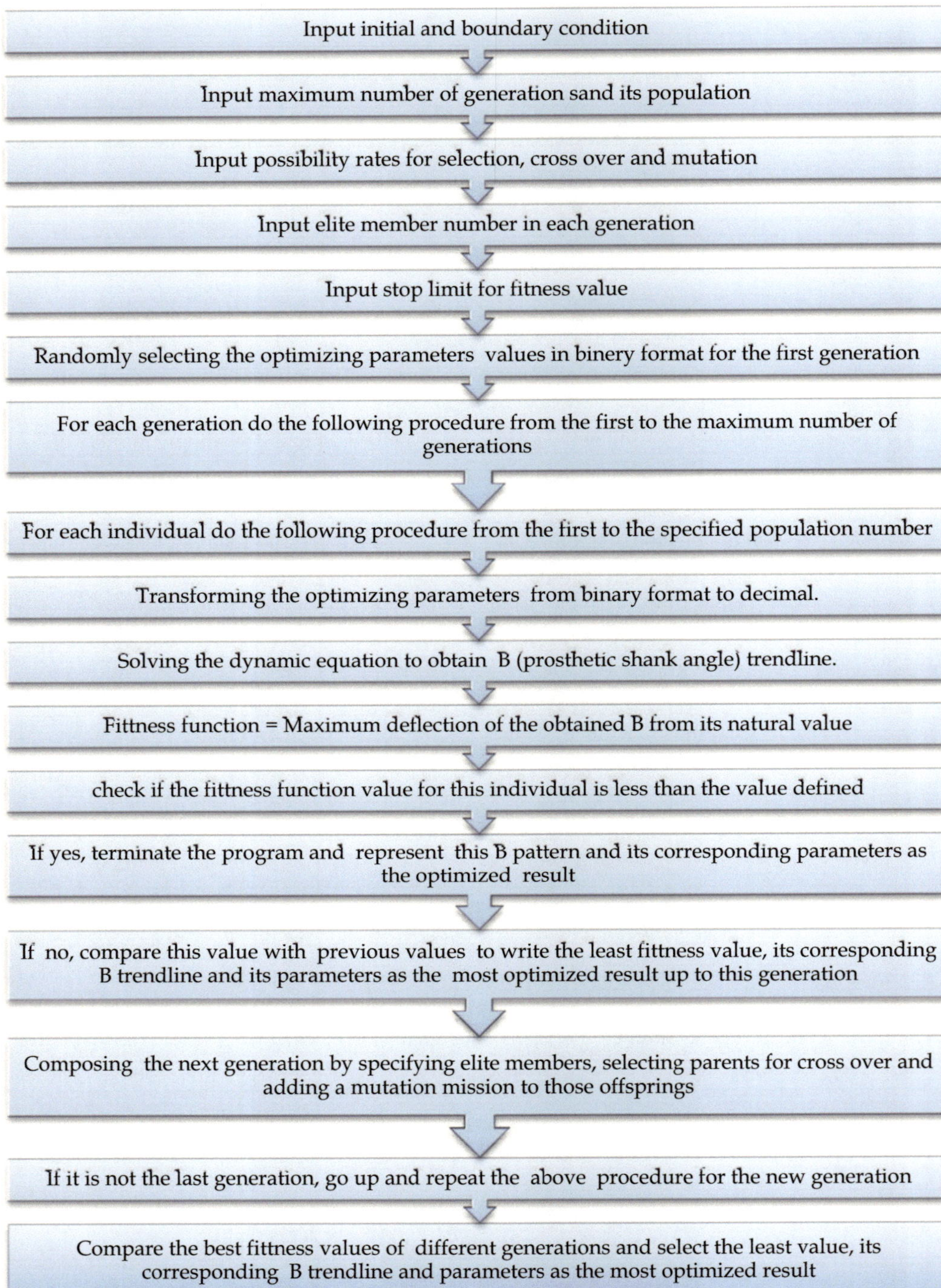

Fig. 7. Optimizing program code of physical properties as the optimizing parameters.

4. Results

AK prosthesis models represented acceptable results in comparison to natural walking. The physical parameters of the prosthesis which have shown in Table4 are optimized to minimize the deviation of resulted shank angle from the natural pattern according to walking gait data and its relevant anthropometry. The maximum deviation resulted in optimization of each model is represented in the fitness value column in the table.

Models	k (Nm/Rad)	c (NmS/Rad)	m_1 (Kg)	l_1 (m)	Fitness value (Rad)
Passive Prosthesis	13	20.8	8.143	0.455	0.0965
SEP Prosthesis	3	3	4.4	0.331	0.0463

Table 4. Physical parameters of the prosthesis.

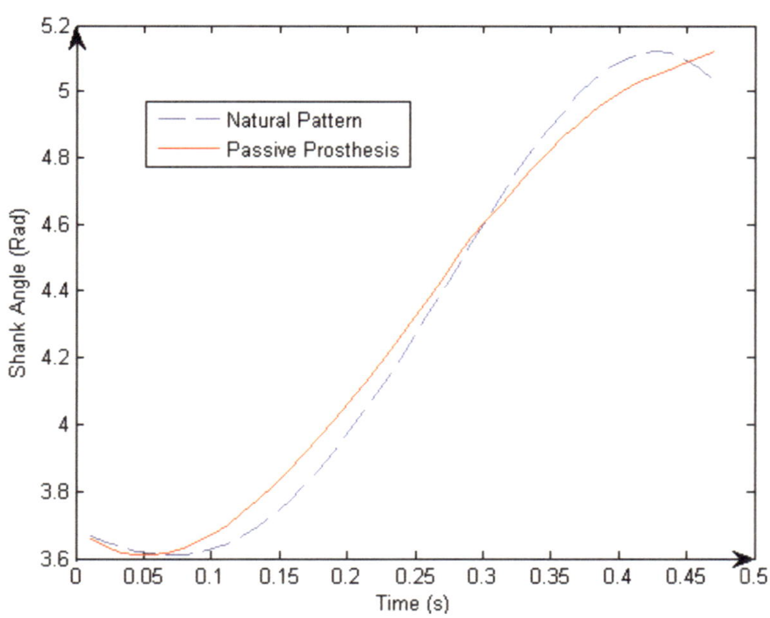

Fig. 8. The resulted passive prosthesis shank angles during swing phase.

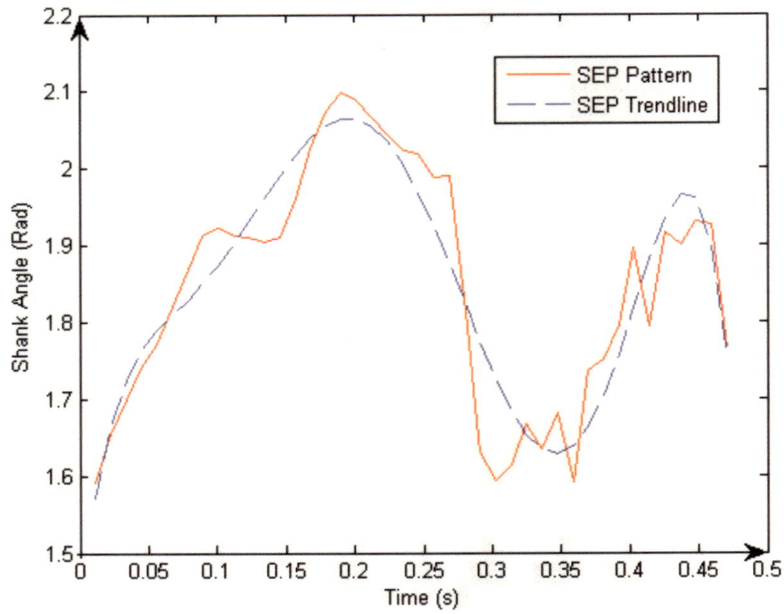

Fig. 9. The resulted SEP pattern during swing phase.

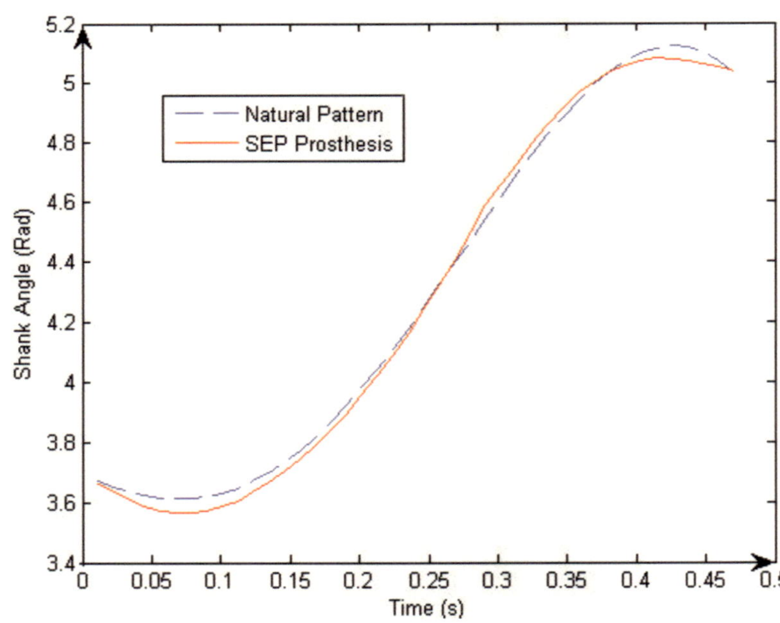

Fig. 10. The resulted SEP prosthesis shank angles during swing phase.

Passive prosthesis optimization also results into the shank angle pattern which is represented in Figure 8 in comparison to the natural pattern. On the other hand SEP prosthesis optimization initially determines the SEP pattern which is depicted in Figure 9.

The shank angle pattern of the optimized SEP prosthesis and its natural pattern are also shown in Figure 10.

5. Conclusion

In this study the prosthesis physical parameters were optimized via genetic algorithm method and led us to the following conclusions:

Beside the undeniable effect of a controlling parameter in making a prosthesis multi behaviour it improves performance of the prosthesis to make more natural behaviours. According to the resulted physical properties, using a controlling parameter (SEP) reduces the prosthesis mass which is highly appreciated and also decreases the amount of damping coefficient and dissipative energy.

6. References

Anderson, F. C., & Pandy, M. G. (2001). Dynamic optimization of human walking. *Biomech. Eng.*, Vol. 123, pp. (381-390).

Baines, A. G. (2005) .Knee design for a bipedal walking robot based on a passive-dynamic Walker. *BS Thesis*, Department of Mechanical Engineering, Massachusetts Institute of Technology.

Basmajian, J. V. and Tuttle, R. (1973). EMG of locomotion in gorilla and man. *Control of Posture and Locomotion*, pp. (599–609)

Baydal, J.M., Barbera, R., Lois, J.M.B., Page, A., & Prat, J. Application of Genetic Algorithms as Optimization Methodology in the design of Orthosis, Retrieved from < www.iai.csic.es/gait/documents/Publications/Genetic.pdf >

Blumentritt, S., Scherer, H.W., Michael, J. W., & Schmalz, T. (1998). Transfemural Amputees walking on a rotary hydraulic prosthetic knee mechanism. *J. Prosthet. Orthot.*, Vol. 10, No. 3, pp. (61-70)

Gage, J.R., Deluca, P.A., & Renshaw, T.S. (2008). Gait analysis: principles and applications. *Journal of bone and Joint Surgery*, Vol. 77, pp. (1607-1623)

Herr, H., & Wilkenfeld, A. (2003). User-adaptive control of a magnetorheological prosthetic knee. *Ind. Robot*, Vol. 30, No. 1, pp. (42–55)

Kapti, A. O., & Yucenur, M. S. (2006). Design and control of an active artificial knee joint. *Mech. Mach. Theory*, Vol. 41, pp. (1477–1485)

Karimi, G., (2010). Optimization of kneed prosthetic leg by biomechanical considerations. *MS Thesis*, Department of Mechanical Engineering, Islamic Azad University, Mashhad Branch, Mashhad.

Kim, J. H., & Oh, J. H. (2001). Development of an above knee prosthesis using MR damper and leg simulator. *Proceedings of the IEEE International Conference on Robotics 8 Automation*, pp. (3686-3691), Seoul, Korea. May 2001

Lotfi, B., Jahanian, O., & Karimi, G. (2006). Statistical modeling of a 2D straight leg passive dynamic walker Machine. *Proceedings of the International Conference on Modeling and Simulation*, Kuala Lampur, Malaysia, April 2006

McGeer, T. (1990). Passive dynamic walking. *International Journal of Robotics Research*, Vol.9, pp. (62-82)

McGeer, T. (1990). Passive walking with knees. *Proceedings of the IEEE Conference on Robotics and Automation*, pp. (1640-1645), 1990

Mochon, S. and McMahon, T. A. (1980). Ballistic walking, *J.Biomech*, Vol. 13, pp. (49-57)

Nordin, M. & Frankel, V.H. (2001). *Basic biomechanics of the musculoskeletal system*. Lippincott Williams & Wilkins.

Sentinella, M.R., & Casalino, R. (2009). Hybrid Evolutionary Algorithm for the Optimization of Interplanetary Trajectories. *Journal of Spacecraft and Rockets*, Vol. 46, No. 2, pp. (365-372)

Tahani, M., & Karimi, G., (2010). A new controlling parameter in design of above knee prosthesis. *World Academy of Science Engineering and Technology*, Vol. 70, No. 69, pp. (926-933)

Tsai, C. S., & Mansour, J. M. (1986). Swing phase simulation and design of above knee prostheses. *Biomech. Eng.*, Vol. 108, pp. (65-72)

Villalpando, E. C. M. & Herr, H. (2009). Biomimetic active prosthetic knee with antagonistic actuation. *Dynamic Walking 2009*, Simon Fraser University, Vancouver, Retrieved from < www.dynamicwalking.org/dw2009>

Villalpando, E. C. M. & Herr, H. (2009). Agonist-antagonist active knee prosthesis: A preliminary study in level-ground walking. *J. Rehabil. Res. Dev.*, Vol. 46, No. 3, pp. (361–374)

Winter, D. A. (2009).*Biomechanics and motor control of human movement* (4), John Wiley & Sons Inc., 978-0-470-39818-0

Yeadon, M. R. & Morlock, M. (1989). The appropriate use of regression equations for the estimation of segmental inertia parameters. *J. Biomech.*, Vol. 22, pp. (683-689)

Zahedi, S. (2004). Lower Limb Prosthetic Research In the 21st century, In: *Atlas of Amputations and Limb Deficiencies: Surgical, Prosthetic and Rehabilitation Principles* (3), American Academy of Orthopaedic Surgeons, Retrieved from < www.endolite.com>

Zarrugh, M. Y., & Radcliffe, C. W. (1976). Simulation of Swing Phase Dynamics in Above Knee Prostheses. *J. Biomech*, Vol. 9, pp. (283-292)

Part 2

GAs in Scheduling Problems

6

Genetic Algorithms Application to Electric Power Systems

Abdel-aal H. Mantawy
Ain Shams University, Faculty of Engineering, Electrical Power and Machines Department, Egypt

1. Introduction

The economic operation problem in electric power systems involves the scheduling of both thermal and hydro generating units to minimize the cost of supplying the power requirements of the system over a certain period under specified system constraints.

With the opening of the power industry to competition, the power system structure is changing. According to these changes, power system operation, planning, and control need modifications. In the past, utilities had to produce power to satisfy their customers with objective to minimize costs and all demand/reserve were met. However, it is not necessary in a restructured system. Under new structure, generation companies schedule their generators with objective to maximize their own profit without regard for system social benefit. Power and reserve prices become important factors in decision process.

The optimal scheduling of thermal generating units in the electrical power system is called thermal UC. The Unit Commitment Problem (UCP) is the problem of selecting the generating units to be in service during a scheduling period and for how long. The committed units must meet the system load and reserve requirements at minimum operating cost, subject to a variety of constraints. To solve the UCP, another crucial problem must simultaneously be solved; the economic dispatch problem.

The Economic Dispatch Problem (EDP) is the optimal allocation of the load demand among the running units while satisfying the power balance equations and the unit's operating limits [1-3].

The UCP is obtained by considering many factors, including:

- Unit operating costs/constraints
- Generation and reserve constraints; and
- Plant start-up and shut down constraints.

The objective of this report is to introduce the general UCP and discuss various considerations involving the chapter solution of this problem. It also aims to summarize the methods that have been used to solve this problem. Moreover an interest will be given to the Genetic Algorithms [4, 5] technique as a powerful tool to solve the UCP as one of the complex optimization problems.

This chapter includes seven sections organized as follows: In section 2, a literature survey for the UCP solution methods is presented. Section 3 introduces the problem formulation. In section 4, genetic algorithm background is presented. Section 5, outlines the genetic algorithm solution to the UCP. In section 6, general conclusions of the chapter report are presented. Section 7 includes the chapter report references.

2. Literature survey

The solution of the UCP is really a complex optimization problem. It comprises the solution of the EDP as well. The UCP can be considered as two linked optimization problems. The first is the UCP, which is considered as a combinatorial problem, and the second is the EDP, which is a nonlinear programming problem. The exact solution of the UCP can be obtained by a complete enumeration of all feasible combinations of generating units, which could be a massive number. Then, the EDP is solved for each feasible combination. Basically, the high dimension of the possible solution space is the real difficulty in solving the problem.

The solution methods being used to solve the UCP can be divided into four categories [1-74]:

- Classical optimization methods such as: Dynamic Programming, Integer and Mixed Integer Programming, Lagrangian Relaxation, Linear Programming, Network Flow Programming, Probabilistic Methods and other methods [6-18].
- Heuristic methods such as Priority List and Expert Systems [19-21].
- Artificial Intelligence methods such as: Neural Networks, Simulated Annealing, Tabu Search and Genetic Algorithms [22-57].
- Hybrid Algorithms: hybridization of two or more of the previously mentioned methods [58-74].

In the following, a survey of the classical optimization methods that have been reported in the literature is presented.

2.1 Artificial intelligence methods

The growing interest for the application of Artificial Intelligence (AI) techniques to power engineering has introduced the potentials of using the state-of-the art in many problems in power systems.

AI methods seem to be promising and are still evolving. Currently, four methods that are perceived as affiliated in some measure with the AI field have gained prominence as frameworks for solving different problems. AI techniques have been applied successfully to solve the UCP [99-163].

- Neural Networks (NN), [22-26],
- Simulated Annealing (SA), [27-28],
- Tabu Search (TS), [29-30], and
- Genetic Algorithm (GA), [31-57].

GA, NN and TS are inspired by principles derived from biological processes, and SA is derived from material sciences. These methods need not be viewed competitively, and they comprise the emergence of promise for conquering the combinatorial explosion in a variety of decision-making arenas. NN have claimed intriguing successes in pattern-recognition applications, but have generally performed less than impressively in optimization settings. SA, TS and GA have the attractive feature of assured convergence under appropriate assumptions.

In the following section a brief description of the applicability of the GA for the UCP is presented:

2.2 Genetic algorithms application to the UCP

Genetic Algorithms (GAs) have become increasingly popular in recent years in science and engineering disciplines [31-34]. The GA, as a powerful tool to achieve global optima, has been successfully used for the solution of this complex optimization problem. Several papers have been published in solving the UCP using the GA [35-57].

The solution coding is the most important point in applying the GA to solve any optimization problem. Coding could be in a real or a binary form. Coded strings of solutions are called "chromosomes." A group of these solutions (chromosomes) are called population. Moving from one population of chromosomes to a new population is set by selection, together with a set of genetic operators of crossover, mutation and inversion. Since the UCP lends itself to the binary coding in which zero denotes the OFF state and a one represents the ON state, all published works used the binary coding. A candidate solution is a string whose length is the product of the number of generating units and the scheduling periods.

Fitness function is the second issue in solving the UCP using GA. In the literature the fitness function is constructed as the summation of the operating costs and penalty terms for constraints violations.

A basic advantage of the GA solution is that it can be easily converted to work on parallel computers. A disadvantage of the GA is that, since they are stochastic optimization algorithms, the optimality of the solution they provide cannot be guaranteed. However, the results reported indicate good performance of the method.

The following is a summary of a literature survey on solving the UCP using the GA [35-57]:

In 1994, D. Dasgupta et al. [35] presented a paper, which discusses the application of GA to solve the short term UCP. In this work, the problem is considered as a multi-period process and a simple GA is used for commitment scheduling. Each chromosome is encoded in the form of a position-dependent gene (bit string) representing the status of units available in the system, (on/off), at a specific time period. The fitness function is formulated by using a weighted sum of the objective function, and values of the penalty function based on the number of constraints violated and the extent of these violations.

Hong-Tzer Yang, Pai-Chuan Yang and Ching-Lien Huang, 1995, [36], proposed an innovative GA (GA) approach to solve the thermal UCP in power generation industry through a constraint satisfaction technique. Due to a large variety of constraints to be satisfied, the solution space of the UCP is highly nonconvex, and therefore the UCP cannot be solved efficiently by the standard GA.

Hong-Tzer Yang, Pai-Chuan Yang and Ching-Lien Huang [37] modified their previous algorithm [36]. Ramp rate constraints on the units being started up or shut down are tackled in the economic dispatch subprogram by limiting the associated maximum available capacities for generating. The proposed approach is shown to be well amenable to parallel implementation.

In 1995, X. Ma et al. [38] presented a new approach based on the GA to solve the UCP. The coding scheme used was the binary coding. A forced mutation operator was adopted to correct the solutions (or chromosomes) that do not satisfy the load demand and reserve constraints. The fitness function was constructed from the objective function and penalty terms for constraints violation.

S. A. Kazarlis et al. [39], 1996, presented a GA solution to the UCP. The coding was implemented in a binary form. Fitness function was constructed from the objective function and penalty terms of constraints violation. A nonlinear transformation was used for fitness function scaling. With the technique of the varying quality function, the GA finally manages to locate the exact global optimum.

In 1996, P. C. Yang et al. [40] presented a practical approach for using the GA to solve the UCP. The implemented algorithm deals with the constraints in a different manner. The proposed algorithm, along with SA and LR is applied to solve a Taiwan power system consisting of 38-unit over a 24-hour period. With a reasonable computation time, the cost of the solution obtained by the GA approach was found to be the lowest among the three methods (GA, SA and LR).

S. O. Orero [41], 1996, proposed an enhanced GA approach for the UCP. The major difference between this approach and the previous ones is that it incorporates what was called 'a sequential decomposition logic', to provide a faster search mechanism. In this approach, the selection, mutation, and crossover operators are restricted to a single time interval. An advantage of this approach is that any constraints, which are already satisfied, cannot be violated later in the sequence.

G. B. Sheble' et al. [42], 1996, presented a paper to discuss the applicability of the GA approach to the UCP and the EDP. The first half of the paper presented the problems that the author has faced, when applying the GA to the UCP. The two main problems encountered when using a GA with penalty methods are the crossover operator can introduce new constraints violations that were not in either parent, and the problem of selecting penalty values for satisfying the five considered constraints is hopeless. These two problems resulted in each generation of population members having a similar fitness or similar UC schedule cost as the preceding generation. In the second half of the paper an algorithm of solving the EDP using GA is implemented and successfully tested and compared with the lambda iteration method.

Maifeld, T.T. and Sheble, G.B. [43], presented a new UC scheduling algorithm. The proposed algorithm consists of using a GA with domain specific mutation operators. The proposed algorithm can easily accommodate any constraint that can be true hosted. Robustness of the proposed algorithm is demonstrated by comparison to a Lagrangian relaxation UC algorithm on three different electric utilities.

Arroyo, J.M, Conejo, A. and Jimenez, N. [44], addressed the UCP with a new idea of implementing an interior point GA conducted through heuristics to get a near optimal solution to the problem. The modeling framework provided was less restrictive than the frameworks provided by other approaches such as dynamic programming or Lagrangian relaxation. The CPU time requirement to solve problems of realistic size was moderate.

In 1997, Mantawy, A.H., Abdel-Magid, Y.L. and Selim, S.Z. [45], presented a new GA approach to solve the UCP in electric power systems. In the proposed algorithm, coding the UCP solution is based on mixing binary and decimal representations. A fitness function is constructed from the total operating cost of the generating units without penalty terms. Genetic operators are implemented to enhance the search speed and to save memory space. The UCP is divided into two subproblems a combinatorial optimization problem and a nonlinear programming problem. The former is solved using the proposed GA while the latter problem is solved via a quadratic programming routine.

Mantawy, A.H., Abdel-Magid, Y.L. and Selim, S.Z. [46], presents an improved algorithm to the one in [143]. To improve the fine-tuning capabilities of the GA and escape from entrapment in local minimum, a special mutation operator based on a local search algorithm is designed. The new operator enhanced the speed of convergence and improved the quality of solution.

Zhao Hongwei, Yi Liangting, Wang Buyun, Cheng Gang and Yang Haiping [47], presented a revised GA for UCP. The model adjusts the parameters of GA automatically with the population evolution and different chromosomes. A new convergence rule is also given to enhance the convergence speed with global optimum reserved.

Hong-Tzer Yang, Pai-Chuan Yang and Ching-Lien Huang [48], proposed a parallel GA approach to solving the thermal UCP by using a constraint handling technique. The proposed topology of dual-direction ring is shown to be well amenable to parallel implementation of the GA for the UCP.

Zhu Mingyu, Cen Wenhui, Wang Mingyou and Zhang Peichao [49], proposed an enhanced GA to solve the UCP. The new features of the proposed algorithm include chromosome mapping, problem specific operators and local search technique. Significant improvements have been achieved with this implantation.

In 1999, Juste, K.A., Kita, H., Tanaka, E. and Hasegawa, J.[50] proposed algorithm to employ the evolutionary programming (EP) technique, in which populations of contending solutions are evolved through random changes, competition, and selection. The practical implementation of this procedure yielded satisfactory results.

F [50] proposed modification to counter the drawbacks of the GA which are their slow processing speed and their solution inconsistency. The method proposes a sequential UC implementation. It decouples a 24-hour UCP into 24 individual scheduling problems. The proposed modified GA algorithm was successfully tested with 6 generators system.

Christiansen, J.C., Dortolina, C.A. and Bermudez, J.P. [52] presented a new implementation of GA to solve the UCP. The proposed algorithm includes the basic GA operators (cross over and mutation) besides five particular operators that proved to be very useful in order to obtain faster and more accurate solutions lowering the possibility of reaching local optimums.

In January 2002, Senjyu, T., Yamashiro, H., Uezato, K. and Funabashi, T. [53] present a new approach for thermal UCP. To handle the UCP constraints, some cording methods have been proposed. However, these methods require computation time. To overcome these problems, a new genetic operator based on unit characteristic classification and intelligent techniques generating initial populations are introduced.

In February 2002, Swarup, K.S. and Yamashiro, S. [54] presented a solution methodology of UCP using GA. Problem specific operators are proposed for the satisfaction of time dependent constraints. Problem formulation, representation and the simulation results for a 10 generator-scheduling problem are presented

Haoyong Chen Xifan Wang [55] presented a new cooperative co-evolutionary algorithm (CCA) for UCP. CCA is an extension of the traditional GA (GA), which appears to have considerable potential for formulating and solving more complex problems by explicitly modeling the coevolution of cooperating species. This method combines the basic ideas of Lagrangian relaxation technique (LR) and GA to form a two-level approach.

In November 2002, Arroyo, J.M. and Conejo, A.J. [56] addressed the UCP of thermal units. This paper proposed a novel repair GA conducted through heuristics to achieve a near optimal solution to this problem. This optimization technique is directly parallelizable.

In August 2003, Mashhadi, H.R. and Shanechi, H.M. Lucas, C. [57] proposed an improved GA to solve the UCP. In order to improve the convergence of the GA, a new local optimizer for the UCP based on Lamarck theory in the evolution, has been proposed. This local optimizer, which tries to improve the fitness of one chromosome in the population, effectively uses the information generated in calculating the fitness.

2.3 Hybrid algorithms

Hybrid algorithms are also well known techniques for solving engineering problems. Hybrid algorithms try to make use of the merits of different methods. Hence, the aim is to improve the performance of algorithms that are based on a single method. The main objective of proposing an algorithm as a hybrid of two or more methods is to speed up the convergence and/or to get better quality of solutions than that obtained when applying the individual methods.

Different hybrid algorithms, used to solve the UCP, are available in the literature [58-74]. These algorithms consist of two or more of the following methods: Classical Optimization (e.g. DP, LP, and LR), Heuristics, and Artificial Intelligence, (e.g. NN, and GA).

The following survey is divided into two parts: hybrid algorithms without the GA and hybrid algorithms with the GA

2.3.1 Hybrid algorithms with the GA

Many AI and classical optimization techniques have been hybridized with the GA to solve the UCP. The following is a summary of these algorithms:

In 1994, Gerald B. Sheble' et al. [62] presented a genetic-based UCP algorithm. The algorithm uses the ES to satisfy some of the UCP constraints. The advantage of the algorithm is that the EDP routine is only used with the initialization and mutation subroutines. Since the mutation is a technique that changes a small percentage of the on/off status of the generating unit schedule, the only times ED is needed is for the hours where a mutation has occurred. An adaptive mutation operator is used.

In 1995, S. O. Orero et al. [65] proposed an algorithm to incorporate a PL scheme in a hybrid GA to solve the UCP. In the GA coding process, the solution string length is the product of the scheduling period T, and the number of generating units N. Accordingly; the search space of the GA is then equal to $2^{T \times N}$ which is a very large number. Due to this problem, a premature convergence of the GA search has occurred. To counteract this problem, a method of decomposition was proposed to limit the GA search space to 2^N.

Mantawy, A.H., Abdel-Magid, Y.L. and Selim, S.Z. [68] presented a new algorithm based on integrating GA, TS and SA methods to solve the UCP. The core of the proposed algorithm is based on GAs. TS is used to generate new population members in the reproduction phase of the GA. A SA method is used to accelerate the convergence of the GA by applying the SA for all the population members. A new implementation of the GA is introduced. In the TS part of the proposed algorithm, a simple short-term memory procedure is used to counter the danger of entrapment at a local optimum, and the premature convergence of the GA. A simple cooling schedule has been implemented to apply the SA test in the algorithm.

Chuan-Ping Cheng, Chih-Wen Liu and Chun-Chang Liu [70-72] presented an application of a combined GA and LR methods for the UCP (LRGA). The proposed LRGA incorporates GA into LR method to update the Lagrangian multipliers and improve the performance of LR method in solving combinatorial optimization problems such as the UCP.

Mantawy, A.H., Abdel-Magid, Y.L. and Selim, S.Z. [67] presented a new algorithm based on integrating GA and TS to solve a fuzzy UCP model. The core of the proposed algorithm is based on the GA while TS is used to generate new population members in the reproduction phase of the GA. The uncertainties in the load demand and the spinning reserve constraints are formulated in a fuzzy logic (FL) frame. A fitness function is constructed from the total operating cost of the generating units with penalty term related fuzzy spinning reserve and load demand membership functions. In the TS part of the proposed algorithm, a simple short-term memory procedure is used to counter the danger of entrapment at a local optimum, and the premature convergence of the GA.

Mantawy, A.H [71] presented a fuzzy model for the UCP. The model takes the uncertainties in the forecasted load demand and the spinning reserve constraints in a fuzzy frame. The genetic algorithm (GA) approach is then used to solve the proposed fuzzy UCP model. In the implementation for the GA, coding of the UCP solutions is based on mixing binary and decimal representations. A fitness function is constructed from the total operating cost of the generating units plus a penalty term determined due to the fuzzy load and spinning reserve membership functions.

Gwo-Ching Liao and Ta-Peng Tsao. [73], introduced a hybrid GA/fuzzy system and tabu search method (GAFS-TS) for solving short-term thermal generating UCP. This system makes three important improvements to the GA. First, it generates a set of feasible UC schedules and then put the solution to TS. The GAFS has good global optima search capabilities, but poor local optima search capabilities. The TS method has good local optima search capabilities.

3. Unit Commitment Problem formulation

The Unit Commitment Problem (UCP) is the problem of selecting the generating units to be in service during a scheduling period and for how long. The committed units must meet the system load and reserve requirements at minimum operating cost, subject to a variety of constraints. The Economic Dispatch Problem (EDP) deals with the optimal allocation of the load demand among the running units while satisfying the power balance equations and units operating limits [1].

The solution of the UCP using artificial intelligence techniques requires three major steps:

- A problem statement or, system modeling,
- Rules for generating trial solutions, and
- An efficient algorithm for solving the EDP.

Problem Statement: Modeling of power system components affecting the economic operation of the system is the most important step when solving the UCP. The degree of details in components modeling varies with the desired accuracy and the nature of the problem under study. The basic components of a power system include generating power stations, transformer, transmission network, and system load.

This work is concerned with thermal generating units scheduling. Hence it is assumed that the network is capable of transmitting the power generated to the load centers without neither losses nor network failures. This means that the network is assumed to be perfectly reliable. Consequently, the following basic engineering assumptions are made [1-3]:

- The network interchange between the system under study and other systems is fixed.
- Adding or removing generating units does not affect the load demand.
- The operating cost of a generating unit is assumed to be composed of three components; start-up cost, spinning (no load) cost, and production (loading) cost.

In the UCP under consideration, one is interested in a solution, which minimizes the total operating cost during the scheduling time horizon while several constraints are satisfied.

The objective function and the constraints of the UCP are described in Sections 3.1 and 3.2.

3.1 The objective function

The objective function of the UCP is represented by the total operating cost of thermal generating units, which contains two major parts; the production costs and the start-up costs.

3.1.1 The production cost

The major component of the operating cost, for thermal and nuclear units, is the power production cost of the committed units. The production cost is mainly the cost of fuel input per hour, while maintenance and labor contribute only to a small extent. Conventionally the unit production cost is expressed as a quadratic function of the unit output power as follows:

$$\mathbf{F_{it}(P_{it}) = A_i P^2_{it} + B_i P_{it} + C_i} \ \ \$/\mathrm{HR} \tag{3.1}$$

3.1.2 The start-up cost

The second component of the operating cost is the start-up cost. The start-up cost is attributed to the amount of energy consumed to bring the unit "ON" line. The start-up cost depends upon the down time of the unit. This can vary from maximum value, when the unit is started from cold state, to a much smaller value, where the unit was recently turned off.

Calculation of the start-up cost depends also on the treatment method for the thermal unit during down time periods. There are two methods for unit treatment during the OFF hours; the cooling method and the banking method.

The former method allows the boiler of the unit to cool down and then reheat back up to the operating temperature when recommitted on line.

In the latter method, the boiler operating temperature is maintained during the OFF time using an additional amount of energy.

The cooling method is used in the present work, due to its practicability when applied to real power systems. In this work, the start-up cost, for a unit i at time t, based on the cooling method, is taken in a more general form as follows:

$$\mathbf{ST_{it} = So_i[1 - D_i exp(-Toff_i / Tdown_i)] + E_i} \quad \$ \tag{3.2}$$

Accordingly, the overall operating cost of the generating units in the scheduling time horizon (i.e. objective function of the UCP) is

$$\mathbf{F_T = \sum_{t=1}^{T} \sum_{i=1}^{N} (U_{it} F_{it}(P_{it}) + V_{it} ST_{it} + W_{it} SH_{it})} \quad \$ \tag{3.3}$$

3.2 The constraints

The UCP is subject to many constraints depending on the nature of the power system under study. The constraints, which are taken into consideration in this work, may be classified into two main groups: system constraints and unit constraints.

3.2.1 System constraints

The system constraints, sometimes called coupling constraints, include also two categories: the load demand and the spinning reserve constraints.

1. Load demand constraints

The load demand constraint is the most important constraint in the UCP. It basically means that the generated power from all committed units must meet the system load demand. This is formulated in the so-called balance equation as follows:

$$\mathbf{\sum_{i=1}^{N} U_{it} P_{it} = PD_t \quad ; 1 \le t \le T} \tag{3.4}$$

2. Spinning reserve constraint

The spinning (operating) reserve is the total amount of generation capacity available from all units synchronized (spinning) on the system minus the present load demand. It is important to determine the suitable allocation of spinning reserve from two points of view: the reliability requirements and the economic aspects.

There are various methods for determining the spinning reserve [1,20,34,52]:

The reserve is computed as a percentage of the forecasted load demand, or

It is determined such that the system can make up for a loss of the highest rating unit in a given period of time, or

Determination of the reserve requirements as a function of the system reliability, which is evaluated on a probabilistic basis.

The most commonly used approach is computing the reserve as a given prespecified amount, which is a percentage of the forecasted load demand, i.e.

$$\sum_{i=1}^{N} U_{it} Pmax_i \geq (PD_t + R_t) \; ; \qquad 1 \leq t \leq T \tag{3.5}$$

3.2.2 Unit constraints

The constraints on the generating units (sometimes called local constraints) are described as follow:

1. Generation limits

The generation limits represent the minimum-loading limit below which it is not economical to load the unit, and the maximum loading limit above which the unit should not be loaded.

$$U_{it} Pmin_i \leq P_{it} \leq Pmax_i U_{it} \; ; \; 1 \leq t \leq T \, , \; 1 \leq i \leq N \tag{3.6}$$

2. Minimum up/down time

If the unit is running, it cannot be turned OFF before a certain minimum time elapses. If the unit is also down, it cannot be recommitted before a certain time elapse.

$$\begin{matrix} T_{off_i} \geq T_{down_i} \\ T_{on_i} \geq T_{up_i} \end{matrix} \; ; \; 1 \leq i \leq N \tag{3.7}$$

These constraints could be formulated in a mathematical form as follows:

$$\sum_{l=0}^{T_{up_i} - 1} U_{i,t+l} \geq V_{it} T_{up_i} \; ; \qquad 1 \leq t \leq T \, , \; 1 \leq i \leq N \tag{3.8}$$

$$\sum_{l=0}^{T_{down_i} - 1} (1 - U_{i,t+l}) \geq W_{it} T_{down_i} \; ; \qquad 1 \leq t \leq T \, , \; 1 \leq i \leq N \tag{3.9}$$

$$V_{it} \geq U_{it} - U_{i,t-1} \; ; \qquad 2 \leq t \leq T \, , 1 \leq i \leq N \tag{3.10}$$

$$W_{it} \geq U_{i,t-1} - U_{it} \; ; \qquad 2 \leq t \leq T \, , \; 1 \leq i \leq N \tag{3.11}$$

$$\mathbf{V_{i1} = U_{i1}} \; ; \qquad \mathbf{1 \le i \le N} \tag{3.12}$$

$$\mathbf{W_{i1} = 1 - U_{i1}} \; ; \qquad \mathbf{1 \le i \le N} \tag{3.13}$$

3. Units initial status constraint

The status of unit (e.g. hours of being ON or OFF) before the first hour in the proposed schedule is an important factor to determine whether its new status violates the minimum up/down constraints. Also, the initial status of the unit affects the start-up cost calculations.

4. Crew constraints

If the plant consists of two or more units, they cannot be turned ON at the same time due to some technical conditions or manpower availability.

5. Unit availability constraint

Due to some abnormal conditions, e.g. forced outage or maintenance of a unit, the unit may become *unavailable.* The unit may also be forced in service to increase reliability or stability of the system, hence the unit becomes *must run* or *fixed at a certain output.* Otherwise the unit is *available.* The availability constraint specifies the unit to be in one of the following different situations; *unavailable, must run, available, or fixed output (MW).*

6. Units derating constraint

During the lifetime of a unit its performance could be changed due to many conditions, e.g. aging factor, the environment, etc. These conditions may cause derating of the generating unit. Consequently, the unit maximum and minimum limits are changed.

3.3 The economic dispatch problem

The economic dispatch problem (EDP) is an essential problem when solving the UCP. Once a trial solution is generated, the corresponding operating cost of this solution is calculated by solving the EDP. Consequently, using an efficient and fast algorithm for modeling and solving the EDP improves the quality of the UCP solution, and therefore, the performance of the overall UCP algorithm.

In brief, the EDP for a one-hour in the scheduling time horizon could be formulated as the minimization of the summation of production costs of the committed units in this hour subjected to the load demand and unit limits constraints as follows:

$$\text{Minimize } \sum_{i=1}^{N} \mathbf{F_{it}(P_{it}) = A_i P^2{}_{it} + B_i P_{it} + C_i} \qquad \$/\text{HR} \tag{3.14}$$

Subject to:

$$\sum_{\mathbf{i=1}}^{\mathbf{N}} \mathbf{P_{it} = PD_t} \quad ; \mathbf{1 \le t \le T} \tag{3.15}$$

and

$$\mathbf{Pmin_i \le P_{it} \le Pmax_i} \;\; ; \mathbf{1 \le t \le T} \, , \, \mathbf{1 \le i \le N} \tag{3.16}$$

Since the EDP is formulated in a quadratic function, the EDP is solved using a quadratic programming routine.

4. Genetic algorithms approach

4.1 Overview

Genetic algorithms (GAs) have been developed by John Holland, his colleagues, and his students at the University of Michigan in the early 1970's [3,5, 122-128]. GAs have become increasingly popular in recent years in science and engineering disciplines. GAs have been quite successfully applied to optimization problems like wire routing, scheduling, adaptive control, game playing, cognitive modeling, transportation problems, traveling salesman problems, optimal control problems, etc.

GAs are general-purpose search techniques based on principles inspired from the genetic and evolution mechanisms observed in natural systems and populations of living beings. Their basic principle is the maintenance of a population of solutions to a problem (genotypes) in the form of encoded information individuals that evolve in time.

GAs are search methods based on the mechanics of natural selection and natural genetics. They combine survival of the strongest among string structures with a structured, yet random, information exchange. In every generation, a new set of artificially developed strings is produced using elements of the strongest of the old; an occasional new element is experimented with for enhancement. Although random in nature, genetic algorithms are not random search. They efficiently utilize historical information to predict new search points with expected improved performance. Furthermore, they are not fundamentally restricted by assumptions about the search space (assumptions concerning continuity, existence of derivatives uni-modality, and other matters). The genetic algorithm is an example of an optimization procedure that utilizes random choice as a mechanism to control the search through a coding of a parameter space.

GAs require the parameters of the optimization problem to be coded as a finite length string over some finite alphabet. In many optimization methods we migrate from a single point in the search space to the next using a transition rule to determine the next point. This point-to-point method is dangerous because it may lead to locating local minima (maxima) in multimodal (many peaked) search spaces. On the other hand, GAs work from a population of strings at the same time, climbing several peaks in parallel; hence, reducing the possibility of locating a false peak over methods that go point to point. The mechanics of a genetic algorithm are extremely simple, only involving copying strings and swapping partial strings.

A simple genetic algorithm that produces satisfactory results in many applications problems must have five components:

A genetic representation for potential solution to the problem; "solution coding"

A way to create an initial population of potential solutions; "Initialization"

An evaluation function that plays the role of the environment, rating solutions in terms of their "fitness function",

Genetic operators that alter the composition of children "Genetic operators",

Values for various parameters that the GA uses (e.g. population size, probabilities of applying genetic operators, etc.); "parameters settings and selection"

4.2 Solution coding

GAs require the natural parameters set of the optimization problem to be coded as a finite-length string over some finite alphabet. Coding is the most important point in applying the GA to solve any optimization problem. Coding could be in a real or a binary form. Coded strings of solutions are called "chromosomes". A group of these solutions (chromosomes) are called population.

In this step, a coding scheme is selected to code the parameter subject to optimization. This will allow access to parameter features that are not apparent using the parameter default code. This access will allow more freedom and resolution for modifying the parameter features to arrive at the optimal solution.

4.3 Fitness function

The fitness function is the second important issue in solving optimization problems using GAs. It is often necessary to map the underlying natural objective function to a fitness function through one or more mappings. The first mapping is done to transform the objective function into a maximization problem rather than minimization to suit the GA concepts of selecting the fittest chromosome, which has the highest objective function.

A second important mapping is the scaling of the fitness function values. Scaling is an important step during the search procedures of the GA. This is done to keep appropriate levels of competition throughout a simulation. Without scaling, early on there is a tendency for a few superindividuals to dominate the selection process. Later on, when the population has largely converged, competition among population members is less strong and simulation tends to wander. Thus, Scaling is a useful process to prevent both the premature convergence of the algorithm and the random improvement that may occur in the late iterations of the algorithm. There are many methods for scaling such as linear, sigma truncation, and power law scaling [4]. Linear scaling is the most commonly used and will be discussed in details in Section 5.3. In the sigma truncation method, population variance information to preprocess raw fitness values prior to scaling is used. It is called sigma (σ) truncation because of the use of population standard deviation information; a constant is subtracted from raw fitness values as follows:

$$\mathbf{f}' = \mathbf{f} - (\mathbf{f}' - \mathbf{c}.\sigma) \tag{5.1}$$

In equation (5.1) the constant c is chosen as a reasonable multiple of the population standard deviation and negative results ($\mathbf{f}'$<0) are arbitrarily set to 0. Following sigma truncation, fitness scaling can proceed as described without the danger of negative results.

4.4 Genetic algorithms operators

There are usually three operators in a typical GA; reproduction, crossover and mutation

Reproduction is a process in which individual strings are copied according to their pay-off function values, which can be thought of as a measure of profit, utility or goodness that we want to maximize. This means that copying strings according to their fitness values will give strings with higher fitness value a higher probability of generating one or more offspring in the following generation. So the reproduction operator is simply makes one or more copies of any individual that posses a high fitness value in the current generation to the next generation; otherwise, the individual is eliminated from the solution pool.

Crossover is the second operator (also known as the "recombination"). This operator selects two individuals within the generation and a crossover site and performs a swapping operation of the string bits to the right hand side of the crossover site of both individuals. The crossover operator serves two complementary search functions. First, it provides new points for further testing within the hyperplanes already represented in the population. Second, crossover introduces representatives of new hyperpalnes into the population, which is not represented by either parent structure. Thus, the probability of a better performing offspring is greatly enhanced.

Mutation is the third operator. This operator acts as a background operator and is used to explore some of the unvisited points in the search space by randomly flipping a "bit" in a population of strings. Since frequent application of this operator would lead to a completely random search, a very low probability is usually assigned to its activation. Mutation is needed because, although reproduction and crossover effectively search and recombine information contained in the strings, occasionally they may fail and lose some potentially useful genetic material (1 or 0 at particular locations in the case of binary coding). In artificial genetic systems, the mutation operator protects against such an irrecoverable loss. In the simple GA, mutation is the occasional (with small probability) random alteration of the value of a string position. When used randomly with reproduction and cross over, it is a guaranty against early loss of important notions.

4.5 Parameters settings and selection

Based on the results of the fitness evaluation step, certain individuals of the population are selected for further processing. The selection is based on a predetermined threshold of fitness level. The selection of chromosomes for applying various GA operators is based on their scaled fitness function in accordance to the roulette wheel selection rule. The roulette wheel slots are sized according to the accumulated probabilities of reproducing each chromosome.

The search for the optimal GA parameters setting is a very complex task. To achieve good performance of the GA, many experiments for the system under study must be performed to get the most suitable parameters for a specific problem. An adaptive scheme to control the probability rate of performing the crossover and mutation operators is designed.

The crossover rate controls the frequency with which the crossover operator is applied. The higher the crossover rate, the more quickly new structures are introduced into the population. If the crossover rate is too high, high-performance structures are discarded faster than selection can produce improvements. If the crossover rate is too low, the search may stagnate due to the lower exploration rate.

Mutation is a secondary search operator, which increases the variability of the population. A low level of mutation serves to prevent any given bit position from remaining forever converged to a single value in the entire population, and consequently increases the probability of entrapment at local minima. A high level of mutation yields an essentially random search, which may lead to very slow convergence.

4.6 Constraints handling (Repair mechanism)

Constraints handling techniques for the GAs can be grouped into a few categories. One way is to generate a solution without considering the constraints but to include them with penalty factors in the fitness function.

Another category is based on the application of a special repair algorithm to correct any infeasible solution so generated.

The third approach concentrates on the use of special representation mappings (decoders), which guarantee (or at least increase the probability of) the generation of a feasible solution or the use of problem-specific operators, which preserve feasibility of the solutions. However, due to applying the crossover and mutation operations the some constraints might be violated. A mechanism to restore the feasibility is applied according to the problem under study.

4.7 Merits and demerits

The GA technique has the following advantages:

- GAs work with a coding of the parameters of the function they optimize, not the parameters themselves.
- GAs search from a group (population) of points, not a single point.
- GAs use penalty (objective function) information, not auxiliary knowledge such as derivatives or other information.
- GAs use probabilistic transition rules, not deterministic rules.

The followings are some of the shortcomings of the GA technique:

- GA's do not work for large problems due to stochastic algorithm
- Its convergence depend on problem specific parameters that are not clearly defined
- It suffers from convergence and computational requirements

4.8 A general Genetic algorithm

A genetic search starts with a randomly generated initial population within which each individual is evaluated by means of a fitness function. Individuals in this and subsequent generations are duplicated or eliminated according to their fitness values. Further generations are created by applying GA operators. This eventually leads to a generation of high performing individuals.

The followings are the major steps of a basic general GA for any optimization problem:

Step 1. Select a suitable coding of the parameters in the problem under study.

Step 2. Initialize a population of chromosomes.
Step 3. Evaluate each chromosome in the population.
Step 4. Create new chromosomes by mating current chromosomes; apply mutation and recombination as the parent chromosomes mate.
Step 5. Delete members of the population to make room for the new chromosomes.
Step 6. Evaluate the new chromosomes and insert them into the population.
Step 7. If the termination criterion is satisfied, stop and return the best chromosomes; otherwise, go to Step (3).

5. Unit commitment solution using Genetic algorithms approach

5.1 Overview

Many GA implementations for the UCP are proposed in the literature. They differ from each other in three respects. First, the UCP solution coding which could be binary or real or mix between binary and real representations. Second, the fitness function could include, in addition to total operating cost, penalty terms for constraints violations or without penalty terms. Third, the GA operators are also differing from one implementation to another. Some algorithms used the basic GA operators only, while others used special operators in order to enhance the solution and speed up the convergence.

Generally speaking the GA for the UCP starts by coding the variables, randomly selecting several initial values, calculating the resultant objective function by solving the EDP based on the UCP decision variables, selecting a subset of the initially selected variables based on highest savings, cross mating the coded locations and mutating the resultant code to arrive at a better solution.

The major steps of the GA as applied to the UCP could be summarized as follows (Fig (5.1)):

- Creating an initial population by randomly generating a set of feasible solutions (chromosomes).
- Evaluating each chromosome by solving the economic dispatch problem.
- Determining the fitness function for each chromosome in the population.
- Applying GA operators to generate new populations as follows:
    - Copy the best solution from the current to the new population
    - Generate new members (typically 1-10% of the population size), as neighbors to solutions in the current population, and add them to the new population.
    - Apply the crossover operator to complete the members of the new population.
    - Apply the mutation operator to the new population.

In the following sections, the implementations of the different components of the GA for the UCP are presented.

5.2 Solution coding

Since the UCP lends itself to the binary coding in which a zero denotes the OFF state and a one represents the ON state, most of the published works used the binary coding [129-140]. The UCP solution is represented by a binary matrix (U) of dimension TxN (Fig.(5.2-a)). A candidate solution in the GA could then be represented by a string whose length is the product of the scheduling periods and the number of generating units TxN. In the GA a number of these solutions, equal to the population size (NPOP), is stored. The required storage size is then equal to NPOPxTxN, which is a large value even for a moderate size system.

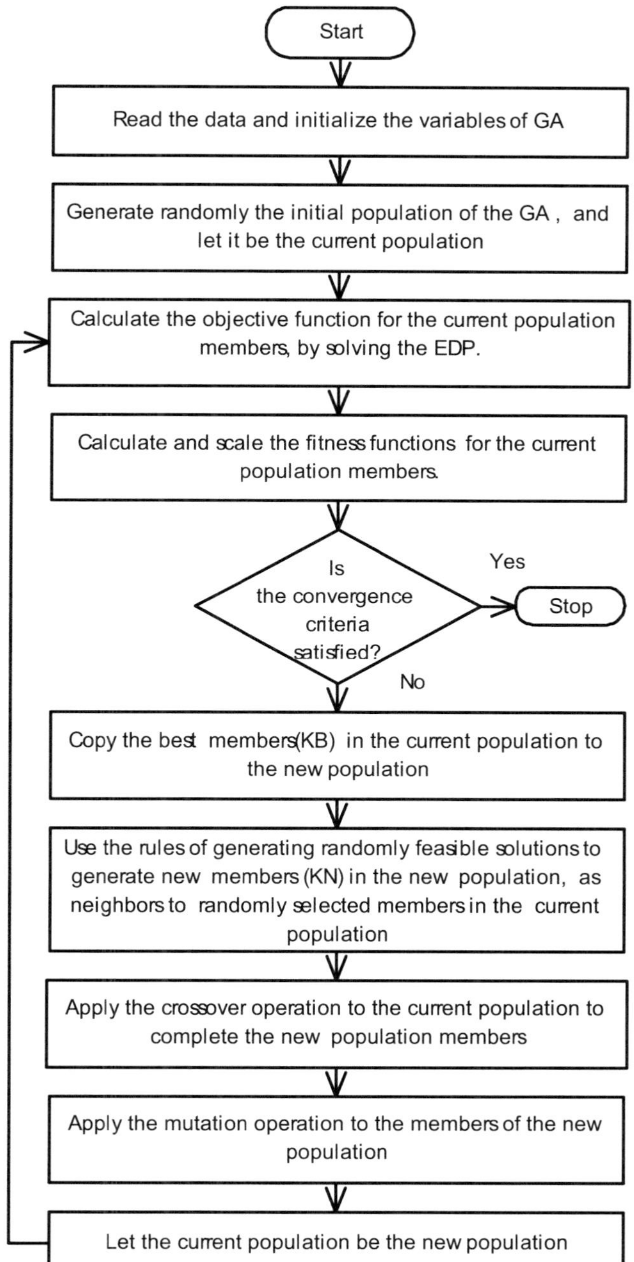

Fig. 5.1. Flow char of the GA for the UCP

Another method of coding presented is based on a mix between a binary number and its equivalent decimal number [141-142]. Each column vector of length T in the solution matrix (which represents the operation schedule of one unit) is converted to its equivalent decimal number. The solution matrix is then converted into one row vector (chromosome) of N decimal numbers, (U1, U2,....UN); each represents the schedule of one unit as shown in Fig.(5.2-b). Typically the numbers U1, U2, ..,UN are integers ranging between 0 and $\mathbf{2^N - 1}$. Accordingly, a population of size NPOP can be stored in a matrix of dimension NPOPxN as arbitrarily shown in Fig.(5.2-c). Hence, the proposed method requires only 1/T of the storage required if a normal binary coding is used.

HR	Unit Number 1 2 3 4 . . . N
1	1 1 0 0 . . . 1
2	1 1 0 0 . . . 1
3	1 0 1 0 . . . 0
.	. . . .
.	. . . .
T	0 1 0 1 . . . 0

Fig. 5.2-a. The binary solution matrix U

U1	U2	U3	U4	.	.	.	UN

Fig. 5.2-b. The equivalent decimal vector (1xN) (One chromosome)

23	14	45	56	.	.	.	62
34	52	72	18	.	.	.	91
.	.	.	.	.	.	.	.
51	36	46	87	.	.	.	21

Fig. 5.2-c. Population of size NPOPxN (NPOP chromosomes)

5.3 Fitness function

Unlike the previous solutions of the UCP using GA [129-140], the fitness function is taken as the reciprocal of the total operating cost in (3.1), where all new generated solutions are feasible.

The fitness function is then scaled to prevent the premature convergence. Linear scaling is used. This requires a linear relationship between the original fitness function (f) and the scaled one ($\mathbf{f_s}$) as follows [4]:

$$\mathbf{f_s = af + b} \tag{5.2}$$

$$a = (c - 1)f_{av} / (f_{max} - f_{min}) \tag{5.3}$$

$$b = (1 - a)f_{av} \tag{5.4}$$

Where: c: is a parameter between 1.2 and 2,

f_{max}, f_{min}, f_{av}: are maximum, minimum and average values of the original fitness functions respectively.

5.4 Selection

The selection of chromosomes for applying various GA operators is based on their scaled fitness function in accordance to the roulette wheel selection rule. The roulette wheel slots are sized according to the accumulated probabilities of reproducing each chromosome.

5.5 Crossover

To speed up the calculations, the crossover operation is performed between two chromosomes in their decimal form. A two points crossover operation is used. The following steps are applied to perform the crossover operation:

Select two parents according to the roulette wheel rule.

Select randomly two positions in the two chromosomes.

Exchange the bits between the two selected positions in the two parents to produce two children (Fig. (5.3)).

Decode the two children into their binary equivalent and check for reserve constraints violation.

If the reserve constraints are not satisfied apply the repair mechanism (described in Section 4.6) to restore feasibility of the produced children.

12	34	**45**	**62**	**93**	72	82	32

52	81	**69**	**55**	**26**	38	57	76

Two Parents

12	34	**69**	**55**	**26**	72	82	32

52	81	**45**	**62**	**93**	38	57	76

Two children

Fig. 5.3. Two points cross over example

5.6 Mutation

The crossover operation explained in the last section is not enough for creating a completely new solution. The reason is that it exchanges the schedule of units as black boxes among different chromosomes without applying any changes in the schedules of the units themselves.

Two new types of mutation operators are introduced to create changes in the units' schedules [141-142]. The mutation operation is applied after reproducing all the new population members. It is done by applying the probability test to the members of the new population one by one. The mutation operation is then applied to the selected chromosome. The details of the two mutation operators are described in the following sections.

5.6.1 Mutation operator (1)

The first mutation operator is implemented as follows:

1. Select a chromosome as explained before and decode it into its binary equivalent.
2. Pick randomly a unit number and a time period.
3. Apply the rules in Section 2.4 to reverse the status of this unit keeping the feasibility of the unit constraints related to its minimum up/down times.
4. For the changed time periods, check the reserve constraints.
5. If the reserve constraints are violated, apply the proposed correction mechanism and go to the next step, otherwise go to the next step.
6. Decode the modified solution matrix from binary to decimal form and update the new population.

5.6.2 Mutation operator (2)

The second mutation operator is based on a local search algorithm to perform fine-tuning on some of the chromosomes in the new generated population. The selection of chromosomes for applying this type of mutation could be random or based on the roulette wheel method.

1. The local search algorithm steps are described in details as follows:
2. Decode the selected chromosome into its binary form.
3. Sort the time periods in a descending order according to the difference between the committed units capacity and the load demand.
4. Identify the time periods at which the committed units capacity is greater than 10% above the load plus the desired reserve. These time periods have a surplus of committed power capacity.
5. At the time periods of surplus capacity, sort the committed units in an ascending order according to their percentage loading.
6. Identify the units that have a percentage loading less than 20% above their minimum output limits. These units are the costlier units among the committed units in the respective time periods, since they are lightly loaded.
7. Take the time periods, according to their order found in (2) and consider switching off the underloaded units one at a time, according to their order.
8. Check the feasibility of the solution obtained. If it is feasible, go to Step (8), otherwise go to Step (6).
9. Calculate the objective function of the solution obtained by solving the economic dispatch problem for the changed time periods.
10. Decode the new solution obtained to its decimal equivalent and replace the old one in the new population.

5.7 Adaptive GA operators

The search for the optimal GA parameters setting is a very complex task. To achieve good performance of the GA, an adaptive scheme to control the probability rate of performing the crossover and mutation operators is designed.

The crossover rate controls the frequency with which the crossover operator is applied. The higher the crossover rate, the more quickly new structures are introduced into the population. If the crossover rate is too high, high-performance structures are discarded faster than selection can produce improvements. If the crossover rate is too low, the search may stagnate due to the lower exploration rate. In our implementation, the crossover rate is initialized with a high value (typically between 0.6 and 0.8) and is then decreased during the search according to the convergence rate of the algorithm (decrement value is 0.01).

Mutation is a secondary search operator, which increases the variability of the population. A low level of mutation serves to prevent any given bit position from remaining forever converged to a single value in the entire population, and consequently increases the probability of entrapment at local minima. A high level of mutation yields an essentially random search, which may lead to very slow convergence. To guide the search, the mutation rate starts at a low value (between 0.2 and 0.5) then it is incremented by 0.01 as the algorithm likely converged to a local minimum.

6. Numerical examples

In order to test the proposed algorithm, three systems are considered. Preliminary experiments have been performed on the three systems to find the most suitable GA parameters settings. The following control parameters have been chosen after running a number of simulations: population size=50, initial value of crossover rate=0.8, decrement value of crossover=0.01, initial value of mutation rate=0.2, increment value of mutation=0.01, local search mutation rate=0.1, elite copies=2, and the maximum number of generations=1000.

Different experiments were carried out to investigate the effect of the local search mutation on the results. It was found that the proposed algorithm with local search performs better than the simple GA without local search , in terms of both solution quality and number of iterations.

Table(6.1) presents the comparison of results obtained in the literature (LR and IP) for Examples 1 and 2.

Fig.(6.1) shows progress in the best objective function versus the generation number. The algorithm converges after about 400 generations, which is relatively fast.

Tables (6.2), (6.3) and (6.4) show detailed results for Example 1 [4.29]. Table (6.2) shows the load sharing among the committed units in the 24 hours. Table (6.3) gives the hourly load demand and the corresponding economic dispatch costs, start-up costs, and total operating cost. Table (5.4) presents the final schedule of the 24 hours, given in Table (6.2), in the form of its equivalent decimal numbers.

Tables (6.5), to (6.8) also present the detailed results for Example 3 with a total operating cost of $661439.8

	Example	LR [29]	IP [41]	GA
Total Cost ($)	1	540895	-	537372
"	2	-	60667	59491
% Saving	1	-		0.65
"	2	-		1.93
Generations No	1	-		411
"	2	-		393

Table 6.1. Comparison between LR, IP, and the proposed GA

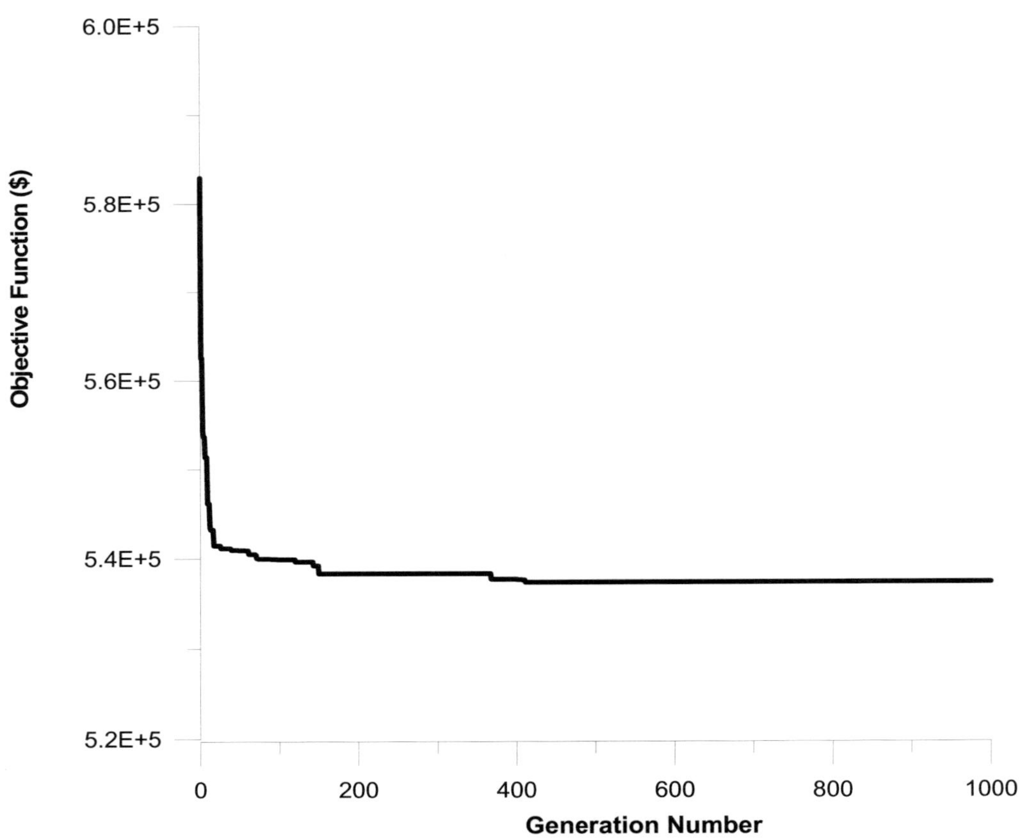

Fig. 6.1. Convergence of the proposed GA

HR	Unit Number**							
	2	3	4	6	7	8	9	10
1	400.0	0.0	0.0	185.0	0.0	350.3	0.0	89.7
2	395.4	0.0	0.0	181.1	0.0	338.4	0.0	85.2
3	355.4	0.0	0.0	168.7	0.0	301.0	0.0	75.0
4	333.1	0.0	0.0	161.8	0.0	280.1	0.0	75.0
5	400.0	0.0	0.0	185.0	0.0	350.3	0.0	89.7
6	400.0	0.0	295.7	200.0	0.0	375.0	0.0	129.3
7	400.0	0.0	343.0	200.0	0.0	375.0	507.0	145.0
8	400.0	295.6	396.7	200.0	0.0	375.0	569.9	162.8
9	400.0	468.1	420.0	200.0	0.0	375.0	768.0	218.9
10	400.0	444.6	420.0	200.0	358.1	375.0	741.1	211.3
11	400.0	486.3	420.0	200.0	404.9	375.0	789.0	224.9
12	400.0	514.1	420.0	200.0	436.1	375.0	820.9	233.9
13	400.0	479.4	420.0	200.0	397.1	375.0	781.0	222.6
14	400.0	389.0	420.0	200.0	295.6	375.0	677.2	193.2
15	400.0	310.1	410.8	200.0	250.0	375.0	586.6	167.5
16	400.0	266.6	368.3	200.0	250.0	375.0	536.7	153.4
17	400.0	317.3	417.9	200.0	250.0	375.0	594.9	169.9
18	400.0	458.5	420.0	200.0	373.7	375.0	757.0	215.8
19	400.0	486.3	420.0	200.0	404.9	375.0	789.0	224.9
20	400.0	0.0	420.0	200.0	442.2	375.0	827.2	235.7
21	400.0	0.0	404.9	200.0	0.0	375.0	579.6	165.6
22	400.0	0.0	0.0	200.0	0.0	375.0	675.0	0.0
23	400.0	0.0	0.0	191.6	0.0	370.1	338.2	0.0
24	377.6	0.0	0.0	175.6	0.0	321.8	275.0	0.0

**Units 1,5 are OFF all hours.

Table 6.2. Power sharing (MW) of Example 1

HR	LOAD	ED-COST	ST-COST	T-COST
1	1025	9670.04	0.00	9670.04
2	1000	9446.62	0.00	9446.62
3	900	8560.91	0.00	8560.91
4	850	8123.13	0.00	8123.13
5	1025	9670.04	0.00	9670.04
6	1400	13434.10	1705.97	15140.00
7	1970	19217.70	2659.11	21876.80
8	2400	23815.50	2685.07	26500.60
9	2850	28253.90	0.00	28253.90
10	3150	31701.70	3007.58	34709.30
11	3300	33219.80	0.00	33219.80
12	3400	34242.10	0.00	34242.10
13	3275	32965.50	0.00	32965.50
14	2950	29706.30	0.00	29706.30
15	2700	27259.70	0.00	27259.70
16	2550	25819.80	0.00	25819.80
17	2725	27501.60	0.00	27501.60
18	3200	32205.70	0.00	32205.70
19	3300	33219.80	0.00	33219.80
20	2900	28899.00	0.00	28899.00
21	2125	20698.40	0.00	20698.40
22	1650	15878.20	0.00	15878.20
23	1300	12572.80	0.00	12572.80
24	1150	11232.00	0.00	11232.00

Total operating cost = $537371.94

Table 6.3. Load demand and hourly costs ($) of Example 1

Unit Number 1,6	2,7	3,8	4,9	5,10
0	16777215	524160	2097120	0
16777215	1048064	16777215	16777152	2097151

Table 6.4. The UCT of Example 1 in its equivalent decimal form (best chromosome)

HR	Unit Number												
	1	2	3	4	5	6	7	8	9	10	11	12	13
1	0.00	0.00	0.00	0.00	0.00	0.00	0.00	0.00	4.00	0.00	76.00	54.80	15.20
2	0.00	0.00	0.00	0.00	0.00	0.00	0.00	0.00	4.00	0.00	0.00	76.00	50.00
3	2.40	0.00	0.00	0.00	0.00	0.00	0.00	0.00	4.00	0.00	0.00	28.40	15.20
4	2.40	0.00	0.00	0.00	0.00	0.00	0.00	0.00	4.00	0.00	0.00	15.20	15.20
5	2.40	0.00	0.00	0.00	0.00	0.00	0.00	0.00	4.00	0.00	0.00	58.40	15.20
6	2.40	0.00	0.00	0.00	0.00	0.00	0.00	0.00	4.00	76.00	76.00	66.40	15.20
7	0.00	0.00	2.40	0.00	0.00	0.00	0.00	0.00	4.00	76.00	76.00	76.00	76.00
8	0.00	0.00	2.40	0.00	0.00	0.00	0.00	0.00	4.00	76.00	76.00	76.00	76.00
9	0.00	0.00	2.40	0.00	0.00	0.00	0.00	0.00	4.00	76.00	76.00	76.00	76.00
10	0.00	0.00	2.40	0.00	0.00	0.00	0.00	0.00	4.00	76.00	76.00	76.00	76.00
11	0.00	0.00	2.40	0.00	0.00	0.00	0.00	0.00	4.00	76.00	76.00	76.00	76.00
12	0.00	0.00	2.40	0.00	0.00	0.00	0.00	0.00	4.00	76.00	76.00	76.00	76.00
13	0.00	0.00	2.40	0.00	0.00	0.00	0.00	0.00	4.00	76.00	76.00	76.00	76.00
14	0.00	0.00	2.40	0.00	0.00	0.00	0.00	0.00	4.00	76.00	76.00	76.00	76.00
15	0.00	0.00	0.00	0.00	0.00	0.00	0.00	0.00	4.00	76.00	76.00	76.00	76.00
16	0.00	0.00	0.00	0.00	0.00	0.00	0.00	0.00	4.00	76.00	76.00	76.00	76.00
17	0.00	0.00	0.00	0.00	0.00	0.00	0.00	0.00	0.00	76.00	76.00	76.00	76.00
18	0.00	0.00	0.00	0.00	0.00	0.00	0.00	0.00	0.00	76.00	76.00	76.00	76.00
19	0.00	0.00	0.00	0.00	0.00	0.00	0.00	0.00	0.00	76.00	76.00	76.00	76.00
20	0.00	0.00	0.00	0.00	0.00	0.00	0.00	0.00	0.00	76.00	76.00	76.00	76.00
21	0.00	0.00	0.00	0.00	0.00	0.00	0.00	0.00	0.00	76.00	76.00	76.00	76.00
22	0.00	0.00	0.00	0.00	0.00	0.00	0.00	0.00	0.00	76.00	76.00	76.00	76.00
23	0.00	0.00	0.00	0.00	0.00	0.00	0.00	0.00	0.00	76.00	76.00	76.00	64.10
24	0.00	0.00	0.00	0.00	0.00	0.00	0.00	0.00	0.00	15.20	15.20	15.20	15.20

Table 6.5. Power sharing (MW) of Example 3 (units 1-13)

HR	Unit Number 14	15	16	17	18	19	20	21	22	23	24	25	26
1	0.00	0.00	0.00	155.00	155.00	155.00	155.00	0.00	0.00	0.00	350.00	350.00	350.00
2	0.00	0.00	0.00	155.00	155.00	155.00	155.00	0.00	0.00	0.00	350.00	350.00	350.00
3	0.00	0.00	0.00	155.00	155.00	155.00	155.00	0.00	0.00	0.00	350.00	350.00	350.00
4	0.00	0.00	0.00	155.00	155.00	155.00	155.00	0.00	0.00	0.00	343.20	350.00	350.00
5	0.00	0.00	0.00	155.00	155.00	155.00	155.00	0.00	0.00	0.00	350.00	350.00	350.00
6	0.00	0.00	0.00	155.00	155.00	155.00	155.00	0.00	0.00	0.00	350.00	350.00	350.00
7	0.00	0.00	69.60	155.00	155.00	155.00	155.00	0.00	0.00	0.00	350.00	350.00	350.00
8	0.00	100.00	100.00	155.00	155.00	155.00	155.65	150.65	68.95	0.00	350.00	350.00	350.0
9	100.00	100.00	100.00	155.00	155.00	155.00	155.00	197.00	122.60	0.00	350.00	350.00	350.00
10	100.00	100.00	100.00	155.00	155.00	155.00	155.00	197.00	122.60	0.00	350.00	350.00	350.00
11	100.00	100.00	100.00	155.00	155.00	155.00	155.00	197.00	142.60	0.00	350.00	350.00	350.00
12	100.00	100.00	100.00	155.00	155.00	155.00	155.00	197.00	102.60	0.00	350.00	350.00	350.00
13	100.00	100.00	100.00	155.00	155.00	155.00	155.00	197.00	112.60	0.00	350.00	350.00	350.00
14	100.00	100.00	100.00	155.00	155.00	155.00	155.00	197.00	92.60	0.00	350.00	350.00	350.00
15	100.00	100.00	100.00	155.00	155.00	155.00	155.00	153.05	68.95	0.00	350.00	350.00	350.00
16	100.00	100.00	34.10	155.00	155.00	155.00	155.00	68.95	68.95	0.00	350.00	350.00	350.00
17	100.00	100.00	78.10	155.00	155.00	155.00	155.00	68.95	68.95	0.00	350.00	350.00	350.00
18	100.00	100.00	100.00	155.00	155.00	155.00	155.00	137.05	68.95	0.00	350.00	350.00	350.00
19	100.00	100.00	100.00	155.00	155.00	155.00	155.00	197.00	109.00	0.00	350.00	350.00	350.00
20	100.00	100.00	100.00	155.00	155.00	155.00	155.00	197.00	149.00	0.00	350.00	350.00	350.00
21	100.00	100.00	100.00	155.00	155.00	155.00	155.00	197.00	129.00	0.00	350.00	350.00	350.00
22	100.00	100.00	100.00	155.00	155.00	155.00	155.00	137.05	68.95	0.00	350.00	350.00	350.00
23	0.00	25.00	25.00	155.00	155.00	155.00	155.00	68.95	68.95	0.00	350.00	350.00	350.00
24	0.00	25.00	25.00	155.00	155.00	155.00	155.00	68.95	68.95	0.00	331.30	350.00	350.00

Table 6.6. Power sharing (MW) of Example 3 (units 14-26)

HR	LOAD	ED-COST	ST-COST	T-COST
1	1.82E+03	1.79E+04	0.00E+00	1.79E+04
2	1.80E+03	1.76E+04	0.00E+00	1.76E+04
3	1.72E+03	1.66E+04	0.00E+00	1.66E+04
4	1.70E+03	1.63E+04	0.00E+00	1.63E+04
5	1.75E+03	1.70E+04	0.00E+00	1.70E+04
6	1.91E+03	1.93E+04	1.60E+02	1.94E+04
7	2.05E+03	2.17E+04	1.00E+02	2.18E+04
8	2.40E+03	2.98E+04	7.00E+02	3.05E+04
9	2.60E+03	3.42E+04	1.00E+02	3.43E+04
10	2.60E+03	3.42E+04	0.00E+00	3.42E+04
11	2.62E+03	3.46E+04	0.00E+00	3.46E+04
12	2.58E+03	3.37E+04	0.00E+00	3.37E+04
13	2.59E+03	3.39E+04	0.00E+00	3.39E+04
14	2.57E+03	3.35E+04	0.00E+00	3.35E+04
15	2.50E+03	3.18E+04	0.00E+00	3.18E+04
16	2.35E+03	2.87E+04	0.00E+00	2.87E+04
17	2.39E+03	2.92E+04	0.00E+00	2.92E+04
18	2.48E+03	3.12E+04	0.00E+00	3.12E+04
19	2.58E+03	3.35E+04	0.00E+00	3.35E+04
20	2.62E+03	3.44E+04	0.00E+00	3.44E+04
21	2.60E+03	3.40E+04	0.00E+00	3.40E+04
22	2.48E+03	3.12E+04	0.00E+00	3.12E+04
23	2.15E+03	2.47E+04	0.00E+00	2.47E+04
24	1.90E+03	2.14E+04	0.00E+00	2.14E+04

Total operating cost = 661439.8125

Table 6.7. Load demand and hourly costs ($) of Example 3

Unit Number						
1	2	3	4	5	6	7
8	9	10	11	12	13	14
15	16	17	18	19	20	21
60	0	16320	0	0	0	0
0	65535	16777184	16777185	16777215	16777215	4194048
16777088	16777152	16777215	16777215	16777215	16777215	16777088
16777088	0	16777215	16777215	16777215		

Table 6.8. The UCT of Example 3 in its equivalent decimal form(best chromosome)

7. Summary

GA is one of the most powerful techniques for solving optimization problems and the UCP as well. The major components of the GA as applied to the UCP, which are different from one implementation to another, are: First, the UCP solution coding which could be binary, real or mix between binary and real representations. Second, the fitness function, which is basically, the total operating costs with or without adding penalty terms for constraints violations. Third, the GA operators: reproduction, crossover and mutation in addition to special operators that might be used to improve the solution speed and quality.

Discussions of the available GA implementations, as applied to the UCP, are summarized.

A complete GA implementation as applied to the UCP is presented. The features of the presented algorithm are: First, the UCP solution is coded using a mix between binary and decimal representations. Second, the fitness function is based only on the total operating cost and no penalties are included. Third, to improve the fine local tuning capabilities of the proposed GA, a special mutation operator based on a local search procedure, is designed.

8. List of abbreviations

UC	Unit Commitment
UCP	Unit Commitment Problem
EDP	Economic Dispatch Problem
Gas:	Genetic Algorithms
GA:	Genetic Algorithm
NN	Neural Networks
SA:	Simulated Annealing
TS:	Tabu Search
DP	Dynamic Programming
LR	Lagrangian Relaxation
IP	Integer Programming
MIP	Mixed Integer Programming
PL	Priority List
ES	Expert Systems
HR	Hour
MW	Mega Watt

9. Nomenclature

The following notations are used throughout the thesis:

$\mathbf{A_i, B_i, C_i}$	Cost function parameters of unit i (\$/ MW^2.HR, \$/MW.HR, \$/HR)
$\mathbf{D_i, E_i}$	Start-up cost coefficients for unit (\$).
$\mathbf{F_{it}(P_{it})}$	Production cost of unit i at time t (\$/HR).
$\mathbf{F_T}$	Total operating cost over the scheduling horizon (\$)
$\mathbf{F_i^k}$	The total operating cost for a current solution i at iteration k
N	Number of available generating units.

P_{it} Output power from unit i at time t (MW).

P_i^k Output power from all units for a current solution i iteration k.

P_{min_i} Unit i minimum generation limit (MW).

P_{max_i} Unit i maximum generation limit (MW).

PD_t System peak demand at hour t (MW).

R_t System reserve at hour t (MW).

ST_{it} Start-up cost of unit i at hour t.

SH_{it} Shut-down cost of unit i at hour t.

So_i Unit i cold start-up cost .

T Scheduling time horizon, (24 HRs).

T_{upi} Unit i minimum up time.

T_{downi} Unit i minimum down time.

T_{oni} Duration during which unit i is continuously ON.

T_{offi} Duration during which unit i is continuously OFF.

T_{shuti} Instant of shut down of a unit i.

T_{starti} Instant of start-up of a unit i.

$U(0,1)$ The uniform distribution with parameters 0, and 1

U_{it} Unit i status at hour t.
= 1 if the unit is ON and 0 if OFF at hour t.

U_i^k Unit status matrix for a current solution i at iteration k.

V_{it} Unit i start-up status at hour t.
= 1 if the unit is started at hour t and 0 otherwise.

V_i^k Unit start-up/shut-down matrix for a current solution i at iteration k

W_{it} Unit i shut-down status at hour t.
= 1 if the unit is turned off at hour t and 0 otherwise

10. References

[1] Allen J. Wood and B. F. Wollenberg, "Power Generation, Operation, and Control", John Wiley & Sons Ltd. 1984.

[2] M. E. El-Hawary and G. S. Christensen, "Optimal Economic Operation of Electric Power Systems", Academic Press, Inc. 1979.

[3] J. Nagrath and D. P. Koathari, "Modern Power System Analysis", TATA McGraw Hill Publishing Co., 1987.

[4] D. E. Goldberg, " Genetic Algorithms in Search, Optimization and Machine Learning, Reading, Mass., Addison Wesely, 1989.

[5] L. Davis (Ed), " Handbook of Genetic Algorithms", Van Nostrand, N. York, 1991.

[6] P. G. Lowery, " Generating Unit Commitment by Dynamic Programming", IEEE Trans. on PAS-85, No. 5, Page(s): 422-426, May 1966.

[7] W. L. Snyder, H. D. Powell, and J. C. Rayburn, "Dynamic Programming Approach to Unit Commitment", IEEE Trans. on Power Systems, Volume PWRS-2, No. 2, May 1987, Page(s): 339-350.

[8] Mantawy A. H., " Optimal Scheduling of Thermal Generation in Electric Power Systems", A Master Thesis, Ain Shams University, Cairo, Egypt, 1988.

[9] G. B. Sheble', and G. N. Fahd, "Unit Commitment Literature Synopsis", IEEE Trans. on Power Systems, Volume 9, No. 1, February 1994, Page(s): 128-135.

[10] Merlin, and P. Sandrin," A New Method for Unit Commitment At Electricite De France", IEEE Trans. on PAS, Volume PAS-102, No. 5, May 1983, Page(s): 1218-1225.

[11] J. F. Bard, " Short-Term Scheduling of Thermal-Electric Generators Using Lagrangian Relaxation", Operation Research, Volume 36, No. 5, September-October 1988, Page(s): 756-766.

[12] S. J. Wang, S. M. Shahidehpour, D. S. Kirschen, S. Mokhtari, and G. D. Irisarri, "Short-Term Generation Scheduling With Transmission and Environmental Constraints Using An Augmented Lagrangian Relaxation", IEEE Trans. on Power Systems Volume 10, No. 3, August 1995, Page(s): 1294-1301.

[13] R. Zhu, C. Fu, and S. Rahamn, "Network Programming Technique for Unit Commitment", Electrical Power & Energy Systems, Volume 17, No. 2, Page(s): 123-127, 1995.

[14] S. Takriti, J. R. Birge, and E. Long, "A Stochastic Model for Unit Commitment Problem", A New Decomposition Framework", IEEE Trans. on Power Systems, Volume 11, No. 3, August 1996, Page(s): 1497-1508.

[15] Ma, H.; Shahidehpour, S.M.; "Unit commitment with transmission security and voltage constraints", IEEE Transactions on Power Systems, Volume: 14, Issue: 2, May 1999, Page(s): 757 - 764.

[16] Motto, A.L.; Galiana, F.D.; "Equilibrium of auction markets with unit commitment: the need for augmented pricing", IEEE Transactions on Power Systems, Volume: 17, Issue: 3, Aug. 2002, Page(s): 798-805.

[17] Momoh, J.A.; Jizhong Zhu; "Optimal generation scheduling based on AHP/ANP", IEEE Transactions on Systems, Man and Cybernetics, Part B, Volume: 33, Issue: 3, June 2003, Page(s): 531-535.

[18] Jing Wang; Redondo, N.E.; Galiana, F.D.;" Demand-side reserve offers in joint energy/reserve electricity markets", IEEE Transactions on Power Systems, Volume: 18, Issue: 4, Nov. 2003, Page(s): 1300 - 1306.

[19] F. N. Lee, "Short-Term Thermal Unit Commitment -- A New Method", IEEE Trans. on Power Systems, Volume 3, No. 2, May 1988, Page(s): 421-428

[20] S. Mokhtari, J. Singh, and B. Wollenberg, " A Unit Commitment Expert System", IEEE Trans. on Power Systems, Volume 3, No. 1, February 1988, Page(s): 272-277.

[21] Z. Ouyang, and S. M. Shahidepour, " Short-Term Unit Commitment Expert System ", Electric Power System Research, 20 (1990) 1-13.

[22] Ronne-Hansen, P.; Ronne-Hansen, J. "Neural networks as a tool for unit commitment", Proceedings of the First International Forum on Applications of Neural Networks to Power Systems, 1991, Page(s): 266 -270.

[23] Ouyang, Z.; Shahidehpour, S.M. "A hybrid artificial neural network-dynamic programming approach to unit commitment", IEEE Transactions on Power Systems, Volume: 7, No.1, Feb. 1992, Page(s): 236 -242.

[24] Sasaki, H.; Watanabe, M.; Kubokawa, J.; Yorino, N.; Yokoyama, R. "A solution method of unit commitment by artificial neural networks", IEEE Transactions on Power Systems, Volume: 7, No. 3, Aug. 1992, Page(s): 974–981.

[25] Walsh, M.P.; O'Malley, M.J., "Augmented Hopfield network for unit commitment and economic dispatch", IEEE Transactions on Power Systems, Volume: 12 4, Nov. 1997, Page(s): 1765 -1774.

[26] M. E El-Hawary, "applications of artificial neural networks in electric power systems operational plannibg", Engineering Intelligent Systems, Vol. 7, No. 1, March 1999, Page(s): 49-61.

[27] Zhuang, F.; Galiana, F.D. "Unit commitment by simulated annealing", IEEE Transactions on Power Systems, Volume: 5, No. 1, Feb. 1990, Page(s): 311-318.

[28] Mantawy, A.H.; Abdel-Magid, Y.L.; Selim, S.Z., "A simulated annealing algorithm for unit commitment", IEEE Transactions on Power Systems, Volume: 13, No.1, Feb. 1998, Page(s): 197 -204.

[29] Mori, H.; Usami, T. "Unit commitment using Tabu search with restricted neighborhood", International Conference on Intelligent Systems Applications to Power Systems, 1996. Proceedings, ISAP'96, Page(s): 422 -427.

[30] Mantawy, A.H.; Abdel-Magid, Y.L.; Selim, S.Z. "Unit commitment by tabu search ", Generation, Transmission and Distribution, IEE Proceedings- Volume: 145, No. 1, Page(s). 1998, Page(s): 56–64.

[31] Zbigniew Michalewicz, "Genetic Algorithms + Data Structures = Evolution Programs", Springer-Verlag Berlin Heidelberg New York, 1992.

[32] John J. Grefenstette, and James E. Baker," How Genetic Algorithm Work: A Critical Look At Implicit Parallelism", The Proceedings of The Third International Conference on Genetic Algorithms, Morgan Kaufmann Publishers, San Mateo, California, 1989.

[33] David E. Goldberg, K. Deb and James H. Clark, "Genetic Algorithms, Noise, and the Sizing of Populations", Complex systems 6 (1992) 333-362.

[34] K. S. Tang, K. F. Man, S. Kwong and Q. He, "Genetic algorithms and their applications", IEEE Signal processing magazines, Issue: November 1996, Page(s): 22–37.

[35] Dasgupta, D.; McGregor, D.R.; "Short term unit-commitment using genetic algorithms", Proceedings of the Fifth International Conference on Tools with Artificial Intelligence, TAI '93, 8-11 Nov. 1993, Page(s): 240–247

[36] Hong-Tzer Yang; Pai-Chuan Yang; Ching-Lien Huang; "Applications of the genetic algorithm to the unit commitment problem in power generation industry", Proceedings of the IEEE International Joint Conference of the Fourth IEEE International Conference on Fuzzy Systems and The Second International Fuzzy Engineering Symposium, Volume: 1, 20-24 March 1995, Page(s): 267–274.

[37] Hong-Tzer Yang; Pai-Chuan Yang; Ching-Lien Huang; "Optimization of unit commitment using parallel structures of genetic algorithm", Proceedings of the International Conference on Energy Management and Power Delivery, EMPD '95, Volume: 2, 21-23 Nov. 1995, Page(s): 577-582.

[38] X. Ma, A. A. El-Keib, R. E. Smith, and H. Ma, " A Genetic Algorithm Based Approach to Thermal Unit Commitment of Electric Power Systems", Electric Power Systems Research 34 (1995) 29-36.

[39] S. A. Kazarilis, A. G. Bakirtzis, and V. Petridis, " A Genetic Algorithm Solution to the Unit Commitment Problem", IEEE Trans. on Power Systems, Volume 11, No. 1, February 1996, Page(s): 83-92.

[40] Pai-Chuan Yang, Hong-Tzer Yang, and Ching-Lien Huang, "Solving the Unit Commitment Problem With A Genetic Algorithm Through A Constraint Satisfaction Technique", Electric Power Systems Research 37 (1996), 55-65.

[41] S. O. Orero and M. R. Irving, "A Genetic Algorithm for Generators Scheduling in Power Systems", Electric Power & Energy Systems, Volume 18, No. 1, 1996, Page(s): 19-26.

[42] G. B. Sheble', T. T. Maifeld, K. Birttig, G. Fahd, and S. Fukurozaki-Coppinger, "Unit Commitment by Genetic Algorithm With Penalty Methods and A Comparison of Lagrangian Search and Genetic Algorithm-Economic Dispatch Example", Electric Power & Energy Systems, Volume 18, No. 6, 1996, Page(s): 339-346.

[43] Maifeld, T.T.; Sheble, G.B.; "Genetic-based unit commitment algorithm" IEEE Transactions on Power Systems, Volume: 11, Issue: 3, Aug. 1996, Page(s): 1359-1370.

[44] Arroyo, J.M; Conejo, A.; Jimenez, N., "A genetic algorithm approach to solve the unit commitment problem", Intelligent System Application to Power Systems (ISAP'97), July 6-10, 1996, Seoul Korea, Page(s): 182-187.

[45] Mantawy, A.H.; Abdel-Magid, Y.L.; Selim, S.Z. "A new genetic algorithm approach for unit commitment", Second International Conference On Genetic Algorithms In Engineering Systems: Innovations and Applications, GALESIA 97, (Conf. Publ. No. 446), 1997, Page(s): 215 -220.

[46] Mantawy, A.H.; Abdel-Magid, Y.L.; Selim, S.Z. "A genetic algorithm with local search for unit commitment", Intelligent System Application to Power Systems (ISAP'97), July 6-10, 1996, Seoul Korea, Page(s): 170-175.

[47] Zhao Hongwei; Yi Liangting; Wang Buyun; Cheng Gang; Yang Haiping "A new genetic algorithm for unit commitment", IEEE International Conference on Intelligent Processing Systems, 1997, ICIPS '97, Volume: 1, Page(s): 606–610.

[48] Hong-Tzer Yang; Pai-Chuan Yang; Ching-Lien Huang, "A parallel genetic algorithm approach to solving the unit commitment problem: implementation on the transputer networks", IEEE Transactions on Power Systems, Volume: 12, No. 2, May 1997, Page(s): 661 -668

[49] Zhu Mingyu; Cen Wenhui; Wang Mingyou; Zhang Peichao; "Using an enhanced genetic algorithm to solve the unit commitment problem", IEEE International Conference on Intelligent Processing Systems, ICIPS '97, Volume: 1, 28-31 Oct. 1997, Page(s): 611 - 614.

[50] Juste, K.A.; Kita, H.; Tanaka, E.; Hasegawa, J.; "An evolutionary programming solution to the unit commitment problem", IEEE Transactions on Power Systems, Volume: 14, Issue: 4, Nov. 1999, Page(s): 1452 - 1459.

[51] Richter, C.W., Jr.; Sheble, G.B.; "A profit-based unit commitment GA for the competitive environment", IEEE Transactions on Power Systems, Volume: 15, Issue: 2, May 2000, Page(s): 715-721.

[52] Christiansen, J.C.; Dortolina, C.A.; Bermudez, J.P.; "An approach to solve the unit commitment problem using genetic algorithm", IEEE Power Engineering Society Summer Meeting, 2000, Volume: 1, 16-20 July 2000, Page(s): 261-266.

[53] Senjyu, T.; Yamashiro, H.; Uezato, K.; Funabashi, T.; "A unit commitment problem by using genetic algorithm based on unit characteristic classification", IEEE Power Engineering Society Winter Meeting, Volume: 1, 27-31 Jan. 2002, Page(s): 58–63.

[54] Swarup, K.S.; Yamashiro, S.; "Unit commitment solution methodology using genetic algorithm", IEEE Transactions on Power Systems, Volume: 17, Issue: 1, Feb. 2002, Page(s): 87-91.

[55] Haoyong Chen; Xifan Wang; "Cooperative co evolutionary algorithm for unit commitment", IEEE Transactions on Power Systems, Volume: 17, Issue: 1, Feb. 2002, Page(s): 128- 33.

[56] Arroyo, J.M.; Conejo, A.J.; "A parallel repair genetic algorithm to solve the unit commitment problem", IEEE Transactions on Power Systems, Volume: 17, Issue: 4, Nov. 2002, Page(s): 1216-1224.

[57] Mashhadi, H.R.; Shanechi, H.M.; Lucas, C.; "A new genetic algorithm with Lamarckian individual learning for generation scheduling", IEEE Transactions on Power Systems, Volume: 18, Issue: 3, Aug. 2003, Page(s): 1181-1186.

[58] Hans P. Van Meeteren, "Scheduling of Generation and Allocation of Fuel, Using Dynamic and Linear Programming", IEEE Trans. on Power Apparatus and Systems, Volume PAS-103, No. 7, July 1984, Page(s): 1562-1568.

[59] K. P. Wong and K. P. Doan, "Artificial Intelligence Algorithm for Daily Scheduling of Thermal Generators", IEE Proc. C, 1991, 138,(6), Page(s): 518-534.

[60] Z. Ouyang, and S. M. Shahidehpour, "An Intelligent Dynamic Programming for Unit Commitment Application", IEEE Trans. on Power Systems, Volume 6, No. 3, August 1991, Page(s): 1203-1209.

[61] Z. Ouyang, and S. M. Shahidehpour, "A Hybrid Artificial Neural Network-Dynamic Programming Approach to Unit Commitment", IEEE Trans. on Power Systems, Volume 7, No. 1, February 1992, Page(s): 236-242.

[62] G. B. Sheble', and T. T. Maifeld, " Unit Commitment by Genetic Algorithm and Expert System", Electric Power Systems Research 30 (1994) 115-121.

[63] Ruey-Husn, and Yuan-Yih Hsu, "A Hybrid Artificial Neural Network-Differential Dynamic Programming Approach for Short-Term Hydro Scheduling", Electric Power Systems Research 33 (1995), 77-86.

[64] Khanh Doan and Kit Po Wong, "Artificial Intelligence-Based Machine-Learning System for Thermal Generator Scheduling", IEE Proc. -Gener. Transm. Distrib., Volume 142, No. 2, March 1995, Page(s): 195-201.

[65] S. O. Orero, and M. R. Irving, "Scheduling of Generators With A Hybrid Genetic Algorithm", Genetic Algorithms in Engineering Systems: Innovation and Applications, IEE Conference, September 1995, Page(s): 200-206.

[66] Mantawy, A.H.; Abdel-Magid, Y.L.; Selim, S.Z. "A new simulated annealing-based tabu search algorithm for unit commitment", IEEE International Conference on Computational Cybernetics and Simulation., Systems, Man, and Cybernetics, 1997., Volume: 3, Page(s): 2432–2437.

[67] Mantawy, A.H.; Abdel-Magid, Y.L.; Selim, S.Z. "A new genetic-based tabu search algorithm for unit commitment problem", Journal of Electric Power Systems Research 49 (1999), Page(s): 71-78.
[68] Mantawy, A.H.; Abdel-Magid, Y.L.; Selim, S.Z.; "Integrating genetic algorithms, tabu search, and simulated annealing for the unit commitment problem", IEEE Transactions on Power Systems, Volume: 14, Issue: 3, Aug. 1999, Page(s): 829-836.
[69] Mantawy, A.H.; Abdel-Magid, Y.L.; Abido, M.A., " A simulated annealing algorithm for fuzzy unit commitment problem", IEEE Transmission and Distribution Conference, 1999, Volume: 1, Page(s): 142 -147.
[70] Chuan-Ping Cheng; Chih-Wen Liu; Chun-Chang Liu; "Unit commitment by Lagrangian relaxation and genetic algorithms", IEEE Transactions on Power Systems, Volume: 15, Issue: 2, May 2000, Page(s): 707-714
[71] Mantawy, A.H.; "A genetic-based algorithm for fuzzy unit commitment model", IEEE Power Engineering Society Summer Meeting, Volume: 1, 16-20 July 2000, Page(s): 250–254.
[72] Jimenez-Redondo, N.; Chuan-Ping Cheng; Chih-Wen Liu; Chun-Cheng Liu; "Unit commitment by Lagrangian relaxation and genetic algorithms [discussion and closure]", IEEE Transactions on Power Systems, Volume: 16, Issue: 4, Nov. 2001, Page(s): 938– 39.
[73] Gwo-Ching Liao; Ta-Peng Tsao; "The use of genetic algorithm/fuzzy system and tabu search for short-term unit commitment", Proceedings OF the International Conference on Power System Technology, PowerCon 2002, Volume: 4, 13-17 Oct. 2002, Page(s): 2302 - 2307.
[74] Rajan, C.C.A.; Mohan, M.R.; Manivannan, K.; "Neural-based tabu search method for solving unit commitment problem", Generation, Transmission and Distribution, IEE Proceedings-, Volume: 150, Issue: 4, 14 July 2003 Page(s): 469-474.

Genetic Algorithms Implement in Railway Management Information System

Jia Li-Min[1] and Meng Xue-Lei[2]
[1]*State Key Laboratory of Rail Traffic Control and Safety, Beijing Jiaotong University, Beijing,*
[2]*School of Transport and Traffic, Lanzhou Jiaotong University, Lanzhou, China*

1. Introduction

The railway system is a complex system and accordingly, the processes of railway operations are very complicated. The essence of railway operations is to meet the demand assigned to railways through the optimization of usage of the railway transportation specific resources. So problem-solving oriented optimization algorithms or techniques form the basis, especially in the era when information technologies prevail, of modern railway operation, in which the most typical cases are, not limited to, as follows.

- Railway management information systems design
- Transportation resources allocation
- Traffic control through dynamical transportation resources re-allocation

These problems feature large scale, combinatorial complexity and nonlinearity etc and need optimization algorithms with searching efficiency, scale insensitivity, embedded heuristics and certainty of solution-finding. Genetic Algorithms (GA) have been proved suitable for the above mentioned railway application oriented problems solving.

The chapter consists of two parts. The first part will cover some recent development of and improvement to the generic GA. And the second part will outline several typical applications of GAs to solving optimization problems arising from railway management information system design, transportation resources allocation and traffic control for railway operation.

2. Improvement on GA

GA is the most popular type of EA. One seeks the solution of a problem in the form of strings of numbers (traditionally binary, although the best representations are usually those that reflect something about the problem being solved), by applying operators such as recombination and mutation (sometimes one, sometimes both) (Bäck 1996). The most important development on GA is the improvement on its efficiency and precision. And the other achievement we got at hand is that the implement of GA in optimization algorithm, which is not only used to solve single objective problem, but also used to solve multi-objective problem. We will introduce this improvement to the GA from our research group. We mainly introduce a variation of GA: The new kind of fast global convergent multi-objective genetic algorithm (Meng 2005).

The key step of genetic algorithm is to select the best chromosomes of each generation to generate the next generation, and the sorting methods of chromosomes are the most important, which determines the selecting results. So we focus on the sorting methods for selection and propose a new kind of sorting method---Improved Non-dominated Sorting method, constructing the basis of the fast global convergent multi-objective genetic algorithm.

2.1 Improved non-dominated sorting method

First, we calculate the number of dominating individuals for individual i --- n_1; then, we propose the sets of dominated individuals by individual i--- S_1. The steps are as follows.

Step 1. To find the individuals which satisfy the equation $n_1 = 0$ and store them into F_1.

Step 2. To propose S_i. For every individual j in S_i, there are n_j-1 dominating individuals. If n_j-1=0, then store individual j into another set H.

Step 3. Set F_1 to be the first dominating individuals set. Continue these steps to deal with H till each individual is graded.

The time complexity of the algorithm is $O(mN^2)$. m is the number of the objects and N is the population size of the chromosomes. P is the population, F is the non-dominating individuals set (It is the non-inferior solutions set). The algorithm is as follows.

Algorithm

For every $p \in P$

  For every $q \in P$

    if $p \prec q$, then $S_p = S_p \cup \{q\}$

    if $p \prec q$, then $n_p = n_p + 1$

    if $n_p = 0$, then $F_1 = F_1 \cup \{p\}$

  $i = 1$

while $F_1 \neq \Phi$

  $H = \Phi$

  for every $p \in F_1$

    for every $q \in S_p$

      $n_q = n_q = 1$

      if $n_q = 0$ then $H = H \cup \{q\}$

  $i = i + 1$

  $F_1 = H$

2.2 Dynamic virtual adaptability strategy

The selection probability of the individual is usually based on the adaptability according to a direct ratio. As a result, the value of the virtual adaptability can affect the selection probability of the individuals. If the difference between the adaptabilities of different groups is obvious, the group which has the bigger adaptability is selected and the individuals in the group will get the dominating positions, which is an obstacle to maintain the diversity of the individuals. We propose a dynamic virtual adaptability strategy to avoid the effect.

As discussed above, the virtual adaptability functions f_1 of individual i is as follows, with its grade $Level$.

$$f_i = \frac{1}{A\left(\frac{Maxgen - gen}{Maxgen}\right) + B^{*}Level} \tag{1}$$

In the function definition, $Maxgen$ is the maximal iteration times, gen is the current generation. $Level$ is the grade of the individual *i*. A and B are the two adjustable parameters, which can be used to adjust the change speed of the difference between different grades according to the grades and the algebra. Take it for granted that the individuals can be divided into 50 grades and the changing graph can be attained according to equation (1), as shown in Figure 1. The smaller the generation is, the smaller the differences between the adaptabilities of different groups are. The difference becomes bigger and bigger when the iteration continues. And the higher the grade of the individual belongs to, the bigger adaptability the individual will get. Then, the probability of being selected is bigger which is propitious to make the process of searching the optimal solution convergent.

2.3 Maintenance of the diversity of individuals

The local convergence can often be found when solving the multi-objective problem, so something must be done to maintain the diversity of the individuals. To share the adaptability is a method. The basic idea is to take the adaptability as the public resources and to adjust the adaptability according to the number of the similar individuals and the similarity of an individual. This can lead to two results. One is to form a niche among the similar individuals. The other is to control the number of the individuals generated by the similar individuals which can help to maintain the diversity the individuals. The shared function $Sh(\bullet)$ is introduced to measure the similarity between the individuals, which is defined as follows, shown in equation (2).

$$Sh\left(d_{ij}\right) = \left\{ \begin{array}{l} 1-\left(\frac{d_j}{\sigma_{share}}\right)^{\alpha}, \text{if } d_{ij} < \sigma_{share} \\ 0, \text{else} \end{array} \right\} \tag{2}$$

α is a constant, σ_{share} is the radii of the niche which can be estimated according to the expected minimal dividing degree of the individuals. d_{ij} is the distance between i and j.

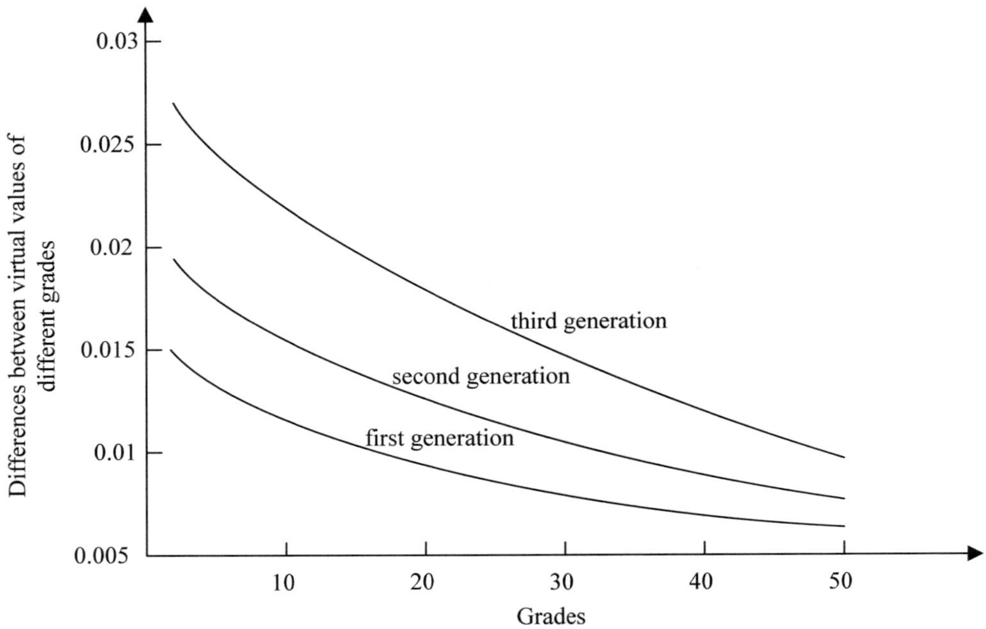

Fig. 1. Differences between virtual values of different grades

When the adaptability sharing function is defined, the adaptability of the individual $i \in P$ is the quotient of the adaptability before sharing operation and the number of niche --- m_i .

$$f_i = \frac{f_i}{m_i} \tag{3}$$

$$m_i = \sum_{j=i}^{pop\_size} Sh\left(d_{ij}\right) \tag{4}$$

According the different definitions of d_{ij}, the sharing methods can be divided into two kinds: the share in the objectives and the share in the solutions space. Here we introduce the first kind of method. d_j is defined as equation (5).

$$d_{ij} = d\left(f_i^{'}, f_j^{'}\right) \tag{5}$$

2.4 Elitist strategy

To hire the elitist strategy can greatly improve the convergence of the Pareto solution set. There are many kinds of methods for selection of elitists. Usually it can be selected from the non-inferior solutions set in which the solutions have been sorted. The number of the individuals to be selected is decided according to the problem condition. The methods to realize the elitist strategy are as follows. One is to add the elitist individuals into the current generation and delete some of the individuals which are worst. The other is to add the elitist individuals into an external set $\overline{P}$, and select some of the individuals from $\overline{P}$ and replace some of the individuals of each generation. Then some of the elitist individuals of the current generation are selected to be added into $\overline{P}$. And some methods are designed to control the number of the elements in $\overline{P}$ and the number of the similar individuals in $\overline{P}$.

We design a new method here. Each individual in the first grade after grading is added into the elitists pool (the external set $\overline{P}$). And the new generation $P^{'}$ is generated after selection, crossover, and mutation. Each individual (the number is suspended to be K) in elitists pool is added into $P^{'}$ directly. And to maintain the population size $N, N-K$ non-elitist individuals are deleted randomly.

2.5 Algorithm flow

The steps of the algorithm are as follows.

Step 1. The initial population $P(0)$ is generated through fake random method.
Step 2. To grade the individuals.
Step 3. To refresh the individuals in elitists pool. To store the individuals of the first grade in the elitists pool.
Step 4. To calculate the virtual adaptability according to equation (1).
Step 5. To apply the share strategy in objectives functions space according to equation (2) ~ equation (5).
Step 6. Selection: To select the individuals according to the adaptability ratio method (roulette).
Step 7. To crossover.
Step 8. To mutate.
Step 9. To generate the new generation $P^{'}$.
Step 10. To apply the elitist strategy and add the individuals in elitists pool into the new generation $P^{'}$ and delete the non-elitist individuals in $P^{'}$ randomly.
Step 11. To adjust the size of the new generation. Set the size to be N. The new generation is P.
Step 12. To check if the ceasing condition is satisfied. If no, go to step 2; else, cease.

The flow chart is shown in Figure 2.

3. Railway management information systems design

The most important work in railway management information system design is to design the physical structure. The essence of physical structure optimization is to allocate the physical resources of railway in order to realize logical structure, minimizing the costs and time.

The optimization objectives include customer satisfactory degree, response time, costs and so on. The constraints are reliability, safety and etc. So we can see the physical structure optimization problem features objective variety, combinatorial complexity and objective index nonlinearity etc.

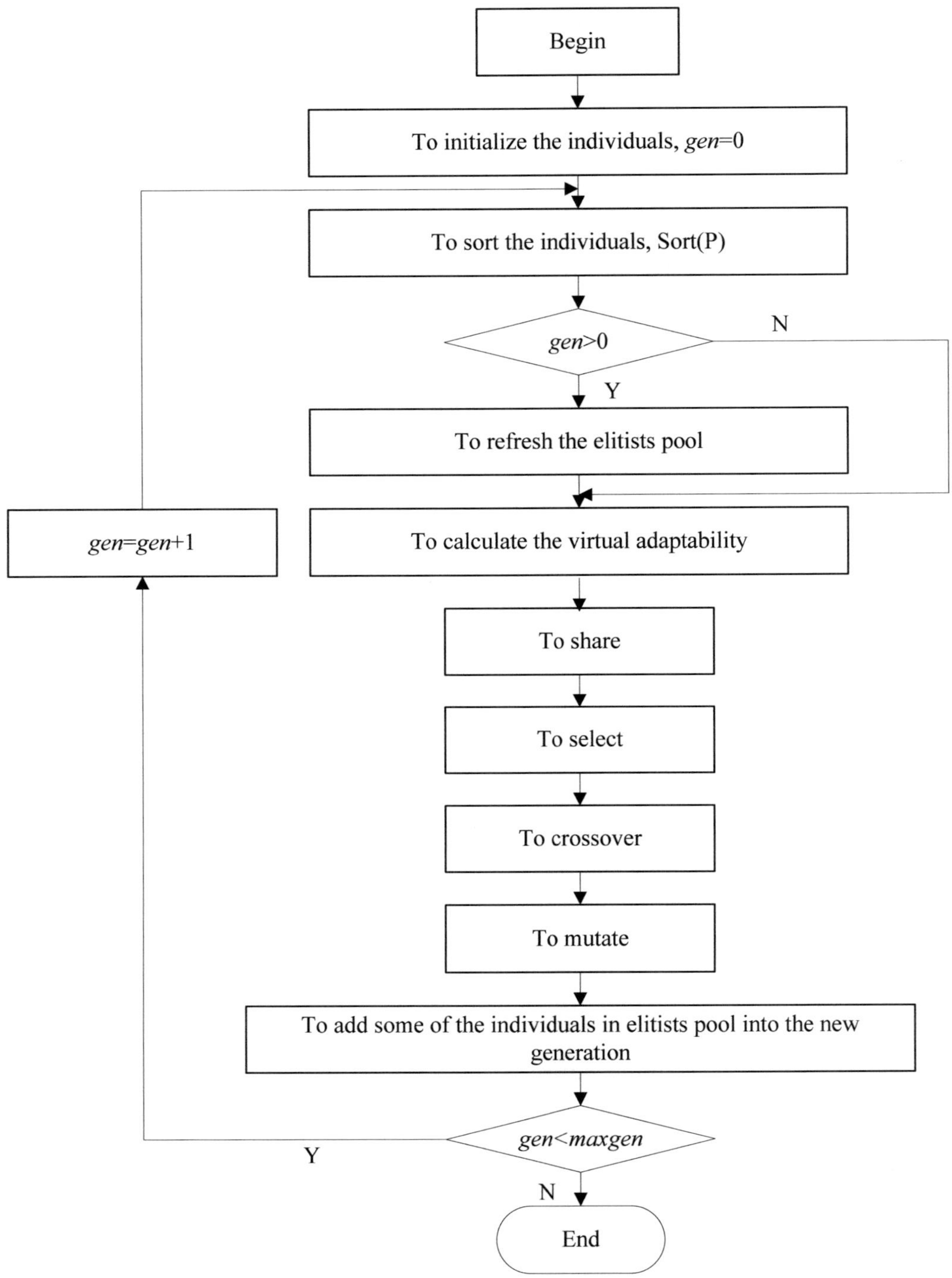

Fig. 2. Flow chart of the new genetic algorithm

A typical application of GA in railway management information system design is the physical structure optimization of emergency succoring system. The key points of implementing GA in the physical structure optimization of emergency succoring system are as follows.

(1) To describe the allocation plan of the physical equipments, the chromosome will be designed to be formed with two integers. The first integer denotes the allocation pattern of each function unit in the sub-systems while another describes the allocation pattern on the equipments of logical procedure.

(2) The objectives, the computing ability and operation cost can both be described with the chromosomes codes, forming the adaptive function formulas.

(3)The optimizing process is to find the optimal adaptive function value through all the iterations, with the chromosomes being selected, crossed over and mutated, deciding the optimal chromosome and the generation it belongs to.

A typical application of GA in railway management information system design is the physical structure optimization of emergency succoring system. Here we give the detailed implementing process of GA in physical structure optimization of emergency succoring system through a computing case study (Meng 2005).

3.1 The description of the physical structure optimization of emergency succoring system problem

The system is divided into 5 physical sub-systems, which are marked with $v_i\left(i=1,2,3,4,5\right)$.The goal is to optimize the calculating ability of the whole system $\left(f_i\left(x\right)\right)$ and minimize the operating cost of the system $\left(f_2\left(x\right)\right)$, which can be described as follows.

$$\min\left(f_1\left(x\right),f_2\left(x\right)\right) \tag{6}$$

The Data Flow Diagram (DFD) of emergency succoring system is shown in Figure 3. The logic processes of the emergency succoring system can be abstracted into 18 function units. They are {1},{2,3},{8,9},{4,5,6,7},{10},{11,12,13},{15,16,17},{19,20,21},{23,24,25}, {27},{28,29,30}, {31},{32},{33},{34},{35},{36,37},{38,39}. The meta-services can be described with the nodes lists as follows.

3.2 The computing case

(1) Coding approach

To distribute the meta-services on the physical sub-systems and optimize the allocation of the processes on the equipments, the genetic codes are designed to be planar. The chromosome consists of two integers shown in Figure 4. The first denotes the distributing modes of the function units on the system. For example, S denotes the number of the sub-system that the function unit F_i belongs to and n is the total number of the function units. The second describes the allocating modes of the logic processes on the system equipments. For instance, ID_i^k denotes the equipment number of process P_i^k allocated on physical system v_i . m is the total number of logic processes in v_i .

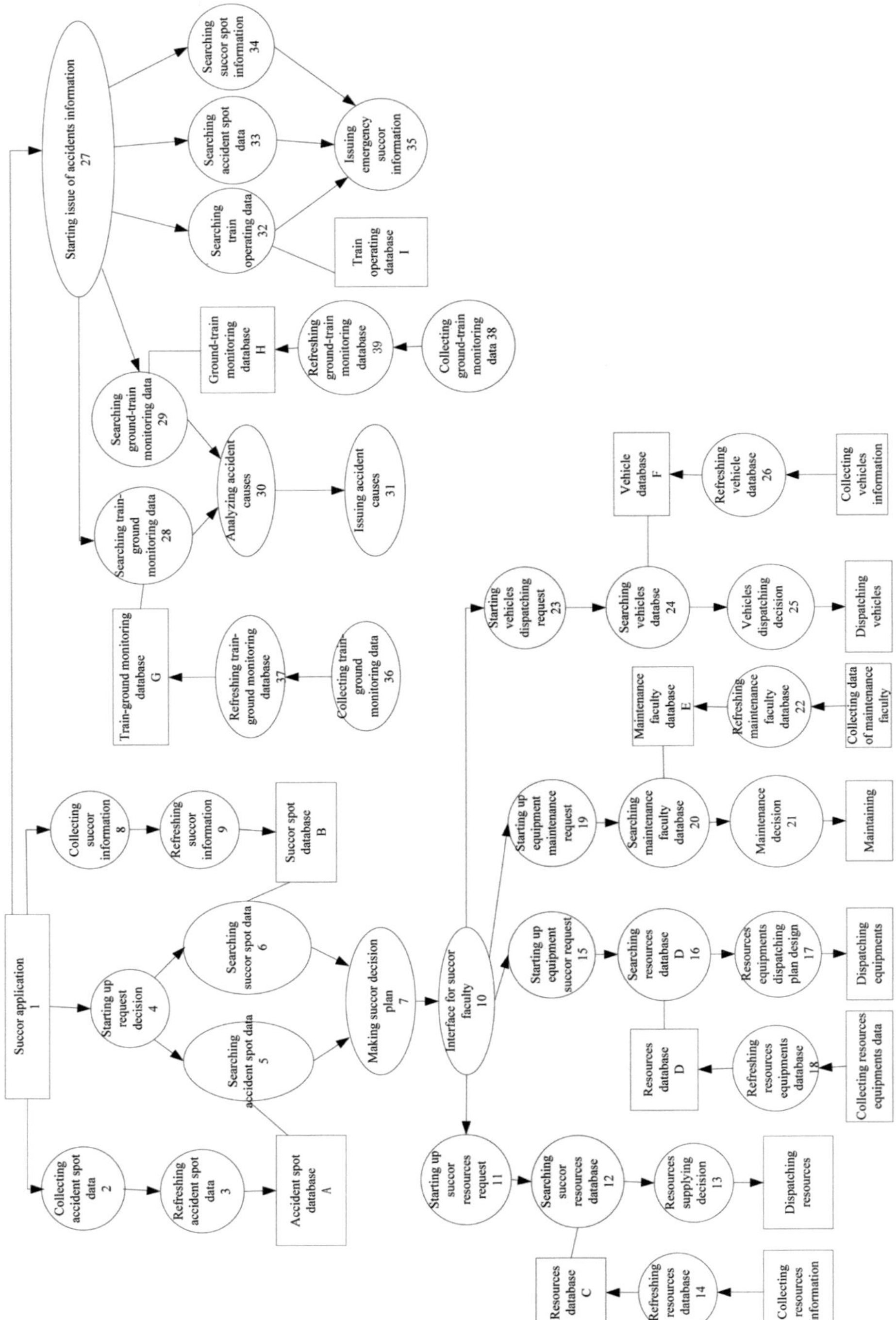

Fig. 3. DFD of emergency succoring system

Materials supply (meta-service 1):{1,4,(5,6),7,10,11,12,13}

Dispatching of materials and equipments (meta-service 2):{1,4,{5,6},7,10,15,16,17}
Maintaining service (meta-service 3):{1,4,{5,6},7,10,19,20,21}
Dispatching of cars (meta-service 4): {1, 4, {5, 6}, 7, 10, 23, 24, 25}
Issuance of causation of accidents (meta-service 5): {1, 27, ((28, 30), (29, 31))}
Issuance of succoring information (meta-service 6): {1, 27, (32, 33, 34), 35}
Collecting of information of accidents scenes (meta-service 7) :{ 1, 2, 3}
Collecting of succoring information (meta-service 8) :{ 1, 8, 9}
Inspection of trains to ground equipments (meta-service 9): {36, 37}
Inspection of ground equipments to trains (meta-service 10): {38, 39}

S_1	S_2	…	S_k	…	S_{n-1}	S_n

ID_i^1	ID_i^2	…	ID_i^k	…	ID_i^{m-1}	ID_i^m

Fig. 4. Coding of Chromosomes for RITS physical structures optimization

(2) Parameters setting

Take it for granted that the all the physical sub-systems have a full-linking relation. That is to say, any sub-system can communicate with all the other sub-systems. There are five kinds of network links today, listed in Table 1. The FDDI (Fiber Distributed Data Interface), Ethernet 1 and Ethernet 2 can be used in LAN (Local Area Network), and DDN (Defense Data Service), T1 link and 56k link can be used in long-distance link.

Type	Transmission(Mbit/s)
FDDI	103~104
Ethernet 1	100
Ethernet 2	10
DDN	2
T1 link	1.544
56k link	56k

Table 1. Types of the links and the transit speed

To calculate the economic and technical indexes, the other parameters are designed, as shown in Table 2 and Table 3.

Economic cost		Computation performance	
hardware cost	communication cost	Parameters about time	Transmission time
3000¥/ Computer	LAN: 0¥/Mbit	Band width: LAN: 100Mbit Internet: 10Mbit	Random delayed time Engorged temporarily
	Internet: 8¥/Mbit	Computer performance 200MIPS	

Table 2. Parameters setting in physical structure optimization

Nodes	Amount of calculation(10^5MI)	Nodes	Amount of calculation(10^5MI)
1	1	21	100
2	30	22	5
3	5	23	1
4	3	24	20
5	20	25	100
6	20	26	5
7	100	27	3
8	30	28	30
9	5	29	100
10	10	30	200
11	1	31	5
12	20	32	15
13	100	33	20
14	5	34	30
15	1	35	5
16	20	36	10
17	100	37	20
18	5	38	20
19	1	39	30
20	20	40	

Table 3. Amount of data processed of DFD graph nodes

(3) Constraints setting

The constraints are as follows. (1) The number of the equipments constraint. In this case the number is set to be 5. (2) Some of the nodes must be allocated in some certain sub-systems. Thus the optimization process is to allocate other nodes in the sub-systems. The constraints are shown in Table 4.

Sub-systems(v_1)	Sub-systems names	Nodes constraints
v_1	User sub-system	
v_2	Central management system	
v_3	Train sub-system	36
v_4	Rail- sideward sub-system	38
v_5	Station sub-system	

Table 4. Constraints of nodes positions

(4) Computing results and analysis

The computing results of the example of optimize the physical structure of the emergency succoring system are as follows.

(a) The results of the first calculation

The parameters are as follows. The size of the population *Popsize* =300 and the maximal iteration number is 100. The intersecting probability is 0.9 and the mutation probability is 0.02. The computing results are shown in Figure 5.

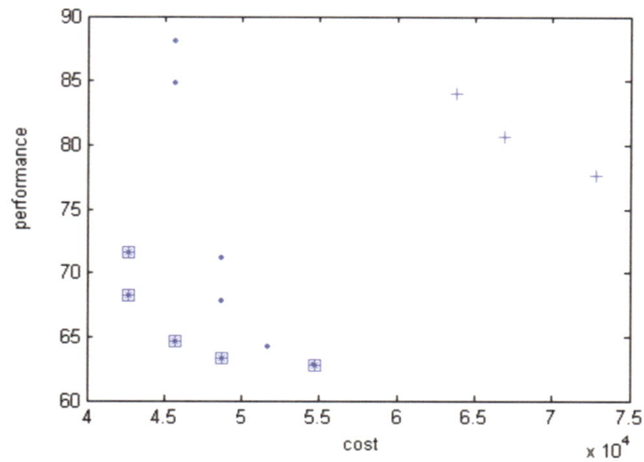

Fig. 5. Results of the first calculation

The problem is a kind of integer programming problem and the non-inferior solutions distribute discretely. '+' denotes the optimal individual chromosome after 10 iterations. '.' denotes the optimal individual chromosome after 60 iterations and '*' for 100. The number of the non-inferior solution is 37.

(b) The results of the second calculation

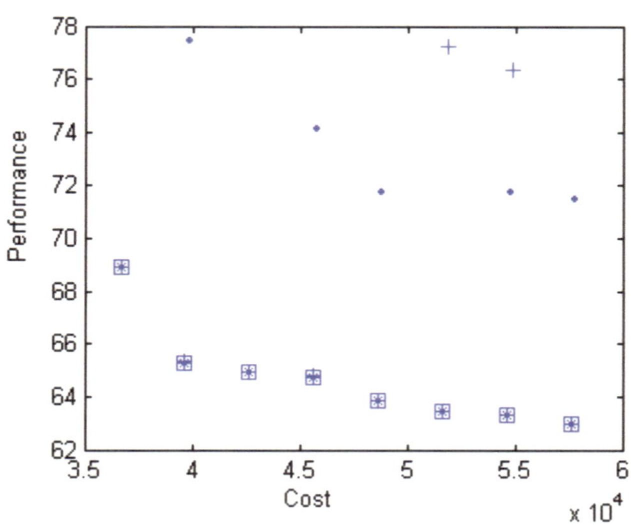

Fig. 6. Results of the second calculation

The parameters are as follows. The size of the population $Popsize = 500$ and the maximal iteration number Max_gen is 100. The intersecting probability is 0.9 and the mutation probability is 0.02. The computing results are shown in Figure 6.

'+' denotes the optimal individual chromosome after 20 iterations. '.' denotes the optimal individual chromosome after 30 iterations and 'Y' for 40, '*' for 100. The number of the non-inferior solution is 53. The typical solution is shown in Table 5.

	Sub-system 1	Sub-system 2	Sub-system 3	Sub-system 4	Sub-system 5	Cost (¥)	Capability (s)
1	{ 1 32 33 35 }, { 27 28 29 34 }, { 30 31},	{ 2 3 }, { 4 5 6 7 }, { 8 9 },	{ 36 37 },	{ 38 39 },	{ 10 11 12 13 15 }, { 16 17 23 }, { 19 20 21 24 25 },	45640	64.745
2	{ 1 27 32 33 35 }, { 28 29 34 }, { 30 31},	{ 2 3 }, { 4 5 6 7 }, { 8 9 },	{36 37 },	{ 38 39 },	{ 10 11 12 13 15 }, { 16 17 23 }, { 19 20 21 24 25 },	48640	63.845
3	{ 1 }, { 27 28 29 32 33 34 35 }, { 30 31},	{ 2 3 }, { 4 5 6 7 }, { 8 9 },	{ 36 37 },	{ 38 39 },	{ 10 11 12 13 15 }, { 16 17 23 }, { 19 20 21 24 25 },	39640	65.29
4	{ 1 }, { 27 32 33 35 }, { 28 29 }, { 30 31 34 },	{ 2 3 }, { 4 5 6 8 9 }, { 7 },	{ 36 37 },	{ 38 39 },	{ 10 15 16 17 }, { 11 12 13 23 }, { 19 20 21 24 25 },	57640	62.955
5	{ 1 }, { 27 28 29 32 33 34 35 }, { 30 31 },	{ 2 3 }, { 4 5 6 7 }, { 8 9 },	{ 36 37 },	{ 38 39 },	{ 10 15 16 17 }, { 11 12 13 23 }, { 19 20 21 24 25 },	42640	64.915
6	{ 1 27 32 33 35 }, { 28 29 }, { 30 31 34 },	{ 2 3 }, { 4 5 6 7 }, { 8 9 },	{36 37 },	{ 38 39 },	{ 10 15 16 17 }, { 11 12 13 23 }, { 19 20 21 24 25 },	51640	63.47
7	{ 1 27 32 33 35 }, { 28 29 34 }, { 30 31 },	{ 2 3 }, { 4 5 6 8 9 }, { 7 },	{36 37 },	{ 38 39 },	{ 10 11 12 13 23 }, { 1516 17 }, { 19 20 21 24 25 },	54640	63.33
8	{1 }, { 27 28 29 32 33 34 35 }, { 30 31},	{ 2 3 }, { 4 5 6 7}, { 8 9 },	{36 37 },	{ 38 39 },	{ 10 11 12 13 }, { 15 16 17 }, { 19 20 21 }, { 23 24 25 },	36720	68.9

Table 5. Optimization mapping results of typical emergency succoring sub-systems

We can see from Table 5 that the distributions of the function units on the system according to different solutions are similar. For example, according to most of the plans, 3 equipments are allocated in sub-system 1, to receive the succoring application, retrieve information from the database and issue the accidents causations and etc. And 3 equipments are allocated in sub-system 2 to search for the succoring information, collect information of accidents scenes and plan for succoring. In addition, the plans for sub-system 3 and for sub-system 4 are the same. An equipment is allocated in the two sub-systems respectively to realize the functions of inspection of trains to ground equipments and inspection of ground equipments to trains. 3 equipments are allocated in sub-system 5 to dispatch the resources, equipments, maintaining services and succoring cars.

To sum up, the solutions are reasonable and the decision makers can choose one of the solutions. A typical solution is shown in Figure 7.

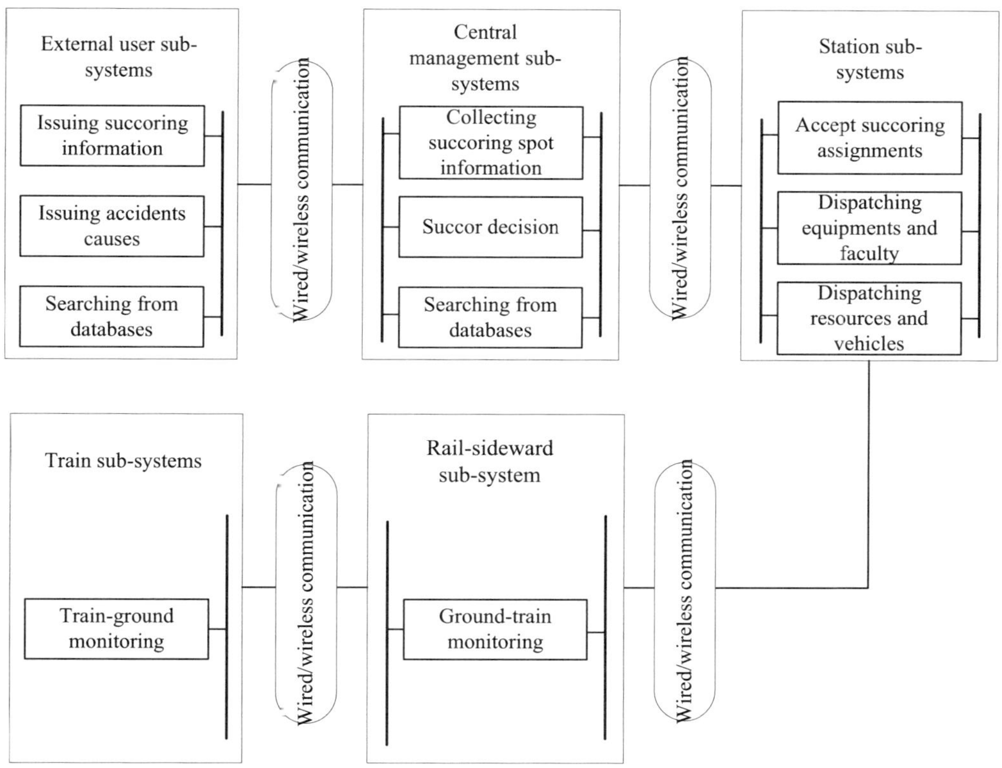

Fig. 7. An example of emergency succoring system structure

4. Train stops setting optimization

Train stops setting optimization problem is a typical problem of transportation resources allocation. In this case, the railway resources are the trains, which are the most important resources of railway. The coefficient of utilization of this kind of resource determines the service quality of the passenger transportation. So train stops setting is a key problem in railway resources allocation study. In this section, we will introduce GA application in train stops setting problem.

(1) Line planning

Line plan is the allocation of trains respected to passenger transportation demand, which determines the grade, type original stations and destination stations, number, paths, stops of passenger trains. It is also the basis of the train timetable, which is the most important arrangement of resources for railway transportation organization.

General line planning is an extremely complex and difficult problem; even its sub-problems considered separately are already NP-hard from a computational complexity point of view. Its process is based on the following input: a public demand, the available railway line, a set of trains. The goal is to obtain a set of lines and associated timetables to which trains are assigned.

A typical sub-problem of line planning is to generate the stops plan of trains. A most valuable advantage of GA in line planning is that the codes in chromosome can exactly describe whether the trains will stop at all the stations, 0 standing for non-stop and 1 for stop. And the stop operation will cause costs, while it meets the passenger transportation demand. The costs and the benefits caused by meeting the passenger transportation demand can both be formulated by the chromosomes codes, generating the adaptive function formulas. Thus, the optimizing process is to find minimal costs adaptive function value and maximal benefits adaptive function value through the iterations.

4.1 Designing the stops of the trains

The problem to select the stops of a train is very hard. It can be described as a planning problem, with 0 standing for the train does not stop at a station and 1 denoting the train stops at a station. The searching space is very large and the decision variables are in great volume. So the heuristic algorithm has the superiority to solve this problem. Genetic algorithm is hired (Zha, Liu and Li 2008) and Simulate Anneal Arithmetic algorithm is used to solve the problem (Wang, Peng and Xie 2006). Tabu Searching algorithm is hired (Deng, Shi and Zhou 2009).

The steps of the algorithm are follows.

Step 1. To design the code of the problem;
Step 2. To initialize the population $X(0)=(x_1,x_2,.....x_n)$;
Step 3. To calculate the value of adaptive function $F(x_i)$ of each chromosome in population $X(t)$;
Step 4. To create the middle generation $X_r(t)$;
Step 5. To create the new generation $X(t+1)$ based on the middle generation $X_r(t+1)$;
Step 6. $t=t+1$; If the exiting condition does not exist, go step 4.

The algorithm is designed for the train stops setting problem as follows.

(1) Solution coding of the problem

Coding is to express the feasible solution as a characteristic string, which can describe the characteristic of the problem. And it is required that the codes are easy to be dealt with. The train stops can be coded as string and there is a 0 or 1 at each bit. 0 denotes that the train will not stop at a certain station and 1 denotes that it will. When the strings of all the trains are linked, a chromosome is formed.

In this section, the code of a single train stops is designed as a one-dimensional array x_i. The length is i.

$$i = \sum_{j=1}^{p} q\left(L_j\right) \tag{7}$$

p is the number of the sections that the trains run through. $q\left(L_j\right)$ denotes the number of the stops when train j runs through section L_j. The code of a chromosome is constructed as shown in Figure 8.

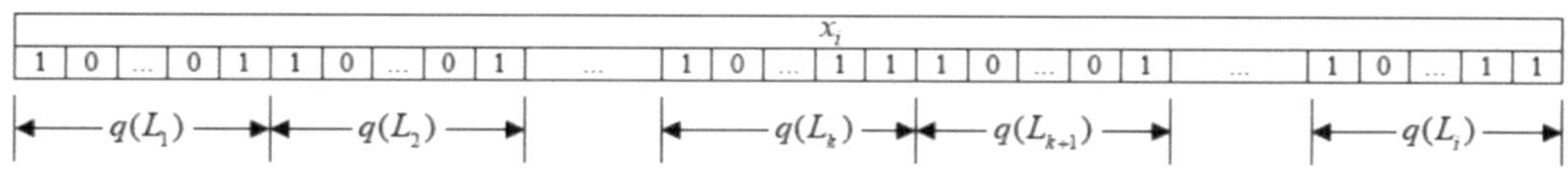

Fig. 8. Coding representation

(2) Initialization of the population

Initialization of the population is to construct the original population as the initial solution of the problem. To create the population of the initial solution is to generate *pop_size* chromosome, which is shown in Figure 8. And it is a constraint to meet the station capacity requirement. So it is necessary to judge whether the capacity constraint is satisfied during generating of the initial solution.

(3) Evaluating of the population

It is a must to evaluate the population to judge the quality of the population. The index is the value of the adaptive function. The adaptive function value is the symbol of the adaptability of the chromosome. The bigger the function value is, the more opportunity to survive the chromosome has. The adaptive function and the objective function are closely related to each other. The objective function can be seen as the mutation of the adaptive function. Generally speaking, the adaptive function can be used as the objective function when the objective function is non-negative or it is a maximal optimizing problem. When the objective function is negative or it is a minimum optimizing problem, the objective function can be designed as an equation that an enough large real number minus the objective functions. In this section, the passenger distributing speed is taken as the objective function and it is non-negative. And it is a maximal optimizing problem, so the adaptive function is designed to be equal to the objective function.

(4) Selection

Selection is to select an outstanding chromosome from a generation and past its excellent gene to the next generation. The roulette method is often taken in programming. Roulette method is a proportion strategy. Its main idea is to select the chromosome by the adaptive function value. The four steps of roulette are as follows.

a. To calculate the adaptive value $eval\left(v_k\right)$ of every chromosome v_k.
b. To calculate the summary of the adaptive value of all the chromosomes.
c. To calculate the selecting probability p_k of chromosome v_k.
d. To calculate the accumulated probability q_k of every chromosome v_k.

Then a plate is formed and it is cycled for pop_size times. Every time one chromosome is selected to create the new generation.

a. To generate a pseudo-random number $r \in [0,1]$.

b. If $r \le q_1$, then select the first chromosome v_1; Otherwise, select the kth chromosome v_k to meet the requirement $q_{k-1} \le r \le q_k$.

(5) Crossover.

The crossover operation includes one-point crossover, multi-point crossover, part- crossover and etc. In this section the one-point crossover is hired. To select a single one-point place for the two father chromosomes, then from the crossover place, the two chromosome exchange the value of every bit till the end of the chromosome.

(6) Mutation.

The task of the mutating is to change the value of a certain bit. In this section, mutating is to negate on the bit. That is to say, to change 1 into o and 0 to 1. It has two steps. The first step is to select a place to determine the bit to execute mutation operation. The second is to execute the negating operation. Then the new generation is created after step (2) to step (6).

(7) To judge if the loop can be cancelled. If it can then exit, else go step (2).

4.2 Calculating the number of the two types of the trains

In this section, a multiple unit contains 16 cars and its capacity A_c is 1200. The low speed train contains 17 cars and has the capacity of 1400. We first calculate out the numbers of the two types of the trains, which is shown in Table 6.

Running section	Number of the two types of trains	
	Multi Unit	Low speed trains
Shangqiu--Xuzhou--Bengbu—Nanjing	0	3
Shangqiu--Xuzhou—Bengbu	0	3
Xuzhou--Bengbu—Nanjing	52	4
Bengbu--Huainan--Hefei	0	3
Fuyang--Huainan--Hefei	0	3
Hefei--Nanjing	2	1
Xuzhou—Shangqiu	0	6
Xuzhou—Bengbu	9	0
Xuzhou--Xinyi	0	3
Bengbu—Nanjing	0	5
Fuyang—Huainan	0	4
Huainan--Hefei	0	3
Xuzhou--Shangqiu--Fuyang--Huainan--Hefei	0	2
Shangqiu--Xuzhou--Xinyi	0	2
Shangqiu--Fuyang--Huainan--Hefei	0	4
Yangzhou—Nanjing	0	1
Fuyang--Huainan--Hefei—Nanjing	0	1

Table 6. Running sections, numbers and grades for train operation under accident disaster

4.3 Stops setting

We first set the intersecting probability to be 0.6 and mutation probability to be 0.1. The maximal iteration number is 10000.

The adaptive function raised value to its peal value 263.1k after 580 iterations. Then we get the stops plan through interpreting the best chromosome. The information about the stops is shown in Table 7.

Running section	Number of the two kind of trains		Stop plan
	G	T	
Xuzhou--Shangqiu--Fuyang--Huainan--Hefei--Nanjing	0	22	One stops at Fuyang,, one stops at Hefei, others have no stop.
Xuzhou--Xinyi--Yangzhou—Nanjing	0	2	One stops at Yangzhou, another has no stop.
Xuzhou--Bengbu—Nanjing	28	8	5 stop at Bengbu
Shangqiu--Xuzhou--Bengbu—Nanjing	0	3	3 stop at Xuzhou.
Shangqiu--Xuzhou—Bengbu	0	3	All have no stops.
Bengbu--Huainan—Hefei	0	3	All have no stops.
Fuyang--Huainan—Hefei	0	9	7 stop at Huainan.
Hefei--Nanjing(high speed rail)	2	0	All have no stops.
Xuzhou—Shangqiu	0	6	All have no stops.
Xuzhou--Bengbu(high speed rail)	9	0	All have no stops.
Xuzhou—Xinyi	0	3	All have no stops.
Xuzhou--Shangqiu--Fuyang--Huainan—Hefei	0	6	4 stop at Shangqiu.
Shangqiu--Xuzhou—Xinyi	0	2	All have no stops.

Table 7. Train operation plan for section Xuzhou-Bengbu

5. Train rescheduling

The dynamic transportation resources allocation optimization is to give online, real time solution of the resources allocation problem to assure the railway transportation system operate safely. Train rescheduling is a typical dynamic transportation resources optimization problem.

Train rescheduling is to reset the inbound and outbound time of trains at stations when the operating plan is affected by disturbances. Similar with timetable optimization, the interval time and buffer time must be considered to assure the feasibility and stability of the timetable. And most of the constraints in train rescheduling are as the same as that in timetable optimization problem. The difference is that there is disturbance, and the train rescheduling is an online dynamic process, which requires more efficient algorithm to give solution in time to dispatch the trains.

A typical application of GA in dynamical transportation resources re-allocation is train rescheduling. The approach to apply GA in train rescheduling is very similar with that in timetable optimization. We will hire the variation of GA to obtain higher calculating efficiency, generating satisfactory solution, not necessarily the optimal solution.

5.1 The mathematic model of train rescheduling problem

The variables are as follows.

m: number of stations in the dispatching section.

n: number of trains that needs to be rescheduled.

g*: the planned timetable. $g* = \{(g_{i,j}^{a,*}, g_{i,j}^{d,*}) | i = 1,2,.....,n; j = 1,2,....m\}, g_{i,j}^{a,*}$, is the arriving time of train i at station j according to $g*$. $g_{i,j}^{d,*}$ is the departing time of train i from station j according to $g*$.

G: The set that is made of all the timetables. $G = \{g \mid g \text{ is a possible timetable}\}$,

$g = \{(g_{i,j}^{a}, g_{i,j}^{d}) | i = 1,2,.....,n; j = 1,2,....m\}, g_{i,j}^{a}$, is the arriving time of train i from station j according to g. $g_{i,j}^{d}$ is the departing time of train i at station j according to g.

Set $\forall p,q \in G$. Then the *distance* between p and q is

$$d(p,q) = \sum_{i=1}^{n}\sum_{j=1}^{m}\sqrt{(p_{i,j}^{a} - q_{i,j}^{a,*}) + (p_{i,j}^{d} - q_{i,j}^{d,*})} \tag{8}$$

Tthe destination of train rescheduling problem is to minimize $d(p,q*)$.

It can be described as follows.

$$f = \min_{\forall p \in G} d(p,g^*) \tag{9}$$

That is to say, the goal of train rescheduling is to find a timetable which has the minimal distance from the planned timetable. And the trains are clarified into different grades, the goal is changed, added a weight variable w_i. The goal is described as follows.

$$\min f = \sum_{i=1}^{n}\sum_{j=1}^{m} w_i \bullet \sqrt{(p_{i,j}^{a} - g_{i,j}^{a,*}) + (p_{i,j}^{d} - g_{i,j}^{d,*})} \tag{10}$$

Note: $w_1 > 0$. The bigger w_1 is, the higher grade train i belongs to. $p_{i,j}^{a}$ and $p_{i,j}^{d}$ are the decision variables. Now we discuss the constraints.

First, the departing time can not be earlier than that in the planned timetable. So

$$p_{i,j}^{d} \geq g_{i,j}^{d,*} \, (j = 1,2,...,m) \tag{11}$$

$$\text{Set } s^t_{i,j} = \begin{cases} 1, \text{train } i \text{ occupyingarail line of thestation} \\ 0, \text{otherwise} \end{cases}$$

If there are D_j rail lines in the station, then

$$\sum_{i=1}^{n} s^t_{i,j} \le D_j \tag{12}$$

Another constraint is about the running time of the trains in the sections.

$$p^a_{i,j+1} \ge p^d_{i,j} + T_{\min}\left(j = 1,2,...,m-1\right) \tag{13}$$

$T_{\min}$ is the minimal running time of train i in section $[j,j+1]$.

According to the minimal headway time constraint,

$$| p^d_{i,j} - p^d_{k,j} | \ge I\left(i \ne k, j = 1,2,....,m\right) \tag{14}$$

I is the minimal headway time.

And there must be skylight time reserved to do the maintaining work. So

$$p^a_{i,j}, p^d_{i,j} \le t_b \text{ or } p^a_{i,j} \ge t_c\left(i = 1,2,...,n; j = 1,2,...,m\right) \tag{15}$$

t_b is the beginning time of skylight time and t_c is the end time of skylight time.

5.2 Train rescheduling problem solving based on genetic algorithm

The train rescheduling problem is actually nonlinear optimization problem with constraints. The problem can be solved with genetic algorithm (H. Wang, Q. Zhang, J. Wang, Z. Wang and Y. Zhang 2006). Now we design the algorithm for it.

5.2.1 Coding design

The train rescheduling problem is to reset the arriving and departing time of trains to optimize the goal. To simplify the description of the time, number of minutes from zero o'clock are designed to represent the arriving time and departing time. For example, 01:06 can be replaced with 66, for 66 is the number of minutes from 00:00 to 01:06. So the chromosome can be coded with such integers. The chromosome is shown in Figure 9. And it can be seen that the maximal length is $2nm$.

$p^a_{1,1}$	$p^d_{1,1}$	…	$p^a_{1,m}$	$p^d_{1,m}$	…	$p^a_{i,m}$	$p^d_{i,m}$	…	$p^a_{n,m}$	$p^d_{n,m}$

Fig. 9. Coding of chromosome in train rescheduling problem

5.2.2 The fitness function

The fitness function is a function that evaluates the ability that the chromosome is adaptive to the environment. The bigger the fitness function value, the greater ability the chromosome has.

According to constraint described in equation (10), the departing time can not be earlier that the planned departing time. So this constraint can be dealt with penalty function.

Constraints described in equation (11) can be adjusted to be adapted with the genetic algorithm.

Function f_1 is defined as follows.

$$f_1 = \begin{cases} 0, \sum_{i=1}^{n} s_{i,j}^t \le D_j (j=1,2,...,m) \\ M, \text{otherwise} \end{cases} \tag{16}$$

Function f_2 is defined for constraint described in equation (12) as follows.

$$f_2 = \begin{cases} 0, p_{i,j+1}^a \ge p_{i,j}^d + T_{\min} (i=1,2,...,m) \\ M, \text{otherwise} \end{cases} \tag{17}$$

Function f_3 is defined for constraint described in equation (13) as follows.

$$f_3 = \begin{cases} 0, |p_{i,j}^d - p_{k,j}^d| \ge I (i \ne k, j=1,2,...,m) \\ M, \text{otherwise} \end{cases} \tag{18}$$

Function f_4 is defined for constraint described in equation (14) as follows.

$$f_4 = \begin{cases} 0, p_{i,j}^a, p_{i,j}^d \le t_b \text{ or } p_{i,j}^a \ge t_c (i=1,2,...,n.j=1,2,...,m) \\ M, \text{otherwise} \end{cases} \tag{19}$$

M is a positive integer.

Then the fitness function can be defined as follows.

$$\begin{aligned} f(\vec{p}_1, \vec{p}_2, ..., \vec{p}_i, ...\vec{p}_n) = C_{\max} &- \sum_{i=1}^{n}\sum_{j=1}^{m} w_i \bullet \sqrt{\left(p_{i,j}^a - g_{i,j}^{a,*}\right)^2 + \left(p_{i,j}^d - g_{i,j}^{d,*}\right)^2} \\ &- \sum_{i=1}^{n}\sum_{j=1}^{m} w \bullet \sqrt{\left(p_{i,j}^d - g_{i,j}^{d,*}\right)^2 \operatorname{sgn}\left(p_{i,j}^d - g_{i,j}^{d,*}\right)} - f_1 - f_2 - f_3 - f_4 \end{aligned} \tag{20}$$

$C_{\max}$ is the maximal positive integer that the computers can generate. $\vec{p}_i = \left(p_{i,1}^a, p_{i,1}^d, ..., p_{i,m}^a, p_{i,m}^d\right), i = 1,2,...,n$; w is the penalty factor of constraint described in equation (11). S gn is the sign function.

In fact, constraints described in equation (12) to (15) are also processed with penalty function where M is the penalty factor.

5.2.3 Crossover operator

The crossover operation is the main characteristic that genetic algorithms are different from other algorithms, which is the method to generate the next generation of chromosomes. The two-point intersecting approach is taken here, as shown in Figure 10.

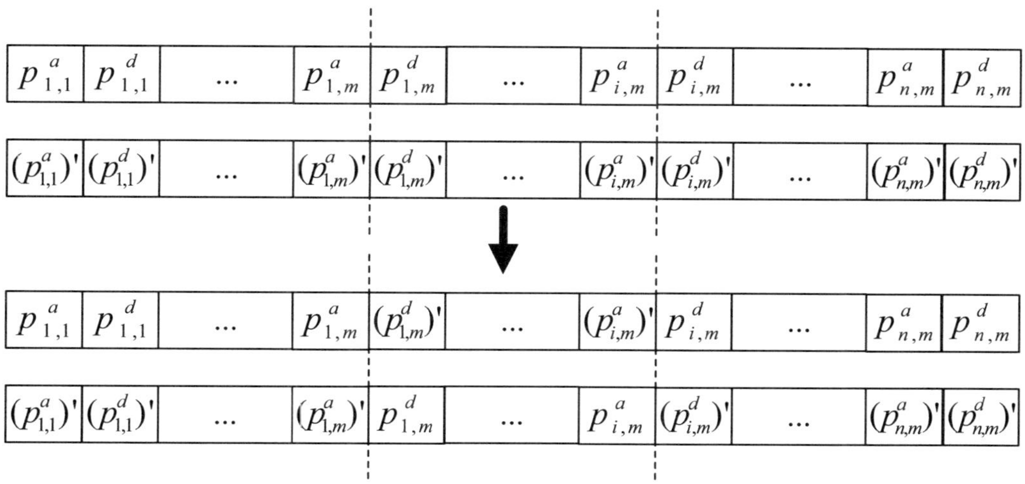

Fig. 10. Crossover pattern

5.2.4 Mutation operator

Mutation is to avoid the premature of the chromosomes, which makes some of the genes in chromosomes to mutate according to a certain probability. Here the mutation is designed as follows.

$$S: p \rightarrow p+\alpha, \alpha \in [-30,30] \tag{21}$$

α is a variable which distributes uniformly. That is to say, the mutation operator disturbs p with a certain probability and the range is less than 1 minute.

5.3 Case study

To prove the feasibility of the algorithm, we propose a case and analyze the computing results. The basic data is taken from the real train timetable of China railway, which makes the case more credible and proves the feasibility of algorithm more directly.

5.3.1 Basic parameters

(1)Number of stations M=6,(2)Number of trains N=11,(3)Train level,(4) The minimal running time of different types of trains,(5) The added time for train stopping operation,(6) The added time for train speeding operation,(7) The operating time of four types of trains (min),(8) The interval time I =4min,(9) The skylight: 0-6 h,(10) The weights of four types of trains $w=[4\ 3\ 2\ 1]$.

$$R_{\min} = \begin{bmatrix} 20 & 24 & 30 & 36 \\ 25 & 32 & 39 & 48 \\ 29 & 36 & 44 & 54 \\ 9 & 11 & 14 & 17 \\ 23 & 28 & 35 & 44 \end{bmatrix} \quad T = \begin{bmatrix} 2 & 2 & 2 & 3 \\ 0 & 0 & 0 & 0 \\ 3 & 3 & 3 & 4 \\ 0 & 0 & 0 & 3 \\ 2 & 2 & 2 & 4 \end{bmatrix}$$

The planned timetable is shown in Table 8.

		Trains										
Stations		1	2	3	4	5	6	7	8	9	10	11
1	Arrive	7:00	7:07	7:14	7:21	8:00	8:10	8:20	8:30	9:00	9:10	9:20
	Depart	7:06	7:13	7:20	7:27	8:08	8:18	8:28	8:38	9:06	9:16	9:26
2	Arrive	7:27	7:34	7:41	7:48	8:46	8:56	9:06	9:16	9:33	9:43	9:53
	Depart	--	--	--	--	--	--	--	--	--	--	--
3	Arrive	7:53	8:00	8:07	8:14	9:38	9:48	9:58	10:07	10:11	10:17	10:27
	Depart	--	--	--	--	--	--	--	10:31	--	--	--
4	Arrive	8:23	8:30	8:37	8:44	10:34	10:44	10:54	11:26	10:58	11:02	11:08
	Depart	8:29	8:36	8:43	8:50	10:42	10:52	11:18	11:34	11:04	11:08	11:14
5	Arrive	8:40	8:47	8:54	9:01	11:00	11:10	11:36	11:52	11:24	11:28	11:32
	Depart	--	--	--	--	11:08	11:18	11:44	12:00	--	--	--
6	Arrive	9:06	9:13	9:20	9:27	11:54	12:03	12:30	12:46	12:07	12:11	12:15
	Depart	9:12	9:19	9:26	9:33	12:02	12:05	12:38	12:54	12:13	12:17	12:21

Notes:

" – " denotes that the departing time of a train at a certain station is the same with the arriving time.

Then, it is assumed that the fifth train arrived at the first station five minutes later than it is planned in the timetable and other trains run according to the planned timetable. Then we began to reschedule the timetable. First, the rescheduling rules are listed as follows.

Table 8. The planned timetable

5.3.2 Rescheduling rules

There are many rules in train rescheduling, which should be applied in the algorithm. Here are the main rules.

1. The grades of the trains can not be changed in rescheduling
2. The higher grades trains can surpass the lower grades trains and the trains of the same grade can not surpass each other
3. A higher grade train can surpass many lower grade trains and a lower grade train can be surpassed by many higher grades trains.

5.3.3 Parameters setting

The population size of the chromosomes is 30, the crossover probability is 0.8 and the mutation probability is 0.001. The maximal number of iteration is 100.

5.3.4 Results and analysis

The planned timetable is turned to the style described in section 4.2.1. And the timetable is rescheduled according to the method proposed in this section. Then, the arriving time and departing time are turned into the original time style, as shown in Table 9.

Stations		Trains 1	2	3	4	5	6	7	8	9	10	11
1	Arrive	7:00	7:07	7:14	7:21	8:05	8:10	8:20	8:30	9:00	9:10	9:20
	Depart	7:06	7:13	7:20	7:27	8:11	8:18	8:28	8:38	9:06	9:16	9:26
2	Arrive	7:27	7:34	7:41	7:48	8:47	8:56	9:06	9:16	9:33	9:43	9:53
	Depart	--	--	--	--	--	--	--	--	--	--	--
3	Arrive	7:53	8:00	8:07	8:14	9:38	9:48	9:58	10:07	10:11	10:17	10:27
	Depart	--	--	--	--	--	--	--	10:31	--	--	--
4	Arrive	8:23	8:30	8:37	8:44	10:34	10:44	10:54	11:26	10:58	11:02	11:08
	Depart	8:29	8:36	8:43	8:50	10:42	10:52	11:18	11:34	11:04	11:08	11:14
5	Arrive	8:40	8:47	8:54	9:01	11:00	11:10	11:36	11:52	11:24	11:28	11:32
	Depart	--	--	--	--	11:08	11:18	11:44	12:00	--	--	--
6	Arrive	9:06	9:13	9:20	9:27	11:54	12:03	12:30	12:46	12:07	12:11	12:15
	Depart	9:12	9:19	9:26	9:33	12:02	12:25	12:38	12:54	12:13	12:17	12:21

The adaptive function value is 10.

Table 9. Computing result of timetable in original time style

We can see from Table 9 that the operating time at station is compressed to 6 minutes, while the planned operating time is 8 minutes, which requires the station workforce to fasten the operation work. And it is still 3 minutes late when it departs from the first station. Then the running time from the first station to the second station is compressed to 36 minutes and the train is re-planned to arrive at the second station at 8:11. Thus it is only 1 minute late. The operating time is not changed at the second station. The train recovers to operate according to the planned timetable at the third station.

It can be concluded that the rescheduled timetable is reasonable and executable from the analysis above. And the algorithm is feasible and practical and the method can be embedded in the train dispatching system to support the operation work.

6. Conclusion of this chapter

The main findings are as follows.

1. The improvement to GA brings high calculating precision and efficiency, meeting the calculating requirements of large scale optimization problem with combinatorial complexity and nonlinearity.
2. GA is suitable for railway application oriented problems solving. Although the solution may not be the optimal solution, the calculating time cost is much more acceptable.
3. GA is very easy to apply in optimization problem, not only reflecting in decision variables description, but also in objective function formulas.

And GA can also be applied in many other fields of railway applications, such as the crew scheduling, station operating plan optimization etc. Its optimization ability affords the possibility to solve the optimization problems in railway applications with high precision and efficiency. It is no doubt that GA has a bright future in the field of railway applications.

7. References

Honggang Wang, Qin Zhang, Jianying Wang, Zhuangfeng Wang, Yijun Zhang. "GA-based model of train operation adjustment for high-speed railway. China railway science." *China railway science* 27: 3(May 2006): 96-100.

Lianbo Deng, Feng Shi, Wenliang Zhou. "Stop Schedule Plan Optimization for Passenger Train." *China Railway Science* 30:4(July 2009): 102-109.

Thomas Bäck. *Evolutionary Algorithms in Theory and Practice: Evolution Strategies, Evolutionary Programming, Genetic Algorithms.* Oxford County: Oxford University Press,1996.

WeiXiong Zha, Huilin Liu, Jian Li. *Theory and Example of Railway Passengers and Trains Flow.* Chengdu: Southwest Jiaotong University Press, 2008.

Yan Meng. *Structure design methodology for the railway intelligent transportation systems.* Beijing: China Academy of railway sciences, 2005.

Zhi Wang, Qiyuan Peng, Xiaosong Xie. "Research on Optimization of Railway Passenger Train Path Based on Genetic Algorithms." *Railway Computer Application* 15:12 (December 2006): 4-6.

Part 3

GAs in Electrical and Electronics Engineering

8

Efficient VLSI Architecture for Memetic Vector Quantizer Design

Chien-Min Ou[1] and Wen-Jyi Hwang[2,*]
[1]*Department of Electronics Engineering, Ching-Yun University, Chungli,*
[2]*Department of Computer Science and Information Engineering,*
National Taiwan Normal University, Taipei,
Taiwan

1. Introduction

Memetic algorithms (MA) (Eiben & Smith, 2003; Molina, Lozano & Herrera, 2010; Moscato, 1999; Santos & Alves, 2010) have been found to be effective for evolutionary computation (Areibi, Moussa & Abdullah, 2001; Merz & Freisleben, 1999). It can be viewed as the hybrid genetic algorithms (GA) (Eiben & Smith, 2003) consisting of local refinement to genetic search results. Because the algorithms involve both the global and local searches, one challenging issue of the MAs is to reduce the computational complexity. One simple way to lower the computational time is to reduce the population size. Nevertheless, this approach is not favorable because small population size usually traps the MA in poor local optimum.

Another way to accelerate the execution of the MA is to implement the algorithm in hardware (Hwang, Hsu, Li, Weng & Yu, 2010). However, existing hardware architectures are mostly designed only for GA. No architecture for local refinement is available. In addition, existing GA hardware implementations (Choi & Chung, 2000; Nedjah & Mourelle, 2005; Tommiska & Vuori, 1996) have a number of drawbacks. First of all, large storage size is required for processing the genetic strings. Usually two set of population memories are used for the regeneration process. One memory contains the parent strings; the other stores the child strings after the regeneration. Moreover, there is overhead for switching one memory to another at the beginning of a new generation. The second drawback is that the regeneration process is based on the fitness function. The selection of parents therefore may need large chip area for hardware implementation. The mutation and crossover operations also result in high area cost when concurrent processing over all the genetic strings is desired. The third drawback is that the existing GA architectures (Choi & Chung, 2000; Nedjah & Mourelle, 2005; Tommiska & Vuori, 1996) contains only single population. Distributed or parallel evolutions are usually desired for attaining a near global optimal performance.

The objective of this paper is to present a novel hardware architecture for fast parallel MA optimization. In this chapter, we consider the applications of MA for vector quantizer (VQ) (Gersho & Gray, 1992) design. When applied for VQ training, the MA requires large storage

---

* Corresponding Author

size and long training time (Hwang & Hong, 1999). Therefore, the VQ design is a good example for verifying the effectiveness of the proposed MA architecture.

In the proposed architecture, each population of the parallel MA is associated with a hardware module for independent memetic evolutions. Each hardware module consists of population memory unit, mutation and crossover unit, C-Means (Gersho & Gray, 1992) unit, and survival test and update unit. In our design, the mutation and crossover unit is used for global search, while the C-Means unit is used for local refinement.

Each hardware module contains only one population memory for reducing the area cost. Both the mutation and crossover operations are performed concurrently for accelerating the MA. In addition, a pipeline architecture with direct memory access (DMA) operation is adopted for the C-Means operation. A hardware sorting structure is adopted for survival test. The proposed architecture has been implemented on field programmable gate array (FPGA) devices (Hauck & Dehon, 2008) so that it can operate in conjunction with a softcore CPU (NIOS II Processor Reference Handbook, 2008). Using the reconfigurable hardware, we are then able to construct a system on programmable chip (SOPC) system for the genetic VQ design. As compared with its software counterparts, numerical results reveal that the proposed FPGA-based MA architecture attains higher performance with significantly lower training time for VQ design. These fact demonstrate the effectiveness of our design.

2. Preliminaries

The goal of a VQ for data clustering is to partition a large data set $\mathbf{X} = \{\mathbf{x}_1,...,\mathbf{x}_t\}$ into N non-overlapping clusters $C_1,...,C_N$, where $N << t$. The partitioning process is based on a set of codewords $\{\mathbf{y}_1,...,\mathbf{y}_N\}$, where the codewords and the vectors in $\mathbf{X}$ are of the same dimension w. Given a vector $\mathbf{x} \in \mathbf{X}$, the $\mathbf{x}$ will be assigned to the cluster C_i when

$$i = \alpha(\mathbf{x}) = \arg \min_{1 \le j \le N} d(\mathbf{x}, \mathbf{y}_j), \tag{1}$$

where $d(\mathbf{u},\mathbf{v})$ denotes a distance measure between two vectors $\mathbf{u}$ and $\mathbf{v}$. In this paper, the squared distance is adopted as the distance measure. When applied for data reduction applications such as data compression, a vector $\mathbf{x}$ will be represented by the codeword $\mathbf{y}_i$ when $i = a(\mathbf{x})$. One cost function for the data reduction is the average distortion for representing $\mathbf{x}$ by $\mathbf{y}_i$, as shown below

$$D = \frac{1}{wt} \sum_{i=1}^{t} d\left(\mathbf{x}_i, \mathbf{y}_{\alpha(\mathbf{x}_i)}\right) \tag{2}$$

Given a data set $\mathbf{x}$, the objective of the VQ design is to find a set of codewords $\{\mathbf{y}_1,...,\mathbf{y}_N\}$ minimizing D in eq.(2).

In the basic MA (termed MA (I)) for VQ design, there are P genetic strings for the genetic operations. Each string r represents a set of N codewords $\{\mathbf{y}_1,...,\mathbf{y}_N\}_r$. Note that these strings are strings of vectors, not strings of binary numbers.

Let $S(k)$ and $D(k)$ denote the set of P strings and the value of current minimum distortion D after the execution of the k-th generation of the basic MA, respectively. Let s^* be the current optimum string during the course of genetic operations. Suppose that the $(k-1)$-th iteration is completed, and the execution of the k-th ($k \geq 1$) is to be done. We then perform the following operations sequentially on the strings in $S(k-1)$.

Regeneration: Since each string in $S(k-1)$ for the genetic operations is in fact a codebook of VQ, its corresponding D can be computed using eq.(2). The inverse of D is used as fitness function for each string. The regeneration process is then conducted using the roulette-wheel technique. Once a string has been selected for reproduction, an exact replica of it is made as a regeneration string. In the algorithm, P regeneration strings are created after the regeneration operation.

Crossover: On each regeneration string r, $\{\mathbf{y}_1, \mathbf{y}_2, ..., \mathbf{y}_N\}_r$, one point crossover is applied with probability P_c. Out of the total population, a partner string r', $\{\mathbf{z}_1, \mathbf{z}_2, ..., \mathbf{z}_N\}_{r'}$, is randomly chosen. Then an integer random number n between 1 and N is generated. Both strings are cut into two portions at position n and the portions $\{\mathbf{y}_{n+1}, ..., \mathbf{y}_N\}$ and $\{\mathbf{z}_{n+1}, ..., \mathbf{z}_N\}_r$ are mutually exchanged.

Mutation: Mutation is performed on each codeword of each string with a small probability P_m. Suppose now the string $r = \{\mathbf{y}_1, \mathbf{y}_2, ..., \mathbf{y}_N\}_r$ is to be mutated. One of the N codewords, $\mathbf{y}$, is chosen at random. Among the w numbers in $\mathbf{y}$, we also select one number at random. Then a random number, taking the binary values b or $-b$, is generated, and is added to the chosen component.

Local Refinement: The C-Means algorithm is used for the local refinement in the MA. Each string r in the population after mutation is used as the initial codebook to C-Means algorithm. The output codebook of C-Means algorithm then is result of local refinement of r. All the strings after local refinement then form the set $S(k)$. The average distortion of each string in $S(k)$ is then computed for updating $D(k)$.

In the MA algorithm, the iteration continues until the convergence of the sequence $D(k)$. The current optimum string s^* after the completion of MA algorithm is then chosen as the desired result.

It may be difficult to implement the MA (I) algorithm in hardware. This is because two population memories are required in the algorithm. One population memory contains the parent strings. The other is used for storing the strings after the regeneration process. The roulette-wheel technique may also become the bottleneck for the hardware. In addition, the crossover, mutation and C-Means operations should operate over all the P regenerated strings. The corresponding hardware complexity therefore may be very high.

3. The proposed MA architecture

In this chapter, two alternative MA algorithm (termed MA (II) and MA (III) algorithms) is adopted for the VQ design. The MA (II) is based on the steady-state GA for global search, which has superior performance over the basic generational GA for a number of applications (Rasheed & Davisson, 1999). There is no concept of generation in steady-state

GA. Let S be the population of P genetic strings, which are called the parent strings. Initially, the P strings in S are randomly generated. Two strings (denoted by r_1 and r_2) in S will be selected for mutation and crossover for creating a new child string (denoted by c). The new string then is used as the initial codebook to the C-Means algorithm for local refinement.

The fitness value of the child string after local refinement is then evaluated and compared with the fitness value of all the parent strings in S. If the new string is inferior to all the parent strings in S, no parent string will be removed. Otherwise, the parent string with lowest fitness value is replaced by the child string.

Note that because each string for the VQ design is actually a codebook, the memory access time for string retrieval may be long. Consequently, the retrieval process for r_1 and r_2 may be time-consuming. To reduce the memory access time, in the algorithm, the previous r_1 becomes the new r_2 and then the new r_1 is chosen randomly from S. This selection scheme reduces the memory access time by half.

As the process of selection, crossover, mutation, local refinement, and survival/replacement continues, the overall fitness of population will increase and the survival rate of new off-spring will diminish. At some point, the offspring survival rate will drop to zero. At this point, evolution has probably ceased and the algorithm may be terminated. The MA (II) algorithm is more effective for the hardware design. Only one population memory is required. In addition, crossover and mutation operations only operate on r_1 and r_2 instead of all strings in the population memory. Finally, C-Means operation only operate on the new child string c. Therefore, only one crossover and mutation module, and one C-Means module are necessary for hardware implementation. These facts effectively reduce the area cost for FPGA design.

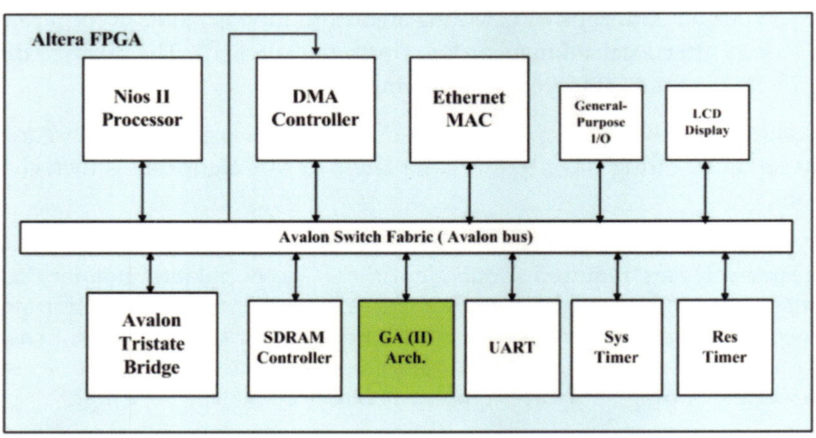

Fig. 1. The employment of SOPC for the MA (II) architecture

In the MA (III) algorithm, there are M populations. Each population evolves independently using the MA (II) algorithm. After all the populations are converged, the optimal strings from different populations are compared. The string having the highest fitness value is then the selected string for the VQ design.

The hardware architecture of the MA (II) and MA (III) can be viewed as a user logic in the NIOS-based SOPC system (NIOS II Processor Reference Handbook, 2008), as shown in Figure 1. Because the proposed architecture is used for the VQ design, the training data is required. The goal of using the SOPC is to provide the training data for the hardware architecture. The training data can be stored in a SDRAM, and delivered to our architecture via the Avalon bus. The DMA can be used to speed up the delivery. Alternatively, the training data can be obtained from a remote host via the internet.

Figure 2 shows the hardware architecture of the MA (II) algorithm. It contains population memory, crossover & mutation unit, C-Means unit, survival test & update unit, and Avalon bus interface. Both the population memory and crossover & mutation unit contain random number generators (RNGs).

In this architecture, the population memory unit is devoted for storing the genetic strings. Moreover, the random selection of parent strings for subsequent crossover and mutation operations is also included here. This selection is based on the RNG inside the population memory unit. All the crossover and mutation operations are performed concurrently in the crossover & mutation unit for producing a new child string c. The fitness value of the resulting string is then evaluated by the fitness evaluation unit.

Based on the fitness value, the goal of the survival test & update unit is to determine whether the child string c will survive. If it is the case, the parent string in the population memory unit with the worst fitness value will be replaced by the child string. Each unit in Figure 2 will be described in detailed as shown below.

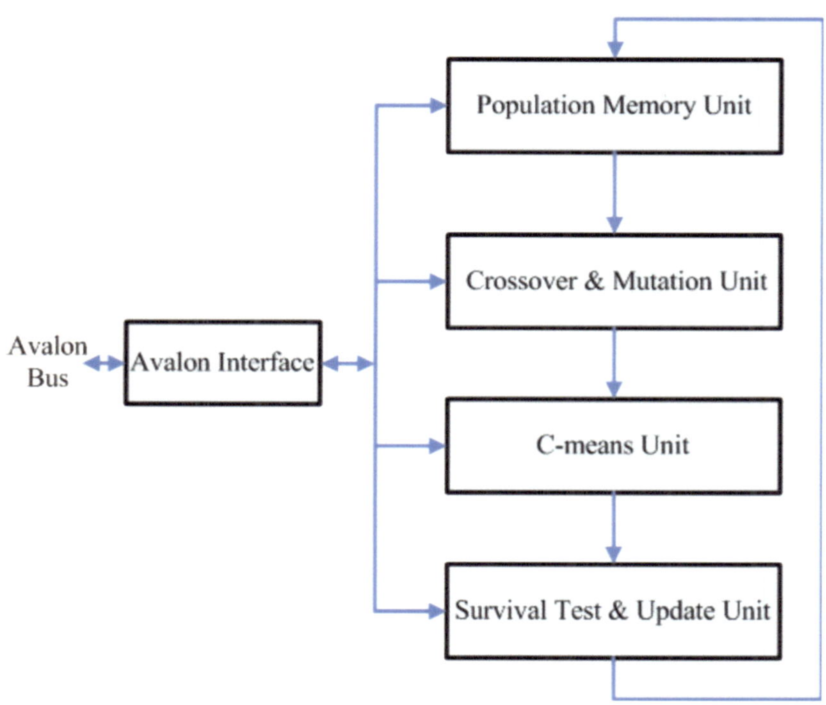

Fig. 2. The proposed hardware architecture for MA (II)

Population Memory Unit: The population memory contains a 2-port RAM and a RNG unit. The 2-port RAM contains S, the set of P genetic strings. In our design, the implementation of the RAM is based on the embedded memory, which is provided by some FPGA devices such as Altera Stratix II. The goal of RNG unit in the population memory unit is to select randomly a string for the subsequent crossover and mutation operations. In our design, the cellular automata (CA) is adopted for the VLSI implementation of random number generator due to its simplicity and regularity of the design.

Mutation and Crossover Unit: Figure 3 shows the basic structure of the mutation and crossover unit, which contains three shift registers for storing the strings r_1, r_2 and c, respectively. A number of RNGs, comparators, multiplexers and counters are then used for crossover and mutation. The major advantage of this architecture is that the crossover and mutation can be performed concurrently with low are a cost.

As shown in Figure 3, SHIFT REGISTER 1 and SHIFT REGISTER 2 contain strings r_1 and r_2, respectively. Note that the architecture does not randomly select new r_1 and r_2 from the population memory. In fact, only new r_1 is chosen from population memory. The new r_2 is actually the previous r_1. The memory access time and routing overhead can then be significantly reduced. Based on the algorithm, in the architecture, The SHIFT REGISTER 1 obtains r_1 from the population memory unit. The SHIFT REGISTER 2 obtains r_2 from SHIFT REGISTER 1.

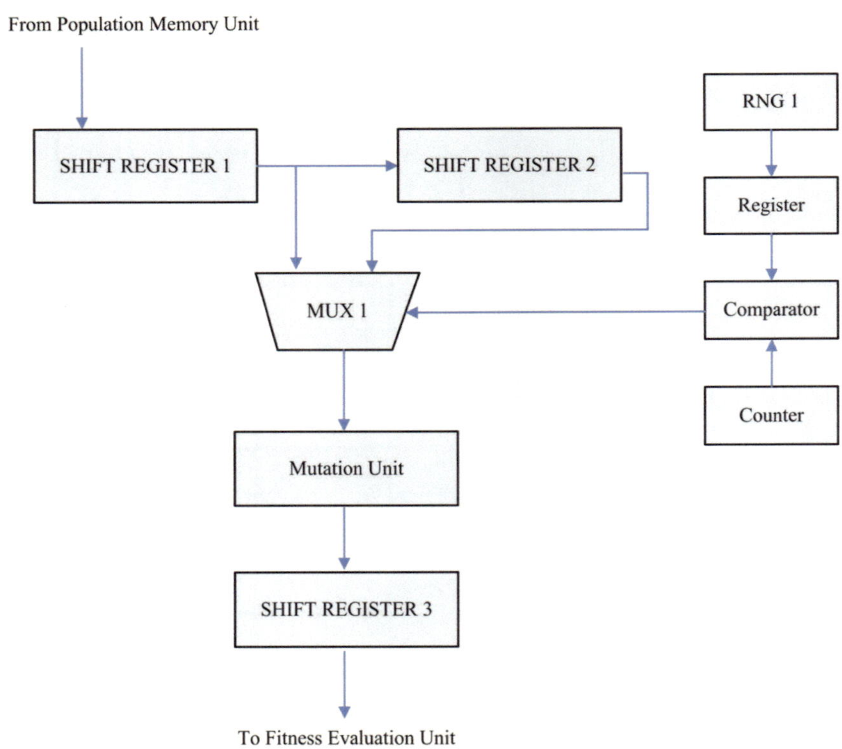

Fig. 3. The architecture of crossover and mutation unit

The crossover operations are accomplished by concurrently shifting the strings in SHIFT REGISTER 1 and SHIFT REGISTER 2 to MUX 1. Each shift register will shift one codeword at a time. As shown in Figure 3, MUX 1 is a switch selecting the codewords of either r_1 or r_2, and route them to SHIFT REGISTER 3, which contains the resulting child string c. The control line of MUX 1 is connected to a comparator, which compares the value of RNG 1 to that of a counter. The counter records the number of shifts made by the shift registers. The value of RNG 1 serves as a threshold here. When the counter value is less than the threshold, codewords of SHIFT REGISTER 1 (i.e., r_1) goes to SHIFT REGISTER 3. Otherwise, codewords of will be selected. Consequently, the value of RNG 1 determines the crossover point. The value will be randomly generated prior to the shifting operations.

We also observe from Figure 3 that the output codeword of MUX 1 will pass through the mutation unit before arriving the SHIFT REGISTER 3. Figure 4 shows the architecture of the mutation unit. As shown in the figure, all w components of the output codeword mutate concurrently. The mutation circuit for each component i consists of 2 RNGs (termed RNG ia and RNG ib), one register (termed register i), one comparator (termed comparator i), one multiplexer (termed mux i).

The probability for mutation P_b is stored in a separate register, and is broadcasted to all the mutation circuits. In the mutation circuit for each component i, the value of RNG ia is first compared with the P_b. The component i will be mutated when the value of RNG ia is less than P_b. The mutated value is then determined by RNG ib.

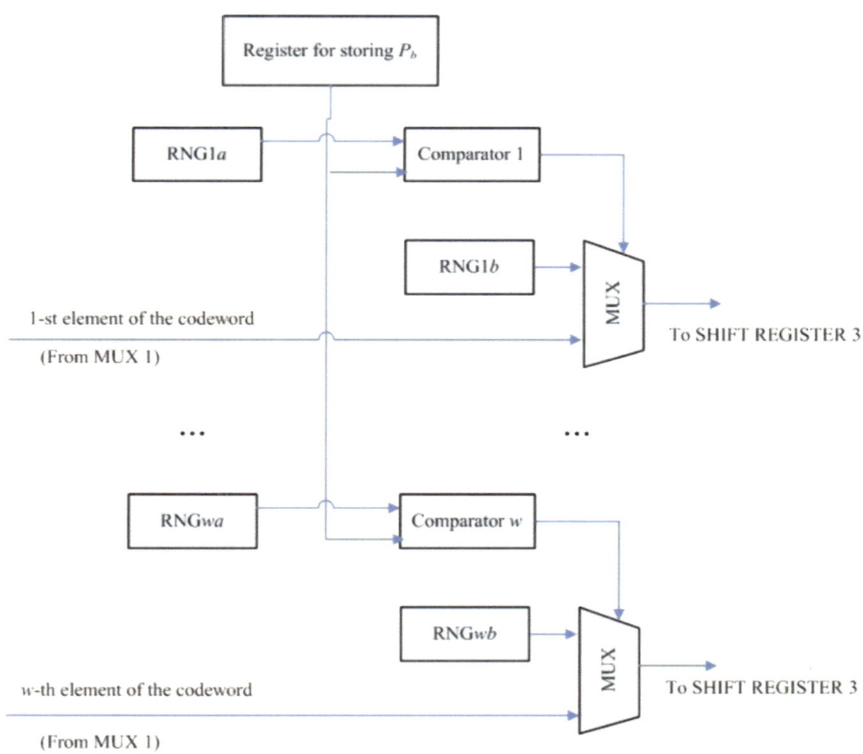

Fig. 4. The architecture of mutation unit

C-Means Unit: The goal of the C-Means unit is to locally refine the mutated child string stored in SHIFT REGISTER 3 using the C-Means algorithm. As shown in Figure 5, the proposed C-Means architecture can be decomposed into two units: the partitioning unit and the centroid computation unit. These two units will operate concurrently for the local refinement process. The partitioning unit uses the codewords stored in the register to partition the training vectors into N clusters. The centroid computation unit concurrently updates the centroid of clusters. Note that, both the partitioning process and centroid computation process should operate iteratively in software. However, by adopting a novel pipeline architecture, our hardware design allows these two processes operate in parallel for reducing the computational time. In fact, our design allows the concurrent computation of $N+2$ training vectors for the C-Means operations.

Figure 6 shows the architecture of the partitioning unit, which is a N-stage pipeline, where N is the number of codewords (i.e., clusters). The pipeline fetch one training vector per clock from the input port. The i-th stage of the pipeline compute the squared distance between the training vector at that stage and the i-th codeword of the codebook. The squared distance is then compared with the current minimum distance up to the i-th stage. If distance is smaller than the current minimum, then the i-th codeword becomes the new current optimal codeword, and the corresponding distance becomes the new current minimum distance. After the computation at the N-th stage is completed, the current optimal codeword and current minimum distance are the actual optimal codeword and the actual minimum distance, respectively. The index of the actual optimal codeword and its distance will be delivered to the centroid computation unit for computing the centroid and overall distortion.

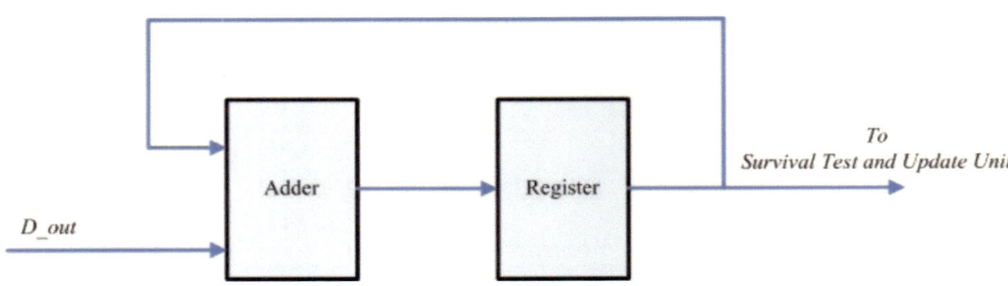

Fig. 5. The architecture of the C-Means unit

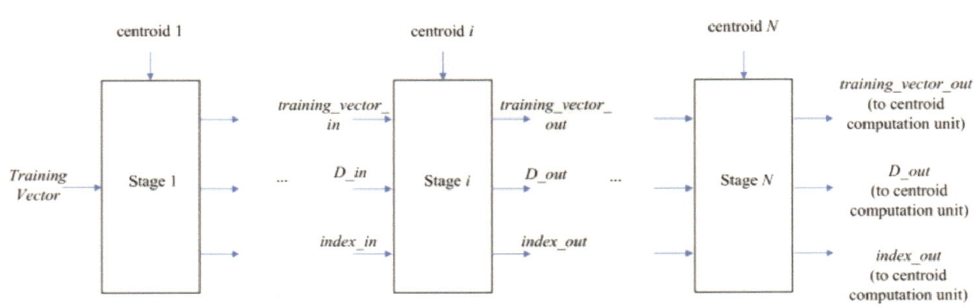

Fig. 6. The architecture of the partitioning unit

Figure 7 depicts the architecture of the centroid computation unit, which can be viewed as a two-stage pipeline. In this paper, we call these two stages, the accumulation stage and division stage, respectively. Therefore, there are $N+2$ pipeline stages in the C-Means unit. The concurrent computation of $N+2$ training vectors therefore is allowed for the local refinement operations.

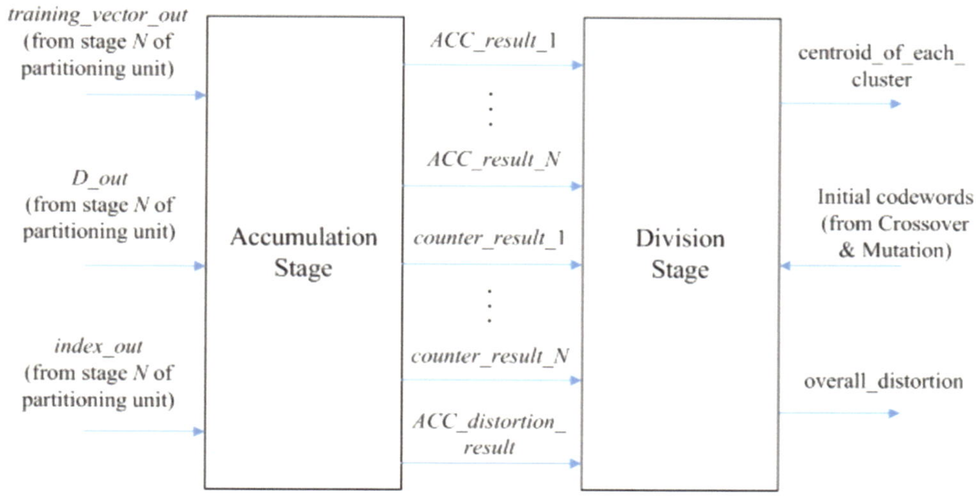

Fig. 7. The architecture of the centroid computation unit

As shown in Figure 8, there are N accumulators (denoted by $ACCi, i=1,...,N$) and N counters for the centroid computation in the accumulation stage. The i-th accumulator records the current sum of the training vectors assigned to cluster i. The i-th counter contains the current number of training vectors mapped to cluster i. The i-th counter contains the current number of training vectors mapped to cluster i. The training_vector_out, D_out and index_out in Figure 8 are actually the outputs of the N-th pipeline stage of the partitioning unit. The index_out is used as control line for assigning the training vector (i.e. training_vector_out) to the optimal cluster found by the partitioning unit.

The circuit of division stage is shown in Figure 9. There is only one divider in the unit because only one centroid computation is necessary at a time. Suppose the final index_out is i for the i-th vector in the training set. The centroid of the i-th cluster then need to be updated. The divider and the i-th accumulator and counter are responsible for the computation of the centroid of the i-th cluster. Upon the completion of the j-th training vector at the centroid computation unit, the i-th counter records the number of training vectors (up to j-th vector in the training set) which are assigned to the i-th cluster. The i-th accumulator contains the sum of these training vectors in the i-th cluster. The output of the divider is then the mean value of the training vectors in the i-th cluster.

It can be observed from the Figure 9 that the division stage also evaluates the overall distortion of the codebook. This can be accomplished by simply accumulates all the minimum distortion associated with each training vector after the completion of the partitioning process. The overall distortion is used for both the fitness evaluation and the convergence test of the C-Means algorithm.

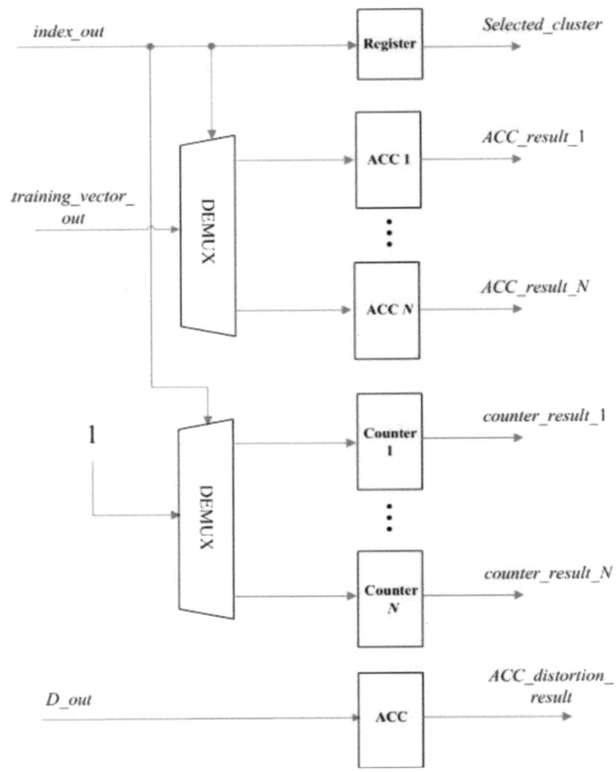

Fig. 8. The architecture of the accumulation stage in the centroid computation unit

Survival Test and Update Unit: This unit contains a hardware sorting circuit (Hwang, Li, Yeh & Chan, 2008), which sorts the parent strings in a descending order according to their fitness values. After the fitness evaluation operation is completed, the fitness value of the child string is used as the input to the sorting circuit. When the distortion of the string is larger than the parent string with lowest fitness value, the child string is not survival, and no updating operation is necessary. Otherwise, the parent string with highest distortion is replaced by the child string. The sorting circuit is then activated to determine the new parent string with the highest distortion.

Figure 10 depicts the architecture of MA (III) algorithm, which contains modules. Each module is a hardware realization of MA (II) algorithm. Therefore, the architecture of each module is shown in Figure 2. Although the genetic strings in different modules (i.e., different populations) evolve independently, they all need the same set of training vectors for C-means algorithm and fitness evaluation. Independent requests for training vector delivery from different modules demand very high memory bandwidth. This may become the bottleneck of the architecture for MA (III) implementation. To solve the problem, the C-means operation of all the architectures operate synchronously. Therefore, training vectors from main memory can be broadcasted to all the modules for C-means training. In addition, the DMA is used for further accelerating the data delivery. To implement synchronous C-means operations among different modules, we first note that all the string selection, mutation crossover, and survival test operations take fixed number of clock cycles. The same operation will take the same number of clocks in different modules. Consequently, when all the modules start MA operations at the same time, the synchronization among the modules can be achieved.

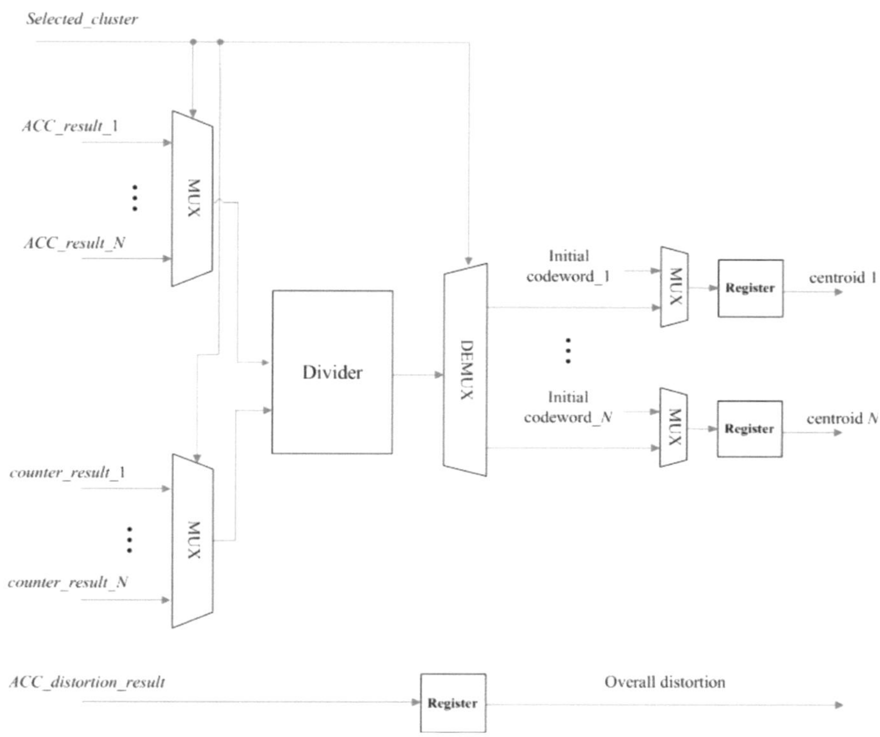

Fig. 9. The architecture of the division stage in the centroid computation unit

3. Experimental results

This section presents some physical performance measurements of the proposed FPGA implementation. The target FPGA device for the hardware design is Altera Stratix II 2S60 (Stratix II Device Handbook, 2008). The Altera Quartus II version 7.2 with SOPC Builder is used as the platform for the system development. The vector dimension of codewords is $w = 2 \times 2$. The mutation probability is $P_b = 0.03125$.

Figure 11 compares the average distortion of the proposed MA (II) implementation with that of basic MA(I) under the same population size $P = 64$ and number of codewords $N = 64$. The software implementation of MA (I) is executed on the 3-GHz Pentium D CPU. In the experiment, we execute each implementation 300 times independently. The training set contains 65536 training vectors from the image "Lena."

Based on the training set, the average distortion of each execution is computed according to eq.(2). Figure 11 then reveals the distribution of the average distortion. It can be observed from Figure 11 that both implementations have similar average distortion distributions. Therefore, our architecture simplifying the string random selection process does not degrade the performance of memetic VQ design.

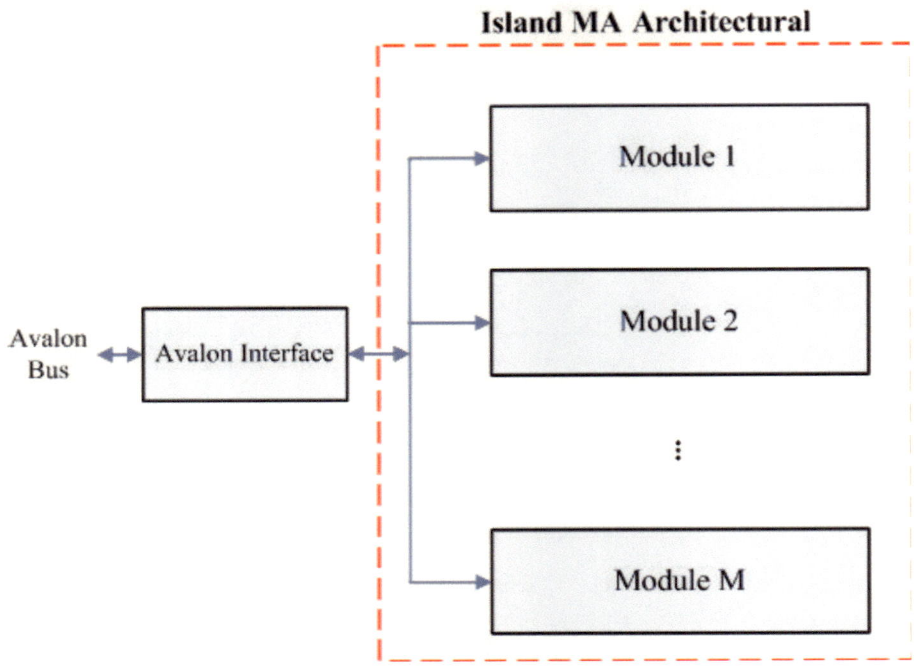

Fig. 10. The architecture of the MA (III) Algorithm.

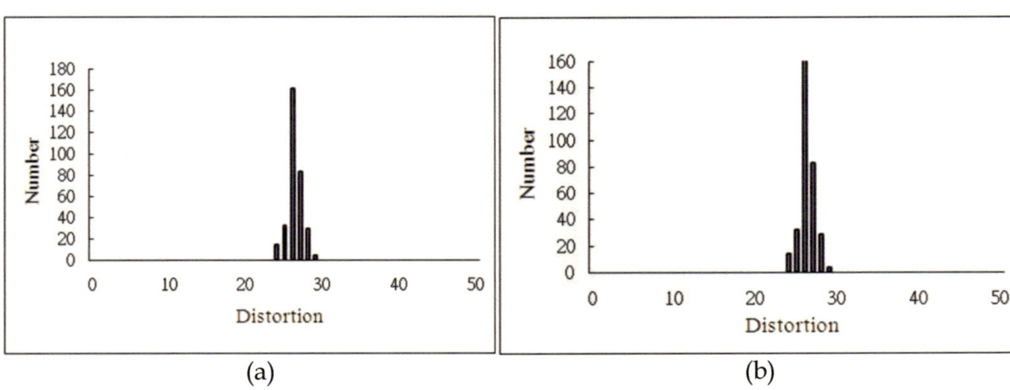

Fig. 11. Distribution of average distortion of various MA algorithms:(a) MA(I) algorithm,(b) MA(II) algorithm

Figure 12 shows the distribution of the mean-squared distortion of MA(II) algorithm implemented by our proposed architecture for 100 independent runs with $N = 64$ and $P = 64$. Each run starts with different set of genetic strings randomly selected from training images. The distribution of distortion of C-Means algorithm and steady-state GA algorithm for 100 independent runs are also included in Figure 12 for comparison purpose. From Figure 12, it can be observed that the C-Means algorithm has a broad distribution of local optima. On Figure 12: Distortion Distribution of proposed MA(II) architecture, C-Means architecture and steady-state GA architecture.

On the other hand, from Figure 12, we see that the distribution of distortion of the MA(II) has a better concentration. The worst case of MA(II) has distortion Only 9 of the distortion of VQs designed by C-Means algorithm are lower than that of the worst case of the MA(II) algorithm. The best case of the MA(II) has The difference between the worst and best cases is only 2. Moreover, we can observe from Figure 12 that the MA(II) algorithm significantly outperforms the steady-state GA algorithm for 100 independent runs.

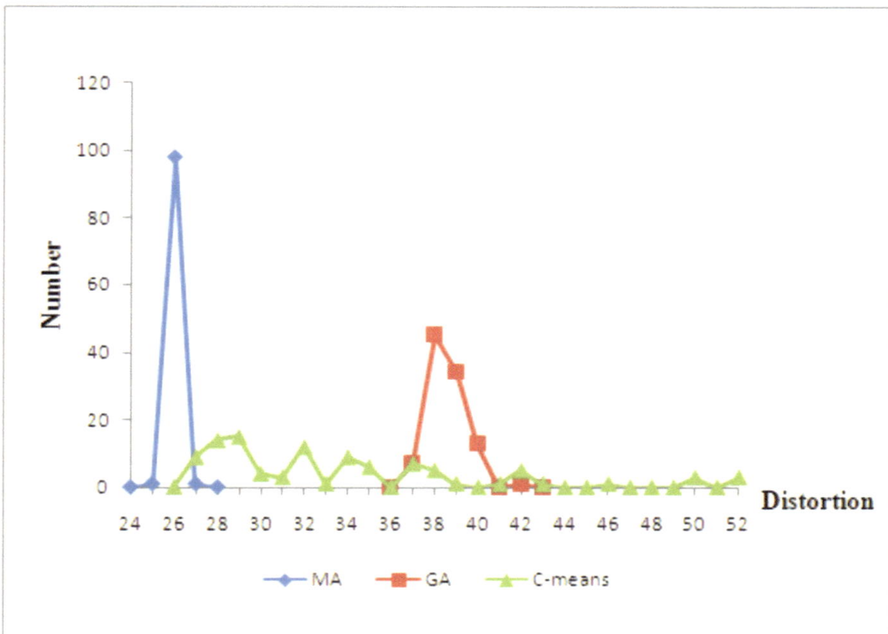

Fig. 12. Distortion Distribution of proposed MA(II) architecture, C-Means architecture and steady-state GA architecture.

Table 1 shows the area costs, average distortion and execution time of the proposed SOPC system for various population size We fix for the experiment. The distortion and execution time are obtained by averaging those of 100 independent executions. It can be observed from Table 1 that the area cost of the entire system becomes only slightly higher as increases. The average execution time grows linearly with In addition, the average distortion can be effectively reduced as becomes larger.

Table 1 shows the area costs, average distortion and execution time of the proposed SOPC system for various population size P. We fix $N = 64$ for the experiment. The distortion and execution time are obtained by averaging those of 100 independent executions. It can be observed from Table 1 that the area cost of the entire system becomes only slightly higher as

P increases. The average execution time grows linearly with P. In addition, the average distortion can be effectively reduced as P becomes larger.

Table 2 investigates the impact of the number of codewords N on the area cost, average distortion and execution time of the proposed SOPC system for MA (II) implementation. The population size P is fixed to 64 for this experiment. The distortion and execution time are obtained by averaging those of 100 independent executions. From Table 2, we see that the number of ALMs and embedded memory bits consumed by the circuit grows with N. The average distortion is effectively lowered as N increases.

P	Average Distortion	Average CPU Time	ALMs (Entire SOPC)	Embedded Memory Bits(Entire SOPC)
16	26.88	366.8ms	22,487	629,504
32	26.65	580.5ms	22,793	662,272
64	26.50	1001.0ms	23,456	727,808
128	26.48	1801.4ms	24,935	858,880

Table 1. The area costs, average distortion and execution time of the proposed SOPC system for MA (II) algorithm for various population size P

N	Average Distortion	Average CPU Time	ALMs (Entire SOPC)	Embedded Memory Bits (Entire SOPC)
8	85.15	909.8ms	9,068	613,120
16	54.49	933.7ms	10,444	629,504
32	37.12	971.0ms	14,569	662,272
64	26.50	1001.0ms	23,456	727,808

Table 2. The area costs, average distortion and execution time of the proposed SOPC system for MA (II) for various number of codewords N

We can also observe that the average CPU time only slightly increase with N. Note that the computational complexity of C-Means algorithm may be large when the number of codewords is high, due to the fact that the partitioning process is based on exhaustive search. However, in the proposed architecture, the C-Means algorithm is implemented by an efficient $(N+2)$-stage pipeline. Therefore, the average CPU time for the VQ design can still be low even when N increases, as shown in Table 2.

Table 3 shows the average CPU time and average distortion of various SOPC systems for VQ design. The measurements are based on the average values of 100 independent runs. All the SOPC systems are running on the same NIOS II softcore CPU with 50 MHz operating frequency. The number of codewords is $N=64$. Moreover, the MA(II) and steady-state GA have the same population size $P=64$.

For comparison purpose, we also implement the software counterpart of each SOPC system using only C code running on Pentium D 3.0 GHz CPU. Note that, the SOPC system and its software counterpart may not have the same distortion for each algorithm shown in the table. This is because the SOPC system and its software counterpart are based on different RNG for initial codewords selection and genetic operations. Nevertheless, the difference in distortion is very small.

	SOPC systems			Software		
	MA (II)	C-Means (Hwang, Hsu, Li, Weng & Yu, 2010)	Steady-State GA(Ou, 2010a)	MA(II)	C-Means	Steady-State GA(Ou, 2010b)
CPU Time (ms)	1001.0	7.36	400.2	366669.3	1922.35	37495.47
Distortion	26.50	35.10	37.62	27.67	37.40	37.48

Table 3. The average CPU time and average distortion of various SOPC systems and software programs for VQ design

It can be observed from the table that each SOPC system has significantly lower CPU time than its software counterpart. In particular, the CPU time of the SOPC system and software for MA(II) design are 1001.0 ms and 366669.3 ms, respectively. The speedup of the proposed SOPC over its software counterpart is 366.3. In addition, as shown in Table 3, the MA(II) algorithm has lowest average distortion as compared with the C-Means and steady-state GA algorithms.

The performance of MA(II) algorithm can be further improved by the employment of MA(III) algorithm. Table 4 compares the performance of the proposed MA(II) and MA(III) architectures, and their software counterparts. The number of modules for MA(III) implementation is $M=3$. The CPU time and average distortion measurements are based on the average values of 100 independent runs. The area cost of the hardware implementations are also included in the table for comparison purpose. To achieve meaningful comparisons, both the architectures have the same number of codewords $N=16$ and the same number of total genetic strings $P=24$. They are also implemented on the same target FPGA device Altera Stratix II 2S60. The software counterpart executes on the processor 4GHz Intel I7.

It can be observed from Table 4 that the MA(III) architecture has lowest average CPU time and lowest average distortion. The average CPU time of the MA(III) architecture is 0.47 second, which is only 43.93 % and 1.36 % of the CPU time of the MA(II) architecture and the software counterpart of MA(III), respectively. Note that, each module for MA(III) architecture has only 8 genetic strings. By contrast, the MA(II) architecture has 24 genetic strings. Therefore, because each module for MA(III) architecture has smaller population, its memetic operations are able to achieve faster convergence. In addition, the best string is selected from multiple populations. Its average distortion is lower than that of the basic memetic algorithm containing only one population, as shown in Table 4.

Although each module has smaller population for MA(III) architecture, the total number ofgenetic strings of the MA(III) architecture is identical to that of the MA(II) architecture. As a result, we can see from Table 4 that both the hardware architectures consume the same number of embedded memory bits. On the other hand, the MA(III) architecture uses more ALMs and DSP blocks for hardware implementation. This is because the architecture consists of 3 modules, and each module has independent mutation and crossover unit, and C-means units. These units utilizes large number of ALMs and DSP blocks. Therefore, when both the area cost and speed are the important concerns, the MA (II) architecture can be used. All these facts demonstrate the effectiveness of the proposed architectures.

Algorithms	ALMs	Embedded Memory Bits	DSP Blocks	Average CPU Time	Average Distortion
MA (III) Architecture	19281	12288	288	0.47 (sec)	54.62
MA (II) Architecture	7203	12288	96	1.07 (sec)	55.27
Software				34.55(sec)	55.23

Table 4. Comparisons of the performance of various MA implementations

4. Conclusion

The proposed MA (II) and MA (III) architectures have been shown to be effective for fast VQ training. Selections of genetic strings one at a time for crossover and mutation are able to reduce area cost for hardware implementation while maintaining the performance for VQ training. Moreover, the DMA for training vector delivery and pipeline architecture for C-Means algorithm are beneficial for local refinement and fitness evaluation. Experimental results show that the proposed architectures attains high speedup over its software counterpart. It also has lower average distortion as compared with C-means and steady-state GA algorithms.

5. References

Areibi, S., Moussa, M., & Abdullah, H., (2001). A Comparison of Genetic/Memetic Algorithms and Heuristic Searching, *Proc. International Conference on Artificial Intelligence*, pp.660-666, June 2001.

Choi, Y. H., & Chung, D.J., (2000) VLSI Processor of Parallel Genetic Algorithm, *IEEE Asia Pacific Conf. on ASICs*, pp.143-146, 2000.

Eiben, A. E., & Smith, J. D., (2003) Introduction to Evolutionary Computing, *Springer*, 2003.

Gersho, A., and Gray, R.M., (1992). Vector Quantization and Signal Compression, Kluwer, *Norwood, Massachusetts*, 1992.

Hwang W.J., Hsu C.C., Li H.Y., Weng S.K., & Yu T.Y., (2010). High Speed C-means Clustering in Reconfigurable Hardware, *Microprocessors and Microsystems*, pp.237-246, 2010. (SCI)

Hwang, W.J., & Hong, S. L., (1999). Genetic entropy-constrained vector quantization, *Optical Engineering*, Vol. 38, pp.233-239, 1999.

Hwang, W.J., Li, H.Y., Yeh, Y.J. & Chan, K.F., (2008). FPGA Implementation of Competitive Learning with Partial Distance Search in the Wavelet Domain, *Progress in Neurocomputing Research*, pp.203-221, NOVA Science Publisher, 2008.

Hauck, S., & Dehon, A., (2008). Reconfigurable Computing, *Morgan Kaufmann*, 2008.

Merz, P., & Freisleben, B., (1999). A Comparison of Memetic Algorithms, Tabu Search, and Ant Colonies for the Quadratic Assignment Problem, *Proc. the IEEE Congress on Evolutionary Computation*, pp.2063-2070, 1999.

Molina, D.; Lozano, M., & Herrera, F., (2010). MA-SW-Chains: Memetic algorithm based on local search chains for large scale continuous global optimization, *the IEEE Congress on Evolutionary Computation*, pp.1-8, 2010.

Moscato, P., (1999). Memetic Algorithms: A Short Introduction," *New Ideas in Optimization*, pp.219-234, McGraw-Hill, 1999.

Nedjah, N., & Mourelle, L., (2005). Hardware Architecture for Genetic Algorithms, *Lecture Notes in Computer Science*, pp. 554-556, Vol. 3533, 2005.

Ou, C.M., (2010a). FPGA implementation of genetic vector quantizers, *Neurocomputing*, pp. 2125-2131, vol. 73, no. 10-12, Jun. 2010.

Ou, C.M., (2010b). Vector Quantization Based on Steady-State Memetic Algorithm, *Journal of Marine Science and Technology (JMST)*, vol. 18, no. 4, pp. 553-557, Aug. 2010.

Rasheed, K., & Davisson, B.D., (1999). Effect of global parallelism on the behave of a steady state genetic algorithm for design optimization, In Proceedings of the Congress on Evolutionary Computation, Washington, DC, 1999.

Tommiska, M., & Vuori, J., (1996). Implementation of genetic algorithms with programmable logic devices, *Proc. 2nd Nordic Workshop on Genetic Algorithms and Their Applications*, pp.111-126, 1996.

Santos, P.V.; Alves, J.C., (2010). FPGA Based Engines for Genetic and Memetic Algorithms, *Field Programmable Logic and Applications (FPL)*, pp.251-254, 2010.

Stratix II Device Handbook, 2008, Altera Corporation. http:// www.altera.com/ literature/ lit-nio2.jsp.

NIOS II Processor Reference Handbook, 2008, Altera Corporation. http://www.altera.com/literature/ lit-nio2.jsp.

9

Multiple Access System Designs via Genetic Algorithm in Wireless Sensor Networks

Shusuke Narieda
Akashi National College of Technology
Japan

1. Introduction

Recently, a distributed estimation, a type of parameter estimation problem, has been widely studied from the viewpoint of wireless sensor network (WSN) applications (1) (2). In particular, distributed estimation has been well-studied for certain WSN applications, such as environmental monitoring and precision agriculture (3)-(8). In such applications, measurements are acquired by the combination of a large number of deployed sensors which are equipped with a radio communication transceiver and a fusion center (FC), which collects measurement information from sensors to obtain a final estimate. Such measurement systems require some multiple access systems such as time division multiple access (TDMA), frequency division multiple access (FDMA) (9), frequency and time division multiple access (FTDMA) (10). However, most of related works ignore the effect of multiple access techniques on distributed estimation in WSNs.

This chapter describes a distributed estimation technique that uses genetic algorithm (GA) (11) to optimize the FTDMA which offers high reliability and spectral efficiency and is employed in several WSN systems (12) (13) and RFID systems as a multiple access technique (14). Mobile fusion center based WSN systems that enables ubiquitous physical data collection anywhere have been presented (15). However, because the devices involved in such systems do not typically employ an expensive or considerable hardware, their communication requirements are strictly limited. For instance, a high performance digital signal processor is required to cancel in-band channel interference at baseband in a low-IF receiver (16)-(23). First, the optimization problem based on a mean-squared error (MSE) function to obtain the final estimate is defined. Next, the effects of FTDMA-based measurement environment with WSN on the energy constrained distributed estimation are described, and we show that time slots and frequency bands should be allocated appropriately to avoid the effect of a large power interference (24). We define this problem as a combination optimization, and employ GA to solve this problem. Also, from these, we develop an algorithm to obtain the suboptimal time slot, frequency band and transmit power allocation for each sensor.

2. Preliminary notion

2.1 Frequency and time division multiple access

Fig.1 shows FTDMA models as the multiple access tecnique. In this model, the time is divided into N_T time slots with the same length and the available frequency is divided into N_F

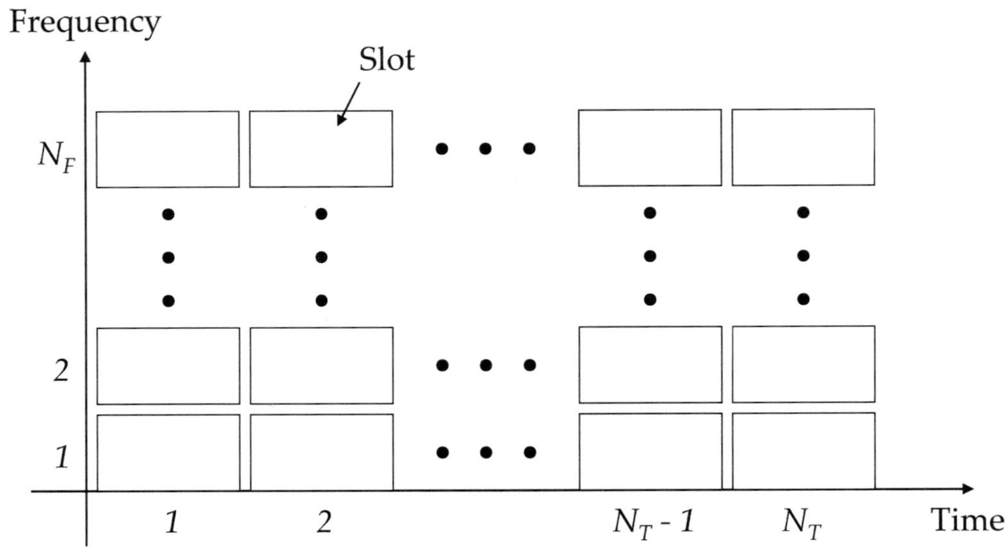

Fig. 1. FTDMA system

frequency bands with the same bandwidth. Also, N_F time slots are transmitted at the same time for all available frequencies. Time slots are allocated to sensors to transmit observed quantities to the FC.

2.2 Multisensor measurement system with best linear unbiased estimator

In this subsection, we describe the distributed estimation model in FTDMA-based WSNs as shown in Fig.2. In this model, N spatially deployed senosrs observe unknown phenomena θ with zero mean and variance σ_θ^2. A local measurement at the ith node is corrupted by an additive noise as

$$x_i = \theta + n_i, \quad 1 \le i \le N \tag{1}$$

where n_i is spatially independent zero-mean additive measurement noise with variance $\sigma_{n_i}^2$. We assume that all $\sigma_{n_i}^2$ are known at the FC. Due to the bandwidth limitation, each sensor quantizes x_i with a quantization function $\mathcal{Q}(\cdot)$ into b-bit messages as

$$m_i = \mathcal{Q}(x_i), \quad 1 \le i \le N. \tag{2}$$

In this chapter, we adopt an uniform quantization scheme as $\mathcal{Q}(\cdot)$. The quantization message m_i can be written with a quantization error as

$$m_i = x_i + q_i, \quad 1 \le i \le N \tag{3}$$

where q_i is the quantization error uniformly distributed with zero mean and variance $\sigma_{q_i}^2 = W^2/(3 \cdot 2^{2b_i})$, where $[-W, W]$ is the available signal amplitude range and b_i is the allocated

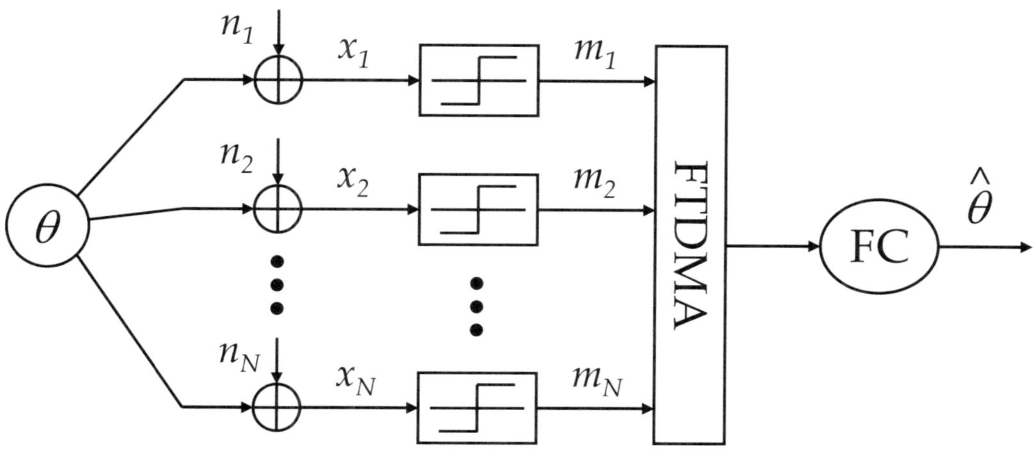

Fig. 2. System model

bit to ith sensor. The FC is gathered quantization message m_i and combined to generate final estimate of $\hat{\theta}$. $\hat{\theta}$ can be obtained by the best linear unbiased estimator (BLUE) (25) as

$$\hat{\theta} = \left(\sum_{i=1}^{N} \frac{1}{\sigma_{n_i}^2 + \sigma_{q_i}^2} \right)^{-1} \left(\sum_{i=1}^{N} \frac{m_i}{\sigma_{n_i}^2 + \sigma_{q_i}^2} \right). \tag{4}$$

The MSE D is given as

$$D = \left(\sum_{i=1}^{N} \frac{1}{\sigma_{n_i}^2 + \sigma_{q_i}^2} \right)^{-1}. \tag{5}$$

3. Communication systems

3.1 Modulation scheme

In this subsection, we describe communication systems in the distributed estimation model. In this chapter, we consider multilevel quadrature amplitude modulation (QAM) which is a popular digital modulation schemes. To characterize QAM modulated signals, we employ the transmission energy model (26) as

$$\bar{P}_i(b_i) = c_i \cdot d_i^{\alpha} \left(\ln \frac{2}{p_i} \right) \cdot (2^{b_i} - 1), \quad \forall i \tag{6}$$

where c_i, d_i, α and p_i is a system constant related with an analog circuit, a transmission distance between ith sensor and the FC, the pathloss exponent, and a probability of bit error, respectively. In this chapter, we assume that the electrical and communication requirement for all sensor nodes are the same, i.e., $c_i = c$ and $p_i = p$, and we define a normalized transmission energy model as

$$P_i(b_i) = d_i^{\alpha} \cdot (2^{b_i} - 1), \quad \forall i. \tag{7}$$

Here, we consider the effect of a decision error of a bit in quantized messages m_i on D. It can be seen that error free communication systems are considered in previous subsection. However, modulated signals are distorted from the additive white Gaussian noise, and received messages $\hat{m}_i$ may be not equal to m_i. As a result, an obtained MSE $\hat{D}$ may be larger than D. From these, it can be considered that D represents a lower bounds of the obtained MSE. Although D can be interpreted as mentioned above, we assume that D is the MSE which is defined in eq.(5) to simplify description and explanation.

3.2 Adjacent and in-band channel interferences

Heterodyne receivers may be most widely used architecture in narrowband communication systems. In the architecture, a low intermediate frequency (IF) receiver can be implemented with high degree of integration, and it is suited to the wireless communication terminal which is required the transceiver miniaturization. The low-IF architecture is equipped an analog-to-digital converter (ADC) at the processing stage of an IF signal, and the fact provides a good performance for an in-band and adjacent channel interference cancellation because of digital signal processing techniques, e.x., filtering (16)-(23). However, a digital filter for such processing is required a steep characteristic, and it causes the computational complexity.

In this subsection, we describe the narrowband wireless communication systems with $\bar{N}$ communication channels. The receiver model discussed in this chapter is shown in Figs.3 and 4. In the architecture, a radio frequency (RF) signal is received by an antenna and passed through a band pass filter (BPF) such as a surface acoustic wave (SAW) filter and a low noise amplifier (LNA). The receiver has Hartley image canceller in analog circuits to cancel image band interferences. Under the assumption that there are no an I/Q imbalance (16) in these analog circuits, IF signals, which is the desired signal and in-band channel interference including the adjacent channel interference, are sampled and quantized at the ADC. A filtered and an amplified RF signal $r_{\mathrm{RF}}(t)$ is down converted into the IF signal $r_{\mathrm{IF}}(t)$ at a quadrature mixer with the frequency f_{LO}, where f_{LO} is the local oscillator frequency and $f_{\mathrm{LO}} = f_{\mathrm{RF}} - f_{\mathrm{IF}}$, f_{RF} and f_{IF} are the RF and IF frequency, respectively. $r_{\mathrm{IF}}(t)$ can be written by

$$r_{\mathrm{IF}}(t) = d_{\mathrm{IF},i}(t) + \sum_{j=0,j\neq i}^{N_{\mathrm{IF}}-2} z_{\mathrm{IF},j}(t) + v_{\mathrm{IF}}(t), \qquad 0 \leq i \leq N_{\mathrm{IF}} - 1 \tag{8}$$

where $d_{\mathrm{IF},i}(t)$, $z_{\mathrm{IF},j}(t)$, $v_{\mathrm{IF}}(t)$, and N_{IF} is the desired IF signal at ith communication channel, the in-band channel interferences IF signal at jth communication channel, the additive gaussian noise and the number of communication channels at IF band, respectively. The value of N_{IF} depends on the bandwidth of the IF filter and the channel index i, therefore, $\bar{N} \leq N_{\mathrm{IF}}$. Also, illustrations of $r_{\mathrm{IF}}(t)$ on a frequency domain are shown in Fig.5. Then, the desired signal has a center frequency f_{IF}. After passing through the ADC, $r_{\mathrm{IF}}(n)$ is down-converted into the baseband signal $r_{\mathrm{B}}(n)$ at a digital quadrature mixer with the frequency f_{IF} as shown in Fig.4. Since the center frequency of the desired signal is f_{IF}, $r_{\mathrm{B}}(n)$ can be written in the following

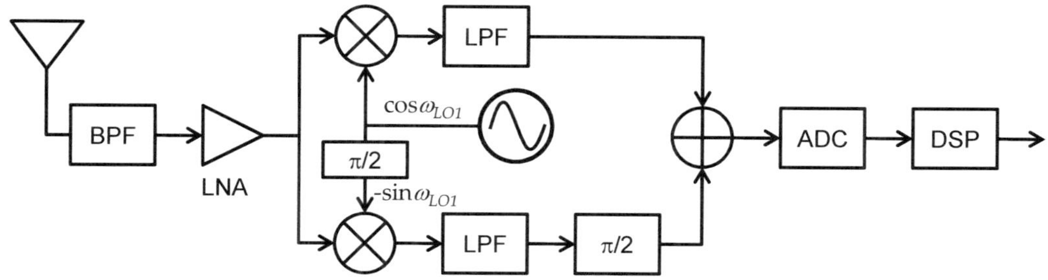

Fig. 3. Low-IF architecture

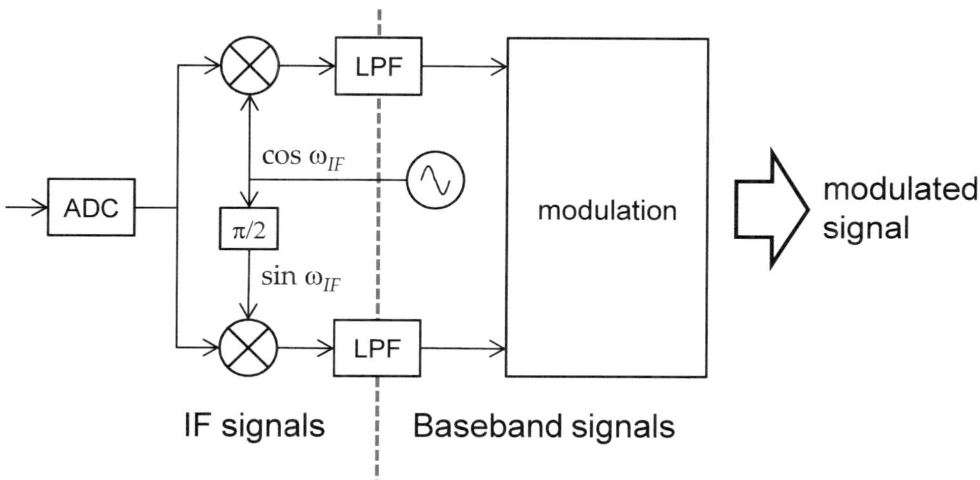

Fig. 4. General digital signal processing part in low-IF receiver

equation,

$$r_{\mathrm{B}}(n) = d_{\mathrm{B}}(n) + \sum_{j=1}^{N_{\mathrm{B}}-1} z_{\mathrm{B},j}(n) + v_{\mathrm{B}}(n) \tag{9}$$

where $v_{\mathrm{B}}(n)$ is the additive gaussian noise, and $v_{\mathrm{B}}(n) \sim \mathcal{N}(0, \sigma_v^2)$, $d_{\mathrm{B}}(n)$ and $z_{\mathrm{B},i}(n)$ are desired signal and interference at ith communication channel respectively. N_{B} is the number of communication channels at baseband and $N_{\mathrm{IF}} \geq N_{\mathrm{B}}$. Also, $z_{\mathrm{B},1}(n)$ is called as the adjacent channel interference. Fig.6 shows baseband signals including the desired signal, adjacent and in-band channel interference in a frequency region. Note that the desired baseband signal is moved to the frequency range around the DC. Let $f_{\mathrm{B,max}}$ denotes the maximum frequency of all baseband signal component including desired signal, adjacent and in-band channel interferences. Although the minimum sampling frequency of the baseband signal $f_{S,\min}$ equals to $2f_{\mathrm{B,max}}$, the sampling frequency of the low-IF receiver is more higher than $f_{S,\min}$ because IF signal with higher frequency than the baseband signal are sampled in the low-IF receiver.

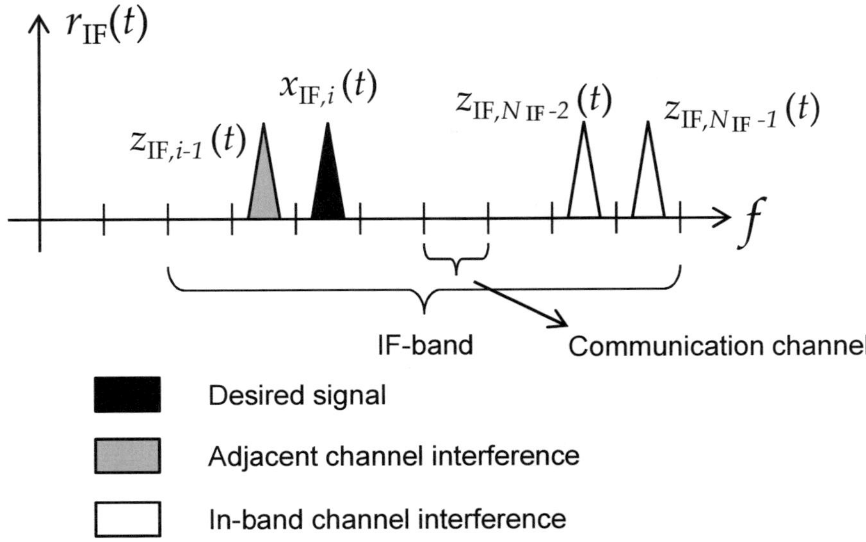

Fig. 5. IF signals in low-IF receiver

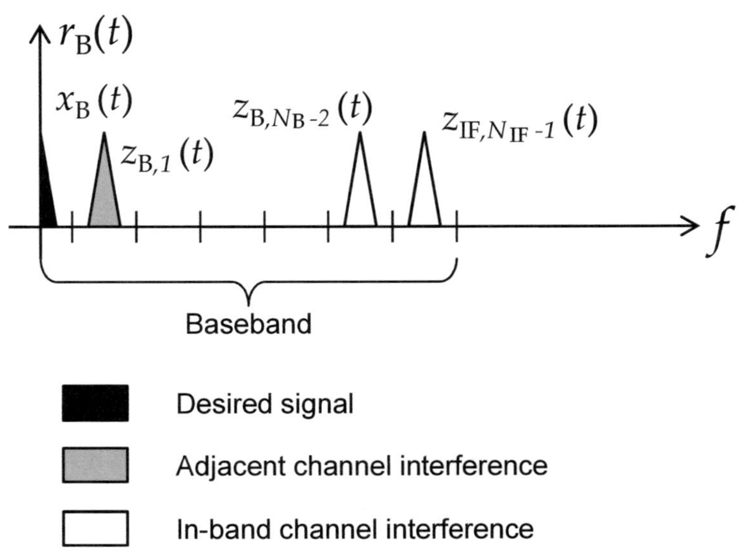

Fig. 6. Baseband signals in low-IF receiver

4. Distributed estimation techniques in FTDMA-based WSN

In this section, we discuss the distributed estimation technique in FTDMA-based WSN. At first, we define an optimization problem to obtain a solution for the distributed estimation.

Next, we derive the equation of the power allocation based on the defined optimization problem. Also, we show that the solution of the problem can not be obtained without optimization of a combination of sensors in tth time slot, and develop the algorithm to obtain suboptimal solution.

4.1 Problem setup

At first, we define an all sensor set $\bar{\mathbb{S}}_0$ as

$$i \in \bar{\mathbb{S}}_0, \quad 1 \leq i \leq N. \tag{10}$$

Also, the set $\bar{\mathbb{S}}_0$ can be partitioned into N_T sensor subsets $\mathbb{S}_t$ as

$$\bar{\mathbb{S}}_0 = \bigcup_{1 \leq t \leq N_T} \mathbb{S}_t. \tag{11}$$

The $\mathbb{S}_t$ means the subset of sensors which transmit message in tth time slot.

Next, we define the problem while keeping a total power constraint which is the sum of transmit powers of individual sensor at the same time. As shown in previous section, received signals in narrowband communication systems are corrupted by the adjacent and in-band channel interferences. Interferences having a large power cannot be canceled without the LPF which has steep characteristics, ans such the LPF is incurred the large number of multiplyer and register because the length of the impluse response of the LPF is very long. Therefore, maximum total power of these interferences at the same time slots is strictly limited. From these, we define the optimization problem as (24)

$$\begin{aligned} &\underset{b_i \in \mathbb{Z}^+}{\arg\min} \left(\sum_{i=1}^{N} \frac{1}{\sigma_{n_i}^2 + \sigma_{q_i}^2} \right)^{-1} \\ &\text{subject to } \mathcal{P}_{tot} \geq \sum_{i \in \mathbb{S}_t} a_i \cdot (2^{b_i} - 1) \\ &\qquad \sigma_{q_i}^2 = W^2 / (3 \cdot 2^{2b_i}) \end{aligned} \tag{12}$$

where $a_i = d_i^{\alpha}$, $\mathbb{Z}^+$ denotes the set of all nonnegative integers, and $\mathcal{P}_{tot}$ is the normalized total power constraint at the same time slots.

However, the solution of eq.(12) can not be obtained via a convex optimization. In this chapter, to facilitate analysis of eq.(12), since $b_i \in \mathbb{Z}^+$, it follows $\sum_{i \in \mathbb{S}_t} a_i(2^{b_i} - 1) \leq \sum_{i \in \mathbb{S}_t} a_i(2^{b_i} - 1)(2^{b_i} + 1)$ and $(2^{b_{\min}} + 1) \leq (2^{b_i} + 1)$ where $b_{\min}$ represents the number of the smallest allocatable bits. From these, we introduce the constraint defined as follows (24),

$$(2^{b_{\min}} + 1)\mathcal{P}_{tot} \geq \sum_{i \in \mathbb{S}_t} a_i(2^{2b_i} - 1). \tag{13}$$

Eq.(13) is the equation based on the constraint in eq.(12), and we can replace the power constraint in eq.(12) by eq.(13) without violating the total power requirement. A similar replacement technique, which represents $\mathcal{P}_{tot} \geq \sum_{i \in \mathbb{S}_t} a_i(2^{2b_i} - 1)$, has been reported (4). As shown in the comparison of two equations, our technique can use the available transmit power effectively. In fact, $b_{\min}$ is equal to zero, in which the case corresponds that there is no allocatable bit to ith sensor.

From these, by performing a change of variable with $\beta_i = 2^{2b_i}$ and some modification, the optimization problem is redefined as

$$\begin{aligned} \underset{\beta_i \in \mathbb{R}^+}{\arg\max} \sum_{i=1}^{N} \frac{Q\beta_i}{\sigma_{n_i}^2 Q\beta_i + 1} \\ \text{subject to } 2 \cdot \mathcal{P}_{tot} \geq \sum_{i \in \mathbb{S}_t} a_i \cdot (\beta_i - 1) \\ \beta_i \geq 0 \end{aligned} \tag{14}$$

where $\mathbb{R}^+$ denotes the set of all nonnegative real number and $Q = 3/W^2$. β_i is relaxed to a nonnegative real number so as to render the problem tractable. In eq.(14), once the optimal β_i is obtained, b_i is determined through upper integer rounding, as (3)-(5).

4.2 Power allocation and sensor selection in FTDMA-based WSN

In eq.(14), when $N_T = 1$, which is similar to conventional method as (3)-(5), the solution of the optimization problem can be obtained by Lagrangian multiplier (27) associated with the equality the total power constraint and inequality constraint. In the case of $1 < N_T < N$, which requires using several frequency bands, the solution of eq.(14) can not be obtained with the solving method for $N_T = 1$. In this subsection, we discuss how to obtain the solution of eq.(14), when $1 < N_T < N$. In this case, the solution of eq.(14) can be obtained by following Lagrangian J

$$J = -\sum_{i=1}^{N} \frac{Q\beta_i}{\sigma_{n_i}^2 Q\beta_i + 1} - \sum_{t=1}^{N_T} \lambda_t \left\{ 2 \cdot \mathcal{P}_{tot} - \sum_{i \in \mathbb{S}_t} a_i \cdot (\beta_i - 1) \right\} - \sum_{i=1}^{N} \nu_i \beta_i \tag{15}$$

where λ_t and ν_i is equality and inequality constraints as Lagrange multiplier, respectively. Eq.(15) leads to the following Karush-Kuhn-Tucker (KKT) conditions (25)

$$\begin{aligned} -\frac{Q}{\left(\sigma_{n_i}^2 Q\beta_i + 1\right)^2} + \lambda_t a_i - \nu_i = 0, \ \forall t, i \in \mathbb{S}_t \\ 2 \cdot \mathcal{P}_{tot} - \sum_{i \in \mathbb{S}_t} a_i \cdot (\beta_i - 1) = 0, \ \forall t \\ \nu_i \beta_i = 0, \ \forall i \\ \nu_i \geq 0, \ \forall i \\ \beta_i \geq 0, \ \forall i. \end{aligned} \tag{16}$$

From the first equation in eq.(16), β_i can be obtained as

$$\beta_i = \frac{Q}{\sigma_{n_i}^2} \left(\frac{1}{\sqrt{Q\lambda_t a_i - \nu_i}} - 1 \right), \quad \forall t, i \in \mathbb{S}_t. \tag{17}$$

Also, we can see from the third equation that for those sensors with $\beta_i \geq 0$, ν_i holds. Therefore

$$\beta_i = \frac{Q}{\sigma_{n_i}^2}\left(\frac{1}{\sqrt{Q\lambda_t a_i}} - 1\right)^+, \quad \forall t, i \in \mathbb{S}_t \tag{18}$$

where $(\mathcal{X})^+$ equals to 0 when $\mathcal{X} < 0$, and is otherwise equals to $\mathcal{X}$. The Lagrange multiplier λ_t can be obtained by substituting β_i into the second equation in eq.(16) as

$$\lambda_t = \left(\frac{Q\sum_{i\in\mathbb{S}_t}^{N_F^{(t)}} \frac{\sqrt{a_i}}{\sigma_{n_i}^2}}{2\cdot\mathcal{P}_{tot} + \sum_{i\in\mathbb{S}_t}^{N_F^{(t)}} a_i\left\{\frac{Q}{\sigma_{n_i}^2}+1\right\}}\right)^2, \quad \forall t. \tag{19}$$

where $N_F^{(t)}$ is the number of active sensors in tth time slot, and $1 \leq N_F^{(t)} \leq N_F$. $N_F^{(t)}$ is determined such that $f\left(N_F^{(t)}\right) \geq 1$ and $f\left(N_F^{(t)} - 1\right) < 1$, where $f(\cdot)$ is the function which is defined as

$$f\left(N_F^{(t)}\right) = \frac{1}{\sqrt{Q\lambda_t\left(N_F^{(t)}\right)a_i}} \tag{20}$$

where $\lambda_t(\cdot)$ is the rewritten version of λ_t and represents the function of the number of active sensor. We assume that sensors are ranked according to a_i such as $a_1 \geq \cdots \geq a_{N_F^{(t)}}$, and the optimal bit load b_i^{opt} can be obtained as

$$b_i^{opt} = \begin{cases} \frac{1}{2}\log_2\left\{\frac{Q}{\sigma_{n_i}^2}\left(f(N)-1\right)\right\} & \text{for } 1 \leq N \leq N_F^{(t)} \\ 0 & \text{for } N_F^{(t)} < N \leq N_F \end{cases} \tag{21}$$

4.3 Selection for combination of sensors in subset $\mathbb{S}_t$

The solving method derived in previous subsection is not yet enough to solve the power (or information bit) allocation problem in FTDMA-based WSN, since the subset $\mathbb{S}_t$ which represents the combination of sensors transmit at tth time slot is not determined. From the solving method, it can be seen that β_i is determined from the distance parameter a_i and measurement noise variance of sensors in $\mathbb{S}_t$. Obtained β_i may be different when combinations of sensors in $\mathbb{S}_t$ are different. Moreover, the MSE D is a nonlinear function for β_i as shown in the following equation which is rewritten version of eq.(5) with β_i,

$$D = \left(\sum_{i=1}^{N}\frac{1}{\sigma_{n_i}^2 + W^2/(3\cdot\beta_i)}\right)^{-1}. \tag{22}$$

Hence, it can be considered that obtaining the MSE depends on combinations of sensors in each $\mathbb{S}_t$, and when $1 < N_T < N$, the combination of sensors in subset $\mathbb{S}_t$ must be determined appropriately, i.e., $\mathbb{S}_t$ optimization. Here, we rewrite the MSE function representation D to $D(\bar{\mathbb{S}}_0)$ as a function of sensors set $\bar{\mathbb{S}}_0$, and this problem can be written as a combination optimization problem as

$$\left[\hat{\mathbb{S}}_1, \cdots, \hat{\mathbb{S}}_{N_T}\right] = \underset{\mathbb{S}_1, \cdots, \mathbb{S}_{N_T}}{\arg\max} \left\{ D\left(\bar{\mathbb{S}}_0\right)^{-1} \right\} \tag{23}$$

$$2 \cdot \mathcal{P}_{tot} \geq \sum_{i \in \mathbb{S}_t} a_i \cdot (\beta_i - 1) \tag{24}$$

$$\beta_i \geq 0, \quad 1 \leq t \leq N_T \tag{25}$$

where $\hat{\mathbb{S}}_t$ is a suboptimal sensors subset. To solve this problem, we employ GA which is utilized to efficiently solve the combination optimization.

From these, we develop an algorithm to obtain a suboptimal combination of sensors in subset $\hat{\mathbb{S}}_t$. The flowchart of the developed algorithm is shown in Fig.7. In Fig.7, at first, M individuals are initialized, where M is population size. The mth individual can be represented by $1 \times N$ vector $\mathbf{k}_{(j,m)}$ as

$$\mathbf{k}_{(j,m)} = \left[\kappa_1^{(j,m)}, \cdots, \kappa_N^{(j,m)}\right], \quad 1 \leq m \leq M \tag{26}$$

where the gene $\kappa_i^{(j,m)}$ represents the time slot index to be ith sensor transmitted and the value of $\kappa_i^{(j,m)}$ can take the integer value as $\kappa_i^{(j,m)} = 0, 1, \cdots, N_T$, and when the number of available time slot is smaller than the number of sensor, $\kappa_i^{(j,m)}$ may be equal to 0. Also, the total number of $\kappa_i^{(j,m)}$ with same value is limited by the available frequency band N_F. Several GA operations, i.e., selection, crossover and so on, are carried out to $\mathbf{k}_{(j,m)}$.

In our developed algorithm, a subset $\hat{\mathbb{S}}_t^{(j,m)}$ which represents the subset of sensors obtained from mth individuals at jth generation can be obtained at every generation. $\hat{\mathbb{S}}_t^{(j,m)}$ is determined by $\mathbf{k}_{(j,m)}$ as

$$\hat{\mathbb{S}}_t^{(j,m)} \ni \left\{ i \middle| \kappa_i^{(j,m)} = t \right\}, \quad \forall i. \tag{27}$$

$\hat{\mathbb{S}}_t^{(j,m)}$ determines the MSE $D_{(j,m)}\left(\bar{\mathbb{S}}_0\right)$ to rank mth individuals at jth generation. Also, the number of $\kappa_i^{(j,m)}$ with the same value is counted after the initialization and GA operation for $\mathbf{k}_{(j,m)}$. If the total number of $\kappa_i^{(j,m)}$ with same value exceeds N_F, it is allocated to other time slot other than N_F sensors.

After finishing the developed algorithm, the $\mathbf{k}_{(j,k)}$ provides a suboptimal combination of sensors in subset $\hat{\mathbb{S}}_t, \forall t$, namely, the time slot and frequency band allocation for all sensors. The allocated power for all sensors can be obtained from eq.(18).

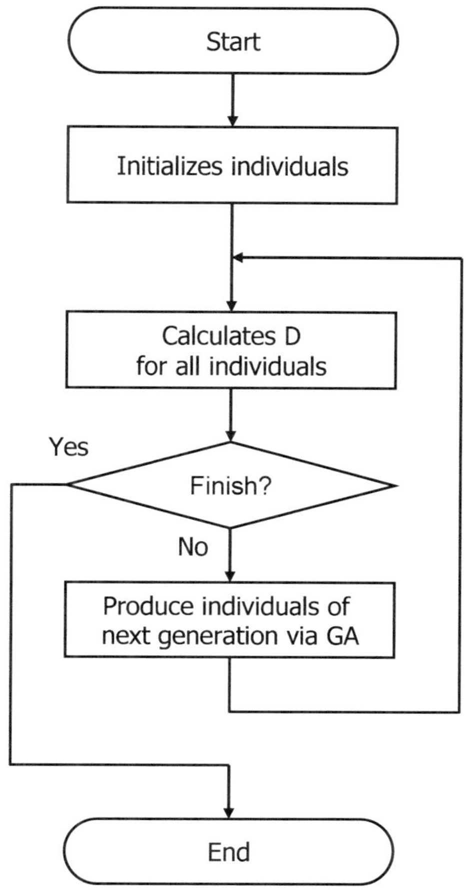

Fig. 7. Flowchart of the algorithm combined power allocation and combination optimization to solve the optimization problem.

5. Numerical examples

In this section, to evaluate the performance of the algorithm shown in Fig.7, numerical simulations are carried out. At first, we show GA operations and parameter employed in this chapter. We employ an elite selection scheme and one point crossover, also, only one gene is mutated at a mutation step in GA. In our numerical simulations, for GA, the number of elite, population and mutation ratios are selected as 5, 50 and 1, respectively. Individual vectors $\mathbf{k}_{(j,m)}$ are initialized uniformly distributed for all time slots in the initialization step. Also, results shown in this section are obtained by averaging over 500 independent trials.

In order to evaluate the algorithm, we compare two curves which were obtained by i) the algorithm shown in previous section, and ii) averaged result in initialized individuals in population. In these, i) corresponds to the results obtained from algorithm with $\mathbb{R}_t$ optimization, and ii) corresponds to the result obtained from conventional sensor selection, i.e., without $\mathbb{R}_t$ optimization. In the following results, σ_θ^2 equals 1, and pathloss coefficients $a_i = d_i^\alpha$ are generated by a uniformly distributed $d_i \in [1, 10]$, and we use $\alpha = 2$ which is the almost same value in literatures (3)-(8) assuming same environments to this chapter. In this chapter, to evaluate the heterogeneous sensor environment, we adopt the normalized deviation of random variables $\psi(\cdot)$ as

$$\psi(R) = \frac{\sqrt{\text{var}R}}{E[R]}. \tag{28}$$

Also, to describe statistical information of sensor noise variance, we adopt the commonly used following equation (3)-(8)

$$\sigma_{n_i}^2 = 0.1 + \gamma\chi_{1,i}^2, \quad 1 \leq i \leq N. \tag{29}$$

where $\chi_{1,i}^2$ is the Chi-square distribution of degree 1, γ controls the underlying variation from the nominal minimum.

Fig.8 shows the MSE performance versus measurement noise variance for several number of time slots when $N_F = 10$, $N = 300$ and $\mathcal{P}_{tot} = N$. For all curves in Fig.8, MSE

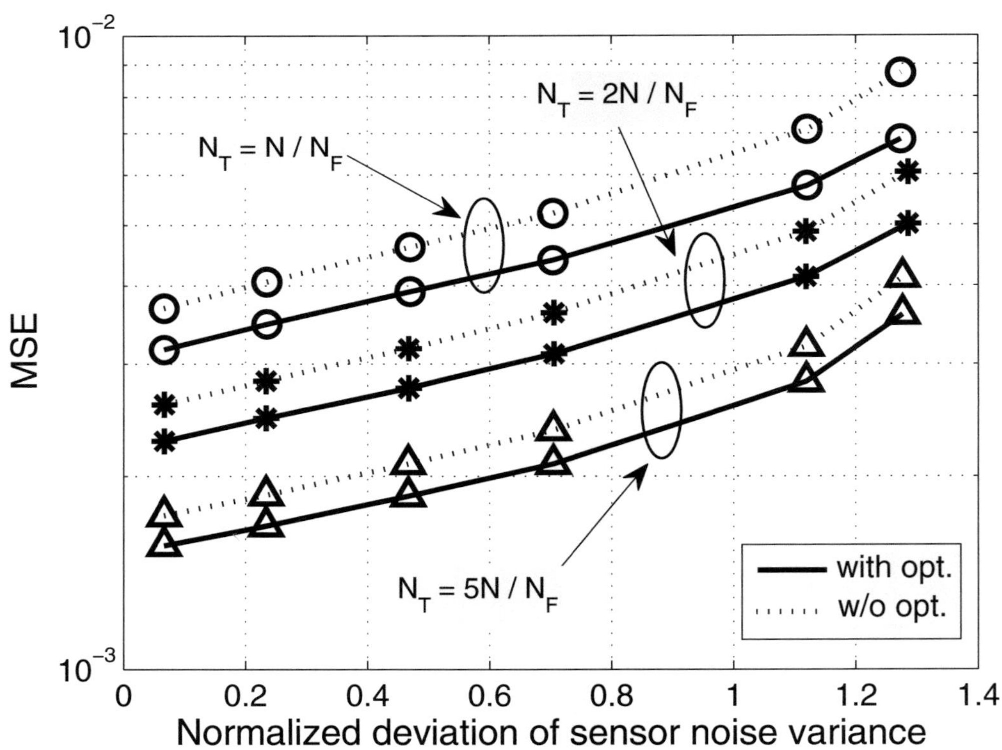

Fig. 8. MSE performance versus normalized deviation of sensor noise variance for the number of different time slot

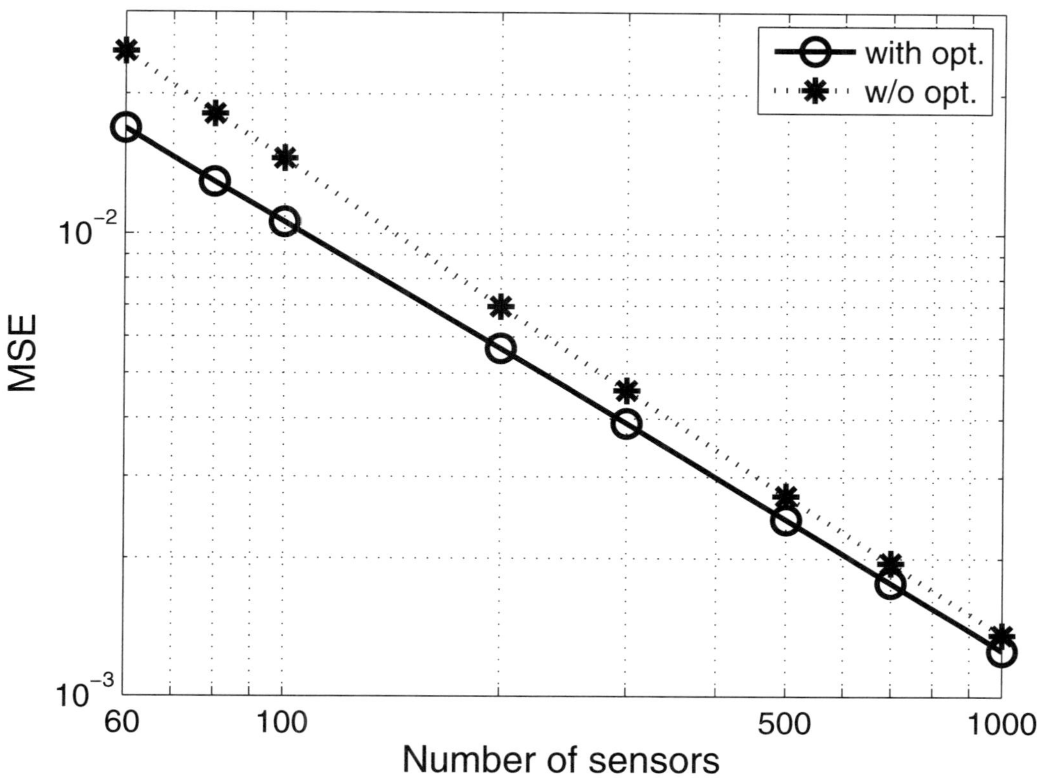

Fig. 9. MSE performance versus the number of sensors with $N_F = 10$, $N_T = N/N_F$, $\psi(n_i) = 0.47$ and $\mathcal{P}_{tot} = 300$.

performances are improved as the number of time slot increases, and it can be considered available transmit power per one active sensor increases as the number of N_T increases. The algorithm outperforms the algorithm without $\mathbb{R}_t$ optimization. Also, it can be seen that MSE performances are improved effectively as the number of N_T decreases, i.e., the density of sensors in FTDMA-based WSN increases.

Fig.9 shows that MSE performances versus the number of sensors when $N_F = 10$, $N_T = N/N_T$, $\mathcal{P}_{tot} = 300$ and $\phi(n_i) = 0.47$, and these conditions represent the number of available frequency band is fixed. From Fig.9, it can be seen that MSE performances are improved as N increases for two curves and our algorithm outperforms the algorithm without $\mathbb{R}_t$ optimization for all plots. In the contrast, the results for the fixed N_T case are shown in Fig.10. In Fig.10, MSE performances versus the number of sensors when $N_T = 10$, $N_F = N/N_T$, $\mathcal{P}_{tot} = 30 \cdot N_F$ and $\psi(n_i) = 0.47$, respectively. It can be seen that the fixed N_F case and the fixed N_T case have similar characteristics. Therefore, for an arbitrary N, $N_F < N_T$ is desirable to achieve measurement systems in FTDMA-based WSN with high spectral efficiency.

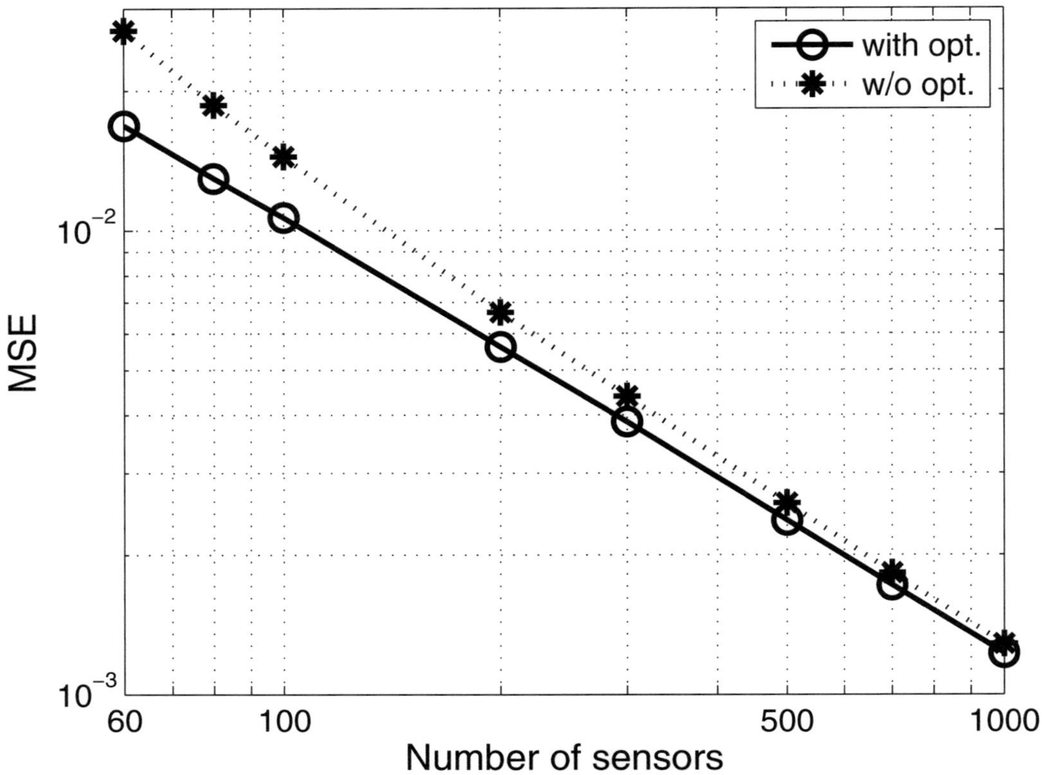

Fig. 10. MSE performance versus the number of sensors with $N_F = N/N_F$, $N_T = 10$, $\psi(n_i) = 0.47$ and $\mathcal{P}_{tot} = 30N_T$.

6. Conclusion

This chapter described the energy constrained distributed estimation in FTDMA-based WSN. The distributed estimation problem in FTDMA-based WSN has been formulated. Several equations for the bit allocation and the replacement technique of total power constraint in the problem have been derived. Also, the effect of FTDMA employed WSN on the distributed estimation has been investigated. We show that the time slot and frequency band to be allocated to each sensor must be optimized for the MSE minimization since the MMSE function is nonlinear for the number of allocated bit to each sensor. The problem of the combination of sensor determination in tth time slot has been defined as the combination optimization, we have employed GA to solve this problem. The algorithm to determine the time slot, frequency band, and the number of allocated bit to each sensor has been developed. Numerical examples have been presented. Our developed algorithm outperforms conventional sensor selection without optimization for the combination of sensors in terms of mean-squared error.

7. References

[1] D. Culler, D. Estrin and M. Srivastava, "Overview of Sensor Networks," *Computer*, vol.37,Ą@issue 8, pp.41-49, Aug., 2004.

[2] I. Akyildiz, W. Su, and E. Cayirci, "Wireless Sensor Networks : A Survey," *Comput. Netw.*, vol. 38, pp.393-422, Mar. 2002.

[3] G. Thatte and U. Mitra, "Sensor Selection and Power Allocation for Distributed Estimation in Sensor Networks : Beyond the Star Topology," *IEEE Trans. Signal Process.*, vol. 56, no. 7, pp. 2649-2661, Jul., 2007.

[4] J. Y. Wu, Q.-Z. Huand, and T.-S. Lee, "Energy-Constrained Decentralized Best-Linear-Unbiased Estimation via Partial Sensor Noise Variance Knowledge," *IEEE Signal Process. Lett.*, vol. 15, pp. 33-36, 2008.

[5] S. Cui, J.-J. Xiao, A. J. Goldsmith, Z.-Q. Luo and H. V. Poor, "Estimation Diversity and Energy Efficiency in Distributed Sensing," *IEEE Trans. Signal Process.*, vol.55, no.9, pp.4683-4695, Dec., 2007.

[6] S. Narieda, ĄgOn the Effect of FTDMA Techniques on a Distributed Estimation in WSNs,Ąh in *Proc. of the IEEE IntĄfl Workshop on Signal Processing Advances in Wireless Communications 2010 (IEEE SPAWC 2010)*, pp.1-5, 2010.

[7] A. Krasnopeev, J.-J. Xiao, and Z.-Q. Luo, "Minimum Energy Decentralized Estimation in a Wireless Sensor Network with Correlated Sensor Noises," *EURASIP J. Wireless Commun. Network.*, vol. 4, pp.473-482, 2005.

[8] S. Cui, J.-J. Xiao, A. J. Goldsmith, Z.-Q. Luo and H. V. Poor, "Estimation Diversity and Energy Efficiency in Distributed Sensing," *IEEE Trans. Signal Process.*, vol.55, no.9, pp.4683-4695, Dec., 2007.

[9] J. G. Proakis, *Digital Communications, Fourth ed.* New York: McGraw-Hill, 2001.

[10] H. Harada, C.-J. Ahn, S. Takahashi, Y. Kamio and S. Sampei, "Dynamic Parameter Controlled Orthogonal Frequency and Time Division Multiple Access," in *Proc. of the IEEE Int'l Conf. on Personal, Indoor and Mobile Radio Communications 2004 (IEEE PIMRC2004)*, vol.4, pp.2648-2652, 2004.

[11] D. E. Goldberg, *Genetic Algorithms in Search, Optimization, and Machine Learning. New Reading*, MA: Addison Wesley, Dec. 1988.

[12] G. Zhou, C. Huang, T. Yan, T. He, J.A. Stankovic and T.F. Abdelzaher, "MMSN:Multi-Frequency Media Access Control for Wireless Sensor Networks," in *Proc. of the IEEE INFOCOM 2006*, Apr. 2006.

[13] H. Soroush, M. Salajegheh, A. Kalis, "HyMAC: Hybrid TDMA/FDMA Medium Access Control Protocol for Wireless Sensor Networks", in *Proc. of the IEEE Int'l Conf. on Personal, Indoor and Mobile Radio Communications 2004 (IEEE PIMRC2007)*, Sep. 2007

[14] International Organization for Standardization, "ISO/IEC 18000-3: Information technology - radio freqnency identification for item management - part3: Parameters for air interface communications at 13.56MHz," 2004.

[15] D. Shah and S. Shakkottai, ĄgOblivious Routing with Mobile Fusion Centers over a Sensor Network,Ąh in Proc. of the IEEE INFOCOM 2007, pp.1541-1549, 2007.

[16] B. Razavi, RF Microelectronics, Prentice Hall, 1998.

[17] S. Narieda, "Downsampling Techniques using Notch Filter for Interference Cancellation in Narrowband Wireless Systems," *Proc. in the IEEE Vehicular Technology Conference 2011 (IEEE VTC2011-Fall)*, Sep., 2011.

[18] J. Crols and M. S. J. Steyaert, "Low-IF topologies for high-performance analog front ends of fully integrated receivers," *IEEE Trans. Circuits and Systems,* vol.45, no.12, pp.269-282, Mar. 1998.

[19] F. J. Harris, C. Dick, and M. Rice, "Digital Receivers and Transmitters Using Polyphase Filter Banks for Wireless Communications," *IEEE Trans. Microw. Tech.,* vol.51, no.4, pp.1395-1412, Apr. 2003.

[20] A. M. Bostamam, Y. Sanada, "Experimental investigation of undersampling for adjacent channel interference cancellation scheme," *in Proc. IEEE PIMRC 2005*

[21] J. E. Adlard, T. C. Tozer, and A. G. Burr, "Interference rejection in impulsive noise for VLF communications," *in Proc. IEEE MILCOM 1999*, pp.296-300, Nov. 1999.

[22] I. Korn, "Effect of adjacent channel interference and frequency-selective fading on outage of digital radio," *IEE Proceedings F, Commun., Radar and Signal Processing,* vol.132, pp.604, Dec. 1985.

[23] S.-J. Jou, S.-Y. Wu, and C.-K. Wang, "Low-power multirate architecture for IF digital frequency down converter," *IEEE Trans. Circuits and Systems II,* vol.45, no.11, pp.1487-1494, Nov. 1998.

[24] S. Narieda, AgDistributed Estimation Techniques for In-band Channel Interference Cancellation of Mobile Fusion Center in FTDMA-based WSNs," *Int'l Journal of Distributed Sensor Networks,* (in submission).

[25] S. M. Kay, *Fundamentals of Statistical Signal Processing: Estimation Theory*. Englewood Cliffs, NJ: Prentice-Hall, 1998.

[26] J.-J. Xiao, S. Cui, Z.-Q. Luo, and A. J. Goldsmith, "Power Scheduling of universal decentralized estimation in sensor networks," *IEEE Trans. Signal Process.,* vol.54, no.3, pp.1131-1143, Mar. 2006.

[27] S. Boyd and L. Vandeberghe, *Convex Optimization.* Cambridge, U.K. : Cambridge Univ. Press, 2003.

10

Genetic Algorithms in Direction Finding

Dario Benvenuti
Elettronica S.p.A.,
Italy

1. Introduction

Passive receiving systems are used to intercept emissions of interest, both communication and Radar, and to measure their characteristic parameters in order to classify and possibly identify them. Direction of Arrival (DOA) is one of the most important parameters to be measured, as it can yield a localization fix by means of triangulation (if more receivers are dislocated on the area), or however it can help designate the target for further operations (Neri, 2006).

There are several ways to estimate the DOA: by measuring signal amplitude received by a rotating directional antenna, or the amplitude difference, phase difference and time difference of arrival between two or more antennas (Wiley, 1985). A more general approach is based on the Array Processing techniques, as described in (Friedlander, 2009), considering the complex signals received by the elements of an array, thus taking into account both amplitude and phase or time, and performing an estimation process.

Rotating antenna DOA can give a good accuracy, in the order of a fraction of its beamwidth, but it works for a continuous emitter or a high rate pulse emitter in order to estimate DOA through the analysis of amplitude shape modulated by the beam pattern on a pulse train, and in order to have a reasonable probability of intercept.

Amplitude monopulse DOA is usually simple though not very performing due to amplitude measurement errors (e.g. antennas ripple, multipath, unbalances).

Time difference of arrival DOA can be quite simple and accurate but it needs a large baseline between the two antennas to have good performance.

Phase goniometry is usually very performing though accurate channel and antennas calibrations are needed to reduce phase mismatch as required.

The optimum performance is given by the array processing techniques: beamforming, maximum likelihood and super-resolution techniques like MUSIC (Smidth, 1986; Poisel, 2002; Friedlander, 2009).

In communication band passive receivers are usually equipped with phase interferometers, as amplitude information is poor. In the next paragraph the basic principle of interferometry is described.

2. Phase goniometry

Here we focus the attention to phase goniometry, which is often used in Communication-band intercept receivers because of the difficulty of having directional antennas at these frequencies; by the way, generalization to other Array Processing techniques is straightforward.

The basic principle of phase goniometry is the simple interferometer depicted in Fig. 1; the phase difference between the two antennas is related to the angle ϕ. Here the angle ϕ is measured counter-clockwise starting from the x-axis as in trigonometry, while DOA is defined, as usual in operative systems, as the clockwise angle starting from a given reference: e.g. North or Platform Heading, giving absolute and relative DOA respectively.

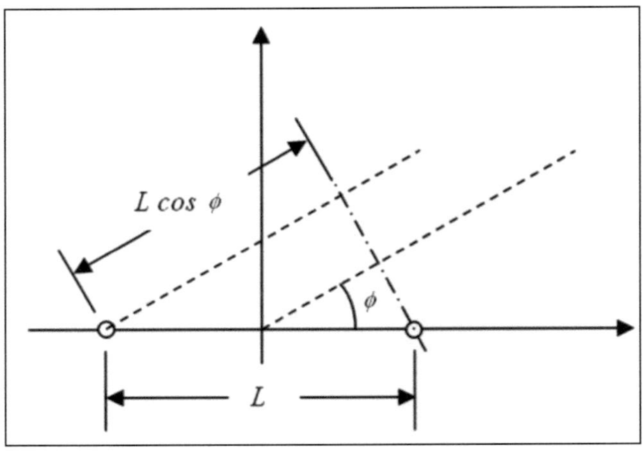

Fig. 1. Basic principle of phase goniometry

The two antennas are separated by the baseline L thus the path difference between a distant emitter[1] and the two antennas is given by

$$\Delta R = L\cos\phi \tag{1}$$

and the phase difference $\Delta\psi$, is obtained multiplying the path difference by the propagation vector $k = 2\pi/\lambda$, where λ is the signal wavelength:

$$\Delta\psi = \frac{2\pi}{\lambda} L\cos\phi \tag{2}$$

If $L < \lambda/2$, phase difference is never ambiguous for every incident angle, while on the contrary more baselines are needed to solve the ambiguity. A short baseline provides a not ambiguous angular estimate and a long baseline gives a more accurate measurements around the former. The ratio between the baselines is limited by the phase measurement error.

A general solution is represented by the phased array, as described in Figure 2.

[1] A distant emitter means that the directions from the two antennas to the emitter can be considered parallel with a negligible error.

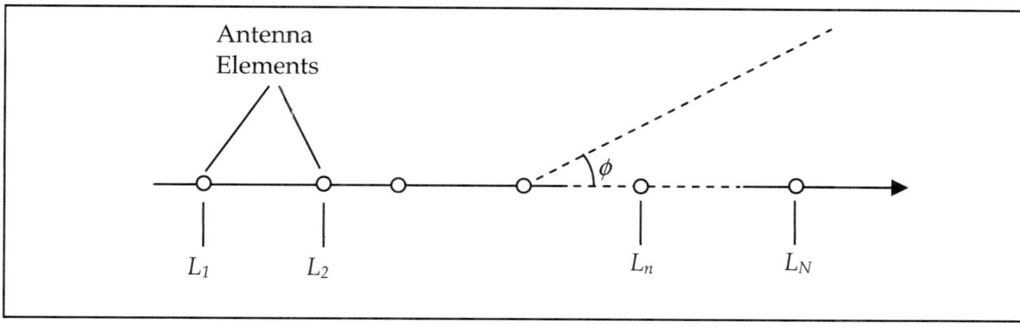

Fig. 2. Schematic of a Phased array

Let L_n be the coordinate of the nth antenna element from the reference point (e.g. the center of the array): generally, elements may be at different distances each other. An array factor can then be defined as:

$$A(\theta)=\begin{bmatrix} \exp\left\{j\dfrac{2\pi L_1\cos\phi}{\lambda}\right\} \\ \exp\left\{j\dfrac{2\pi L_2\cos\phi}{\lambda}\right\} \\ \cdots \\ \exp\left\{j\dfrac{2\pi L_N\cos\phi}{\lambda}\right\} \end{bmatrix} \tag{3}$$

If a regular disposition is used, i.e. all element distances are equal (L) the array n^{th} line becomes:

$$\exp\left\{j\frac{2\pi nL\cos\phi}{\lambda}\right\} \tag{4}$$

In this case the ambiguity is related to the distance between the elements L, while accuracy is related to the total array length (i.e. the number of elements). Linear arrays present their best performance at the broadside direction, while at endfire the beam is wider and DOA accuracy is lower.

To have a good coverage of the whole azimuth a circular array is usually used, which are described below, along with the principles of several DOA estimation algorithms.

2.1 Uniform circular arrays

A uniform circular array is a smart solution to have a good direction finding performance for every angle, while linear arrays suffer from beam broadening when scanning; moreover less coupling between the element is expected with this kind of arrays (Tan et al., 2002). They are composed of several omnidirectional elements (e.g. dipoles) equally spaced on a circle, (cfr. figure 3).

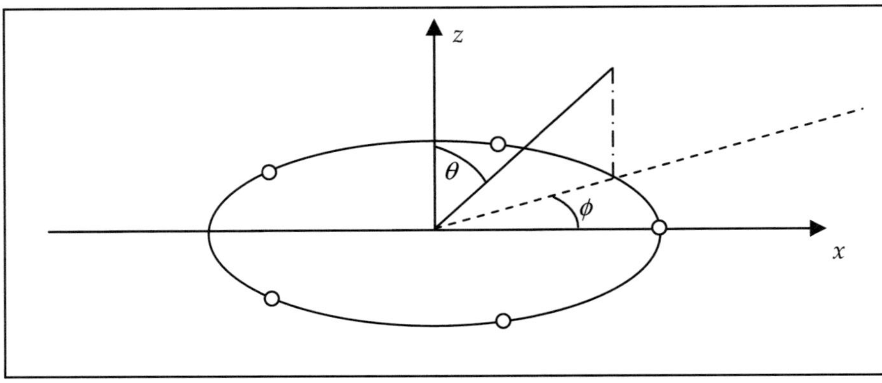

Fig. 3. Example of a Uniform Circular Array

Let ϕ be the azimuth angle measured from x-axis, and θ the polar angle measured from z-axis, the array factor is

$$\left[\exp\left\{j\frac{2\pi r\sin\theta\cos(\phi-\alpha_n)}{\lambda}\right\}\right] \qquad n=1..N \tag{5}$$

where r is the array radius and α_n is the nth element azimuth, $\alpha_n = 2\pi(n\text{-}1)/N$.

When the number of element is odd, and at least five, ideally no ambiguity arises also when wavelength is smaller than the circle radius. Practically noise and non idealities limit frequency to some bandwidth, but these kind of antennas have usually good performance (Lim et al, 2004, Tan et al., 2002, Miller et al., 1985).

2.2 DOA estimation algorithms

The phase difference between the array elements are related to the azimuth and elevation. The estimation of these angles can be done in several ways, which can be grouped into three conceptual classes:

- algorithms that minimize a cost function, like the Beamforming method (Van Veen & Buckley, 1988), the Maximum Likelihood method (Satish & Kashyap, 1996), and many others, like Minimum Variance, Capon variation;
- algorithms based on multiple signal separation like MUSIC (Schmidt and Franks, 1986), ESPRIT (Roy and Kailath, 1989) and others;
- algorithms exploiting calibration information, like the correlative method and some variations of MUSIC.

A complete review of the DOA estimation method can be found in the paper (Godara, 1997) and in its huge reference list.

The Beamforming method takes the name from the ability to steer the main lobe of an array by feeding its antenna elements with a given phase pattern such that their contributions line up in phase in the wanted direction. Conversely, as the antennas are reciprocal objects, if the measured array factor is combined in phase with the theoretical array factor (5), a maximum will appear in correspondence with the true values θ and ϕ. The way to combine in phase the measured and theoretical array factors is the product by the Hermitian conjugate, thus the angular estimation may be found by maximizing the function:

$$\left|a(\phi,\theta)^{H} a_m(\phi_m,\theta_m)\right| \tag{6}$$

The Maximum Likelihood approach considers the probability density function of the observation vector given the unknown parameters, its peak will give their best estimation:

$$L(\phi,\theta) = PDF(\mathbf{x}\,|\,\phi,\theta) \tag{7}$$

If the measurement joint PDF is the multivariate Gaussian:

$$\frac{1}{\left(\pi\sigma^2\right)^N}\exp\left\{-\frac{1}{2}\frac{\left|\mathbf{x}(t)-\mathbf{A}(\phi,\theta)s(t)\right|^2}{\sigma^2}\right\} \tag{8}$$

the Maximum Likelihood can be obtained minimizing the exponent:

$$\left(\hat{\phi},\hat{\theta}\right)_{ML} = \arg\left\{\min_{(\phi,\theta)} Tr\left[\left(1-\mathbf{A}\left(\mathbf{A}^H\mathbf{A}\right)^{-1}\mathbf{A}^H\right)\hat{\mathbf{R}}\right]\right\} \tag{9}$$

where the measurement covariance matrix has been defined:

$$\hat{\mathbf{R}} = \frac{1}{M}\sum_{t=1}^{M}\mathbf{x}(t)\mathbf{x}^H(t) \tag{10}$$

The MUSIC method and its variations first estimates the noise subspace through eigenvalues analysis of the measured array correlation matrix, and then in the orthogonal subspace M peaks can be searched of the function

$$P_{MUSIC}(\phi,\theta) = \frac{1}{\left|a^*(\phi,\theta)\mathbf{E}_N\mathbf{E}_N^*a(\phi,\theta)\right|} \tag{11}$$

where $\mathbf{E}_N$ is composed of the noise column eigenvectors (Schmidth, 1986).

MUSIC method can be also used in conjunction with the Mutual Coupling Coefficient estimation. Mutual coupling affects the phase patterns of the array elements causing DOA errors; the intrinsic symmetry of a uniform circular array makes it easy to set up a model of non ideal phase pattern due to mutual coupling, which acts as a circularly symmetric Toeplitz matrix whose coefficient can be estimated together with DOA (Qi et al., 2005; Weiss & Friedlander, 1992).

The most straightforward way to deal with antennas non idealities is to set up a calibration and to compare measurement with calibrated data to estimate an accurate DOA (Smith et al., 2005). Of course this method has the drawback of the expensive calibration phase that has to be performed in a proper test range, and the memory requirement to store the calibrated data. The peak of the correlation function gives the estimated ϕ and θ

$$CORR(\phi,\theta)=\sum_k \cos\left(\Delta\psi_k^{(meas)}-\Delta\psi_k^{(cal)}(\phi,\theta)\right) \tag{12}$$

where $\Delta\psi$ are the phase differences and the superscripts indicate the measured and the calibrated data.

The described methods for DOA estimation can be all considered as optimization problems, as there is always a function to be minimized or maximized; Genetic Algorithms can be applied easily to them.

3. Genetic Algorithms

The great adaptability of living gave the first hints for an exploitation of this characteristic by computer machine. The pioneer of this approach is John Holland around the 70s: though previous works tried to simulate the evolution, he was the first to use evolution as an optimization tool, and invented the term Genetic Algorithm.

Living beings evolve through Natural Selection: only those who are strong enough to survive till the reproductive age and that win the struggle to mate can propagate their genetic heritage. In other words those who have a high Fitness can proliferate and their offspring have a high probability of inheriting good characters after the partial mixing (Crossover) of the sexed reproduction.

A random Mutation can occur which causes sad effects in our species, but which has the important task of avoiding the characters stagnation in the population, that is the complete equality of one or more genes over the whole population: in such case the Crossover cannot change that gene and the only chance to recover a variability is a random mutation.

These features have been implemented in the so called Genetic Algorithm. The genes represent the points of the search space, that is the domain of the Fitness, the function to be maximized. The gene length is related to the resolution needed for the solution, however it is easy to deal with standard sized words, like bytes, or 16 or 32 bit words.

A starting population is built with random genes values and it evolves through several generations in which Selection, Crossover and Mutation are repeated until a satisfactory solution has been found or a maximum number of iterations has been reached. This is the recipe of a classic GA, described in figure 4; in the following section some variations are described, which in some cases can help the velocity of convergence to a good solution.

Some effort has been performed to provide a satisfactory theoretical explanation of a Genetic Algorithm, the Schemata Theorem (Holland, 1975) being one of the most celebrated, though not earning complete acceptance; Genetic Algorithms maintain the status of a mainly empirical optimization technique for a large variety of applications (Davis, 1991).

It is surely useful when the problem under study is not easily treatable through classical technique: e.g. an analytical model may not exist or may be too complex, or the parameters are so many that a mathematical approach would be too time consuming, while a handful of genes can evolve for some tens of generations giving a satisfactory result (Whitley, 1994).

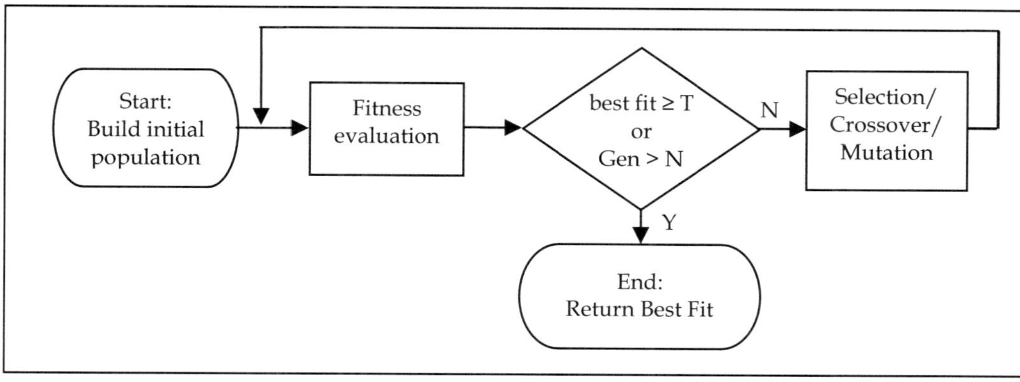

Fig. 4. Schematic diagram of a Genetic Algorithm

3.1 Modified algorithms

In these 30 and more years GA have been used in every field of science and techniques, and each researcher, trying to grab the most of his algorithm, gave a contribution to enrich the Nature own recipe by various modifications: there are thus many variants of Selection, Crossover, Mutation and even Genes Representation. A clear view of this sophistications can be found in (Haupt, 2004).

The Genes Representation for example is often carried on the Real Numbers domain instead of the classical string of bits, performing the so called continuous GA. The Gray encoding has been proposed for integer genes in order to have smooth offsprings variations when the classic encoding is unstable: e.g. when parents are around the value 2^{N-1}, N being the length in bit, it suffices a little change in the gene value to completely shuffle its binary representation, while with Gray Coding always a unitary change in the value is represented by a variation on one bit only. However this problem should be circumvented by the uniform crossover (see below).

Classical selection is random with probability proportional to fitness (Roulette Wheel Selection), while sometimes the best fitting individuals are priorly selected: this is an Elitist Selection.

Also for the Crossover many variants exist like one cut point, two points, uniform; they are depicted in figure 5. The uniform crossover has the advantage of a large exploring power, i.e. the number of different children that are possible from a given couple of parents: one point crossover can generate 2(N-1) different children, where N is the gene length in bit, while the uniform crossover can generate $2^{(N-1)}$ different children increasing dramatically the exploring power. An even greater exploration capability crossover has been investigated in (Coli et al., 1996), where the concept of real-valued GA are used for integer genes. This is based on the interpretation of the classic single point crossover as an arithmetical operation between integer numbers. The cut point (cp) divide a gene x_1 into two substrings that are the quotient and the remainder of the division of x_1 by $2^{(N-cp)}$: classic CO is performed by choosing a random index cp between 1 and *N*. The generalized CO is obtained allowing the divisor to span over a greater set of values.

Let $b \in (1, 2]$ and $M = \lceil N \log_b 2 \rceil$, choose a random index k between 1 and M, and let $c=b^k$, the CO is operated by swapping the remainders of the division by c and then to return to integer numbers by rounding. When b is less than 2 and approaches 1, M becomes greater and greater, i.e. the search space of the CO is incremented. Of course there is a limit given by the rounding effect, for which the optimum b seems to be around 1.05 (Coli et al., 1996).

The result of this generalized CO is a non-random mixing of the two parents that is no more correlated with the bit representation of the genes, but the parents legacy is smeared all over the offspring length.

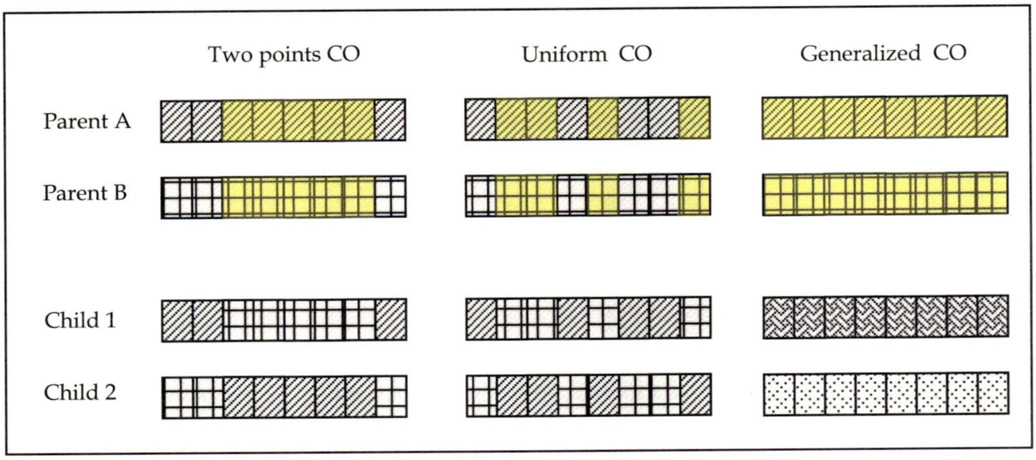

Fig. 5. Schematic view of different kinds of crossover operators

Mutation should theoretically have a low probability, but it can be used with a high probability in the beginning of the evolution and then exponentially decaying to the usual values around 1/N.

Other topics about tuning a GA include population size, growth and control: a variable population size implies a more difficult memory management, and control of twin genes can be useful in some cases but it overload the algorithm with another function to be performed.

Contaminations with other types of algorithms can be foreseen, like hill climbing or random search making a hybrid GA (Haupt, 2004). Hill climbing can speed up the process of final optimization, while random search prevents local minima trapping.

There is not a complete agreement on the utility of these variations, sometimes different applications require different setup, but this can be seen as another interesting features of the GA. In the following the application to the DOA estimation is described, along with the optimization parameters that have been explored.

4. GA application to goniometry

The Genetic Algorithm approach has been implemented to the problem of Direction of Arrival estimation through phase interferometry with a Uniform Circular Array. GA have been used to minimize the Mean Square Error and its performance have been compared to a standard Steepest Descent Algorithm, both for the DOA accuracy and the computational load. A benchmark is set with the Correlative method, which should guarantee the best performance being supported by the calibration data.

The interferometer is a five element array operating in VHF bandwidth, from 30 to 300 MHz, see figure 6, where additional higher bands arrays are shown too. The VHF array is the largest and has a radius of 1.35 m.

Fig. 6. Five element Uniform Circular Array interferometer

The measured phase patterns, at interval of 4 degrees in azimuth 10 degrees in elevation and 5 MHz in frequency, are stored for the correlation algorithm and are used with additive noise to generate the phase measurements. The theoretical and measured phase differences between adjacent array elements are reported in figure 7, along with the estimated angle at frequency f = 200 MHz.

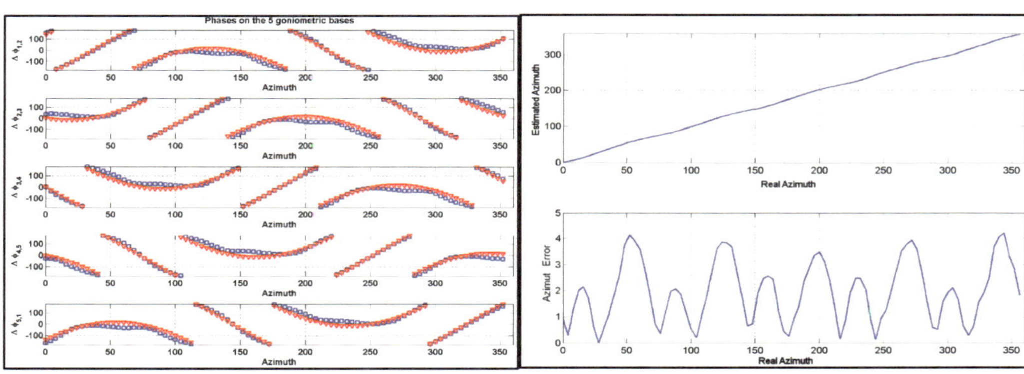

Fig. 7. Phase differences, estimated DOA and DOA error at 200 MHz

4.1 Genetic Algorithm setup

A Genetic Algorithm has been implemented and optimized versus several parameters using a simple one dimensional DOA estimation, having fixed elevation at zero degrees.

Several runs have been executed with different Population Size and Maximum number of Generations in order to have a reasonable setup of the GA, and the results in terms of DOA accuracy and ambiguity fraction have been plotted in figure 8. The Mutation probability was set to 0.1 and the classic 2-points Crossover has been used.

DOA accuracy is the standard deviation of the DOA error over the whole azimuth and frequency band, while the ambiguity fraction is the number of points with an error greater than 90°, divided by the total number of points.

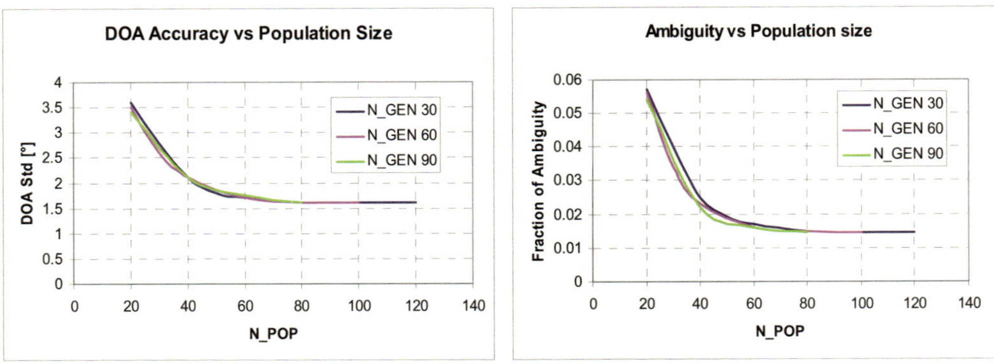

Fig. 8. DOA accuracy and Ambiguity Fraction vs Population Size (N_POP) and Maximum Number of Generations (N_GEN)

These trials show a quick convergence, in fact the results are quite independent of the number of generations, while a population size greater than 40 to 60 individuals seems to be important.

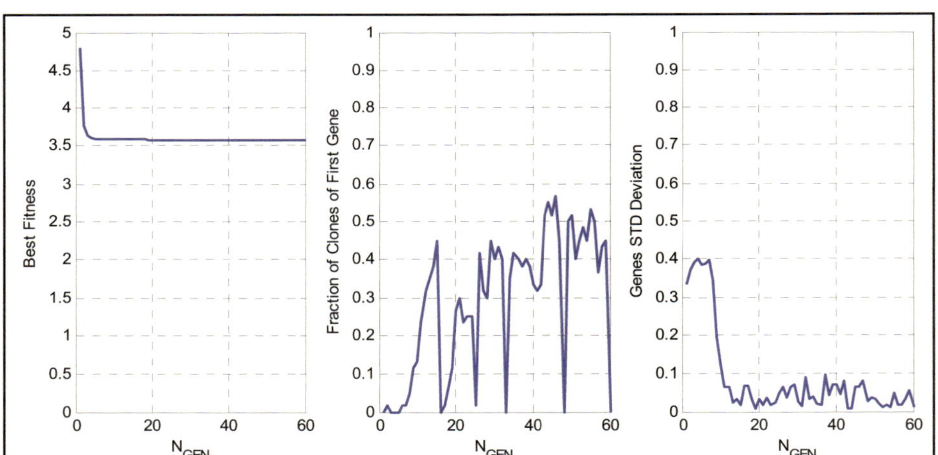

Fig. 9. Convergence of the GA: Minimum Error (left); Fraction of Clones of best gene (middle); Genes Normalized Standard Deviation (rigth)

In figure 9 it is shown the behaviour of the algorithm during the generations. In the left the best fitness is shown (in term of MSE); it can be seen that convergence is very fast as was already mentioned. In the middle graph the fraction of clones of the first gene is reported for each generation: after few iterations population becomes quite biased, about 50% of the population is just a silly copy of the best gene. In the right the genes normalized standard deviation is plotted, which has a complementary trend, after few iterations becomes very low, meaning that the majority of the genes are very near to the best individual.

A set of trials has been executed varying the mutation probability, from 0 to 0.9. The results, shown in figure 10, are quite impressive, being necessary to have a great randomness in the GA to work properly.

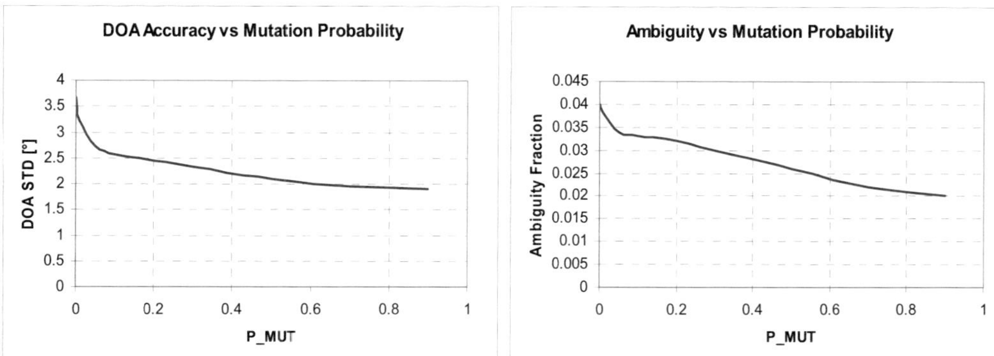

Fig. 10. Effect of Mutation Probability on GA performance

To improve convergence an hybrid random search has been implemented in the GA introducing a renewal of the population: the worst individuals are overwritten with new random genes, and mutation probability has been set to 0.1. The results are very encouraging, the number of generation has been limited to 20, in figure 11 the performance are reported for a 20% population renewal at each generation; population size ranges from 20 to 60 showing better results than previous with less computing power.

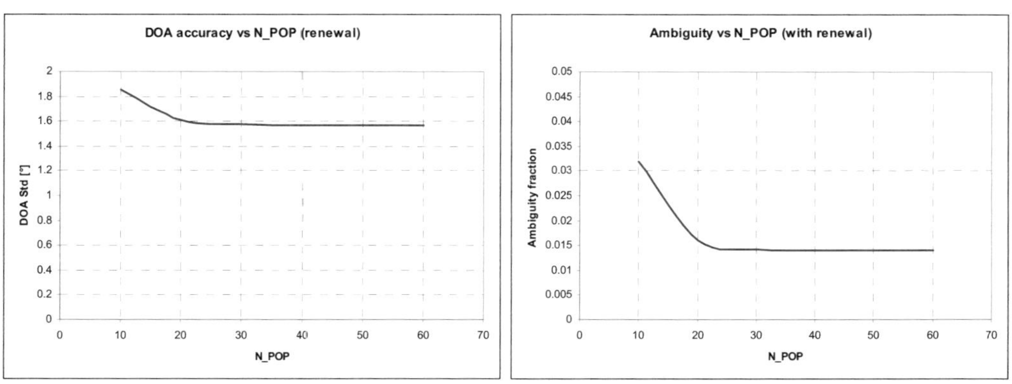

Fig. 11. GA performance with the introduction of Population Renewal

A similar improvement has been achieved also changing the Crossover operator in order to have a more efficient search space exploration. In table 1 the comparison between the 2 points crossover, the uniform and the generalized is reported with and without the population renewal. It seems that this random renewal prevails over the crossover type.

	Standard mutation		Population renewal (20%)	
	DOA std [°]	Ambiguity	DOA std [°]	Ambiguity
2 points crossover	2.6	0.034	1.572	0.0145
Uniform crossover	2.2	0.022	1.573	0.0139
Generalized crossover	1.7	0.028	1.571	0.0154

Table 1. Comparison of different Crossover operators, with and without population renewal

With these hints on GA parameters, an operative simulation has been performed over a full azimuth and elevation estimation in presence of noise and in comparison with a standard minimization algorithm.

4.2 Results of GA in mean square error minimization

The measured array phase pattern has been used to generate the phase differences to which a Gaussian noise has been added. Given the phase difference measurement vector the Square Error Function (13) can be evaluated for every azimuth and elevation, its minimum indicates the best estimate of direction of arrival.

$$MSE(\phi,\theta)=\sum_n \left| \exp\left\{-j\frac{2\pi}{\lambda}r\cos(\phi-\alpha_n)\sin(\theta)+\psi_{n+1}^{(meas)}\right\} - \right.$$
$$\left. -\exp\left\{-j\frac{2\pi}{\lambda}r\cos(\phi-\alpha_{n+1})\sin(\theta)+\psi_n^{(meas)}\right\}\right|^2 \tag{12}$$

The standard minimization method is the Nelder-Mead implemented in Matlab. To avoid ambiguity and local minima trapping several starting points have to be selected, the step of this sampling must be large to limit computation resources, but it must be sufficiently small in order to sample the real maximum, because the error function ripple increase with frequency. Genetic algorithms overcome this problem by the global search.

Comparison of performance versus computational complexity is reported in figure 12. The computational load has been evaluated in terms of number of error function evaluation (fitness in the case of GA); for the Nelder-Mead algorithm every starting point gives rise to a process in which several points are evaluated until a convergence to a local minimum is reached, the number of evaluation has been recorded for every tentative starting point. For the GA this is simply the product of population size by the number of generations. Some accessory functions are present in the GA, like the Crossover, but these have an almost negligible computational complexity with respect to the error function calculation.

The superiority of the Genetic Algorithm approach with respect to the Nelder-Nead minimization is evident: the GA is converging with much less operations to about the same performance. A Signal to Noise Ratio equal to 20 dB was selected, then other simulations were performed at different SNR at the same computational load, in figure 13 the results have been plotted.

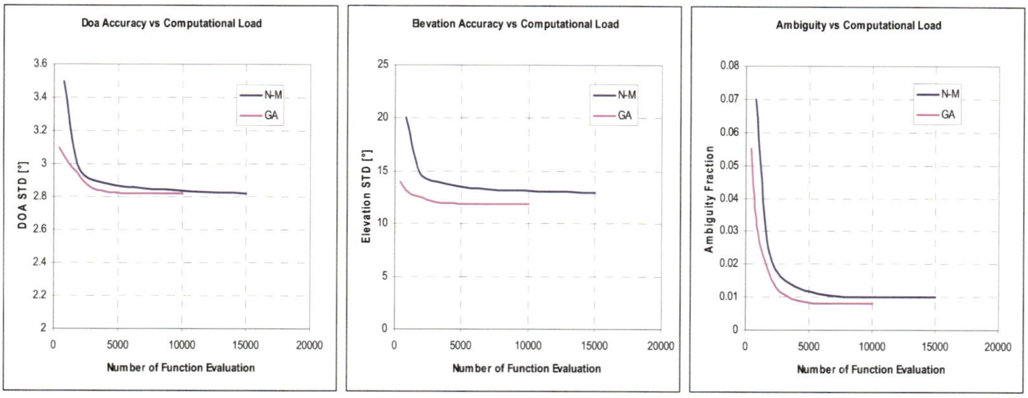

Fig. 12. Comparison between GA and Nelder Mead versus computational load

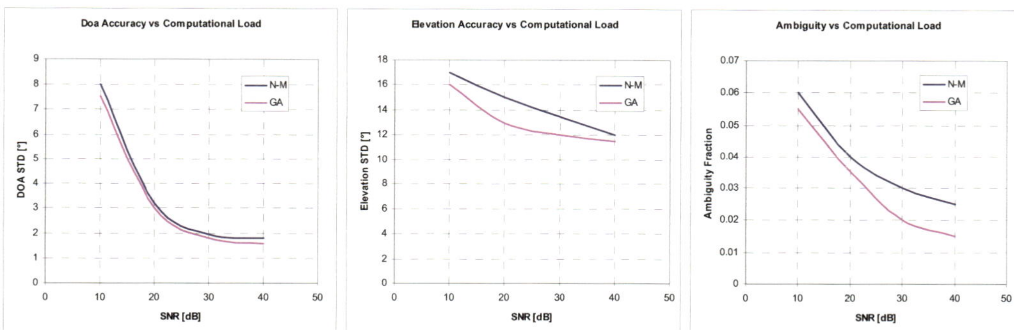

Fig. 13. Comparison between GA and Nelder Mead versus SNR

Having fixed the computational complexity to a middle value the GA has better performance especially for what concerns elevation accuracy and ambiguity. However both algorithms are quite good, considering that the estimation does not take into account the pattern non idealities. This could mean that the antenna has a good pattern which resembles an ideal one. To have a confirm the correlative algorithm has been used as a benchmark.

4.3 Correlative algorithm

As mentioned before, calibration is a straightforward method to account for phase pattern distortions due to mutual coupling between elements and the effect of the mast and the installation. The correlative algorithm makes use of the stored calibrated patterns building up a correlation with the measured phase vector; the peak of the correlation function gives the DOA estimation. An example is reported in figure 14 from (Dinoi et al., 2008).

Here the phase vector is measured from direction 125° azimuth and about 45° elevation. Correlation spans -5 to +5 because the sum of the 5 channels has not been normalized.

From the figure it is clear that the elevation accuracy is much worse than the azimuth accuracy, and this phenomenon is amplified around the horizontal plane, where most of the measurements are taken: the calibrated pattern have been measured at elevation steps of 10° from -30° to 30° and then extrapolated for higher elevations.

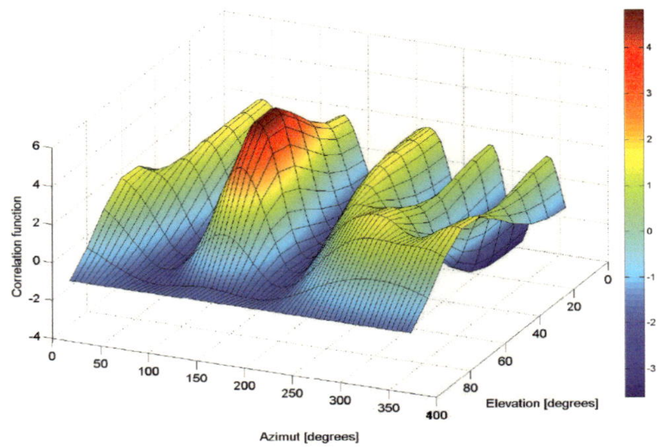

Fig. 14. Example of Correlation function

The correlative method is not very robust for low SNR: in fact it is more subject to gross errors or ambiguities than the MSE based algorithms: this means that noise can raise up a secondary maximum of the correlation function to an higher value than the real maximum. In figure 15 a plot of the minimum SNR required to avoid ambiguities is plotted (red line) together with the minimum SNR to have 1° accuracy (green line) and 2° accuracy (blue line). This plot has been obtained by simulation with ideal patterns.

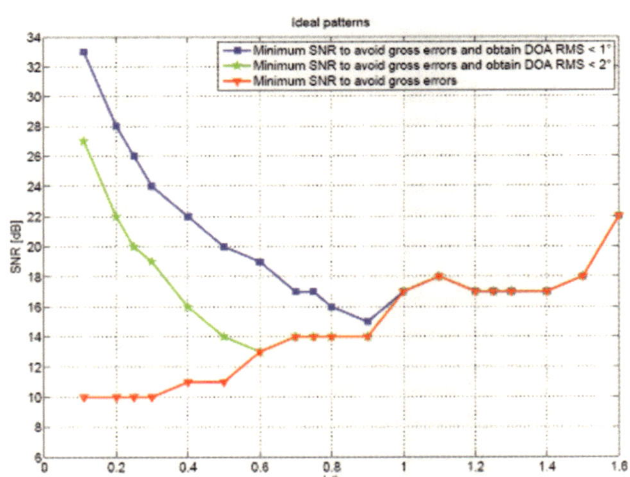

Fig. 15. Minimum SNR to avoid ambiguity versus L/λ ratio (i.e. ~ frequency)

With the real patterns that is more evident: in figure 16 the performance of correlative goniometry with the measured patterns is reported versus SNR. At high SNR this method yields excellent results, but it fails at low SNR, when MSE based methods still work.

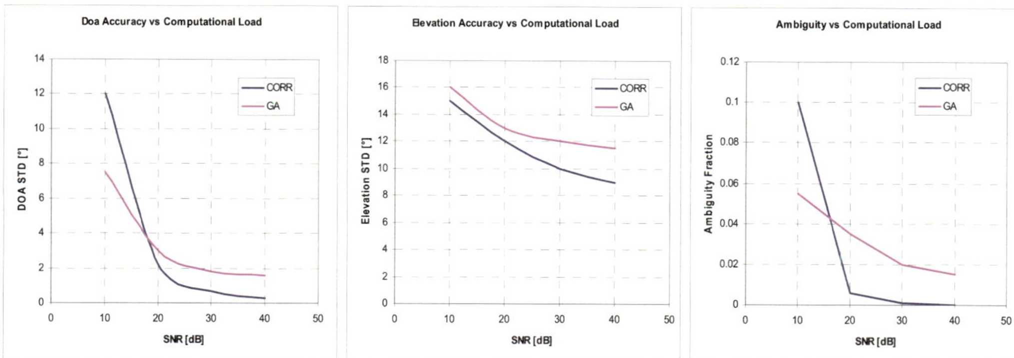

Fig. 16. Comparison of GA and Correlative method versus SNR

5. Conclusion

Genetic Algorithms have been applied to the Direction of Arrival Estimation through a Uniform Circular Array interferometer. After a brief description of the DOA estimation techniques and a view of Genetic Algorithms a sort of parameter tuning for optimization has been performed on a GA; some algorithm variations has been introduced and described. The Genetic Algorithms have been compared to a standard minimization tool, the Nelder-Mead method. The Correlative method, which makes use of the calibrated phase patterns, and thus guarantee the best achievable performance at high SNR, has been used as a benchmark.

Genetic Algorithms reach the same performance of Nelder-Mead optimization technique, but with less computational power. Both techniques reach good performance compared to the correlative method.

The Genetic Algorithms showed a more robust behaviour when low computing power is available, confirming their ability as general purpose optimization tools.

6. Acknowledgment

I would like to thank my responsible in Elettronica SpA, Daniela Pistoia, head of Research and Advanced System Design, and Graziano Lubello, head of Communication Electronic Warfare Advanced Systems, who allowed me to investigate this interesting field of research. Many thanks also to my colleague Libero Dinoi, who supported me in the subject of Correlative Goniometry. This work has surely grown up from the prolific discussions I had with Michele Russo.

7. References

Coli M., Gennuso, G., Palazzari, P., (1996). A New Crossover Operator for Genetic Algorithms, *Proceedings of the 1996 IEEE International Conference on Evolutionary Computation*, ISBN 0-7803-2902-3, Nayoya University, Japan, May 1996

Davis, L. D., (Ed.). (1991). *Handbook of Genetic Algorithms*, Van Nostrand Reinhold, New York

Dinoi, L., Di Vito, A. & Lubello, G., (2008). Direction finding of ground based emitters from airborne platforms, *IEEE Radar Conference*, Rome, May 2008

Friedlander, B., (2009). Wireless Direction Finding Fundamentals, In: *Classical and Modern Direction-of-Arrival Estimation*, Tuncer, E. & Friedlander, B., pp. 1-51, Academic Press, ISBN-13: 978-0-12-374524-8, Burlington, MA, USA

Haupt, R. L. and Haupt, S. E., (2004). *Practical Genetic Algorithms*, John Wiley and Sons, ISBN 0-471-45565-2, New Jersey, USA

Holland, J. H., (1975). *Adaptation in natural and artificial systems*, Ann Arbor: University of Michigan Press, USA

Lim, J. S., Jung, C. G., Chae, G. S., (2004). A design of precision RF direction finding device using circular interferometer, *Proceedings of 2004 International Symposium on ISPACS*, ISBN 0-7803-8639-6, Seoul, Korea, November 2004

Miller, P. A., Lyons, R. S., Weber, B. L., (1985). A Compact Direction-Finding Antenna for HF Remote Sensing, *IEEE Transactions on Geoscience and Remote Sensing, Vol. 23, no. 1*, January 1985

Neri, F. (2006). *Introduction to electronic defense systems*, SciTech Publishing, ISBN 978-1-891121-49-4

Poisel, R. (2002), *Introduction to communication electronic warfare systems*, Artech House, ISBN 1-58053-344-2, Norwood, MA, USA

Qi, C., Wang, Y., Zhang, Y. & Chen, H., (2005). DOA estimation and self-calibration algorithm for uniform circular array, *Electronic Letters, Vol. 41, No. 20*, Sept. 2005

Roy, R. and Kailath, T., (1989). ESPRIT-Estimation of Signal Parameters via Rotational Invariance Techniques, *IEEE Transactions on Acoustics, Speech and Signal Processing, Vol. 37, no. 6*, June 1989

Satish, A. & Kashyap, R. L., (1996). Maximum Likelihood Estimation and Cramer-Rao Bounds for Direction of Arrival Parameters of a Large Sensor Array, *IEEE Transactions on Antennas and Propagation, Vol. 44, no. 4*, April 1996

Schmidt, R. O., (1986). Multiple Emitter Location and Signal Parameter Estimation, *IEEE Transactions on Antennas and Propagations*, March 1986

Smith, R. S., Anderson, H. & Jugler, L., (2005). Correlative Vector Direction Finding, *Watkins Johnson Technical Symposium*, Gaithersburg, MD, 2005

Tan, C. M., Fletcher, P., Beach, M. A., Nix, A. R., Landmann, M. & Thoma R. S., (2002). On the Application of Circular Arrays in Direction Finding. Part I: Investigation into the estimation algorithms. Part II: Experimental evaluation on SAGE with different circular arrays, *1st annual COST 273 Workshop*, Espoo, Finland, May 2002

Van Veen, B. D., Buckley, K. M., (1988). Beamforming: A Versatile Approach to Spatial Filtering, *IEEE ASSP Magazine*, April 1988

Weiss, A. J. & Friedlander, B., (1992). Mutual coupling effects on phase-only direction finding, *IEEE Transactions on Antennas and Propagation, vol. 40, no. 5*, May 1992

Whitley, D., (1994). A Genetic Algorithm tutorial, *Statistics and Computing n 4*, 1994

Wiley, R. G. (1985), *Electronic intelligence: the interception of radar signals*, Artech House, ISBN 0-89006-138-6, Dedham, MA, USA

11

Applications of Genetic Algorithm in Power System Control Centers

Camila Paes Salomon[1], Maurílio Pereira Coutinho[1], Carlos Henrique Valério de Moraes[1], Luiz Eduardo Borges da Silva[1] Germano Lambert-Torres[1] and Alexandre Rasi Aoki[2]

[1]UNIFEI - Itajuba Federal University
[2]LACTEC – Institute of Technology for Development
Brazil

1. Introduction

Nowadays, modern operation control centers have managed electrical power systems, accomplishing functions such as automatic generation control, state estimation, topology analysis, etc. In these centers, operators handle the system using several computational programs to help them in the problem solving.

Usually, these programs are based on traditional numerical computation. However, recently, some applications based on intelligent systems have started to be used in control center. This chapter will present three new developments/applications of these programs based on genetic algorithms: power flow calculation, system restoration process and economic dispatch/unit commitment.

The chapter starts with an introduction about the structure of modern control centers, their relations with the power system, their management structure, and the computational programs available. And then, an overview about the new intelligent computational program applications is presented with focus in genetic algorithm techniques.

After this introductory part, the three applications, power flow, system restoration and unit commitment, will be presented in details. It means, how to use genetic algorithm techniques to solve these problems is presented with illustrative examples and with the possibility to readers reproduce the results.

2. Overview of the modern power control centers

Electric power systems are the structures that have the purpose of generating, transporting and distributing electricity. These structures are composed of energy generating plants, transmission lines, distribution systems and elevating and distribution substations. The biggest challenge of this type of system is that the electrical energy is not a material that can be stored. That is, so it is required by the load (which can be a driver in an industry or the mere light of a lamp in a residence) this energy must be generated, transported and delivered to the user instantly.

Another problem is regarding to a systematic increase of demand and consumption of electric energy, observed mostly in large urban centers and regions where focus greater industrial activity. This also conducts to the growth of complexity to the management, supervision and control in meeting these demands.

There are several ways to design a control system to an electrical system. The hierarchical form is the form most widely used. It holds a system operation center that is responsible for controlling generation of large blocks of energy in the power plants and by monitoring of interconnection transmission lines between the areas. The electrical system is then operated by areas of operation, where each area has its own center for the operation, named area operation center or regional operation center. These area operation centers are responsible for the operation of power plants in their area of control, by the operation of transmission lines and substations into their control areas. They are also responsible for the energy supply of large consumers of electricity in their area. Operation centers receive information from distribution operation centers, coordinate this information and deliver to the system operation centers.

Within an area, there is another division of the electrical system in power distribution centers, which are controlled by distribution operation centers. These centers are responsible for the operation of the lines of sub-transmission, distribution networks and distribution substations. These centers are also responsible for the supply of energy for industrial consumers and small and medium industries and residential consumers of electrical energy existing in your distribution sub-area. Figure 1 shows a possible structure of a power system control with a system operation center (SOC), three area operation centers (AOC), and many distribution operation centers (DOC).

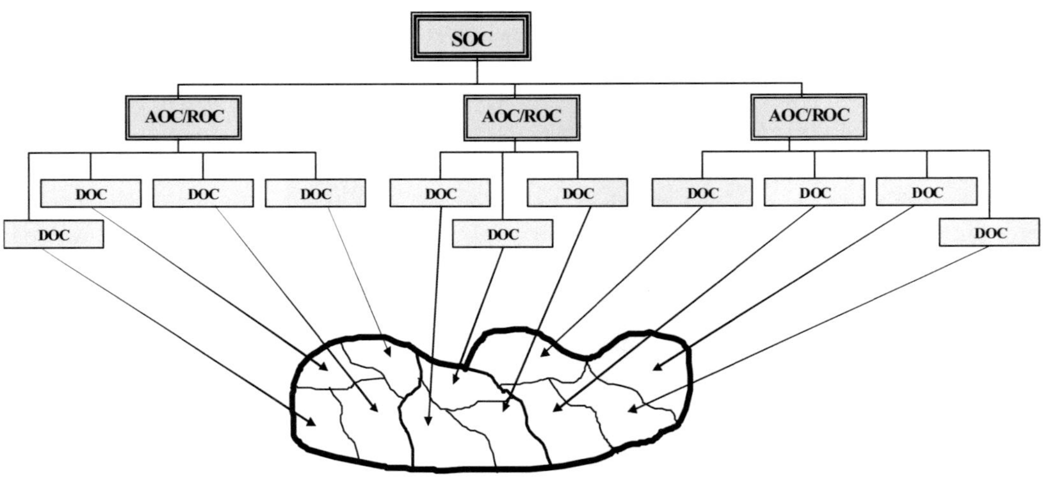

Fig. 1. Hypothetical power system control structure with system operation center (SOC), three area operation centers (AOC), and many distribution operation centers (DOC)

The operation centers, regardless of their type, have structures that are very similar. They are equipped with computers that have two main functions. The first one is to receive the information from the electric system. The size of flow of this information depends on the type of the monitored equipment and the type of measurement that is being monitored. For example, the power flow in a transmission line can have a read performed every second, while the status of operation of a circuit breaker can be read and sent to the operation center each minute. However, with increasingly reduced cost of measurement and telecommunication systems, more measuring points are created and the number of data read has increased a lot. Currently, a mid-size operation center receives something around 3000 to 5000 values per minute.

The second function of computers is to save a set of computer programs for analysis and assistance to the operation of the system. Several existing programs are in operation center computers. For example, one of them is responsible for the reception, validation and delivery of this large volume of data received per minute by control centers, namely SCADA (Supervisory Control and Data Acquisition). Figure 2 shows the structure of an Operating Centre. The path of operation in a control center is the following. The center receives the measurements from the system. These measurements are validated and presented to the operator. He/she runs computational programs in order to obtain the status of the system, and then, if necessary, he/she sends action control commands to the system also by some computational programs. In order to support the power system management, operation and control, the SCADA systems can be integrated with computational tools composing what is usually named EMS (Energy Management System). These systems comprise functions such as state estimator, power flow, optimal power flow, fault calculation, network sensitivity, security analysis, economic dispatch, etc (Wood & Wollenberg, 1996). Some of these applications can be implemented in real-time, and some of them are performed in study modes.

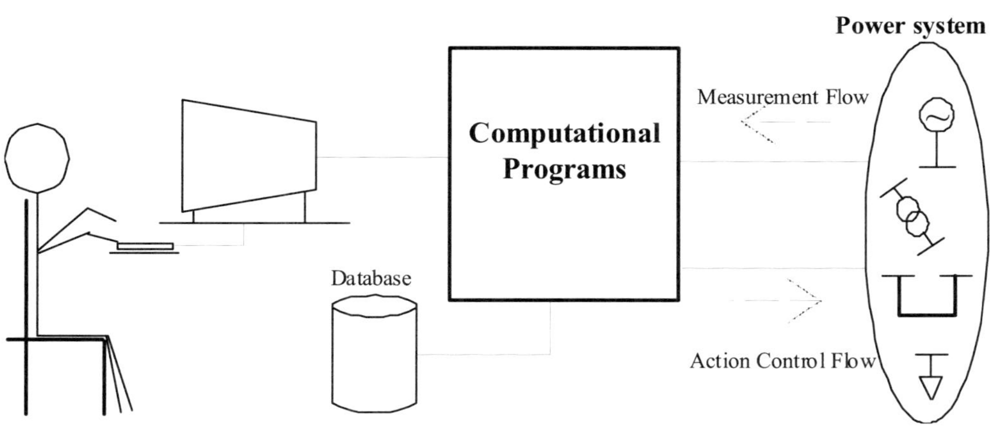

Fig. 2. Structure of a control center with the measurement flow and action control flow (Lambert-Torres et al., 1999)

3. Problem statement

The present section provides an overview on three common activities performed in power system control centers, the power flow studies, the power system restoration after contingencies, and economic dispatch of generator units and their commitment. These mentioned activities will be approached in coming sections through genetic algorithm based methodologies.

3.1 Power flow analysis in electrical power systems

The achievement of many power flow studies is required by most functions performed in power system control centers. Power flow is an electrical engineering known problem which determines the power system operation point in the steady-state. The power flow – or load flow – problem consists in the obtainment of the buses voltages and then in the calculation of the amount of power in the system generation buses as well as the power flow in the system branches. A set of non-linear equations is applied to model this kind of problem, which is commonly solved by numerical computational methods (Stott & Alsac, 1974). Among the traditional numerical methods, the usually applied method in the power flow computation is the Newton-Raphson method, as well as its variations, because it presents a better and a faster convergence. However, such method implies some difficulties because of the complex Jacobian matrix calculation and inversion, and also the dependence on good initial estimated values to guarantee the convergence.

In fact, a power bus in the system has 4 variables, where two of them can be controlled and the other two are related to be system conditions. These variables are: P expresses the values of active power in the bus; Q expresses the values of reactive power in the bus; $|V|$ represents the magnitude of the bus voltage; and, δ represents the phase angle of the bus voltage. The values of P and Q are positive if the active power is injected in the bus – it means, for generation buses, and negative if the active power is taken from the bus – it means, for load buses.

The power system buses are classified according to the variables previously known, in three types:

a. Type 1 or Type PQ: P_i and Q_i are specified and $|V_i|$ and δ_i are calculated – usually, this type represents the load buses of the system.
b. Type 2 or Type PV Bus: P_i and $|V_i|$ are specified and Q_i and δ_i are calculated – usually, this type is used to represent generation buses.
c. Type 3 or Type Vδ (namely "Slack Bus"): $|V_i|$ and δ_i are specified and P_i and Q_i are calculated – this type is a representation of the strongest generation bus of the system.

The buses type 1 usually represents the load buses because the values of P and Q are known by the load. An example is the power required to a motor runs. The user knows these values and can control it. If he/she put more motors in a bus, it is quite simple to know the power. However, it is impossible to the user control the voltage values ($|V|$ and δ). It also occurs in our homes, we know the power required but we don't have any kind of control about the voltage levels.

The buses type 2 usually represents the generation buses because in a power plant the values of P and $|V|$ can be controlled by the operator. If the operator increases the primary source of energy, the value of P increases together, and, vice-versa, it means, if the operator decreases the primary source of energy, the value of P decreases. The same occurs with the value of $|V|$ but in this case the operator changes the excitation system of the generator. However, for this type of bus, the operator can not have any kind of control of the Q and δ values.

Finally, the bus type 3 is generally only one in the power flow calculation. Usually, this bus is the strongest power generation in the system. This bus gives a reference for the system (the values of $|V_i|$ and δ) and receives all balance power required from the system, it means, this generator needs supply all power not given by the other generators to the system.

The power flow study provides the system status in the steady-state; it consists in the determination of the possible power system operational states through the previous knowledge of some variables of the system buses. This study aims to obtain the system buses voltages in order to determine later the power adjustments in the generation buses and the power flow in the system branches. After the system steady-state is calculated, it is possible to obtain the amount of power generation necessary to supply the power demand plus the power losses in the system branches. Besides, the voltage levels must remain within the boundaries and overloaded operations added to those in the stability limit must be prevented (Anderson & Fouad, 2003).

The main idea behind the power flow computation, which is made by iterative form, is to find equilibrium of the known values (controlled values) and the calculated values. For instance, let's a system with 2 buses with voltages V_1 and V_2 and supplying a load with values P and Q, the power flow computation between two buses is given by the following equation:

$$P - jQ - yV_1V_2^* = 0 \tag{1}$$

Or, in general form of the static power flow equations is given by (2):

$$P_i - jQ_i - y_{i1}V_1V_i^* - y_{i2}V_2V_i^* - \ldots - y_{in}V_nV_i^* = 0 \tag{2}$$

Where: $i = 1,\ldots, n$, and it represents the bus number; P_i is the active power generated or injected in the bus i; Q_i is the reactive power generated or injected in the bus i; $|V_i|$ represents the voltage magnitude of the bus i; δ_i is the voltage phase angle of the bus i.

And more, $V_i = |V_i|e^{j\delta_i}$, i. e., the voltage in the polar form; $V_i^* = |V_i|e^{-j\delta_i}$, i. e., the conjugate voltage; y_{ik} = element of the nodal admittance matrix Y_{bus}.

The nodal admittance matrix can be computed as follows: if $i = k$, y_{ik} is the sum of the admittances that come out from the bus i; else y_{ik} is the admittance between the buses i and k, multiplied by -1.

A complex and non-linear equations system is represented by (1), so its solution is obtained through approximations using numeric methods. These methods make the assumption of the initial estimate values to the bus voltages and in the application of the static power flow equations in successive iterations, looking for better approximations. The required accuracy determines the stop criterion.

3.2 Restoration of electrical energy distribution systems

Modern society depends increasingly on power supply, which conducts to the growth in demand and consumption of electrical energy. Therefore, in order to supply this amount of power, electrical power systems have been presenting a natural expansion. The described phenomenon is more evident in large urban centers and in regions of greater industrial concentration. As consequence of the development of the system, the complexity of its supervision, control, and energy demand supply management have been increasing. These mentioned factors highlight the importance of high quality power supply as well as its continuity, low cost and reliability.

At the same time we point out the power system current scenario, the possibility of faults along the line is inherent to the system or even greater due to the rise in electrical system complexity and natural factors. Thus, after system contingencies, it is extremely important that the electric power system restoration be quick to guarantee the power demand supply and the customer's satisfaction. The longer it takes, the greater the loss for the company as well as for the customer. This situation becomes worse when the fault reaches an industrial area (Chiang, et al. 2001). The reconfiguration is a switch shifting (open/closed), loss reduction, load balancing, and restoration process (Lambert-Torres et al., 1997).

Electrical energy transmission systems usually adopt structured procedures to restore a faulted system, following pre-defined rules established by standardization agencies. So the operator has a limited decision power and its main function is to proceed according to the operation steps sequence pre-determined for the system given contingency. Moreover, it is usual the employment of the "*N*-1" criterion, in which, the whole power system, must be restored after a single contingency occurrence. In some particular cases, more rigorous restoration criteria can also be applied (Esmin et al., 2005).

Introducing this problem to electrical energy distribution systems, which usually have less regulation to perform these processes, we will face some peculiarities. The system operator has more decision power in a network reconfiguration process, because of the mentioned difference regarding to less standardization or even lack of network procedures. Each distribution company can adopt a different philosophy to perform a restoration process and the computer programs which support the system operator can play an important role. These computer programs can assist in the choice for a better solution and even reduce time required by the operator for its decision-making (Lambert-Torres et al., 2009).

Moreover, there are differences regarding to the system structure and topology. Electrical energy distribution systems generally present a radial topological structure. In other words, in this kind of system is not usual the presence of meshes. These systems often comprise switches that can be classified in general as NO - Normally Open switches and NC - Normally Closed switches. In the case of all the present switches are closed, so there will be formation of meshes. Then, in order to preserve the radial structure of the topology, for a system composed by k meshes, k switches must to be open. That is, there must be at least one normally open switch in each mesh (Salomon et al., 2011).

Resuming the system restoration process issue, the restoration is defined as the process of changing the open/closed status of switches, loss reduction, load balancing and restoration (Lambert-Torres et al, 1997). This is a decision-making problem of combinatory nature, subject to optimization and system building characteristics constraints. The reconfiguration of the system is performed by closing NO switches in order to restore the system in an optimized way, however retaining the radial topology inherent of electrical distribution systems. Moreover, NC switches may also be opened, providing a network reconfiguration without overloaded branches.

Generally electrical distribution systems comprise lines with NO switches, lines with NC switches and lines without switches. For an optimized reconfiguration, the decision-making involving switching is done so as to maximize the power supply, minimize the switching maneuvers and avoid overloaded branches. This process must happen fast and dynamically. It should provide a simple, objective, and efficient solution to the operator (Lambert-Torres et al., 1997). Considering a single contingency in the distribution system, meeting the characteristics mentioned above, the closing of a single NO switch is enough to restore the system. To avoid overloaded branches, one or more NC switches may also be opened, depending on the contingency consequences for the given system. And, in this case, other NO switches can be closed. This fact generates a new path for energy transmission, to supply the greatest possible power supply after the system contingency.

3.3 Economic dispatch and unit commitment

One of the principal operators' activities in system operation centers is to dispatch the demand and generated energy. However, to accomplish this task the operators need to know different type of information from the system, such as: location of the load demand, situation of the energy generation among the power plant, power flows in the transmission system, and so on. Also they receive some studies previously prepared about the available capacity of each power plant, and the better situation of power dispatch, this study is named economic dispatch and unit commitment.

The economic dispatch study has the aim to establish the better division among the power plants to supply the load demand for a period of time t_j. This study takes into account the cost of primary energy for electric power generation, the cost of transmission system (to take the energy between the power plant and the place where the load is required), and other possible costs related to the dispatch of a generation unit. The main idea behind this study is to minimize all these costs. It can be expressed by (3)

$$F_T = F_1 + F_2 + \ldots + F_N = \sum_{1}^{N} F_i(P_i) \tag{3}$$

Where F_i represents all the generation costs to produce and transport until the load a power P_i by the power unit i, and F_T is the total generation cost the supply a required load in a period t.

The problem is to minimize the value of F_T, subject to the constraint that the sum of each power unit must equal to the required load, expressed in (4).

$$\phi = 0 = P_{Load} - \sum_{1}^{N} P_i \tag{4}$$

P_{Load} represents the total required load during the period t_j. The most traditional method of optimization to solve this problem involves Lagrange function, and it can be expressed by (5), where the Lagrange multiplier λ appears.

$$L = F_T + \lambda\phi \tag{5}$$

And to minimize the Lagrange function must be derivative with respect to the power produced, as expressed in (6).

$$\frac{\partial L}{\partial P_i} = \frac{dF_i(P_i)}{dP_i} - \lambda = 0 \tag{6}$$

So, the conditions and inequalities are completed by the capacity of each power unit expressed by (7). At this time, for N generation units, there are N equations (eq. (6)), 2 N inequalities (eq. (7)), and one constraint (eq. (4)).

$$P_{\min,i} \leq P_i \leq P_{\max,i} \tag{7}$$

Where $P_{min,i}$ and $P_{max,i}$ express the minimum and maximum capacity of generation of unit i.

Different gradient methods have been applied to solve this problem, in special, Newton's method (Wismer, 1971). Also, dynamic programming has been used to solve this problem. In all cases the problem is the computational cost for real-life problems, and some non-convex regions appear in the feasible region.

If the economic dispatch is a "snapshot" of the power generation, the unit commitment can be considered by a "movie", because unit commitment study makes many economic dispatch studies for a period of time t (it involves many periods t_j). Figure 3 shows a hypothetical unit commitment study to supply the required load for three generation units. The largest line represents the required load during the period of study t, and each block represents the generation power P_1, P_2, and P_3 necessary to supply the load.

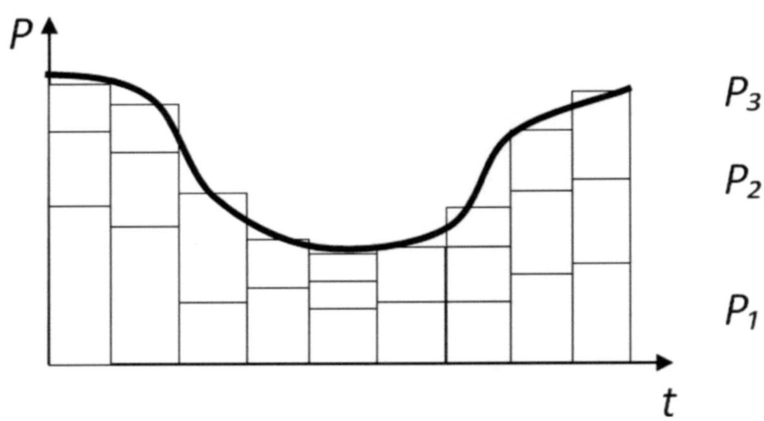

Fig. 3. Hypothetical unit commitment study result for three power units

Of course, unit commitment studies have other elements to take into account to process the economic dispatch. For example, in thermal units, new constraints must be care such as: minimum operational time, minimum time to restart the machine, and so on. And more, aspects such as spinning reserves and fuel reserves are also presented in these studies. Usually, dynamic-programming methods are used to solve this problem (Larson, 1978). The major problems found here are the same of the economic dispatch: computational cost for real-life problems and some non-convex feasible region.

4. Types of genetic algorithm applications in power system problem-solution

The application of modern meta-heuristic methods, in special genetic algorithms, in power system problem-solution can be divided in three types, namely: stand-alone systems, integrated systems, or fused systems.

The first type, stand-alone systems, is where the genetic algorithms run completely alone. It is possible in three ways. The first one is to get the input data, run the genetic algorithm, and give a final answer for the problem. The second way to build stand-alone systems is to help other methodologies to get a final answer. It occurs in two paths: the first one is to run the methodology and then to get the answer of this methodology and to run the genetic algorithm in order to have the final answer. The second paths is to run the genetic algorithm from the initial input data and to have a partial answer and then the methodology runs from these data in order to have the final answer. Figure 4 shows these two types of stand-alone integration system. To be classified as stand-alone system it is important that there is any type of integration between the helped methodology and the genetic algorithm. Example of this type of application is presented below in the chapter for restoration system.

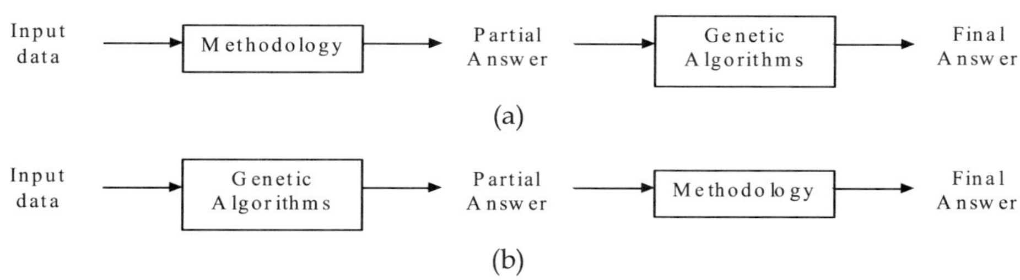

Fig. 4. Two types of stand-alone integration system

Another type of stand-alone systems is a concurrent strategy where helped methodology and genetic algorithm run in parallel, getting the same input data, run each system alone (methodology and genetic algorithm) and each one give their own answer independently. Figure 5 shows this type of stand-alone system. This type of system is applied when sometimes the helped methodology fails to get an answer or gives an incorrect answer for the input data. Example of this type of application is presented below in the chapter for load-flow problem.

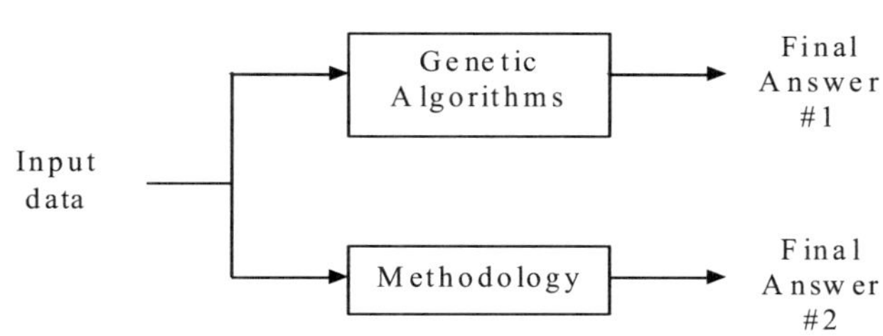

Fig. 5. Two types of stand-alone integration system

The second type is namely integrated systems. In this type, the helped methodology and the genetic algorithms run together, one after other, in cycles. For example, genetic algorithms get some data, run the crossovers and mutations for some generations and give more refined data to the helped methodology. Then, this methodology gets these data, runs its algorithm, and provides an answer. And then, the genetic algorithms get these data, and the process restarts. It occurs many times until to achieve a final answer. An example of this type of integration is when genetic algorithm training a neural network. A good example of this application in power system control is presented in (Farag et al., 1998, Farag et al., 1999). In this example, a genetic algorithm training system is used in a fuzzy-neural model shown in Figure 6. The fuzzy memberships of the fuzzy-neural model are setting by a genetic algorithm strategy to control synchronous generators in power plant. The proposed control can be used for multi-machines and to control the flows in the transmission lines between the areas of the system.

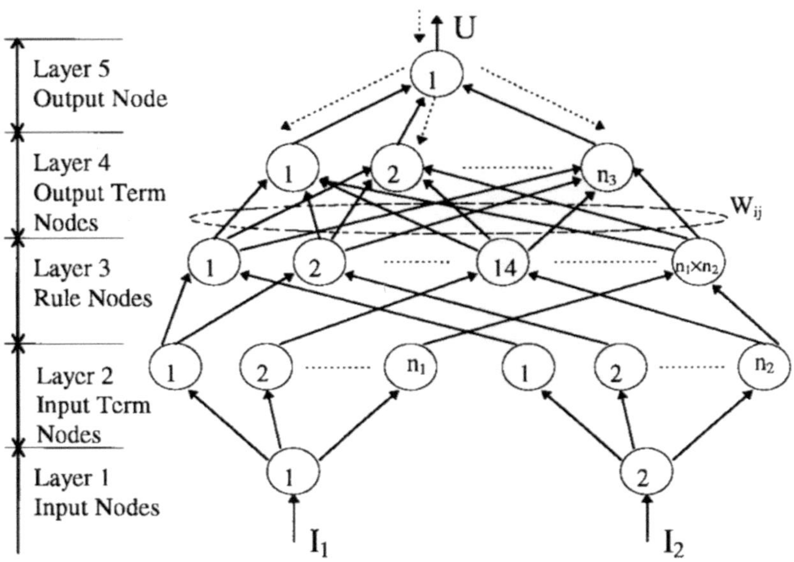

Fig. 6. Example of fuzzy-neural model training by genetic algorithms (Farag et al., 1998)

The third type is named fused systems. In this type, the helped methodology and the genetic algorithms run completely together. It means, it is impossible to have a separation where one methodology finishes and the other methodology starts. It is exactly the difference between fused systems and integrated systems. In the second one, it is possible to change the genetic algorithms for other methodology, meta-heuristic or not, without any kind of compromise of the entire system. For example, in the case presented in Figure 6, the training process could be performed by other meta-heuristic technique, as such, particle swarm optimization (Eberhart & Kennedy, 2001) or ant colonies (Dorigo & Stützle, 2004). In fused systems, this change is impossible without lost of identity of the system. An example of this third type of integration is, for instead, a genetic algorithm with fuzzy parameters, it means where the chromosomes have a fuzzy means and the genetic evaluation has also made by fuzzy arithmetic. An example of this procedure is presented in (de Carvalho et al., 2011). This application for power system operation center has been developed to evaluate the current status of the operational point. This approach reads the operation center database and establishes a set of rules for operation status classification. Then the current measurements from the system are evaluated by this set of rules. The genetic algorithms are used to provide a previous classification of the attributes. Figure 7 shows the chromosomes a_1, a_2, a_3, and a_4, with the ranges of fuzzy memberships and how the crossover is made.

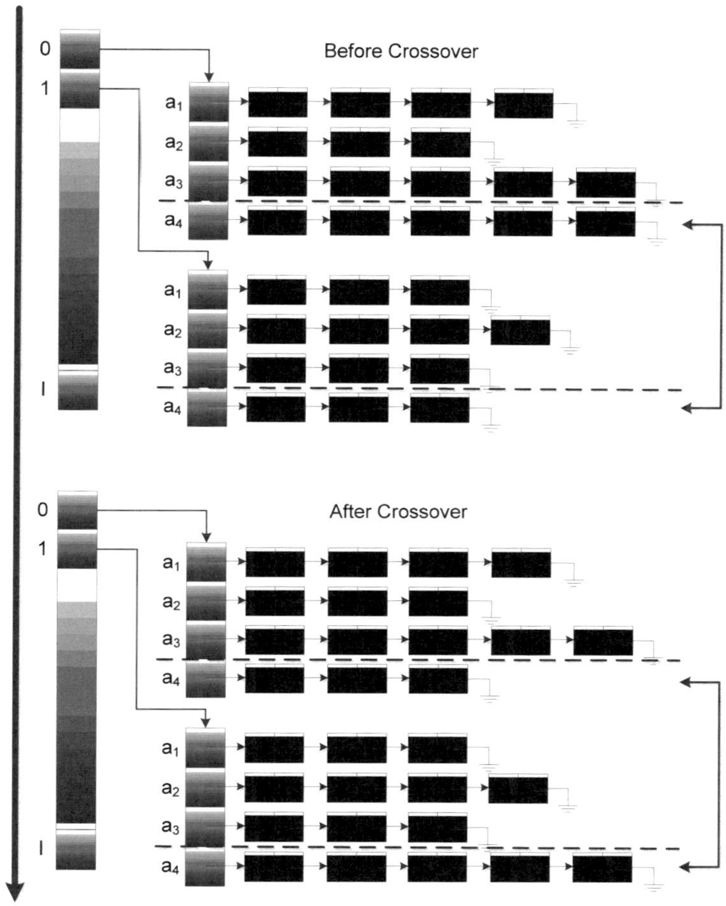

Fig. 7. Example of genetic-fuzzy chromosomes and crossover (de Carvalho et al., 2011)

Another type of classification can be expressed by the kind of the current possible solution for a problem. There are three possible types of classifications: (a) problems with traditional methodologies to solve it but these methodologies have a high computational cost; (b) problems with traditional methodologies to solve it but with some constraints in their application; and (c) problems without any traditional methodologies to solve it. In the first type of classification, a problem has been solved with traditional techniques; however, these techniques have a high computational cost in time or in memory space. Usually, these techniques are not very well scalable, it means, when the size of the problem increases the cost for the solution increases much more. An example of this type of problem is the load-flow. Newton full, Newton-Raphson, and Gauss-Seidel are some traditional methods used to solve load-flow problems. In the second type of classification, we can find problems solving by traditional methodologies; however, these methodologies present some problems to be applied in all possible situations or they don't have an expected performance in all situations.

In the second type of this classification, certain solutions are very-well applied if certain conditions and constraints available. For example, some of them work in convex feasible regions such as the solution of unit commitment problem by dynamic programming. However, when this condition is not satisfied some areas can leave to be explored. The third type of classification occurs when a problem doesn't have any type of traditional numerical solution. The power restoration system is an example of this kind of problem. Usually, only intelligent methods, in special meta-heuristic methods, have been applied to solve this problem.

5. Power flow computation using genetic algorithms

This section presents a methodology using genetic algorithm for accomplishing power flow studies of electrical power systems. The intent of this chapter is to present a novel approach for power flow calculation, providing an easier and more flexible implementation comparing with the traditional methods, and also being potential to overcome some limitations found when executing power flow studies using current computational routines.

The presented genetic methodology is based on the minimization of the power mismatches in the power system buses. The principle of the proposed algorithm consists in adopting the chromosomes as the power system buses voltages, phase angles and magnitudes. The computational routine starts with estimated initial values for the chromosomes parameters, and these values are updated in each iteration process through the genetic operators, and the rule function, which comprises the problem modeling. The chromosome structure model is given as:

$$x_i = \{\delta_2, \delta_3, ..., \delta_k, ..., \delta_n, |V_2|, |V_3|, ..., |V_k|, ..., |V_n|\} \tag{8}$$

Where i represents the chromosome index, related to the population size; n is the number of buses of the system; k is the system bus index, δ_k is the voltage angle at the bus k; and, $|V_k|$ is the voltage magnitude at the bus k. The bus with $k = 1$ is taken as swing bus and it does not compose the chromosome structure.

Let's the test IEEE power system shows in Figure 8. This system contains 14 buses, 15 transmission lines, and 3 transformer branches. The IEEE 14-Bus Test System represents a part of the Midwestern US Electric Power System as of February, 1962. The Bus #1 is chosen as swing bus. The Buses #2, #3, #6, and #8 are buses with generation, and they are the type 2, where P and $|V|$ are known and the values of Q and δ are calculated. The Buses #4, #5, #7, #9, #10, #11, #12, #13 and #14 are load buses and they are type 1, where P and Q are known and the values of $|V|$ and δ are calculated.

In this case the chromosome for the system shown in Figure 8 has the following form:

$$\begin{aligned} x_i = \{&\delta_2, \delta_3, \delta_4, \delta_5, \delta_6, \delta_7, \delta_8, \delta_9, \delta_{10}, \delta_{11}, \delta_{12}, \delta_{13}, \delta_{14}, \\ &|V_4|, |V_5|, |V_7|, |V_9|, |V_{10}|, |V_{11}|, |V_{12}|, |V_{13}|, |V_{14}|\} \end{aligned} \tag{9}$$

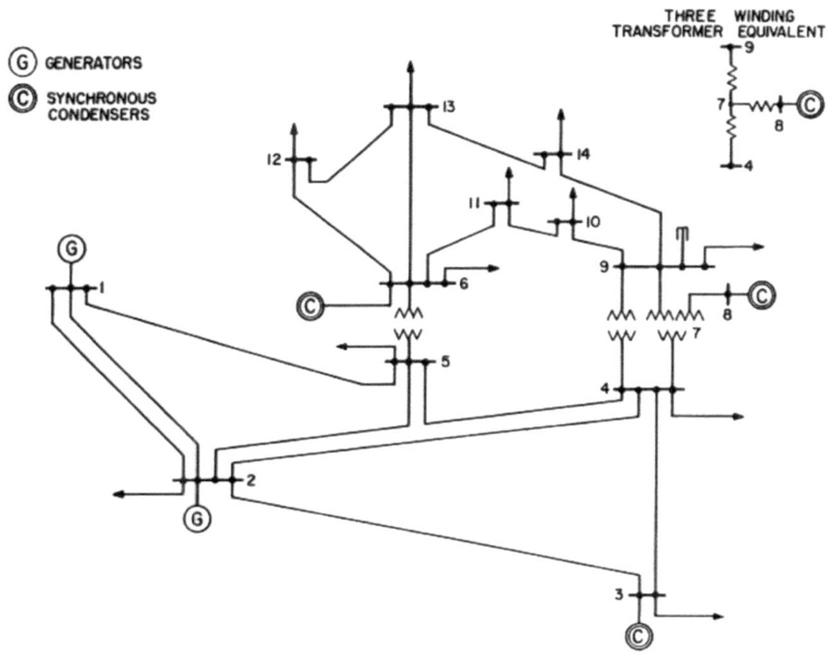

Fig. 8. IEEE 14-bus test system, with all system buses, branches and elements

The definition of the population parameters is made according the power flow problem particular features. The chromosomes are defined as the system buses voltages, so they assume continuing values within the boundaries specified in the system input data. The rule function parameters to be minimized during the genetic algorithm procedure are defined as *scores*. The scores are computed as the arithmetic mean of the buses apparent power. Each chromosome has a *personal score*, and it uses during the creation of individuals in the mating pool.

The algorithm begins with the generation of the initial estimated values for each chromosome. The voltage angle begins with a random initial value within the specified boundary. The voltage magnitude initial value depends on the nature of the bus that the parameter is associated with. In the case of a PQ bus, the voltage magnitude begins with a random value within the specified boundary. On the other hand, in the case of a PV bus, the voltage magnitude receives the related value specified in the input data and this value remains the same during the process iterations, it means, this is a fixed value.

Once all the parameters of the population have the initial estimated values, the iterations are initiated. The procedure detailed as follows is performed for all iterations and for each chromosome.

1. The system buses voltages are assigned with the chromosome values.
2. The reactive power of the PV buses is computed applying the equation (2).
3. The active and reactive power of the Vδ bus is computed applying equation (2).
4. The power flow in the system branches is calculated using the equation (10):

$$S_{ij} = P_{ij} + jQ_{ij} = V_i(V_i * -V_j *)Y_{ij} * +V_iV_i * Y_{sh,i} \tag{10}$$

Where S_{ij} represents the complex apparent power between the buses i and j; P_{ij} is the active power between the buses i and j; Q_{ij} is the reactive power between the buses i and j; V_i is the bus i voltage; V_j is the bus j voltage; $V_i^* = |V_i| e^{j\delta_i}$, i. e., the conjugate voltage; $V_j^* = |V_j| e^{-j\delta_i}$, i. e., the conjugate voltage; Y_{ij} is the admittance between the buses i and j; $Y_{sh,i}$ is the shunt admittance of the bus i.

5. The active and reactive power mismatches of each bus are calculated as the sum of the injected power.in the approached bus. The apparent power mismatches are calculated using the equation (11):

$$\Delta S_k = \sqrt{(\Delta P_k)^2 + (\Delta Q_k)^2} \tag{11}$$

Where k is the system bus index; ΔP_k is the active power mismatch at bus k, ΔQ_k is the reactive power mismatch at bus k; ΔS_k is the apparent power mismatch at bus k.
6. The buses apparent power mismatches arithmetic mean is calculated.
7. The performance index is computed for each chromosome. The performance index is related to the power mismatch obtained by the chromosome. All mismatches produced by each chromosome are summed producing a total mismatch value. Then each mismatch is divided by this total mismatch value producing the individual mismatch degree. After that, all degrees are multiplied by the number of individuals resulting in the final degree of each chromosome.
8. It is obtained the chromosome which has the worst – the bigger – power mismatch until now. This chromosome index is kept and it is used in the mutation operation.

Once all chromosomes have passed through the described routine, it proceeds through the steps described as follows.

9. The elements of the mating pool are composed according the degree of each chromosome. Initially, the entire part of each chromosome contains the number of individuals in the mating pool. For example, if a degree of a chromosome is 4.27, this chromosome has 4 copies in the mating pool. The other chromosomes are chosen by the roulette wheel rules according the not entire value. In the case of the previous chromosome, it has 0.27 to be chosen.
10. The mutation operation is then applied. This operation aims to coverage better the problem domain and to obtain a new chromosome, avoiding a premature convergence to a local best point. The mutation is applied to the worst chromosome of the current iteration, i. e., the chromosome which has the bigger power mismatch value, and because of this philosophy it is called Biased Mutation. The procedure consists in changing random values to the chromosome voltage module and angle, according the minimum and maximum value of the attribute.

Finally, in the end of the iterations, it is obtained the best solution, which is adopted as the power flow study solution. It is important to notice that the genetic algorithm methodology can achieve several acceptable results for the same power flow study, depending on the simulation. It occurs because each chromosome has a random initial estimated value and the genetic operators also make use of random values, so several solutions that are very similar can be achieved for the same initial estimative. However, numeric traditional methods start with the same initial estimative values and achieve the same final results, regardless of the program simulation.

6. Power system restoration computation using genetic algorithms

This section presents a genetic algorithm based decision support tool applied to electrical power system restoration after an incident. The power system restoration is based on the system reconfiguration, which is accomplished by changing switches statuses. This is a NP-hard problem, involving operational optimization constraints and decision-making of combinatory nature. The purpose of the proposed methodology is to support the power system operator providing an optimal solution for system restoration after the occurrence of a single contingency, similar to an N-1 criterion applied to electrical energy distribution systems.

As mentioned previously, electric distribution systems present a radial topological structure that must remain after the system restoration process. The present approach supposes that for each line there must be one switch, and if in the initial configuration it is not on, then, its normal operation status is open. For an optimized reconfiguration, the decision-making involving the switches, which must be closed, is done so as to maximize the power supply and minimize the number of closed switches. Moreover, network configurations with overloaded branches are prevented. Considering fault occurrence on a single line of the distribution system, with the characteristics described above, the closing of a single switch is enough to restore the system. There are contingencies which result in a single possibility for the system restoration, and contingencies which result in several possibilities for the system restoration. Besides, a peculiarity occurs in case the faulted line is of the kind which has normally open switches, because fault occurrence on the line does not compromise the distribution of the system, therefore, the loads supply. In this case the only solution is repairing it, providing necessary technical support.

In the solution provided by genetic algorithm methodology for this problem, each gene of chromosomes presents the information of a switch that composes just one transmission line of system. This switch is normally opened (NO) in the original configuration. The normally closed (NC) switches don´t compose the chromosome. If the original configuration of system presents *N* lines NO then each chromosome will have *N* genes. The gene is a binary number, 0 or 1. The value 0 means that the switch state is open or without energy. The value 1 means that the switch state is closed or with energy. Now it is necessary to structure the information of power system. Each line of the system is represented by two consecutive nodes, according to Figure 9. In this scheme, the full lines are switches NC, the hatched lines are switches NO, and there are three circuits.

The chromosomes require an evaluation procedure for their feasibility. Several functions are presented in order to indentify the chromosomes potentially and its validation.

a. *Unsupplied Loads Function* - This function identifies the amount of loads without energy along the system after a contingency.
b. *Loop Function* - A radial topological structure can't present meshes or *loops*. Then the Loop Function identifies the number of loops formed during the restoration process.

c. *Overload Factor Function* - Each system line possesses a transmission capacity, that is, a maximum power. The Overload Factor Function deals with maximum and current power.

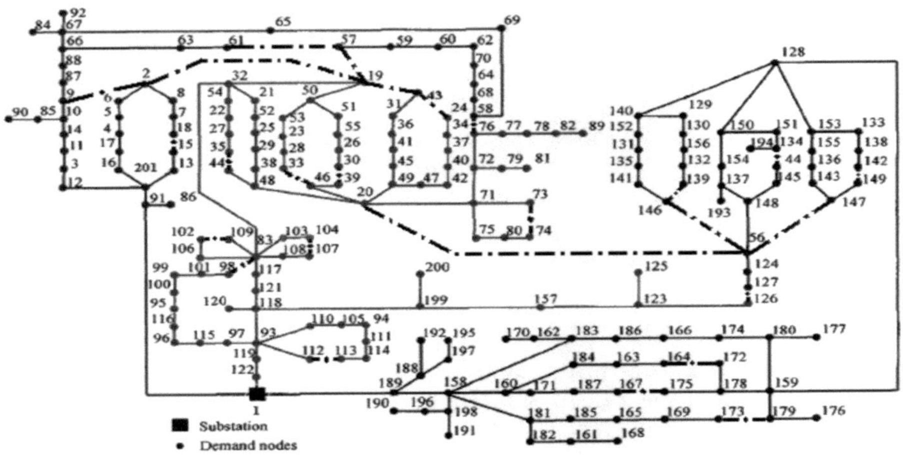

Fig. 9. Distribution test system (Ramírez-Rosado & Bernal-Agustín, 1998)

The maximum power parameter is in the data base but the current power parameter must be calculated from *Power Flow Program,* which is adapted for distribution network analysis. The Overload Factor is determined by (12):

$$OF_i = \frac{\sum_{m=1}^{N}(MP_m - CP_m)}{N} \tag{12}$$

Where i represents the ith chromosome; N is the number of transmission lines closed; OF_i is the Overload Factor for the chromosome i; MP_m is the maximum power of transmission line m; and, CP_m is the current power of transmission line m.

d. *Overload Lines Function* - This function is a sub-product of Overload Factor Function. It determines the number of overload transmission lines. If the current power value is great than maximum power value then this transmission line is overload line.

The proposed genetic algorithm is composed of the following steps:

1. Fitness Function Computation - In this stage each individual receive a *value.* Therefore, how much bigger is the individual value it is better. In other words, how much bigger is the individual value it has more possibility of being the potential solution of restoration. The individual value is determined by (13):

$$\text{Value(individual)}=0.5\times f_1(x)+0.1\times f_2(x)+0.3\times f_3(x)+0.1\times f_4(x) \tag{13}$$

Where:
$f_1(x)$ = Total of supplied loads/ Total of unsupplied loads
$f_2(x)$ = 1/(amount of loops + 1)
$f_3(x)$ = 1/(overload factor)

$f_4(x) = 1/(\text{total of overload lines})$

According to (13), the weights can be chosen empirically. For this approach, the criterion of judgment is based on unsupplied loads with the weight of 0.5, followed by overload factor of system with the weight of 0.3, overload transmission line number with the weight of 0.1, and number of created loops with weight of 0.1.

2. Composition of the Mating Pool - In this stage the better individuals are chosen for constitute the mating pool. To determinate the individuals that will compose the mating pool is necessary to calculate the weight of each one in the group. Therefore, the value of each individual is already applied the fitness function then it is divided by the average of the group value.

   If the individual value gets a weight bigger than 1 then it goes directly to the mating pool, and its weight is deducted by 1, and this operation is repeated until that its weight becomes less than 1. If still exist vacant in the mating pool, it is necessary to use the roulette wheel to decide which individual will compose the mating pool randomly. The roulette wheel needs a straight line composed by the weights of each individual. Therefore, if the random number is between 0 and the first individual weight, then the first individual gets the vacant, else: if the random number is bigger than the first individual weight and smaller or equal than the first individual weight added by the second individual weight, the second individual goes to the mating pool.
3. Crossover Operator - The crossover operator combines the features of two parent structures to form two similar offspring. Two good chromosomes share their good quality; therefore it is possible to produce better chromosomes than before. An arbitrary crossover position along two individuals is selected, beyond which the crossover takes place. They exchange their parts.

   The resulting crossover yields two new individuals where the chromosomes have parts of parent's genetic information. This crossover operation occurs if the random parameter is inferior to crossover rate (probability of crossover).
4. Mutation Operator - In the same way, this mutation operation occurs if the random parameter is inferior to mutation rate (probability of mutation). Mutation is an alteration of a value at a particular position in the individual. This particular position is selected randomly and the gene value is changed. For example, if the gene value is 1 then it is changed to 0.
5. Determination of the New Population - After all this steps, a new population is created. Therefore, the best individuals from previous generations appear in the new population. All steps are executed for the new population again, creating another genetic iteration. The process stops when a pre-defined stopping rule is satisfied.

The restoration system solution provides a switch (or a set of switches) that must have the status changed. Besides, the proposed methodology applies the maximization of power demand supplied, minimization of switching operations, and avoids the overload lines.

7. Economic dispatch and unit commitment studies using genetic algorithms

Initially, this section presents a strategy to use genetic algorithms in economic dispatch studies. The main problem of this study is to get the best composition of generations according some criteria. Usually, these criteria are generation cost and transmission cost. However, in nowadays, another criterion is also taking into account: the environment cost.

This criterion is hard to be express in numbers, and traditional techniques have problems to include this factor in the equation solution.

The economic dispatch problem is a classical optimization problem; it means some elements must to be optimized according some criteria (here expressed by the fitness function). The chromosome for this study is composed by all generated power of each unit, represented by P_i, minus the generation of the swing bus (in our case *index* = 1). The chromosome is shown in (14) for *n* generator.

$$x_i = \{P_2, P_3, ..., P_n\} \tag{14}$$

The generation of the swing bus is not in the chromosome because it promotes the balance between the required load and the power produced by the other generations, in (15).

$$P_1 = P_{Load} - \sum_{j=2}^{n} P_j \tag{15}$$

The fitness function could be expressed by also traditional cost involved (generation and transmission) but also environment cost, political cost, and others aspects required by the system or by the companies, such as: security operation point, maintenance program, fuel constraints. Many of these costs are not necessarily expressed only by equations, but they can be used algorithms or some heuristics.

$$value(P_i) = F_{g,i} + F_{t,i} + F_{o,i} \tag{16}$$

Where $F_{g,i}$, $F_{t,i}$, and $F_{o,i}$ represent the cost of generation, transmission and others for the unit *i* to produce the power P_i.

The proposed genetic algorithm is composed of the following steps:

1. Fitness Function Computation - In this stage each individual receive a *value*, computing by (16). However, the economic dispatch is a minimization problem. Therefore, how much bigger is the individual value it is worst. In other words, how much bigger the individual value is, less possibility of being the potential solution of economic dispatch has. Then, the fitness function is computed by (17):

   $$f_{fitness}(i) = 1 / value(P_i) \tag{17}$$

   The only exception of this fitness function computation process is when the constraints of the swing bus are extrapolated. In this case, the generation of the swing bus can't support generate the required power, and the value of the fitness function is zero.
2. Composition of the Mating Pool - The best individuals are chosen for constitute the mating pool. The strategy describes in the power flow mating pool composition is used here. Use all fitness function to calculate the weight of each individual. The individuals with entire values are represented in the mating pool. The decimal part goes to the roulette wheels.
3. Crossover Operator – By a random process two individuals are chosen to be combined, and another random process decides where they will change their material. And then,

they exchange their parts. This crossover operation occurs if the random parameter is inferior to crossover rate (probability of crossover).

4. Mutation Operator - The mutation operation occurs if the random parameter is inferior to mutation rate (probability of mutation). When one power generator is selected randomly and the gene value is changed for a new value inside of its generation limits, expressed by (7).

This process is repeated until a predefined number of iterations. The best solution found (it means the minimum *value*) until in moment is the solution of the problem.

The unit commitment process uses the economic dispatch shown above. The idea is to start the economic dispatch for the first period of time, t_1. The three best solution are selected, denoted by $S_{1,A}$, $S_{1,B}$, and $S_{1,C}$. Each solution has its own total cost, denoted by $C_{1,A}$, $C_{1,B}$, and $C_{1,C}$.

For the second period of time, t_2, another economic dispatch is run. The three possible best solutions are selected for each best solution selected in the previous period of time. It is important to note that the three possible best solution in the second period for the solution $S_{1,A}$ could not be the same, for example, for the solution $S_{1,B}$. It occurs because there are some constraints to be analyzed such as start-up generator time or minimum time to restart the generator. In Figure 10, the three best solutions for $S_{1,A}$, have been denoted by $S_{2,AA}$, $S_{2,AB}$, and $S_{2,AC}$. For $S_{1,B}$, the selected best solutions are $S_{2,BA}$, $S_{2,BB}$, and $S_{2,BC}$. And, for the solution $S_{1,C}$, the selected solutions are $S_{2,CA}$, $S_{2,CB}$, and $S_{2,CC}$. In this example, the solutions $S_{2,AB}$ and $S_{2,BA}$ are the same solution. The same occurs to $S_{2,AC}$ - $S_{2,BB}$ - $S_{2,CA}$, and $S_{2,BC}$ - $S_{2,CB}$.

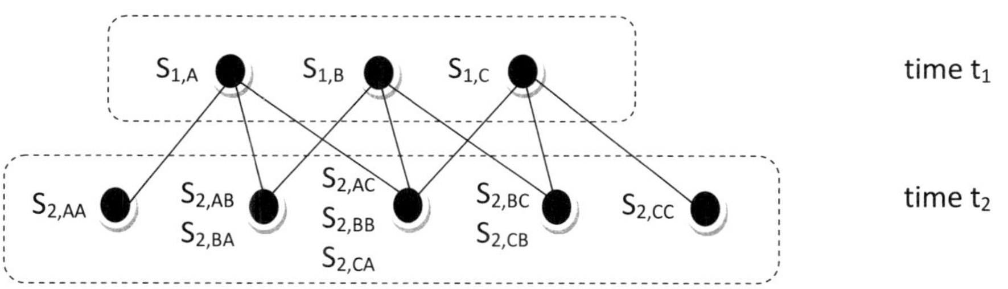

Fig. 10. First and second iteration of the unit commitment process

Each solution of time t_2 also has its own total cost, denoted by $C_{2,AA}$, $C_{2,AB}$, and so on. Of course, the cost of the solutions $S_{2,AB}$ and $S_{2,BA}$ are the same.

For the third period of time t_3, another economic dispatch is run. The three possible best solutions are selected for each best solution selected in the previous period of time, in this case t_2. And the process continues until the last period of time. In this procedure, a search tree is created. There are two possibilities to break one of the possible paths in the search. One possibility is when there is no solution available in the next step of the economic dispatch study for a previous selected state. The other possibility is when the total cost exceeds a predefined value. The total cost is the sum of all previous cost in the path. Figure 11 shows a possible search tree with 6 periods of times (t_1, t_2,..., t_6). Two special remarks have been made in this figure. The first one is the case where there is no solution available in the next period, and then the path is cut. The second one shows a situation where there are only two possible solutions in the next period of time. The search continues for these two solutions.

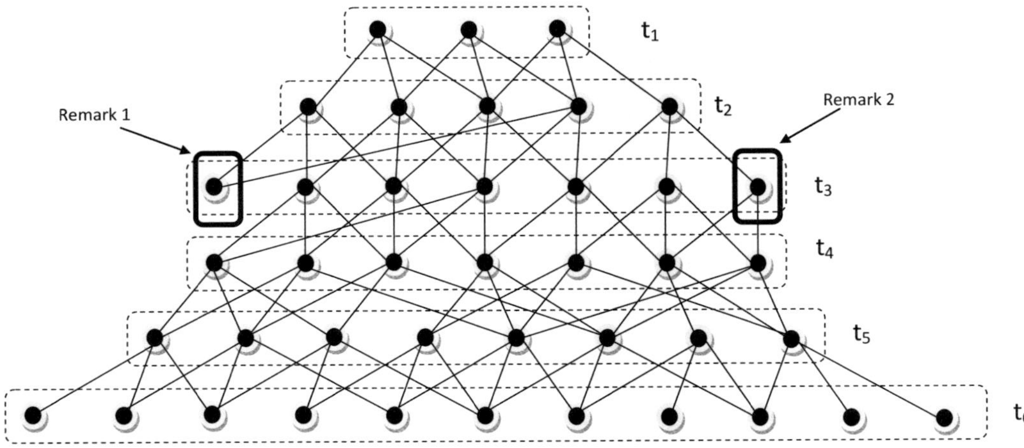

Fig. 11. Complete search tree for unit commitment problem-solving

When the search tree is complete each path has its own total cost which is composed by the sum of each individual solution existed along the path. Figure 12 shows in highlight one possible path (possible solution) for the unit commitment problem. The total cost of this solution is computed by the sum of each individual costs of each solution (C_{1B}, C_{2C}, C_{3D}, C_{4D}, C_{5E}, and C_{6F}) and denoted by $C_{path,k}$, shown in (18). The best solution is that with lowest total cost.

$$C_{path,k} = C_{1B} + C_{2C} + C_{3D} + C_{4D} + C_{5E} + C_{6F} \tag{18}$$

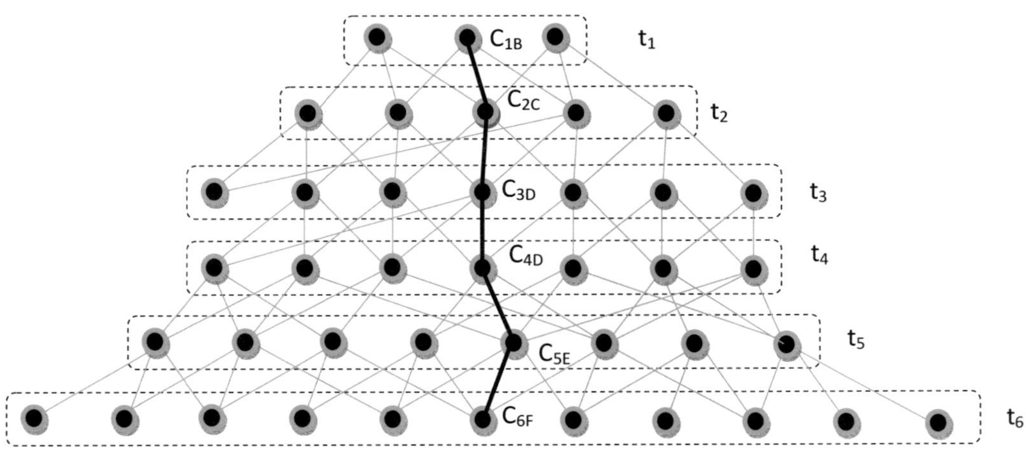

Fig. 12. One possible solution of unit commitment problem with individual costs

Finally, a hint. If the problem requires many periods of time the number of possible paths can be enormous. In this case, intermediary evaluations can occur and a predefined maximum number of paths can continue the search tree.

8. Conclusion

This chapter presented the genetic algorithm application to three functions commonly executed in power control centers - power flow, system restoration and unit commitment. The genetic algorithm based techniques are potential to solve problems whose traditional methodologies to solve them have a high computational cost, problems whose traditional methodologies to solve them hold some constraints in their application, and problems without any traditional methodologies to solve them. This has been well represented by these typical power system control centers applications, and the explanation on how to perform genetic algorithms to compute them.

It is expected that this chapter provided the reader with a comprehensive view of the use of genetic algorithms to solve control center problems and supports them in developing new genetic algorithms based methods for applications of their interest.

9. Acknowledgment

The authors would like to express their thanks to the financial support of this work given by the Brazilian research agencies: CNPq, CAPES, and FAPEMIG.

10. References

Anderson, P.M. & Fouad, A.A. (2003). *Power System Control and Stability*, John Wiley & Sons, ISBN 0471238627, Hoboken, USA.

Chiang, L.H. ; Rusell, E.L. & Braatz, R.D. (2001). *Fault Detection and Diagnosis in Industrial Systems*, Springer-Verlag, ISBN 1852333278, London, UK.

de Carvalho, M.A. ; de Moraes, C.H.V. ; Lambert-Torres, G. & Borges da Silva, L.E. (2011). Transforming Continouous Attributes using GA for Applications of Rough Set Theory to Control Centers, *Proceedings of the 16th International Conference on Intelligent System Applications to Power Systems*, ISAP 2011, Crete, Greece, Sept. 25-28, 2011.

Dorigo, M. & Stützle, T. (2004). *Ant Colony Optimization*, The MIT Press, ISBN 978-0262042192, Massachusetts, USA.

Eberhart, R.C. & Kennedy, J. (2001). *Swarm Intelligence*, Morgan Kaufmann Publishers, ISBN 978-1558605954, San Francisco, USA.

Esmin, A.A.; Lambert-Torres, G. & Souza, A.C.Z. (2005). A Hybrid Particle Swarm Optimization Applied to Loss Power Minimization. *IEEE Transactions on Power Systems*, Vol.20, No.2, (May 2005), pp. 859-866, ISSN 0885-8950.

Farag, W.A.; Quintana, V.H. & Lambert-Torres, G. (1998). A Genetic-Based Neuro-Fuzzy Approach for Modeling and Control of Dynamical Systems, *IEEE Transactions on Neural Networks*, Vol.9, No.5, (September 1998), pp. 756-767, ISSN 1045-9227.

Farag, W.A.; Quintana, V.H. & Lambert-Torres, G. (1999) An Optimized Fuzzy Controller for a Synchronous Generator in a Multi-Machine Environment, *Fuzzy Sets and Systems*, Vol.102, No.1, pp. 71-84, ISSN 0165-0114.

Lambert-Torres, G. ; Abe, J.M. ; da Silva Filho, J.I. & Martins, H.G. (2009). *Advances in Technological Applications of Logical and Intelligent Systems*, IOS Press, ISBN 978-1-58603-963-3, Amsterdam, Holanda, 2009.

Lambert-Torres, G. ; Ribeiro, G. M. ; Costa, C.I.A. ; Alves da Silva, A.P. & Quintana, V.H. (1997). Knowledge Engineering Tool for Training Power-Substation Operators. *IEEE Transactions on Power Systems*, Vol.12, No.2, (April 1997), pp. 694-699, ISSN 0885-8950.

Lambert-Torres, G.; Rossi, R.; Alves da Silva, A.P.; Jardini, J.A. & Quintana, V.H. (1999). Power System Security Analysis based on Rough Classification, In: *Rough-Fuzzy Hybridization: New Trend in Decision Making*, S.K. Pal & A. Skowron, pp. 263-274, Springer-Verlag Co., ISBN 981-4021-00-8, New York.

Larson, R.E. (1978). *Principles of Dynamic Programming*, Marcel Dekker Inc., ISBN 978-0824765897, New York, USA.

Ramírez-Rosado, I. J. & Bernal-Agustín, J.L. (1998). Genetic Algorithms Applied to the Design of Large Power Distribution Systems, *IEEE Transactions Power Systems*, Vol.13, No.2, (May 1998), pp. 696-703, ISSN 0885-8950.

Salomon, C.P.; Coutinho, M.P. ; Lambert-Torres, G. & Ferreira, C. (2011) – Hybrid Particle Swarm Optimization with Biased Mutation Applied to Load Flow Computation in Electrical Power Systems. *Lectures Notes in Computer Science*, Vol. LNCS 6728, pp. 595-605, ISSN 0302-9743

Stott, B. & Alsac, O. (1974). Review of Load-Flow. *Proceedings of the IEEE*, Vol.62, No.2, (July 1974), pp. 916-929, ISSN 0018-9219.

Wismer, D.A. (1971). *Optimization Methods for Large-Scale Systems with Applications*, McGraw-Hill, ISBN 978-0070711549, New York, USA.

Wood, A. J. & Wollenberg, B. F. (1996). *Power Generation, Operation and Control*, John Wiley & Sons Ltd., 2nd Edition, ISBN 0471586994, New York, USA.

Part 4

GAs in Pattern Recognition

12

Applying Genetic Algorithm in Multi Language's Characters Recognition

Hanan Aljuaid

Faculty of Computer Science and Info System, Taif University, Taif, Saudi Arabia

1. Introduction

The character recognition (CR) mechanization is being intensively investigated in the pattern recognition research area. CR automation means translating images of characters into a text; in other words, it represents an attempt to simulate the human reading process. CR is very difficult to accomplish owing to various issues such as the inconsistency of human writing, the segmentation of words into characters, high variability in terms of handwriting styles and shapes, the size of the lexicon, and the writing skew or slant.

There are two main classifications of the problem of handwriting recognition: online recognition and offline recognition; these terms refer to the format of the input handwritings image. Temporal information is available in online recognition, for instance pen tip coordinates as a time function, while in offline recognition, just the handwritings image is obtainable. Several applications require offline handwriting recognition capabilities; these include commercial form reading, bank processing, document archiving, office automation, mail sorting, etc. Up to the present time, offline handwriting recognition is still an open problem, and has been dealt with by several researchers in this field (Benouaretha *et al.*, 2008;Plamondon and Srihari, 2000; Koerich *et al.*, 2003; Vinciarelli, 2002).

While many different methods of solving the OCR problem have been explored, the use of a genetic algorithm to recognize characters has been growing in popularity. "Genetic algorithms offer a particularly attractive approach for this kind of problems since they are generally quite effective for rapid global search. Moreover, genetic algorithms are very effective in solving large-scale problems"(Oliveira *et al.*, 2001).This begs the question of what genetic algorithms (GAs) actually are.

A GAs is an optimization and search technique utilized in computer science to find approximate solutions to problems. It is inspired by processes in biological evolution such as natural selection, inheritance, recombination, and mutation. GAs are generally realized in a computer model, in which a population of runner solutions to an optimization problem progress to better solutions. The evolution starts from a population of completely random individuals and occurs in generations. In each generation, the fitness of the whole population is evaluated, and multiple individuals are selected from the current population based on their fitness. These are modified, mutated, or recombined to create a new population, which becomes current in the next iteration of the algorithm, as shown in Figure

1. Usually, the solutions are represented in strings of 0s and 1s, although different encodings are also possible. So, evolutionary algorithms play on populations, instead of coming to one solution.

This chapter will give an extended illustration of offline character recognition. The system is based on feature extraction and the genetic algorithms approach.

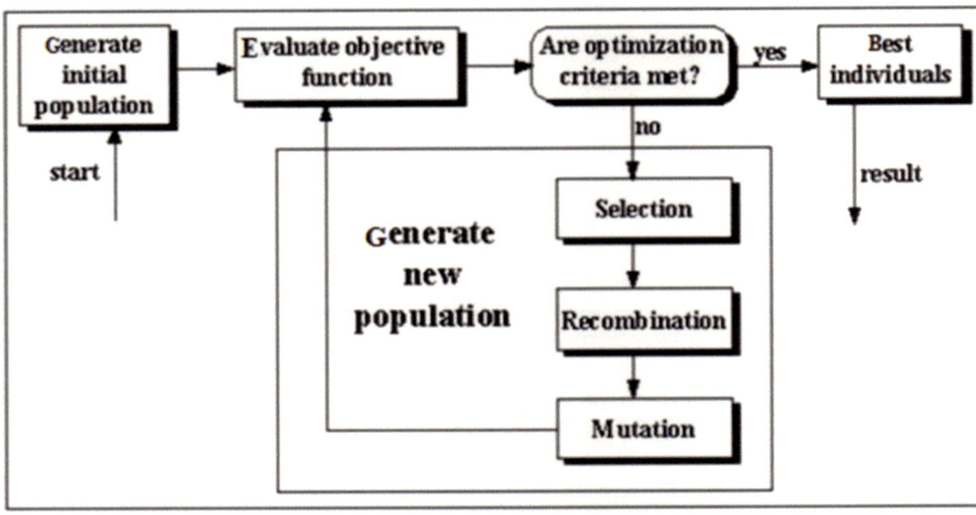

Fig. 1. Structure of a single population evolutionary algorithm

2. Character recognition stages

The character recognition system can be decomposed into several stages: preprocessing, representation, character segmentation, feature detection, and character recognition. Some systems use a subset of these stages. These stages are described in Table 1.

Preprocessing	Noise removal, text detection, etc.
Representation	Skeletons, contours, baseline detection
Segmentation	Segments words, sub-words, characters, strokes, or other units
Features	Information is passed to the recognizer such as shape attributes, pixels
Recognizer	Algorithm that identifies letters

Table 1. Components of OCR recognition

When we focus on these stages, we can see that the recognition method starts by cleaning the image through the use of image processing techniques in the preprocessing stage. Then, the image can be improved to form an extra-short representation. Features of words or characters are identified after the segmentation stage. Finally, from these features, the recognizer proceeds to recognize the wording. The expression "features" refers to any quantities that are recognized. They can be pre-computed through segmentation and computed for individual characters, as shown in Figure 2. The importance of these stages, their impact on the recognition method, and the relation between them will be discussed in the next sections.

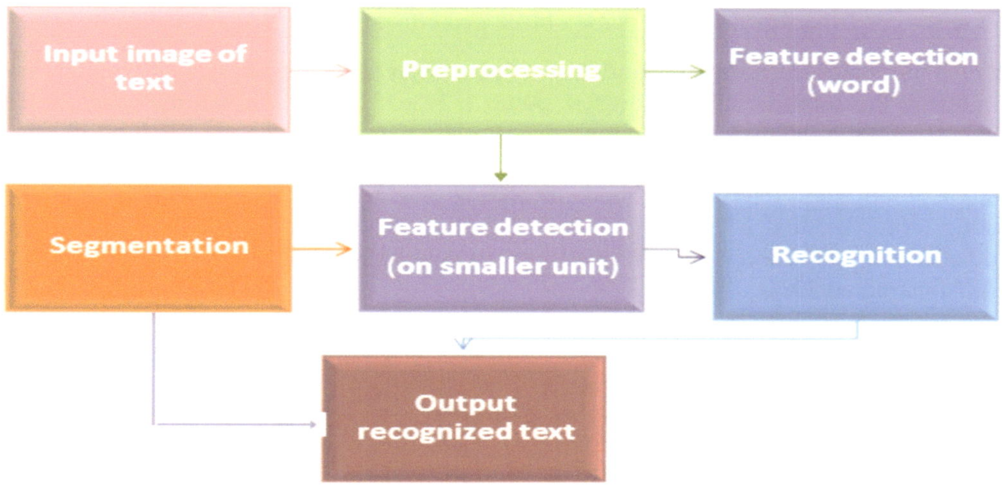

Fig. 2. Character recognition stages

2.1 Pre-processing and representation

The methods of the preprocessing phase are divided into two types of methods according to their function. First, the methods function to construct clean and usable raw data like noise reduction. Second, the smoothing and normalization methods function to prepare the data image to be segmented and recognized in terms of features, for instance: contour tracing, skeleton extraction, and vertical and horizontal projection. These methods represent the preprocessing of the recognition process. However, the segmentation approach can be defined as preparing a short and snappy representation of the word image to be segmented. The common techniques in the representation processes are: vertical and horizontal projection, contour tracing, and skeleton extraction which discussed in the following section.

2.2 Vertical and horizontal projection

The vertical projection methods importance appears in detecting the junction lines between the adjacent characters and the white spaces by counting the black pixels in every column of the image. However, the vertical projection method is not efficient in handwritten recognition owing to overlapping and skew problems. To explore the word image into lines, words, and characters it has been used with horizontal projection,. These techniques take into account that the link between characters is not always as wide as the letters. The projections profile of the image is best achieved in these techniques.

The definition of horizontal projection is as follows:

$$h\ (i) = \Sigma\, p\ (i, j)$$

For vertical projection, it is:

$$v\,(j) = \sum \mathrm{p}\,(i, j)$$

where i is the row number and j is the column number. P is the pixel value. The value is 0 for a white pixel (background) and 1 for a black pixel (foreground).

Figure 3 illustrates the horizontal and vertical projection profiles of an Arabic sentence after eradicating the secondaries. The highest point in Figure 3(c) represents the baseline. The thickness of the baseline is determined by computing the thickness of the longest spike, taking the most repeated column height (Timsari and Fahimi, 1996), or considering the position of loops as a reference, as these are always close to the baseline (Olivier *et al.*, 1996). Among other essential information in the projection profile that can be subtracted is the width, height, and amount of connected components of sub-words (Al-Yousefi and Udpa 1992; Mohammed 2006).

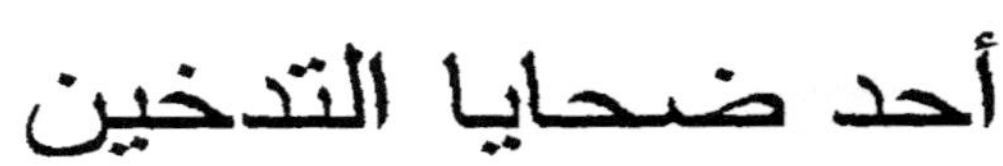

(a) An Arabic sentence

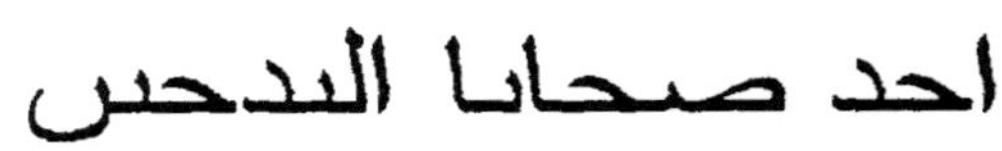

(b) Secondaries are eliminated

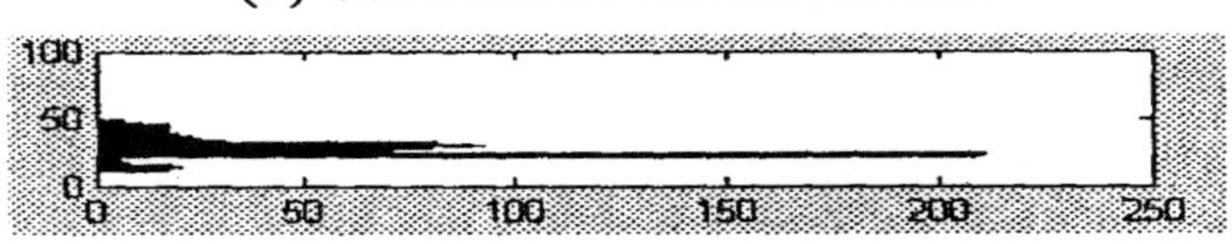

(c) Horizontal projection

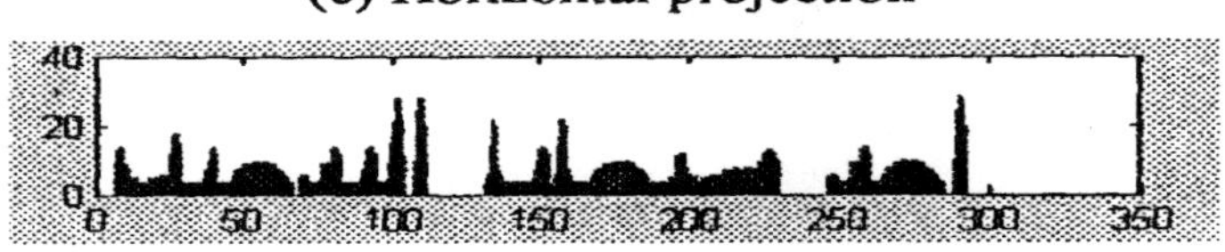

(d) Vertical projection

Fig. 3. Horizontal and vertical projections (Mohammed, 2006)

However, more researchers use the vertical and horizontal projection profile for different functions to prepare the image for recognition. For example, they use it to detect the baseline or to segment the word into characters.

One of the most important functions of projection profiles in character recognition is detecting the baseline. The researcher used dissimilar algorithms to detect the baseline according to the projection profile methods. One of these methods to divide the image into zones according to the intensity of pixels in each zone; the highest intensity zone of black pixels is the baseline. The middle zone is dealt with using the vertical projection in Sarfraz *et al.* (2003), where four regions or zones are identified: the baseline, upper, middle, and lower regions. The zones are defined according to the baseline zone, which has the most black pixels, the middle region is the region on top of the baseline and double the width of the baseline, and has a constructed vertical projection (Sarfraz *et al.*, 2003). The point that all researchers agree on is that the baseline has the highest number of black pixels in the horizontal projection profile (Altuwaijri and Bayoumi, 1995; Hashemi *et al.*, 1995).

On the other hand, the importance of the projection profile appears in the segmentation method. Different methods are used to segment the word into characters using the projection profile. One approach uses a permanent entrance to do so (Nawaz *et al.*, 2003). The connection region between two letters is detected when the projection rate of the middle region is lower than two-thirds of the baseline width. If the outline is larger than one-third of the baseline the start of a new character is detected and the current region tracks the connection region with a better rate. However, other works have applied the vertical projection profile in the direction of determent the pixels of the baseline and secondaries, as in Altuwaijri and Bayoumi (1995).

The necessary information of a shape in character recognition is stored in its skeleton (Zeki, 2005). In other words, the thinning process means creating the skeleton of the image. A skeleton created by highlighting the centerline of the word image, it is a one-pixel-width image. This helps to bring out fundamental information about the word. Figure 4 shows an example of image thinning where the skeleton of the word has one pixel of width.

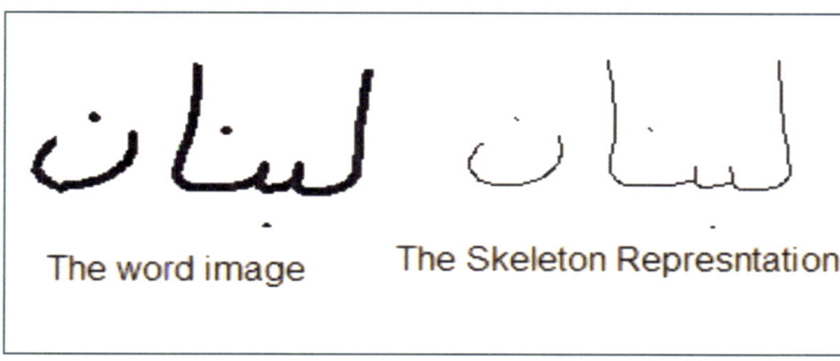

Fig. 4. A word image and its skeleton

The thinning operation improves the ability to recognize and segment characters. However, in the segmentation process, extracting segments from the skeleton graph is more trustworthy than finding the real linked points in a word (Abuhaiba *et al.*, 1994; Khorsheed and Clocksin, 1999). The skeleton can be segmented into strokes. Each stroke begins and ends with a feature point. A feature point could be the end point, branch point, or cross point (Amin *et al.*, 1996; Khorsheed and Clocksin, 1999). Other segmentation techniques begin by determining the baseline of word; after that, the segmentation points are detected by measuring the columns with pixels around the baseline. This point will appear at the middle of the association stroke (Khaly and Sid-Ahmed, 1990). Then, the explore for the starting tip is set in the region of the baseline to extract the stroke; after this, the search for the stroke end point starts by tracing the curve. An end point may be a branch point, a cross point, a point with unexpected modify in the curve following a horizontal movement close to the baseline, or a line end point (Almuallim and Yamaguchi, 1987; Zeki, 2005).

Vertical projection detects the beginning and ending points of characters; these points might be true or applicator points. The true beginning point will be detected, if there is a transformation from zero to nonzero in the vertical projection; the true ending point is detected, if there is a transformation from nonzero to zero (Jambi, 1991; Abandah and Khedher, 2004). This method needs further processing in the presence of vertical overlaps. Other methods have positioned character graph models to recognize isolated letters. Every character's skeleton is transformed to a hierarchy structure that is coordinated to a model through a rule-based recognizer. Every model becomes a state machine through a conversion analogous to the instructions of segments inside the character and with other "fuzzy" restrictions to differentiate some characters from others (Abuhaiba et al., 1994; Lorigo and Govindaraju, 2006).

2.3 Contour tracing

The tracing of the contour is conducted to detect border line pixels or when the contour contains significant information about an item (Khorsheed, 2002). It aims to transform the edge of the word into a series of codes to explore the images features. The coding method begins by discovering the location of an initial pixel then identifies the relations of the following pixels on the contour until it reaches the initial pixel.

RPCT stand for Regional projection contour transformation, it is projected the image in a number of directions which is vertical and horizontal. This was presented with the chain code contour of each projection. The contour was modeled and features were achieved for every segment using a two-dimensional model that took into account the amount of dynamic pixels, slope, and curvature. Individual HMMs were used to create and reproduce split-feature vectors from; the contours of the horizontal and vertical projections were compliant with two HMMs per character. Through recognition, individual categories were incorporated to improve performance (Dehghan, 2001; Lorigo and Govindaraju, 2006).

Tracing the contour also plays a main role in segmentation. It is used in the Segmentation and Recognition of Arabic Printed Text (SARAT) system (Margner, 1992), a segmentation method stand on the external contour of the words. The algorithm starts by detecting the end points of the upper contour. Next, the upper contour segmented into pieces takes place, including a curve of the same symbol.

Techniques depending on tracing the contour keep away from the problems resulting on the thinning procedure since they study the structural of the characters forms according to the scanning. Nevertheless, they are affected by noise on the contour; hence, the contour needs to be thinned first.

2.4 Baseline detection

The baseline is an imaginary line used to connect the characters of the word. It is usually detected in the segmentation stage and helps in characterizing the strokes of the characters. Several methods have been published for detecting the baseline. Kanai *et al.* (1998) used the projection profile technique to detect the fiducial points by interpreting the lowest resolution layer of the image. Detecting the baseline is an ordinary step in many offline handwritten Arabic recognition OACR systems, and it is often an essential step before the segmentation and the feature extraction steps.

For instance, El-Hajj *et al.*'s (2005) system depends on the upper and lower baselines. These are contained by the HMM recognizer in the context of frame-based features, which are integrated features measuring densities, transitions, and concavities in zones defined by the detected baselines. The IFN/ENIT database was used to test the system. For every experiment, three images of the four image sets was used to train the system and tested on the excluded set. In the experimentation, the addition of baseline-dependent features to similar measurements that do not use those zones significantly improved recognition (El-Hajj *et al.*, 2005; Lorigo and Govindaraju, 2006).

2.5 Segmentation

The segmentation stage is necessary when it comes to recognizing Arabic wording. Each mistake in the segmentation method the main form of the characters will generate another representation of the character's form (Amin, 1998). One of the types of recognition strategies needed in the segmentation stage is an analytical strategy, as discussed in Section 2.3. Analytical strategies are sub-classed into two methods that have affected the segmentation mechanism of printed and handwritten Arabic text into individual characters: implicit and explicit segmentation (Amin, 1998).

i. In explicit or external segmentation, the word is segmented into characters after that recognized each character independently. This method is typically more costly because of the greater difficulty of locating the best word.
ii. In implicit or internal segmentation, words are segmented to characters and recognized all together. This category of segmentation is generally considered to facilitate recognition of all the characters through rules. Various rules need to be created manually to obtain excellent accuracy. Thus, the higher the number of rules, the better the recognition.

More researchers have used explicit segmentation to prepare a letter for recognition. In most of their work, the segmentation stage depends on the representation stage. Haraty and Ghaddar use this method to segment the characters and identify ligatures. Their method is based on a thinning technique, along with structural and other features such as the statistics of corner points, loops, division points, and endpoints, and the density and quantity of black pixels. In addition, double neural networks are presently being employed. In these systems, the projected breakpoints were confirmed or rejected by the neural network (Haraty and Ghaddar, 2003).

Conversely, another type of segmentation strategy called (recognition based segmentation), and is an implicit technique. This is unlike the methods discussed above, which were regarded as explicit segmentation techniques. In implicit techniques, the segmentation and recognition of the characters occur at the same time. The basic theory of this approach is that provisional segmentations can be presented through exploiting a changeable window with variable widths that are or are not completed by the categorization (Cheung *et al.*, 2001).

One example of the implicit type of segmentation is that of El-Dabi *et al.* (1990), where the invariant moments are used and checked in terms of their alignment with the feature space of the font. If a character is not found, another column is affixed to the original portion of the word and moments are calculated and checked again. This procedure is repeated until a character is recognized or the end of the word is reached. This method allows the system to handle overlapping and to isolate the connecting baseline between connected characters. The segmentation rate resulting from this method was 83% (El-Dabi *et al.*, 1990).

As can be noticed from the above discussion, the segmentation approach aims to solve the most serious problems of traditional segmentation. Hence, no accurate character segmentation path is necessary. In principle, any of the other approaches can be used here as long as they have some recognition capabilities (Cheung *et al.*, 2001).

2.6 Feature extraction

Feature extraction is used to characterize the tokens that can be applied for a special recognition of every character. Features categorized into two types. First, there are local features; these are typically *geometric* (e.g., curved in their convex parts and types of junctions: intersections, T-junctions, endpoints, secondaries , loops, height and width of stocks, etc.). Second, there are global features that are typically statistical (invariant moments, Fourier transform, etc.) or *topological* (number of connected components, connectivity, number of holes, etc.) (Amin, 1997).

For instance, the Freeman chain code is commonly used for feature extraction moreover than segmentation process or the recognition process (Abdullah, 2007). On the other hand, invariant moments are also used as a feature in some studies, as in El-Dabi *et al.* (1990).

As can be observed from the discussion in previous sections and below, these techniques all use feature extraction and the work cannot succeed without it. This work will be use six local features of characters length, width, loop, left connection, right connection and complementary.

3. Genetic algorithm

GAs can be defined as a "class of optimization and search methods that use randomness to avoid local extreme solutions"(Kherallah *et al.*, 2009). A GA is an iterative algorithm based on many generations of probable solutions, among selection schemes authorization the removal of bad solutions and the reproduction of good ones that can be modified (Kherallah *et al.*, 2009).

Genetic algorithm works with a special fitness to evaluate each individual or string in the population. The evolution starts from population of randomly generations. There are other operation that helps in selected the individuals or strings of the population based on their fitness. The individuals may modify or mutated to form a new population, which used in the next iteration. The algorithm terminates when reached fitness level for the population. If the algorithm has concluded due to a maximum number of generations, a suitable solution may or may not have been reached.

The present chapter depends on the use of GA techniques for character recognition. However, when we focus on research that used GAs for character recognition, there is some works used GAs in character recognition. Wherever, these studies used GAs to recognize online handwriting. Only one study used GAs with NNs, and to recognize offline handwriting, and this was for Latin script. The handwriting recognition model described in this work progresses in three stages: (1) the segmentation of the handwritten text, (2) the recognition of segmented characters with the help of ANNs, and (3) the selection of the best solution from the four ANN outputs with the help of the GA. A strong algorithm for handwriting segmentation has been described, with the help of which individual characters can be segmented from a word selected from an image of a paragraph of handwritten text, which is given as input in the model. The algorithms were tested with 200 handwritten samples; out of these, 142 samples were correctly recognized, representing an overall efficiency of 71% (Mathur *et al.*, 2008).

On the other hand, GAs have used with good results for online Latin character recognition. Menier *et al.* (1994) have presented a genetic algorithm for the online recognition of cursive handwriting. The GAs work with a population of solutions called strings. Each string has a lexical picture and a graphic primitive list that describes how the word is written. Each string is made with construction blocks called allographs. The GAs are used to find the best reconstruction of the word to be analyzed, based on graphic primitives and using the allograph list. This can be seen as an alternative analysis method for word recognition that does not require the definition of a scanning strategy. This system achieved 84% recognition in a manuscript test with a lexical set of 150 words and a small allograph set. The recognition subset consists of 160 words, including ten extra words not belonging to the lexicon (Menier *et al*, 1994).

Ramin Halavati *et al.* (2006) employed a narrative Multiple States Machine as a general tool for elastic pattern recognition and utilized an evolutionary method to generate this machine. The most important scheme after the machine is to expand and sustain special hypotheses about the specified sequence of segments and increasingly confirm or reduce them to reach a single ending result. This is applied using the Persian language, employing a typical feature set and a specific tailored GA. The identification and calculation times were contrasted with a dynamic programming comparison approach. This approach achieved an 89% recognition rate without a dictionary and 96.1% with a dictionary for Persian language groups. Moreover, it was compared with pruned dynamic programming (DP), and shown to present an almost constant recognition speed, whereas DP's computational time increases exponentially when the number of segments increases. Thus, this system gave results more than 10 times faster than DP for 9 segment words, and 100 times faster for words with 13 segments (Halavati *et al.* , 006).

4. Method of feature extraction

In this work, there is a special strategy to segment the word into characters and recognize each character: the whole word is scanned and its features extracted. Each word has eight types of features: (1) quantity of sub-words, (2) quantity of peaks for every sub-word, (3) number of loops for every peak, (4) number and location of complementary characters, (5) the width and (6) height of every peak, and (7) whether there is left and (8) right connection.

After the segmentation of the word, the feature of each character must be detected to recognize the shape of the character. The recognition algorithm is based on six features of each character shape. These features are (1) the length of the character, (2) its width, (3) whether or not it has a loop, (4) whether there is a right character connected to it, (5) whether there is a left character connect to it, and (6) whether there is a complementary character like the hamza, one point, two points, or three points, etc.

(a)

(b)

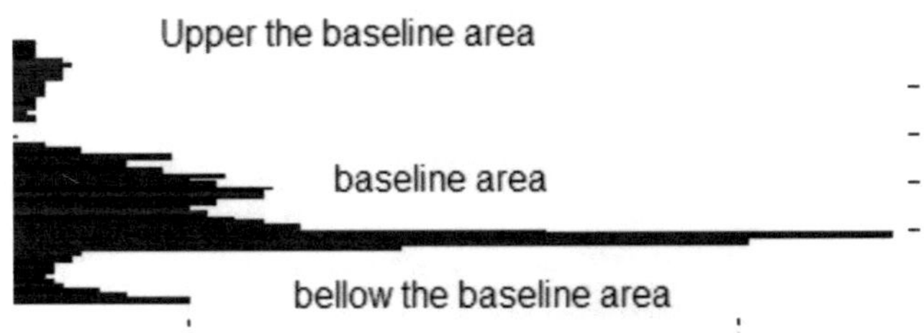

Fig. 6. Detecting the baseline by the horizontal projection profile: (a) handwritten word, (b) horizontal projection profile to detect the baseline.

This algorithm apply in the characters are written cursively and all the characters in the word are based upon the baseline. The feature extraction algorithm depends on this, so in this algorithm the character image is divided to three areas: The first is the baseline area that was detected by the horizontal projection profile; the longest spike represents the baseline, as shown in Figure 6. The second is the area above the baseline; this area usually contains the upper complementary and the upper length of a character, as in ك, ـلin Arabic characters and l, h in Latin characters. The third area is the area below the baseline, which usually contains the lower complementary character and the lower length of the character, as in ،ج، و g, y See Figure 6.

The vertical and horizontal projection profiles are calculated for each area individually, to help in detecting the features of the character. Each character shape has six features that are unique to it; no other shape has that feature combination.

After defining the area of image and its projection profile, the feature extraction algorithm starts by tracing the boundary of the image and traveling around the eight neighbourhoods. One vector array has six cells called feature vectors, where each cell represents one feature of the character's shape using an integer value, as shown in Figure 7, that describes the feature vector of character shape ـه . This character is short, has a small width, has a loop in the baseline, has no right connection, has a left connection, and has no complementary character. This vector is unique for the character shape ـه .

Each feature is detected according to the following strategy:

Length: This is denoted by 0 if the character shape is short or 1 if the character shape is long. The length of the character is detected by the baseline area; if it is in the baseline area only, it is short; otherwise, it is long.

Width: This is denoted by 0 if the character shape has a small width and 1 if the character shape has a large width. The width of the character shape depends in the vertical projection profile of the image and the thinning algorithm where all the images have one pixel width.

Loop	Length	Width	Left connection	Right connection	Complementary character
-1	0	0	1	0	0

Fig. 7. Feature vector representing the character مـ

Loop: This is denoted by 0 if the character shape has no loop; 1 if the character shape has one loop in the baseline area above the baseline like in ـفـ ,a ; -1 if the character shape has one loop below the baseline, مـ ; 2 if the character shape has two loops above the baseline as in B,هـ; 3 if the character shape has an open loop on the left side and it is standing on the baseline, as in حـ ,z ; or -3 if the character shape has an open loop on the right side and it is standing on the baseline, as in عـ ,c,G . The type of loop is detected according to the following algorithm:

a. If the subtraction of the entire nearest pixel row in the same column is >1, and the subtraction of all the nearest pixel column in the same row is >1, the loop type is 1 if the last row is the baseline. Otherwise it is -1.
b. *If the subtraction of the entire nearest pixel row in the same column is >1,* except the first column, which has one pixel only and the second, which has two pixels behind one another, the loop type is 3. Otherwise the loop type is -3.
c. *If there are more than two pixels in the same column, the subtraction of it is >1,* and the subtraction of all the rows in the same column and all columns in the same row is >1, the loop type is 2.
d. Otherwise the loop type is 0.

The right connection: is denoted by 0 if there is no character on the right side; otherwise it is 1. This is detected by the vertical projection profile of the baseline area; if there are ones on the right side of the character width, it denoted by 1; otherwise it is 0.

The left connection; is denoted by 0 if there is no character on the left said; otherwise it is 1. This is detected by the vertical projection profile of the baseline area; if there are ones in the left side of the character width, it is denoted by 1; otherwise it is 0.

The complementary character: is denoted by 0 if there are no complementary character, 1 if there is one dot above the baseline area, -1 if there is one dot below the baseline area, 2 if there are two dots above the baseline area, -2 if there are two dots below the baseline area, if there are three dots above the baseline area, and 4 if there is a hamza above the baseline area. This is detected using the vertical projection profiles of the areas. The devised feature algorithm is illustrated in Figure 8.

5. Applying GA

When the features of the characters in the sub-word are determined, the next phase is to recognize the characters of the sub-word. The genetic algorithm approach will be used for this purpose. The GAs will recognize the character depending on the following strategies:

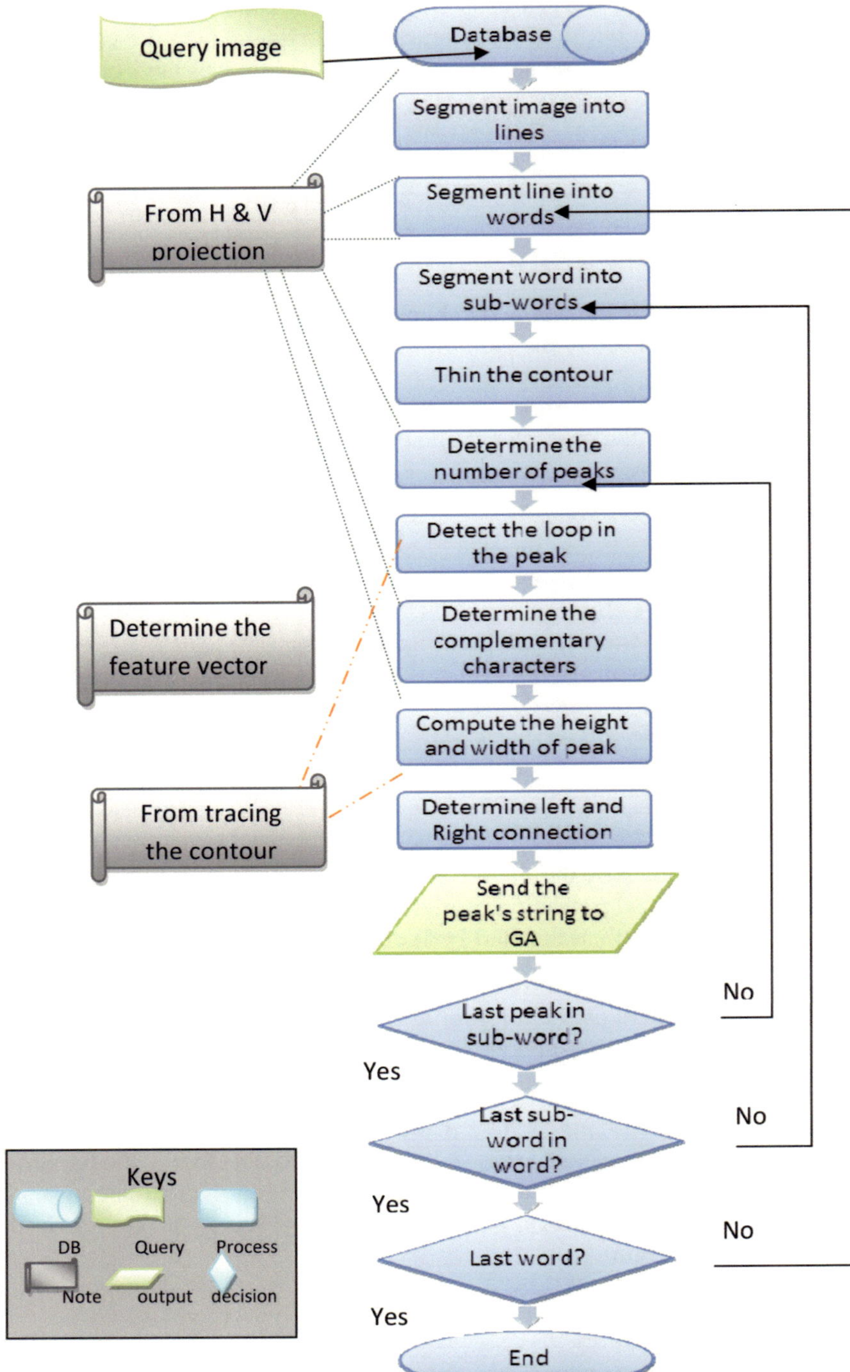

Fig. 8. Feature extraction algorithm

5.1 The fitness function

The value returned from the fitness function for one gene represents the degree of matching between the feature vector of the character represented by that gene and the feature vector of the real character. The fitness function here will be counted as the same number of bits in two feature vectors and returns the value of the same features. If this number is 6, it is the optimal solution. For example, to recognize the characters of the sub-word من, there are two feature vectors shown in Figure 9 for the character shapes مـ and ـن that are used to calculate the fitness function for the character shape ـن . Table 2 shows the summed feature vector values of a character shape with random population values; if the number of one's in the answer is equal to 6, this is the best gene. In Table 2, there are three random genes: the first has a fitness value of 3, the second has a fitness value of 5, and the third has a fitness value of 5. Table 3 shows the fitness function of the population genes of the character shape مـ.

-1	0	0	1	0	0

Feature vector representing the character مـ

0	1	1	0	1	1

Feature vector representing the characterـن

Fig. 9. Feature vectors of مـ and ـن

ن Main feature vector	Random population feature vector	Calculation	F
011011	101010	001110	3
	011010	111110	5
	111011	011111	5

Table 2. Fitness function of the character ـن

Main feature vector	Random population feature vector	Calculation	F
-100100	101010	110001	3
	011011	000000	0
	111011	100000	1

Table 3. Fitness function of the character مـ

5.2 Selection reproduction operator

The importance of this operator is that it reproduces an opposition among diverse feature vectors. The Tournament selection type of selection operation used, where this selection reproduction operator makes sure that better feature vectors are found while the poorer feature vectors are marked as redundant. It establishes new feature vectors within the population, along with the other operators, specifically the crossover operator and the mutation operator. In our example in the character " ـن " in Table 2, the gene with fitness value 3 is the worst one, so it is discarded; the best function has a value of 5, but we have two such feature vectors, so the two feature vectors will be duplicated, as show in Figure 10. In the character "ـه " in Table 3, the fitness value 0 is the worst one, so it is discarded, whereas 3 is the best function, and will be duplicated.

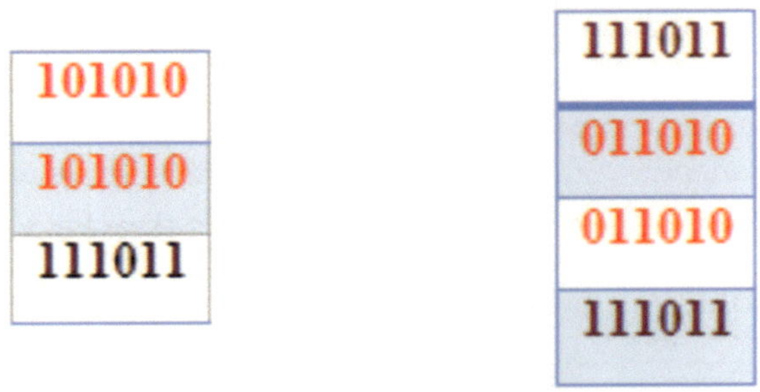

Fig. 10. Example of reproduction operator

5.3 Crossover operator

A single crossover point is applied. Feature vectors are duplicated at random with a higher probability for the feature vectors undergoing crossing. For each parent, a sub-feature vector is chosen where the resultant feature vector is constructed by concatenation of the sub-feature vectors, as shown in Figure 11.

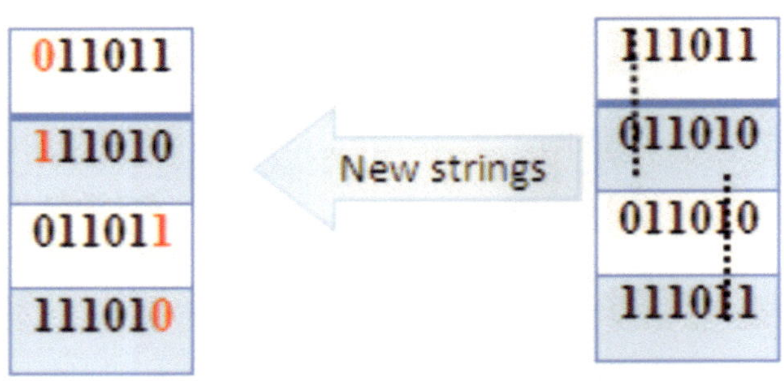

Fig. 11. Example of crossover operator

5.4 Mutation operator

To avoid the recombination of the same feature vectors and to expand the explored solution space, as well as to alternate between some chromosomes, the mutation operator is used in combination with the crossover operator. This gives new and possibly improved solutions, as shown in Figure 12, where the 1 in the fifth index changes to 0.

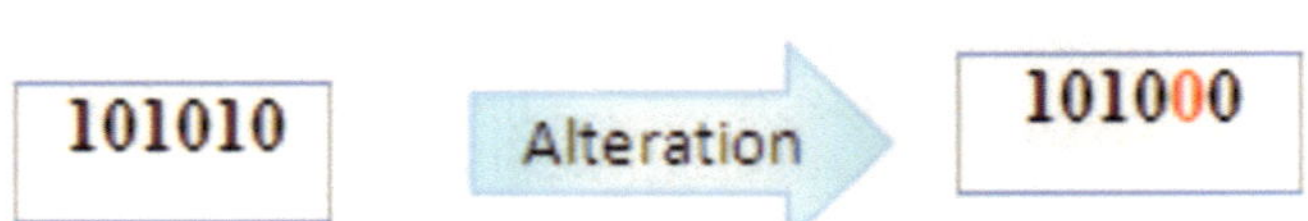

Fig. 12. Example of mutation operator

6. Evaluation

The evaluation of the algorithm depends on the number of words, sub-words, and characters that are recognized, and on the number of words, sub-words, and characters that are unrecognized, out of the number of tested words, sub-words, and characters. The percentage of words recognized will be calculated as:

$$W = \frac{Number\ of\ Sub-words\ that\ are\ recognized}{Number\ of\ tested\ Sub-words} \times 100$$

And the percentage of sub-words recognized will be calculated as:

$$SW = \frac{Number\ of\ Sub-words\ that\ are\ recognized}{Number\ of\ tested\ Sub-words} \times 100\,.$$

Finally, the percentage of characters recognized will be calculated as:

$$L = \frac{Number\ of\ letters\ \ that\ are\ recognized}{Numbers\ of\ letters\ tested} \times 100$$

7. Experiment

In order to determine the correction rate of the developed system, various criteria should exist and be tested in the GA. These include the population size, number of generations, crossing over probability, and mutation probability. These criteria were optimized in the three experiment types and the execution time was calculated for each character. The recognition problem is solved by the GA, which may yield a different solution for the same word each time, depending on the population and number of iteration. However, there is currently high similarity between the original solution and the anticipated one. We remark that if the population size is less than or equal to 100, the tested letters will be better recognized. Nevertheless, in other cases, the population size is about 100 and the executed time augments. The correction rate is 87.81 for all the tested word from Arabic and Latin Characters as show in table 4.

We also re-created the execution with a population of a different range (10, 20, 30, 40, 50, 60, 70, 80, 90, 100, 1000) to analyze how the population affected the recognition score. The recognition rate among a population size of 10 is show in Figure 13; if the population size decreases, the recognition rate increases.

Tested words	Words with correct features	Words with incorrect features	Correction rate
109300	95975	13325	87.81

Table 4. Results of experiments in the recognition stage

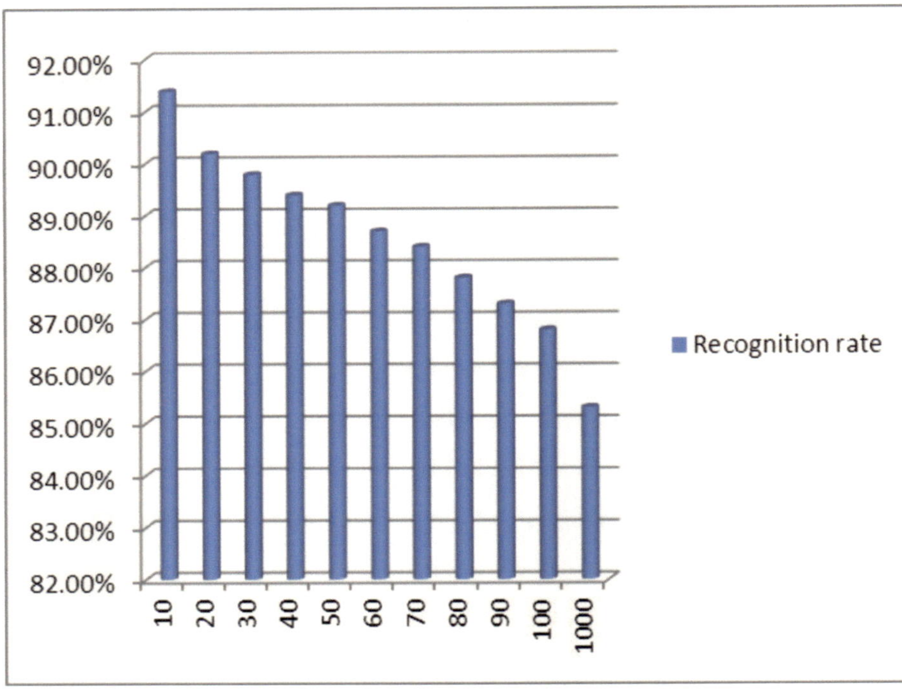

Fig. 13. Relation between population size and recognition rate.

8. References

Abandah, G.A. and Khedher, M.Z. (2004). *Printed and handwritten arabic optical character recognition-initial study.* Technical Report, University of Jordan. Amman, Jordan: August.

Abdullah, S. A. (2007). *Off-line Handwritten Arabic Characters Segmentation using Rotation Invariant Segment Feature (RISF).* Master of Science,USM.

Abuhaiba, I. (2003). A Discrete Arabic Script for Better Automatic Document Understanding. *The Arabian Journal for Science and Engineering, 28* (1B), 77-94.

Al-Hajj, R., Likforman-Sulem, L., and Mokbel, C. (2009). Combining Slanted-Frame Classifiers for Improved HMM-Based Arabic Handwriting Recognition. *IEEE transactions on pattern analysis and machine intelligence, 31. Retreived from http://www.biomedsearch.com/nih/Combining-Slanted-Frame-Classifiers-improved/19443916.html*

Aljuaid, H., Mohamad, D., Sarfraz, M. (2009). "Arabic Handwriting Recognition Using Projection Profile and Genetic Approach". The 5th International conference in Signal Image Technologies and Information based system(SITIS'09). Marrakech: IEEE CPS.

Aljuaid, H., Mohamad, D., Sarfraz,M. (2010)."Evaluation Approach of Arabic character Recognition", International Journal of Computer Vision and Image Processing (IJCVIP), IGI .

Aljuaid,H., Mohamad, D., Sarfraz,M. (2010). "A Tool To Develop Arabic Handwriting Recognition System Using Genetic Approach". Journal of Computer Science, 6(5): 490-495.

Aljuaid, H., Mohamad, D., Sarfraz,M. (2009). ICRIIS09. "Recognition of Arabic Handwriting Using Genetic Approach.

Alimi, A., and Ghorbe, O. (1995). The Analysis in an On-line Recognition System of Arabic Handwritten Characters. *Proc. 3rd Int. Conf. on Document Analysis and Recognition.* Canada, 890-893.

Alimi, A. M. (1997). An Evolutionary Neuro-Fuzzy Approach. *IEEE*, 0-8 186-7898-4/97.

Alma'adeed, S., Higgens, C., and Elliman, D. (2002). Recognition of Off-line Handwritten Arabic Words using Hidden Markov Model Approach. *Proc. 16th International Conference on Pattern Recognition, 3* , 481-484.

Alma'adeed, S., Higgens, C., and Elliman, D. (2004). Off-line Recognition of Handwritten Arabic Words using Multiple hidden Markov models. *Knowledge-Based Systems, vol. 17* , pp. 75-79.

Almuallim, H., and Yamaguchi, S. (1987). A Method of Recognition of Arabic Cursive Handwriting. *IEEE Transactions on Pattern Analysis and Machine Intelligence (PAMI), 9* (5), 715-722.

Al-Sadoun, H. A. (1995). A New Structural Technique for Recognizing Printed Arabic Text. *International Journal of Pattern Recognition and Artificial Intelligence, 9* (1), 101-125.

Altuwaijri , M., and Bayoumi, M. (1995). A New Thinning Algorithm for Arabic Characters using Self-organizing Neural Network. *IEEE International Symposium on Circuits and Systems (ISCAS'95).* Seattle, WA, 3, 1824-1827.

Amin, A. (2000). Recognition of printed arabic text based on global features and decision tree learning techniques. *Pattern Recognition Society* , 1309-1323 , doi:10.1016/S0031-3203(99)00114-4.

Amin, A. (2001). Segmentation of Printed Arabic Text. In *Advances in Pattern Recognition – ICAPR 2001* , Springer Berlin / Heidelberg , 2013/2001, 115-126 , DOI:10.1007/3-540-44732-6).

Amin, A. (2003). Recognition of Hand-printed Characters based on Structural Description and Inductive Logic Programming. *Pattern Recognition Letters, 24,* 3187-3196.

Ben Amara and Najoua Essoukri. (2003). Classification of Arabic Script using Multiple Sources of Information: State of the Art and Perspectives. *International Journal on Document Analysis and Recognition, 5,* 195-212.

Benouareth, A., Ennaji, A., and Sellami, M. (2006). HMMs with Explicit State Duration Applied to Handwritten Arabic Word Recognition. *18th Int. Conf. on Pattern Recognition (ICPR'06). 2,* 897-900.

Benouaretha, A., Ennajib ,A.,and Sellamia,M. (2008). Semi-continuous HMMs with explicit state duration for unconstrained Arabic word modeling and recognition. *Pattern Recognition Letters , 29* (12), 1742-1752 ,doi:10.1016/j.patrec.2008.05.008.

Cheung, A., and Bennamoun, N.W. (2001). An Arabic Optical Character Recognition System using Recognition-based Segmentation. *Pattern Recognition, 34* (2), 215-233.

Cowell, J., and Hussain, F. (2001). Thinning Arabic Characters for Feature Extraction. *IEEE Conference on Information Visualization.* 25-27 July. London, UK, 181-185.

Dehghan, M. K. F. (2001). Handwritten Farsi (Arabic) Word Recognition: A Holistic Approach using Discrete HMM. *Pattern Recognition, 34,* 1057-1065.

El-Dabi, S.S., Ramisis, R., and Kamel, A. (1990). Arabic Character Recognition System: A Statistical Approach for Recognizing Cursive Typewritten text. *Pattern Recognition, 5* (23), 485-495.

El-Hajj, R., Likforman-Sulem, L., and Mokbel, C. (2005). Arabic Handwriting Recognition using Baseline Dependent Features and Hidden Markov Modeling. *Proc. International Conference on Document Analysis and Recognition*. Seoul, Korea, 893-897.

El-Khaly, F., and Sid-Ahmed, M.A. (1990). Machine Recognition of Optically Captured Machine Printed Arabic Text. *Pattern Recognition, 23* (11), 1207-1214.

Fahmy, M. M. M., and Al Ali, S. (2001). Automatic Recognition of Handwritten Arabic Characters using their Geometrical Features. *Jurnal of Studies in Informaticas and Control, 10* (2).

Farah, M. G., Rygh, J.H, Steen, T.W, Selmer, R., Heldal, E., and Bjune, G. (2006). Patient and Health Care System Delays in the Start of Tuberculosis Treatment in Norway. *BMC Infectious Diseases, 6,* 1186/1471-2334-6-33.

Hashemi, M.R, Fatemi, O., and Safavi, R. (1995). Persian Cursive Script Recognition. *3rd international Conference on Document Analysis and Recognition (ICDAR'95)*. Montreal, Canada, 2, 869-873.

http://ar.wikipedia. (2009). Retrieved from http://ar.wikipedia.org/wiki/

Jambi, K. (1991). *Design and Implementation of a System for Recognizing Arabic Handwritten Words with Learning Ability.* Master of Science, Illinois Institute of Technology.

Kandil, A. H., and El-Baily, A. (2004). Arabic OCR: A Centerline Independent Segmentation Technique. *International Conference on Electrical, Electronic and Computer Engineering (ICEEC'04).* 5-7 September. 412-415.

Kherallah, M., *et al.* (2009). On-line Arabic Handwriting Recognition System Based on Visual Encoding and Genetic Algorithm. *Engineering Applications of Artificial Intelligence, 22* (1), 153-170, doi:10.1016/j.

Khorsheed, M. S. (2003). Recognising Handwritten Arabic Manuscripts using a Single Hidden Markov Model. *Pattern Recognition Letters, 24,* 2235-2242.

Khorsheed, M. S., and Clocksin, W. F. (1999). Structural Features of Cursive Arabic Script. *10th British Machine vision Conference (BMV'99).* September. University of Nottingham, UK, 2, 422-431.

Kim, G., and Govindaraju, V. (1997). A Lexicon Driven Approach to Handwritten Word Recognition for Real-time Applications. *IEEE Transactions on Pattern Analysis and Machine Intelligence, 19* (4), 366-379.

Klassen, T. (2001). *Towards Neural Network Recognition of Handwritten Arabic Letters.* MASTER thesis: Dalhousie University.

Koerich, A. S. (2003). Large Vocabulary Off-line Handwriting Recognition: A Survey. *Pattern Anal., 6,* 97–121.

Lee, S.-W., and Kim, Y-J. (1995). A New Type of Recurrent Neural Network for Handwritten Character Recognition. *Proc.3rd Int. Conf. On Document Ananlysis and Recognition.* Canada, 38-41.

Madhvanath, S. G. (2001). The Role of Holistic Paradigms in Handwritten Word Recognition. *IEEE Transactions on Pattern Analysis and Machine Intelligence, 23* (2), 149-164.

Margner, V. (1992). SARAT-A System for the Recognition of Arabic Printed Text. *11th IAPR International Conference on Pattern Recognition Methodology and Systems (ICPR'92).* 30 August - 3 September. Horgue, Netherlands, 2, 561-564.

M¨argner, V., and El Abed,H. (2009). ICDAR 2009 Arabic Handwriting Recognition Competition. *10th International Conference on Document Analysis and Recognition ,* IEEE Computer Society ,(pp. 978-0-7695-3725-2).

Maroy, M. B. (1979). Learning in Syntactic Recognition of Symbols Drawn on a Graphic Tablet. 166-182.

Mohammed, A. M. (2006). *Segmentation of Arabic Characters using Voronoi Diagrams.* Doctor of Philosophy. UKM, Bangi.

Mostafa, M. (2004). An Adaptive Algorithm for the Automatic Segmentation of Printed Arabic Text. *17th Natinal Computer Conference.* Madinah, Saudi Arabia, 437-444.

Nawaz, S. N, Sarfraz, M., Zidouri, A., and Al-Khatib. (2003). An Approach to Offline Arabic Character Recognition using Neural Networks. *10th IEEE International Conference on Electronics, Circuits and Systems (ICECS'03). 3,* 1328-1331. W.G.

Oliveira, L. S., and Sabourin, R. (2003). A Methodology for Feature Selection using Multiobjective Genetic Algorithms for Handwritten Digit String Recognition. *International Journal of Pattern Recognition and Artifical Intelligence, 17* (6), 903-929.

Pernkopf, F., and Bouchaffra, D. (2005). Genetic-based EM Algorithm for Learning Gaussian Mixture Models. *IEEE Transactions on Pattern Analysis and Machine Intelligence, 27 (8),* 1344-1348.

Plamondon, R., and Srihari, S. N. (2000). On-line and Off-line Handwriting Recognition: A Comprehensive Survey. *IEEE Transactions on Pattern Analysis and Machine Intelligence, 22* (1), 63-84.

Sarfraz, M., Nawaz, S. N., and Al-khuraidly, A. (2003). Offline Arabic Text Recognition System. *International Conference on Geometric Modeling and Graphics (GMAG'03).* London, England, 30-36.

Sari, T., Souici, L., and Sellami, M. (2002). Off-line Handwritten Arabic Character Segmentation and Recognition System: ACSA. *8th International Workshop on Frontiers in Handwriting Recognition (IWFHR'8).* Niagara-on-the-lake, CA, 452-457.

Souici-Meslati, L., and Sellami, M. (2004). A Hybrid Approach for Arabic Literal Amounts Recognition. *The Arabian Journal for Science and Engineering, 29,* 177-194.

Vinciarelli, A. B. (2004). Offline Recognition of Unconstrained Handwritten Texts using HMMs and Statistical Language Models. *IEEE Transactions on Pattern Analysis and Machine Intelligence, 26* (6), 709–720.

Wang, Y.-K., and Fan, K.-C. (1996). Applying Genetic Algorithms on Pattern Recognition: An Analysis and Survey.*Proceeding of ICPR'96, 2,740,* HYPERLINK "http://doi.ieeecomputersociety.org/10.1109/ICPR.1996.546921" \t "_blank" *doi.ieeecomputersociety.org/10.1109/ICPR.1996.546921*

Zeki, A. (2005). The Segmentation Problem in Arabic Character Recognition The State Of The Ar. *International Conference on Information and Communication Technologies* , 11 - 26 .

Wikipedia. (2009). Retrieved from http://www.wikipedia.org/

13

Multi-Stage Based Feature Extraction Methods for Uyghur Handwriting Based Writer Identification

Kurban Ubul[1], Andy Adler[2] and Mamatjan Yasin[2]
[1]*School of Information Science and Engineering, Xinjiang University*
[2]*Department of Systems and Computer Engineering, Carleton University*
[1]*China*
[2]*Canada*

1. Introduction

Since starting of civilization era, it has been critical to the human society how to identify and verify the statuses of uncertain people. Consequently, personal identification is widely used in every aspect of society including governmental and commercial sections. However, traditional ways of personal identification, e.g., using identification cards or passwords, have their limitation and weakness that these surrogate representations of identity can easily be shared, lost, manipulated or stolen. Biometrics-based personal identification offers a natural and reliable solution to certain aspects of identity management by utilizing fully automated or semi-automated schemes to recognize individuals based on their characters (Jain et al., 2008). Biometric characteristics usually are physiological (e.g. face, fingerprint, palm print etc.), or behavioural (e.g. handwriting, gait, voice etc.). Among various kinds of biometrics, handwriting based personal recognition and verification have the advantage of easy to access, cheap, reliable (He et al., 2007), so it is widely used and welcomed by the public. As a result, writer identification is attractive enough to both industry and academia (He et al., 2007, 2008; Said et al., 2000; Schomaker & Bulacu, 2004; Srihari et al., 2002).

Writer identification is defined as a task of determining the author based on his/her handwriting from a set of writers (Plamondon & Lorette, 1989). According to the input method, there are generally two types: on-line and off-line writer identification. In on-line system, transducer equipment is connected to the computer that it can convert writing movement into a sequence of signals and then send the information to the computer, while handwriting materials are scanned into a computer in two dimensional image formats for processing in off-line system. The On-line system is get higher identification rate than the off-line system because extra features such as writing speed and pressure are extracted in on-line system. Therefore, off-line writer identification is more challenging task. Off-line research is further subdivided into text-dependent (or text-sensitive) and text-independent (or text-insensitive) approaches (Plamondon & Lorette, 1989; Said et al., 2000). Text-dependent methods refer to the study of one or a limited group of characters, so that they require the writers to write the same text. While text-independent approaches look at a feature set whose components describe global statistical features extracted from the entire image of a text. Text-dependent methods have a better performance on writer identification, but they are inapplicable in many practical applications because of their strict requirement on same the writing content. Off-line, text independent methods are studied in this paper.

1.1 Related work

A number of new approaches on off-line, text-independent writer identification have been proposed in recent years. Many researchers take the handwriting as an image containing some special texture, and they regard the writer identification as texture identification. Said et al. (2000) and Al-Dmemor (2007) treated the writer identification task as a texture analysis problem using multi-channel Gabor filtering and grey-scale co-occurrence matrix (GSCM) techniques. He et al. (2007, 2008) proposed wavelet based generalized Gaussian model (GGD) and hidden Markov tree (HMT) model in wavelet domain to replace the traditional 2-D Gabor filter. The approach which texture features extracted by Gabor and XGabor filters are combined with feature relation graph (FRG) and showed high efficiency for Persian writer identification (Helli & Moghaddam, 2010). Edge based directional probability distributions and connected component contours as features for the writer identification task are proposed (Schomaker & Bulacu, 2004). Li et al. (2009) proposed a text-independent method of writer identification based on grid-window microstructure feature for different multilingual handwritings. In order to reduce the dimensions of the features and to improve identification accuracy, feature selection is implemented by combination of Principal Component Analysis (PCA) and Linear Discriminant Analysis (LDA) (Fukunaga, 1990), and successfully used for text independent Chinese writer identification(Deng et al., 2008). The combined Gabor filter and Independent Component Analysis (ICA) method indicated high accuracy in texture segmentation and classification (Chen, Y & Wang, R, 2006, 2007). So these reports about writer identifications are mostly based on Latin handwriting (Plamondon et al., 1989; Said et al., 2000; Schomaker & Bulacu, 2004; Srihari et al., 2002), and Chinese handwriting (He et al. 2007, 2008; Li et al., 2009), Arabic handwritings (Al-Dmour & Zitar, 2007), even Persian handwritings (Helli & Moghaddam, 2010). However, there are only 4 reports about Uyghur handwriting based writer identification, in which two of them are our previous research (Ubul et al., 2008, 2009) indicated to using Gabor filter and Genetic algorithm (GA), and Gabor filter plus PCA and ICA methods for feature extraction, and get the 92.5% identification rate for 55 different people. Raxidin (2010) also used Gabor filter for feature extraction and achieved an accuracy rate of 79.8%. Li et al. (2009) used grid-window microstructure features for 120 different Uyghur persons handwritings, obtained 91.7% of identification rate. But the identification rate is still need to be improved comparing to other languages' identification. It is challenging task to find and develop methods suitable for Uyghur handwriting based writer identification. Therefore, there is still much research space for implementing existing algorithms or developing new effective algorithms and methods based on the nature of Uyghur handwriting.

1.2 Contribution

The approaches of writer identification methods are dependent on the languages, because letters in different languages have different patterns. In this chapter, we have proposed a method for texture feature extraction and selection by integrating Gabor filters, Genetic algorithm(GA), Principal component analysis (PCA), Kernel Principal component analysis (KPCA) and independent component analysis (ICA) for Uyghur handwriting based writer identification. Considering the diversity of Uygur handwriting, we conducted extensive handwriting data collection. The personal information of the selected people for data collection is different including their age, occupation and education level. A database of writer information was built based those information. Valid handwriting samples were scanned into computer to form a sample database of Uyghur handwriting. The handwriting images in the database were pre-processed based on the character of Uyghur handwriting. The Uyghur texture images were formed by specific pre-processing methods, in which some of the approaches were different from Latin and Chinese. Because the texture feature extraction method was used in this paper, and the style of texture image between different scripts (e.g. Latin, Chinese, and Arabic) is different, the characters of Uyghur handwriting, especially its stroke and local features were studied. Multi-channel Gabor filter suitable for the characters of Uyghur handwriting was designed. In order not to miss any feature of Uyghur handwriting image, 144 features were extracted. The high dimensionality features is computationally expensive, so some optimization (GA) and dimensionality reduction algorithms (PCA, ICA, KPCA) were used to find the best feature selection. Among these strategies, multi-stage based feature extraction and selection methods (such as Gabor + PCA + KPCA) were selected as the most appropriate for dimension reduction. In order to validate the performance of various feature extraction methods, this paper used in four classifiers (ED, WED, NN and KNN) to conduct experiments, and get 89.6% of accuracy for 65 different people. The experimental results shows the effectiveness of the proposed method which to extract more features using Gabor filters and reduce the dimensionality of the features using multi-stage based feature extraction and selection methods.

2. Data acquisition and pre-processing

The common steps of writer identification include data acquisition, pre-processing, feature extraction, and classification. The data acquisition is the first phase for writer identification and verification systems. Subjects are asked to write their handwritings on a paper with their natural writing style. Because of the handwriting images contaminated by noise and letters with different sizes, the efficient features are extracted only after they are pre-processed. Different methods and algorithms (Said et al. 2000; Schomaker & Bulacu, 2004) are used for pre-processing and feature extraction phases based on the handwriting styles. The handwriting is taken as an image containing some special texture, and writer identification is regarded as texture identification here. Uyghur handwriting texture (Fig. 1: e) has its own characters compare to other languages such as Latin, Chinese and Arabic (Fig. 1: b, c, d) so improved methods are implemented in pre-processing and feature extraction steps. The nature of Uyghur handwriting is indicated before description of data acquisition.

2.1 The nature of Uyghur handwriting text

The Uyghur are a Turkic-speaking ethnic group inhabiting Eastern and Central Asia. Today, Uyghurs mainly live in the Xinjiang Uyghur Autonomous Region (hereafter: Xinjiang) in China. Arabic based Uyghur script is an official writing system in Xinjiang, while Cyrillicbased Uyghur script is still used by Uyghurs in former Soviet Union Republics and Latin-based Uyghur script are also in use[1]. The handwriting of Arabic-based Uyghur script (hereafter: Uyghur) used widely in Xinjiang area is studied in this paper.

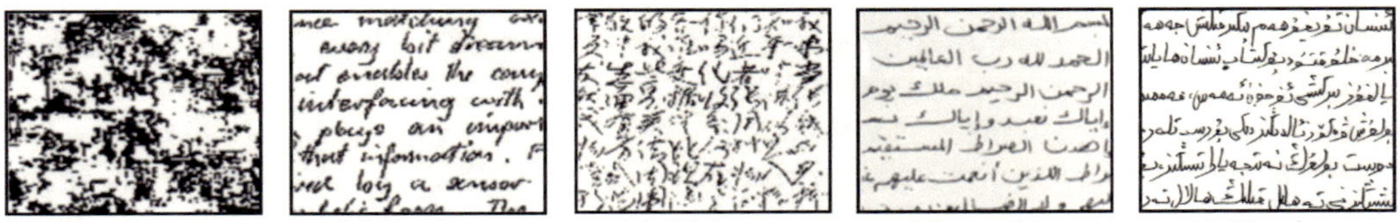

(a) Random texture (b) Latin (c) Chinese (d) Arabic (e) Uyghur

Fig. 1. Random texture image (a) and texture images of different handwriting

Uyghur character is composed of 32 letters including 8 vowel letters and 24 consonant letters, besides 4 kinds of different forms for each character. Thus, 32 letters become more than 120 character styles.

1. The writing direction of Uyghur character is from right to left, from left down right for the line progression. There are 4 different writing forms for Uyghur letter: (i) "initial form": only the suffix is connected with the next character, (ii) "intermediate form": initial and suffix are connected with adjacent letter, (iii) "final form": only the initial is connected with the above letter, and (iv) "isolated form": initial and suffix are not connected with adjacent letter.
2. The vocabulary of Uyghur character is composed of one or several letters. According to rules of writing, these letters will form one or several letter passages by initial and suffix connections. For a block letter or handwriting, the letters are connected along a certain level, which is called base line.
3. Unequal width of letters. This phenomenon happens not only on different letters, but also on the 4 different forms of certain letters. Furthermore, a straight line will be adopted to fill in the spaces among the letter to let a line of text distribute uniformly.
4. The vocabulary of Uyghur character is composed of syllable, which is generally constructed from the combination of vowel and consonant, where vowel is the centre. It is definite that the composition of syllable and vocabulary is regular. There is a blank space between two vocabularies (Fig. 2).

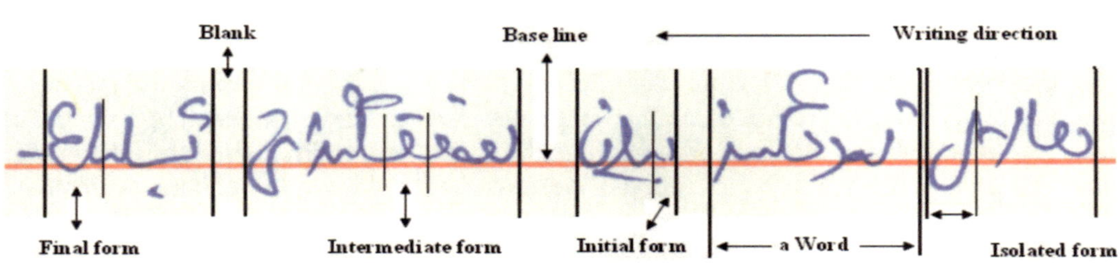

Fig. 2. An example of Uyghur Handwriting

[1] Uyghur alphabet. See http://en.wikipedia.org/wiki/Uyghur_alphabet

5. The stroke of Uyghur character is not fixed. The numbers of strokes for the same Uyghur word are different from person to person. Especially, they are different with position, size, longitude, slant angle and structure. Fig. 4 shows the same word written by different person.

In Fig. 3: (a) to (e), the strokes of the first letter"ش" are consisted of 4, 3, 4, 6, 2 strokes respectively. The situation becomes more complicated if a word or a sentence is concerned without misspelling. Therefore, the local characters of Uyghur handwriting further increased the difficulty level for Uyghur handwriting based writer identification.

(a) (b) (c) (d) (e)

Fig. 3. The Uyghur word "Xinjiang" (in Uyghur - شىنجاڭ) written by 5 different people

2.2 Data acquisition

We selected 353 Uyghur participants for data collection and asked each participant to write anything to fill 3 sheets of letter size paper. They were instructed to write in his/her natural handwriting just by keeping enough spaces between words and lines. They wrote in black or blue ink on the grid paper with red or green lines. To increase the diversity of Uyghur handwriting, the participants are selected respect of their age, gender, education, etc. One part of them is from elementary school to graduate students, while the remainder are adults of various professions. Among them, the oldest person was 80 years old and the youngest was 9. Databases of participants were established including all data collector's personal information (such as age, gender, education, job, etc.). The handwritten documents are digitally scanned using a HP scanner with a resolution of 300 dpi and saved in bmp image format. Thus, the sample database of Uyghur handwriting was set up.

2.3 Pre-processing

The input image contains noise and Uyghur characters of different sizes and spaces between text lines, so original image should be pre-processed before feature extraction. Based on the nature of Uyghur characters similar to Arabic and Persian, the minimum unit to be selected in pre-processing is connected components which are consist of one or several letters unlike Latin and Chinese. Inspired by the work of (He et al., 2008; Schomaker & Bulacu, 2004), we propose a procedure of automatic pre-processing as described below:

1. Removing the background and binarization. Collected handwriting samples were written on a plain graph paper. Although the grid of the graph paper does not affect the writing style, it will affect on accessing handwriting information. The selected cell lines of graph paper are in red colour, while the text colour is black or blue. Therefore, the method to remove the background in this paper is mainly the histograms of the red and green by setting the higher pixel component of the red and green to white, and others to black. It is not only to remove the background, but also to get binarized image as indicated in Fig. 4 (b).

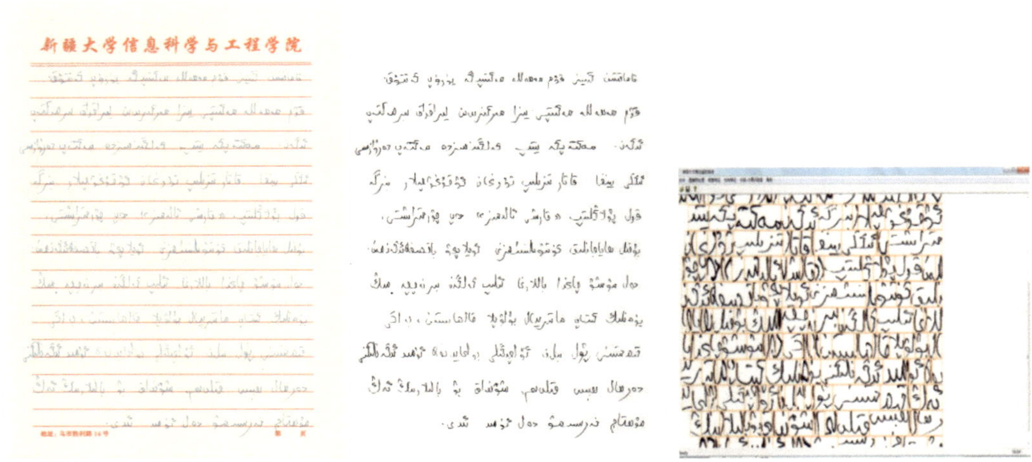

(a) Original image (b) Binarized image (c) Texture image

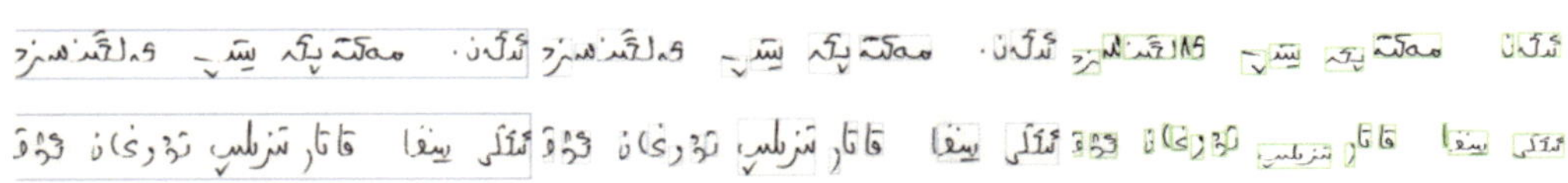

(d) Locating the line (e) Connected component (f) Normalized image

Fig. 4. The steps of Uyghur handwriting image preprocessing

2. The binarized image contains a number of discrete noises. To avoid affecting the feature extraction, the discrete noise is removed. According to the real situation in handwriting samples, the size of the discrete noise threshold is set to 10. If the observation points related to the number of black spots are less than 10, it is considered as noise points and they are filled with white points.
3. Locating the line. Uyghur character has distinctive characteristics of connected letters with different width. A large number of additional components are exist in Uyghur text, so the blank space can be the space between two lines, or the space between additional part and the main part of a character in a line. Thus, a threshold has to be set, where the blank space exceeded the threshold value is the gap between text lines, or it is the gap within a line. Thus, the contour of the text image can be obtained from a text image. Writing along the baseline is a major feature of Uyghur, these characteristics in a line of text images are expressed with pixels concentrated around a particular horizontal line as well as on the baseline domain. When we take the horizontal projection along contour of text line images, two maximum values within the horizontal direction are set as upper and lower boundary in the text baseline domain and boundary of each line can be segmented. (Fig. 4(d))
4. Separating the connected components. After locating each line in Uyghur handwriting, directional statistics was performed for black pixels on each text line where the connected component is the place with small number of black pixels. The distance of blank space for text line images can be obtained through Vertical Projection Profile. From the text line, independent form of letters or their connection is extracted and be indicated as shown in Fig. 4(e). The connected component between letters is linked with relatively flat straight lines.

5. Normalization. The character normalization in writer identification is required for the tilted character, position of stroke and orientation to be stable. Unlike other languages, Uyghur text has significantly connected letters that each word in Uyghur writing is interconnected, so it is enough for adjusting the vertical height of the character. (Fig. 4(f))
6. Making texture image and dividing. After removing the spaces between connected components and lines in normalized image, the handwriting texture image in (Fig. 4(c)) is obtained. The size of texture image here is selected to be 1024 × 1024 pixels. In order to ensure the standard and accuracy of texture feature extraction, we divided the normalized image (size of 1024 × 1024 pixels) into 16 sub-images with the size of not more than 256 × 256 pixels. An example of image pre-processing is shown in Fig. 4.

3. Feature extraction

Multi-channel Gabor wavelet technique is becoming very popular in texture analysis, and has been successfully applied to a broad range of image processing tasks (Jain, & Farrokhnia, 1991). In this paper, we have proposed a method for texture feature extraction and selection by integrating Gabor filters, Genetic algorithm, Principal component analysis, Kernel Principal Component analysis and Independent Component analysis for Uyghur handwriting based writer identification.

3.1 Gabor filter

The two-dimensional Gabor filter (Jain & Farrokhnia, 1991; Plamondon et al., 1989) can be mathematically expressed as:

$$g(x,y) = \frac{1}{2\pi\sigma^2}\exp[-(\frac{x^2+y^2}{2\sigma^2})] \tag{1}$$

We can model each cortical channel by a pair of Gabor filters $h_e(x, y)$ and $h_o(x, y)$ as follows:

$$\begin{cases} h_e(x,y) = g(x,y)\cos[2\pi f(x\cos\theta + y\sin\theta)] \\ h_o(x,y) = g(x,y)\sin[2\pi f(x\cos\theta + y\sin\theta)] \end{cases} \tag{2}$$

where f and θ are the spatial frequency and the orientation of the Gabor envelope, and $h_e(x, y)$ and $h_o(x, y)$ denote the even and odd symmetrical Gabor filters respectively.

Texture feature extraction requires both radial frequency and orientation. Tan (1992) showed that, for any image of size N×N (where N is a power of 2) the important frequency components are within $f \leq N/4$ (cycles/degree). For Uyghur handwriting, N is set to 256, and so frequencies of 2, 4, 8, 16, 32, and 64 cycles/ degree are used. For each central frequency f, filtering is performed at values of 0°, 15°, 30°, 45°, 60°, 75°, 90°, 105°, 120°, 135°, 150°, and 165°, which gives a total of 72 output images (12 for each frequency, as shown in Fig. 5). The mean and standard deviation of the output images are chosen to represent texture features. In this way, a total of 144 features are extracted from a given image. They form a 144 dimensional feature vector which is reduced using the genetic algorithm.

3.2 Two-stage based feature extraction and selection

The two stage-based feature extraction and selection methods in here are indicated to take high dimensional feature vectors based on the character of Uyghur handwriting image first, and then effective features are select using some algorithms such as GA and PCA.

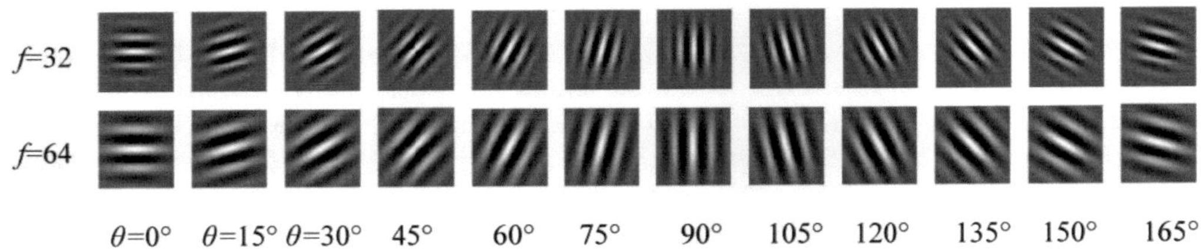

Fig. 5. Real part of Gabor filter with different frequencies (f) and orientations (θ)

3.2.1 Feature extraction using Gabor filter and Genetic algorithm

Genetic algorithms (GA), which are algorithmic models based on a Darwinian-type survival-of-the fittest strategy with sexual reproduction, were firstly introduced by John Holland in 1960s (Holland, 1992). Genetic algorithm is a kind of computerized procedure to search from a group of random initial solutions which are so called population (Goldberg, 1989). Each individual in the population is a possible solution of problem which is so called chromosome (or genes). It is represented in binary as strings of 0s and 1s. These chromosomes are evolved continuously in follow-up iteration, this is called genetic. Fitness is measurement of chromosomes' fair or foul in each generation, and new population created are called offspring which is born through crossover or mutation of previous chromosome. In a new population, the size of population is maintained as a constant based on the fitness selecting parts of offspring and weeding other parts of offspring out. The fitness value of individual with higher probability is selected. Thus, the algorithm converges to the best chromosome through evolving several generations, and it may be the optimum solution of the problem. The feature vectors extracted from Uyghur texture are reduced using the GA and feature selection algorithm (Siedlecki & Sklansky, 1989), as shown Fig. 6.

The input argument of the population is a vector of row indices from the training data. The fitness is a linear combination of the error rate and the posterior probability of the classifier:

$$q(f_j) = 100 \times e(f_j) + 1 - \frac{\sum_{i=1}^{M} r(f_j)}{M} \tag{3}$$

where M is the number of individual features f_j, $e(f_j)$ is the classification error rate, $r(f_j)$ are the maximum values along the columns of $u(f_j)$, and $u(f_j)$ is a matrix containing posterior probabilities that the *k*th training class is the source of the *i*th sample feature. The critical value of fitness $q\ (f_j^*)$ is set to 2.0×10^{-7} here.

3.2.2 Feature extraction using Gabor filter and principal component analysis

Principal component analysis (PCA) is known as Karhunen-Loeve transform. The objective of the study is to perform appropriate linear combination of multi-dimensional data and orthogonal transformation (Dunteman, 1989). By controlling the mean square error in data, dimension reduction and compression are perform for high-dimensional linear space.

The high dimensional vector should be reduced, because Gabor function is non-orthogonal, and redundant information is present in the filtered image (Dunn, 1995), and from the calculation point of view, it is necessary to reduce the dimension of feature vector for classification (Chen & Wang, 2007). From above Gabor filter, we get a high-dimensional Gabor feature vector $F \in R^k$, where k is the dimension of feature vector:

$$k = f \cdot \theta \cdot \mu^2 \tag{4}$$

where f and θ are the centre frequency of Gabor filter and its orientation respectively, and u is the size of filter window.

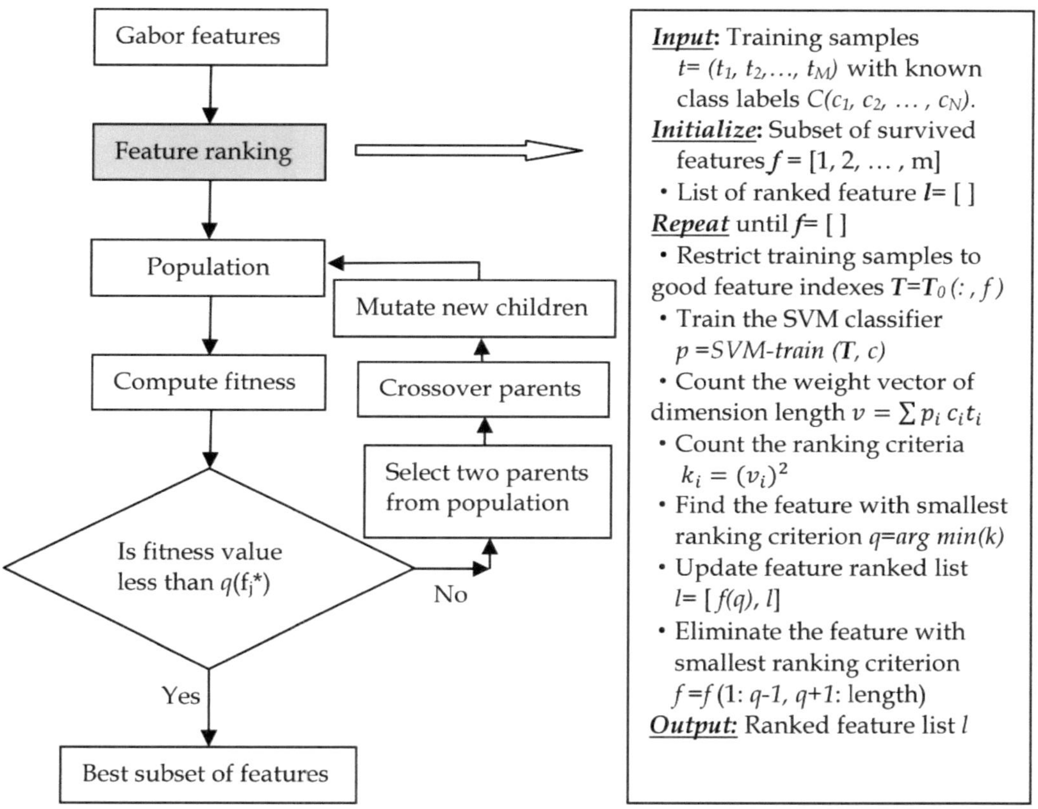

Fig. 6. The flow chart of selecting best features with Genetic algorithm

PCA is a classical dimension reduction method which has the important feature of using low-dimensional subspace to represent the original high-dimensional data based on the minimum mean square error (MSE). To perform PCA dimensionality reduction for high-dimensional Gabor feature vector F:

$$X = PF \tag{5}$$

where $P = (p_1, p_2, ..., p_k)^T \in R^{m \times k}$, $m < k$ is the characteristic matrix, output $X \in R^m$ is low-dimensional feature vector.

It can be seen from the previous procedure that PCA is a linear mapping algorithm, but PCA can only be used to remove the correlation between features (ignoring the non-linear correlation between the features), and it is not obtained the independent components of the feature, and it is a signal analysis method based on second-order statistical properties, cannot use the data in higher order statistics, so the transformed data may still exist between the higher order redundant information.

3.3 Three-stage based feature extraction and selection

Since PCA has some limitation mentioned above, it is necessary to use the combinations of PCA and ICA methods, to implement dimension reduction for high-dimensional feature vector, to remove redundant information in filtered images, and to obtain higher-order statistical characteristics of the handwriting texture in order to make better use of handwriting texture classification.

3.3.1 Feature extraction using Gabor filter plus PCA and ICA

Independent Component Analysis (ICA) is a higher-order statistics-based method of data analysis related to Blind Signal Separation (BSS) (Comon, 1994; Hyvärinen & Oja, 1997). BSS problem assumes that a linear combination of N independent targets (random variable) produces M observed variables, and the purpose of ICA is to identify the mixing matrix from the observed variables. When we perform texture analysis using ICA, the given texture image is considered to be a series of unknown statistical mixture of independent random variables. Jenssen & Eltoft (2003) proposed the concept of ICA filter bank for texture image segmentation and suggested that the performance of segmenting multi-texture image is close to or better than Gabor filters. The paper used ICA techniques for obtaining independent components of high-dimensional feature vector in features, and established an independent Gabor features used for handwriting classification.

We made the output of PCA, $X \in R^m$ as an observed vector for ICA analysis and assume that X is a linear combination of n unknown independent components $S = [s_1, s_2, \ldots, s_n]$, and then the linear relationship can be written as formula form as the model basic of ICA :

$$X=AS \tag{6}$$

where A is m × n unknown mixing matrix of full-rank, S is approximate independent component. The objective of ICA is to find a separation matrix W, making the output:

$$Y=WX \tag{7}$$

When the separation matrix W is the inverse of mixing matrix A, the independent component S can be accurately extracted, or it needs to sort and change the magnitude (Chen & Wang, 2006, 2007). Calculated Y is the last feature vectors used for texture classification. Hyvärinen (1997) proposed more popular matrix separation method according to very small mutual information and equivalence of bigger negative entropy, introduced non-linear monotonic estimated negative entropy function. This algorithm is used in this paper to get independent Gabor features, the formula is as follows:

$$\begin{cases} \vec{W}^{+} = \vec{W} - \dfrac{\mu\left[\vec{C}^{-1}E\{\vec{X}g(\vec{W}^{T}\vec{X})\} - \beta\vec{W}\right]}{E\{g'(\vec{W}^{T}\vec{X})\} - \beta} \\ \vec{W}^{*} = \dfrac{\vec{W}^{+}}{\sqrt{(\vec{W}^{+})^{T}\vec{C}\vec{W}^{+}}} \end{cases} \tag{8}$$

where W^+ and W^* respectively indicate the current and new value obtained by iteration. μ is the step size with initial value of 1, it decreases rapidly with the increased number of iterations, $\beta=E\{W^TXg(W^TX)\}$ is used for normalization to improve the robustness of the algorithm, g is the contrast function, the covariance matrix can be obtained for the observation vector X as $G(u) = u^4 / 4$, $g(u) = u^3.c = E\{XX^T\}$.

3.3.2 Feature extraction using Gabor filter plus PCA and KPCA

Kernel Principal Component Analysis (KPCA) algorithm uses kernel function to obtain the arbitrary high-order correlation between input variants, and the principal components needed through the inner production between input data. After SchÄolkopf et al. (1998) applied Kernel component analysis in feature extraction, it became more popular in image vision, content based retrieval and text classification fields. The PCA outputs are used as the selection vector of KPCA, assumed that the features of mapping is centralized as shown:

$$\sum_{i=1}^{N} \xi(x_i) = 0 \tag{9}$$

where ξ is a non-linear mapping, N is the total entries of mapping feature. After mapping, the features of the covariance matrix C such that:

$$C = \frac{1}{N}\sum_{i=1}^{N} \xi(x_i)\,\xi(x_i)^T \tag{10}$$

The characteristic equation can be found from

$$hV=CV \tag{11}$$

According to the theory of reproducing kernel, feature vector V must be in the space domain, $\{\xi(x_i),\ldots,\xi(x_N)\}$ which is

$$V = \sum_{i=1}^{N} \alpha_i\,\xi(x_i) \tag{12}$$

Defining an N × N matrix K

$$K_{ij} = k(x_i, x_j) = \xi(x_i)^T\xi(x_j) \tag{13}$$

K is called the nuclear matrix. The substitution of (9), (10) and (11) into (13) produces:

$$K\alpha=Nh\alpha \tag{14}$$

By solving (11), the feature vectors V are transformed into the feature vector α of the characteristic equation (14). Based on the above definition, the kernel matrix K is symmetric, positive semi-definite matrix, and its eigenvalues are non-negative according to matrix theory. By solving (14), a group of non-zero eigenvalue h_j and the corresponding α^j ($j = 1, 2, \ldots, p$) are obtained that satisfy the normalization condition (15)

$$h_j\left(\alpha^j,\alpha^j\right)=1 \tag{15}$$

According to (11), the principal components V_j ($j = 1, \ldots, p$) are obtained from the projection of feature space. Let x to be test samples after PCA processing, its projection is V_j

$$\left(V^j\right)^T\xi(x) = \sum_{i=1}^{N} \alpha_i^j\,\xi(x_i)\xi(x) = \sum_{i=1}^{N} \alpha_i^j\,k(x_i, x) \tag{16}$$

Neither (13) nor (16) requires the $\xi(x_i)$ in explicit form, and they are only needed in dot products. Therefore, we are able to use kernel functions for computing these dot products without actually performing the map ξ (SchÄolkopf & Smola, 2001). The dot products are the features selected from KPCA.

4. Writer identification

The classification experiments using selected classifier are processed after extracting and selecting features. This chapter will describe the classifiers to be used and their experimental results based on the size of our database and feature extraction methods.

4.1 Classification

In theory, any kind of classifier can be applicable during the identification phase. Considering the smaller scale of sample data for Uyghur, we use the Euclidean distance classifier, the weighted Euclidean distance classifier, the nearest classifier and K-Nearest Neighbour classifier (Plamondon & Lorette, 1989). Definition of them as following:

1. Euclidean Distance (ED) classifier. Commonly used Euclidean distance is:

$$d_E(u,v) = [(u-v)^T(u-v)]^{\frac{1}{2}} = [\sum_{i=1}^{n}(u_i - v_i)^2]^{1/2} \tag{17}$$

where u_i and v_i are feature vectors and i=1,2,…n.

2. Weighted Euclidean Distance (WED) classifier. Unknown handwriting feature vectors are compared with the trained known samples of handwriting. When the weighted Euclidean distance between the feature vector and k class sample is smallest, the input handwriting is classified as k-class handwriting. Weighted Euclidean distance is calculated as:

$$WED(k) = \sum_{i=1}^{M} \frac{\left(f_l - f_l^{(k)}\right)^2}{\left(\delta_l^{(k)}\right)^2} \tag{18}$$

where f_l is the lth feature of unknown sample, $f_l^{(k)}$ and $\delta_l^{(k)}$ are respectively the sample mean and sample standard deviation of lth feature of write k respectively.

3. Nearest Neighbour (NN) classifier. It classifies the handwriting by decision-making rule. For the nearest neighbour decision-making, assume there are c categories $\omega 1$, $\omega 2$, …, ωc for pattern identification, each class indicates Ni samples to be classified, i=1,2,…,c. The discriminate function for the class can be written as:

$$g_i(x) = \min_k \left\| x - x_i^k \right\|, \ k = 1,2,\dots,N_i \tag{19}$$

where the subscript i of x_i^k indicates ω_i class, k indicates ω_i class. According to above equation, the decision-making rules can be written as:

$$g_{j(x)} = \min_i g_i\,(x), \ \ i = 1,2,\dots,c \tag{20}$$

where decision maker $x \in \omega_j$.

4. K-Nearest (K-NN) Neighbour classifier. When we use K-NN classifier, the ideal characteristics of each trained class K is f_k, the detected characteristics of unknown writer is U. To determine class K of the writer, the similarity of each class is measured by calculating the distance between feature vectors f_k and U. The taken Euclidean distance, which is the distance d_k among the class for unknown writer is:

$$d_k = \left[\sum_{j=1}^{N} \left(U_j - f_{kj}\right)^2\right]^{1/2} \tag{21}$$

The writer assigned to the class R such that:

$$d_R = \min(d_k) \tag{22}$$

where k is the class number, and k=1,2,..., N. We took k=5 in our experiment.

4.2 Experimental results

We selected 65 Uyghur participants' handwritings from our database. In our experiment, we select size as1024 ×1024 pixels. In order to create a number of small images which belong to the same class, each of the1024×1024 images created was divided into non-overlapping 256×256 sub-images, thus forming 16 sub-images from each image. 12 sub-images from the first document were used for the training data set, and 9 sub-images from the second document were used as the testing data set. Four classifiers (ED, WED, NN, and KNN) were used each set of experiments. We performed three kinds of experiments:

1. Result with Gabor filtering. Firstly, features were extracted with frequencies of 8, 16, 32, and 64 cycles /degree. For each central frequency f, filtering was performed at 0°, 45°, 90°, and 165°. Thus a 32 dimensional feature vector was obtained. The results show poor classification rates that indicated as a table 1. Secondly, extracted 144 features as explained in section 3.1, achieved higher identification rates than mentioned above. NN classifier got a top-10 classification rate of 81.1%. Others are illustrated in table 1.

Classifier	Identification accuracy using two types of feature vectors					
	Extractd 32 dimensional features			Extractd 144 dimensional features		
	Top-1	Top-5	Top-10	Top-1	Top-5	Top-10
ED	41.5%	47.1%	51.4%	49.8%	52.3%	54.7%
WED	42.6%	49.9%	58.7%	54.0%	61.5%	66.8%
NN	56.3%	64.2%	71.0%	67.4%	76.9%	81.1%
K-NN	56.8%	63.9%	70.2%	68.7%	75.2%	79.5%

Table 1. Identification accuracy using Gabor features

2. Result using two-stage based feature extraction methods. The 144 dimensional Gabor feature vectors were reduced to 48 and 55 by selecting the appropriate features using GA feature selection model and PCA respectively. The identification rates is higher than the method of using Gabor features directly, the best Top-1 identification accuracy is 78.2% and the Top-10 accuracy reaches 86.9% with K-NN classifier, as shoved in table 2.

Classifier	Identification accuracy using two-stage based feature extraction methods					
	Gabor+GA			Gabor+PCA		
	Top-1	Top-5	Top-10	Top-1	Top-5	Top-10
ED	57.6%	59.5%	62.3%	51.6%	60.7%	69.4%
WED	58.9%	60.8%	61.5%	63.8%	73.0%	76.3%
NN	77.4%	80.1%	82.6%	71.7%	76.5%	83.2%
K-NN	78.2%	81.4%	83.7%	76.2%	82.8%	86.9%

Table 2. Identification accuracy using three-stage based feature extraction methods

3. Result from three-stage based feature extraction methods. The 144 dimensional Gabor feature vectors were reduced to 42 by selecting the most appropriate features using a Gabor plus PCA & ICA method or Gabor plus PCA & KPCA method. We obtain a best Top-1 identification accuracy is 89.6% and the Top-10 accuracy reaches 91.8% with K-NN that is higher than other's in the paper as indicated table 3.

Classifier	Identification accuracy using three-stage based feature extraction methods					
	Gabor+PCA+ICA			Gabor+PCA+KPCA		
	Top-1	Top-5	Top-10	Top-1	Top-5	Top-10
ED	57.7%	63.9%	69.3%	61.0%	64.3%	70.2%
WED	70.1%	73.0%	79.6%	72.5%	75.4%	78.9%
NN	79.8%	82.2%	84.5%	83.2%	86.7%	88.1%
K-NN	87.5%	88.3%	90.0%	89.6%	90.2%	91.8%

Table 3. Identification accuracy using three-stage based feature extraction methods

In order to see the efficiency of the method, it is compared with methods used for Uyghur handwriting based writer identification and related methods used for different languages indicated as following Table 4. and Table 5.

Authers (year)	Used methods	Experimented person No.	Identification rate
Ubul et al. (2008)	Gabor + GA	23 person	88.0%
Ubul et al. (2009)	Gabor+PCA+ICA	55 person	92.5%
Li et al. (2009)	Microstructure feature	120 person	91.7%
Abdiryim (2010)	Gabor	17 person	79.8%
This paper	Gabor+PCA+KPCA	65 person	89.6%

Table 4. Identification accuracy comparing with the methods used for Uyhgur handwriting

Authers (year)	Used feature extraction methods and identification rates (person)				language
	Gabor	Gabor+GA	PCA+LDA	Gabor+PCA	
Said et al. (2000)	96% (40)				Latin
Deng et al. (2008)			88.41% (138)		Chinese
Al-Demor et al. (2007)	85% (22)	90% (22)			Arabic
This paper	81.1% (65)	83.7% (65)		86.9% (65)	Uyghur

Table 5. Comparing with the related methods used for other languages

Among various kinds of approaches used for Uyghur handwriting based writer identification as indicated Table 4, the Microstructure feature based identification method is indicated its high efficiency (91.7% of identification rate), but the three stage based feature extraction approach (Gabor+PCA+KPCA) proposed in this paper still showed higher recognition rates (89.6% of identification rate) than others. It is obvious in Table 5 that the Gabor based feature extraction method is more suitable for Latin (96% of identification rate) than Uyghur (81.1% of identification rate), but its identification rates can be increased by using Gabor plus GA method (83.7% of identification rate) and Gabor plus PCA (86.9% of identification rate) method.

It can be seen from the experimental result that to extract high dimensional feature vectors in texture image are play vital role to increase the identification rates, but needs to large amount of computation. The purposed method which to extract more features and reduce them to with feature selection algorithms is achieved better identification rates than traditional Gabor based method for Uyghur handwriting.

5. Conclusion and future work

Writer identification is a popular research field in many languages such as English, Chinese, Arabic, Uyghur, etc. The approaches of writer identification methods are dependent on the languages, because letters in different languages have different patterns. In this chapter, we have proposed a method for texture feature extraction and selection by integrating Gabor filters, Genetic algorithm(GA), Principal component analysis (PCA), Kernel Principal component analysis (KPCA) and independent component analysis (ICA) for Uyghur handwriting based writer identification. The texture image is firstly formed by connecting components via projection profile on the basis of Uyghur handwriting's nature. It is filtered by a given bank of Gabor filters, and then higher dimensional feature vectors are constructed from the filtered texture images. Next, the dimensionality of these vectors is reduced by means of GA, PCA and KPCA. Finally, the independent components in the resulting vectors with reduced dimensionality are analyzed and extracted. Four classification techniques are used: Euclidean Distance Classifier (ED), Weighted Euclidean Distance Classifier (WED), Nearest Neighbour Classifier (NN), and K-Nearest Neighbour (K-NN) Classifier. Experiments are performed using Uyghur handwriting samples from 65 different people and very promising results of 89.6% correct identification are achieved.

In the future work, the number of samples in Uyghur handwriting database will be further expanded. For the texture feature extraction, on one hand, further research will be carried on the local features of Uyghur handwriting. On the other hand, other effective methods, such as GLCM, X-Gabor, auto-correlation function, the wavelet transform etc will be validated to use the global feature extraction used for the Uyghur texture feature extraction. In addition, combination of the characteristics of Uyghur handwriting with the feature optimization and dimensionality reduction algorithms further improve the performance. About the classifiers, we will try to use other classifiers such as Support Vector Machine (SVM) classifier, artificial neural network classifier (ANN), Linear Discriminate Classifier (LDC), Bayesian classifier, Multi-class classifier or the combinations of classifiers and so on.

6. Acknowledgment

This work is sponsored by the National Natural Science Foundation of China (No. 61163028), the Minorities Special Training Plan Project of Science and Technology Bureau Xinjiang Uyghur Autonomous Region (No. 201023116) and the Open Project of Xinjiang Laboratory of Multi-language Information Technology (No. 049807).

7. References

Al-Dmour, A. & Zitar, R. A. (2007). Arabic Writer Identification based on Hybrid Spectral-statistical Measures. *Journal of Experimental & Theoretical Artificial Intelligence*, Vol. 19, No. 4, (December 2007), pp. 307–332, ISSN 1362–3079

Chen, Y & Wang, R. (2006). Texture segmentation using independent component analysis of Gabor features. *Proceeding of the ICPR 18th International Conference on Pattern Recognition*, Vol. 2, pp. 147-150, ISBN 0-7695-2521-0, Hong Kong, China, August 20-24, 2006

Chen, Y. & Wang, R. (2007). A method for texture classification by integrating Gabor filters and ICA. *Journal of Acta Electronica Sinca*, (in Chinese), Vol. 35, No. 2, (February 2007), pp. 299-303, ISSN 0732-2112

Comon, P. (1994). Independent component analysis, a new concept?. *Signal Processing*, Vol. 36, No. 3, (April 1994), pp. 287–314, ISSN 0165-1684

Deng, W.; Chen, Q & Yan,Y. et al. (2008). Off- line Chinese writer identification based on character-level decision combination. *Procedding of the International Symposiums on Information Processing*, pp. 762 – 765, ISBN 978-0-7695-3151-9, Moscow, Russia, May 23-25, 2008

Dunn, D. & Higgins. W. E. (1995). Optimal Gabor filters for texture segmentation. *IEEE Transactions on Image Processing*, Vol. 4, No. 7, (July 1995), pp. 947 - 964. ISSN 1057-7149

Dunteman, G. H. (1989). *Pricipal Component Analysis*. Sage Publications Ltd. ISBN 978-0-803-93104-6, London, United Kingdom

Fukunaga, K. (1990). *Introduction to Statistical Pattern Recognition* (second edition). Academic Press, ISBN 0-32-269853-7, New York, United States

Goldberg, D. E. (1989). *Genetic Algorithms in Search, Optimization, and Machine Learning, Reading*. Addison-Wesley, ISBN 0201157675, Boston, Massachusetts, United States

He, Z. Y.; You, X. & Tang, Y. Y. (2007). Writer identification of Chinese handwriting documents using hidden Markov tree model. *Pattern Recognition*, Vol. 41, No. 4, (April 2007), pp. 1295 - 1307, ISSN 0031-3203 41

He, Z. Y.; You, X. & Tang, Y. Y. (2008). Writer identification using global wavelet-based features. *Neurocomputing*, Vol. 71, No. 4, (February 2008), pp. 1832–1841, ISSN 0925-2312

Helli, B & Moghaddam, M. E. (2010). A text-independent Persian writer identification based on feature relation graph (FRG). Pattern Recognition, Vol. 43, No. 6 (June 2010), pp. 2199–2209, ISSN 0031-3203

Holland, J. H. (1992). *Adaptation in Natural and Artificial Systems* (second edition), MIT press, ISBN 978-0-262-58111-0, Cambridge, Massachusetts , United States

Hyvärinen, A. & Oja, E. (1997). A fast fixed-point algorithm for independent component analysis. *Neural Computation*, Vol. 9, No. 7, (September 1997), pp. 1483-1492, ISSN 0899-7667

Jain, A. K. & Farrokhnia, F. (1991). Unsupervised texture segmentation using Gabor filters, *Pattern Recognition*, vol. 24, No. 12 (May 1991), pp. 1167-1186, ISSN 0031-3203

Jain, A. K.; Flynn, P. & Ross, A. (2008). *Handbook of Biometrics*. Springer, ISBN 978-0-387-71040-2, New York, United States

Jenssen, R. & Eltoft, T. (2003). ICA filter bank for segmentation of textured images. *Proceeding of the 4th International Symposium on Independent Component Analysis and Blind Signal Separation*, pp. 827-832, ISBN 4-9901531-0-3, Nara, Japan, April 1-3, 2003

Li, X.; Ding, X. & Peng, L. (2009). A microstructure feature based text-independent method of writer identification for multilingual handwritings. *Acta Automatica Sinica* (in *Chinese)*, Vol. 35, No. 9 (September 2009), pp. 1199-1208, ISSN 1874-1029

Plamondon, R. & Lorette, G. (1989). Automatic Signature Verification and Writer Identification - the State of the Art. *Pattern Recognition*, Vol. 22, No. 2, (January 1989), pp. 107–131, ISSN 0031-3203

Raxidin, A. (2010). Study on Gabor wavelet based feature extraction method for Uyghur handwriting. Journal of Hotan Teachers College, Vol. 25, No. 5, (October 2010), pp. 184-185, ISSN 1671-0908

Said, H. E. S.; Tan, T. N. & Baker, K. D. (2000). Personal Identification based on Handwriting. *Pattern Recognition*, Vol. 33, No. 1, (January 2000), pp. 149- 160, ISSN 0031-3203

SchÄolkopf, B. Smola, A. & Mäuller, K. R. (1998). Nonlinear component analysis as a kernel eigenvalue problem. *Neural computation*, Vol.10, No.5, (July 1998), pp.1299-1310, ISSN 0899-7667

SchÄolkopf, B. & Smola, A. J. (2001). *Learning with Kernels: Support Vector Machines, Regularization, Optimization, and Beyond*, MIT Press, ISBN 0262194759, Cambridge, Massachusetts, United States

Schomaker, L. & Bulacu, M. (2004). Writer identification using connected component contours and edge-based featurs of uppercase western script. *IEEE Transactions on Pattern Analysis and Machine Intelligence*, Vol. 26, No. 6, (June 2004), pp. 787–798, ISSN 0162-8828

Siedlecki, W. & Sklansky, J. (1989). A note on genetic algorithms for large-scale feature selection. *Pattern Recognition Letters*, Vol. 10, No. 5, (November 1989), pp. 335–347, ISSN 0167-8655

Srihari, S.; Cha, S.; Arora, H. & Lee, S. (2002). Individuality of handwriting. *Journal of Forensic Science*. Vol. 47, No. 4, (July 2002), pp. 1–17. ISSN 0022-1198

Tan, T. N. (1992). Texture feature extraction via visual cortical channel modeling. *Proceeding of the ICPR 11th International Conference on Pattern Recognition*, Vol. 3, pp. 607–610, ISBN 0-8186-2920, Hague, The Netherlands, August 31 - September 3, 1992

Ubul, K.; Hamdulla, A. & Aysa, A. et al. (2008). Research on Uyghur Off-line Handwriting-based Writer Identification. *Proceeding of the 9th International Conference on Signal Processing*, pp. 1656-1659, ISBN 978-1-4244-2178-7, Beijing, China, October 26-29, 2008

Ubul, K.; Tursun, D. & Hamdulla, A. et al. (2009). A feature selection and extraction method for Uyghur handwriting-based writer identification. *Proceeding of the 1st International Conference on Computational Intelligence and Natural Computing*, Vol. 2, pp. 345 –348, ISBN 978-0-7695-3645-3, Wuhan, China, June 6-7, 2009

14

Towards the Early Diagnosis of Alzheimer's Disease Through the Application of a Multicriteria Classification Model

Amaury Brasil, Plácido Rogério Pinheiro
and André Luís Vasconcelos Coelho
*University of Fortaleza (UNIFOR), Graduate Program in Applied Informatics, Fortaleza (CE)
Brazil*

1. Introduction

The Alzheimer's disease (AD) is a progressive and degenerative disease of the brain which causes a serious impairment over its two main activities: thinking and memory. According to Celsis (Celsis, 2000), AD is the most common form of dementia among the elderly population, comprising up to 75% of all dementia cases. AD causes a gradual loss of intellectual abilities with deterioration in cognition, function, and behavior, affecting many aspects of an individual life.

This way, with the decline of the normal functioning over the nervous and other bodily systems, and with the natural behavioral and personality changes, the identification of what constitutes abnormal impairment becomes a hard task. Davidoff (Davidoff, 1986) argues that the problem over the AD diagnosis is not only related to the current level of understanding of the disease, but also to the comprehension of the normal process involving the patients age. For the author, there are yet no consistent established set of values for what would be a normal level of impairment in the elderly. To overcome these difficulties, some researchers (Braak & Braak, 1997; Elias et al., 2000; Kawas et al., 2003) have demonstrated that the AD first symptoms appears relatively early in life, and it evolves during lifetime. This fact raises the chances of identifying the pathology decades before a clinical diagnosis of dementia can be made.

Trying to detect potential patients with AD as early as possible, many studies (Brasil, Pinheiro & Coelho, 2009; Castro et al., 2007a;b; Mortimer et al., 2005; Nestor et al., 2004) have investigated potential tests and exams that, through a functional and cognitive analysis, may help the early AD detection. In this context, to evaluate the effectiveness of our MCDA classification approach in the early AD detection, we have developed a special-purpose AD-related database by following the recommendations of the Scientific Department of Cognitive Neurology and Aging of the Brazilian Academy of Neurology (Nitrini et al., 2005) and by making use of a neuropsychological battery of exams made available by the well-known Consortium to Establish a Registry for Alzheimer's Disease (CERAD) (Fillenbaum et al., 2008). Various experiments have been performed over this database in a manner as to either fine-tune the components of the MCDA model or to compare its performance level with that exhibited by other state-of-the-art classification algorithms.

In the present study, two Multicriteria Decision Analysis (MCDA) classification approaches, which are developed upon the method recently proposed by Goletsis et al. (Goletsis et al., 2004) (referred to hereafter as *gMCDA classifier*) and the well-known MCDA PROAFTN classification procedure (Belacel, 2000), are employed towards the effective early diagnosis of Alzheimer's disease. The classifiers make use of the concept of prototypes, that is, special alternatives representing the classes of a problem, and has associated with itself some control parameters related to the expert's preference modeling process. As some of the experiments reported here reveal, the appropriate selection of prototypes as well as the calibration of control parameters are key issues to leverage the classifiers' performance. This way, our approach combines two complementary techniques, one based on ELECTRE IV methodology (Roy, 1996) and the other on a customized genetic algorithm (Eiben & Smith, 2003), in order to select the best prototypes and effectively calibrate the control parameters, respectively.

2. Alzheimer disease classification

The very early detection of Alzheimer's disease (AD) has been deeply investigated in numerous studies in the past years. These studies have demonstrated that the pathology usually arises decades before the clinical diagnosis is effectively made, and so a reliable identification of AD in its earliest stages is one of the major challenges clinicians and researchers face nowadays. The following researches evolved to tackle the classification of AD and other dementia.

A classification problem refers to the assignment of a group of alternatives to a set of predefined classes, also known as categories. During the last decades these problems have been tackled using a high variety of statistical and machine learning techniques. Recently, the area of Multicriteria Decision Aid (MCDA) (Figueira et al., 2005; Roy, 1996) has also brought new methodologies and techniques to solve these problems.

The main difference between the MCDA classification methods and others coming from related disciplines, as artificial neural networks (ANN), Bayesian models, rule-based models, decision trees, etc. (Witten & Frank, 2005), lies in the way that the MCDA methods incorporate the decision maker's preferences into the categorization process. In the ANN field, for instance, the work of French et al. (French et al., 1997) performs a comparison between an ANN model and a linear discriminant analysis (LDA) algorithm to classify and to stage the degree of dementia. The results demonstrated that the ANN algorithm clearly outperformed the LDA one in terms of classification accuracy, highlighting the utility of using ANN for group classification of patients with AD and staging dementia severity using neuropsychological data.

Figueiredo et al. (Figueiredo et al., 1995) present an algorithm that classifies individuals into four different groups (i.e., clinically diagnosed groups of elderly normal, demented, AD, and vascular dementia subjects). The classification is performed after the analysis of computer tomography image data from brain and using an optimal interpolative neural network. Another classification work related to dementia disorders among the elderly (Zaffalon et al., 2003) uses a naïve credal classifier to address two different classification problems: discrimination between demented and control patients, and the assignment from among the different types of dementia. The dataset was developed from a set of measures collected among of a series of computerized tests (tasks), which assess some cognitive faculties of the patient.

Sandip et al. (Sandip et al., 2007) realize the AD classification based on a molecular test that evaluates characteristic changes in the concentrations of signaling proteins in the blood, generating a detectable disease-specific molecular phenotype. By this way, through a molecular biomarker in blood plasma, the model classifies the patients into AD or non-AD and identifies those presymptomatic individuals with mild cognitive impairment which will eventually convert to Alzheimer's disease.

In the MCDA field, a decision making model has been recently proposed by Castro and Pinheiro (Castro et al., 2007a;b; 2008) to assist the specialist in the early diagnosis of the Alzheimer's disease. Differently from our approach, this model uses the Macbeth software (Bana et al., 2003) to construct the judgement matrices and the value scales for each fundamental point of view (FPV) already defined. Each patient's information is judged by the decision maker for each FPV; then the Macbeth software generates the value scales that will be used in the final judgment of the patient's diagnosis. Instead of providing the classification itself, this sort of model gives the possibilities of a patient acquiring or not a certain type of dementia in the future.

In the present chapter, some experiments were performed enclosing the Multicriteria Decision Analysis (MCDA) classification techniques, that will be described in next section, towards the effective early diagnosis of the Alzheimer's disease.

3. Multicriteria decision analysis

Zopounidis and Doumpos (Zopounidis & Doumpos, 2002) define that the decision making problems, according to their nature, the policy of the decision maker, and the overall objective of the decision, may require the choice, ranking, or the assignment of the considered alternatives into predefined classes.

The practical approach that concerns the classification problems motivated researches in developing different methods and mathematical models to solve these problems trying to achieve the highest classification rate. A substantial overview on MCDA methods can be found in (Belacel, 2000; Massaglia & Ostanello, 1991; Mousseau et al., 1999) where the authors address the definitions and the problems that are involved in the decision making process.

These methods have been successfully applied to real world problems. The major difficulty during their employment, however, is that, in order to produce models that comply with the decision maker's expectations, a set of control parameters, such as threshold variables, weights, coefficients, etc., needs to be properly set in advance, which turns out to be a hard task to be dealt with. Some authors, like Belacel (Belacel, 2000) and Jacquet-Lagréze & Siskos (Jacquet-Lagréze & Siskos, 2001), have already provided some alternatives to counter this sort of drawback, although their solutions seem to be rather specific to the contexts that were investigated and yet no general recipes are available to be deployed in all methods and circumstances.

As pointed out by Zopounidis and Doumpos (Zopounidis & Doumpos, 2002), the great majority of works conducted on the MCDA classification theme has focused on the development of novel MCDA classification methods, not giving much emphasis on characterizing and comparing their distinctive problems. Likewise, the authors also advocate that future research on this field should consider a more deep investigation into some important practical issues, such as the analysis of the interdependencies of the control parameters of the algorithms, the statistical validation of the generated models, the analysis of performance over large data sets, and the establishment of links between MCDA classifier models and those coming from related disciplines, such as Pattern Recognition, Machine Learning, and Data Mining (Witten & Frank, 2005).

In this context, we have developed an approach, to assist the doctors during the early stages of AD, upon a specific MCDA classification method, which is also composed of two complementary techniques: one responsible for eliciting the values of the classifier's control parameters and the other in charge of selecting the best prototypes from the dataset in accordance with the decision makerŠs preferences. The chosen classifiers and the associated techniques are detailed in the sequel.

3.1 MCDA classification models

The first MCDA classification method that we have chosen to investigate was that proposed by Goletsis et al. (Goletsis et al., 2004). This method makes use of prototypes to serve as references against the new alternatives compared (matched) with it. One distinctive aspect of this scheme with respect to other MCDA-based classifiers is that it presents less control parameters to be adjusted (only some thresholds and criteria weights). In what follows, we provide further details of gMCDA.

As described by Goletsis et al. (Goletsis et al., 2004), during the comparison between an alternative and a prototype the first thing to be computed is the Similarity Index $(SI_j(a, b_p^h))$. This index is calculated for each criterion, and its objective is to model the criteria into a five zone similarity index. In order to compute this index, two thresholds must be specified.

The first threshold that needs to be specified is the similarity threshold, q_j, which represents the maximum allowed criterion difference $|g_j(a) - g_j(b_p^h)|$ between the alternatives and the prototypes. Using this, the alternatives can be judged similar under a specific criterion.

The second threshold used by the $(SI_j(a, b_p^h))$ computation is the dissimilarity threshold, p_j, representing the minimum allowed criterion difference between an alternative a and prototype b_p^h. This threshold needs to be defined in order to consider the criteria totally dissimilar.

The Similarity Index(SI) $(SI_j(a, b_p^h))$ is computed as described below:

$$SI_j(a, b_p^h) = \begin{cases} 1, & \text{if } |g_j(a) - g_j(b_p^h)| \leq q_j \\ \left(\frac{|g_j(a) - g_j(b_p^h)| - p_j}{q_j - p_j}\right), & \text{if } q_j < |g_j(a) - g_j(b_p^h)| < p_j \\ 0, & \text{if } |g_j(a) - g_j(b_p^h)| \geq p_j \end{cases} \tag{1}$$

After the computation of the similarity index, the next step is to compute the concordance index (CI). This index indicates the overall similarity concordance of an alternative a with a prototype b_p^h. This index is computed as follows:

$$CI(a, b_p^h) = \sum_j w_j \, SI_j(a, b_p^h), \tag{2}$$

where w_j is the weight of a specific criterion and $\sum_j w_j = 1$.

Each alternative will have its CI computed for all prototypes of all classes. After that, the next step is the computation of the membership degree (MD) of an alternative a to a category C^h. The best CI of a to all prototypes of C^h is given to the Membership Degree (MD). The MD is computed as follows:

$$MD(a, C^h) = max\{CI(a, b_1^h), \ldots, CI(a, b_{L_h}^h)\} \ . \tag{3}$$

Finally, the last step is the assignment of the alternative a to the category $C(a)$ with the maximum MD calculated in relation to all the groups of prototypes. The formula is presented below.

$$C(a) = arg\ max_h\ MD(a, C^h) \ . \tag{4}$$

The gMCDA method was first applied to the ischemic beat classification problem (Goletsis et al., 2004). According to the authors (Goletsis et al., 2004) the main difficulty encountered when applying their method is the specification of weights and thresholds p_j and q_j. Aiming to achieve better performances and trying to obtain an automated beat classification, the authors have incorporated a genetic algorithm for the adjustment of the parameters of the multicriteria method. Futher information concerning the implementation of this algorithm can be found in (Goletsis et al., 2004).

3.2 PROAFTN classification model

The other MCDA classification method implemented also makes use of prototypes to serve as references against which the new alternatives are compared (matched) with. Differently from the gMCDA, the PROAFTN method (Belacel, 2000) substitutes the similarity relation by the outranking relation, through the calculation of an indifference index based on an alternative and a reference profile (prototype).

The assignment procedure consists of calculating the degree of membership of each alternative to be assigned to each class based on the fuzzy indifference relation between this alternative and each prototype. Belacel (Belacel, 2000) defines the principle in the following way: when the alternative a is judged indifferent to a prototype b_p^h according to the majority of criteria (majority principle) and there is no criterion which uses its veto against the affirrmation "a is indifferent to b_p^h" (minority respect principle), the action a is considered overall as indifferent to a prototype b_p^h. In order to calculate the fuzzy indifference relations it is necessary to build the partial indifference indices using the concordance and non-discordance concepts to aggregate them. As in the gMCDA algorithm the alternative will be assigned into the class with the maximal membership degree value (Belacel, 2000).

In general, the prototype scores are given by intervals, so for each criterion g_j, we associate to each prototype b_p^h the interval $[S_j^1(b_p^h), S_j^2(b_p^h)]$, with $S_j^2(b_p^h) \geq S_j^1(b_p^h)$. The comprehensive indifference index is determined by aggregating the partial indifference indices. These indices indicate if the action a is indifferent or not to a prototype b_p^h according to a criterion g_j. The partial indifference relation is given as follows:

$$aI_j b_p^h \Longleftrightarrow g_j(a) \in [S_j^1(b_p^h), S_j^2(b_p^h)], \tag{5}$$

If the value of the alternative a according to the criterion g_j is equal to $S_j^1(b_p^h)$ or to $S_j^2(b_p^h)$, the alternative a will be indifferent to prototype b_p^h according to Equation 5. However, considering the imperfection and imprecision of the data, the alternative a on the criterion g_j can be assessed as: $g_j(a) = S_j^1(b_p^h) - \epsilon$ or $g_j(a) = S_j^2(b_p^h) - \epsilon$, where ϵ is a real number, which take very small values (Belacel, 2000). In this case, the application of the Equation 5 leads to transform the indifference situation into a non-indifference situation between the alternative a and prototype b_p^h according to criterion g_j, despite the fact that variation is not significant. In order to remedy this inconvenience, Belacel (Belacel, 2000) introduced two discrimination thresholds $d_j^-(b_p^h) \geq 0$ and $d_j^+(b_p^h) \geq 0$, which correspond, respectively to two functions of $S_j^1(b_p^h)$ and $S_j^2(b_p^h)$.

Formally, three comparative situations between the action a and prototype b_p^h according to criterion g_j are obtained using the two discrimination thresholds:

- If $S_j^1(b_p^h) \leq g_j(a) \leq S_j^2(b_p^h)$, then a is clearly indifferent to b_p^h;
- If $[g_j(a) \leq S_j^1(b_p^h) - d_j^-(b_p^h)]$ or $[g_j(a) \geq S_j^2(b_p^h) + d_j^+(b_p^h)]$, then a is not indifferent to b_p^h;
- If $[S_j^1(b_p^h) - d_j^-(b_p^h) < g_j(a) < S_j^1(b_p^h)]$ or $[S_j^2(b_p^h) < g_j(a) < S_j^2(b_p^h) + d_j^+(b_p^h)$, then there is a weak indifference between a and b_p^h.

For each alternative a from the set of alternatives A to be classified and each reference alternative b_p^h of the class C^h, the partial concordance index on the criterion j is computed as follows.

$$C_j(a,b_p^h) = min\{C_j^-(a,b_p^h), C_j^+(a,b_p^h)\}, \tag{6}$$

where,

$$C_j^-(a,b_p^h) = \frac{d_j^-(b_p^h) - min\{S_j^1(b_p^h) - g_j(a), d_j^-(b_p^h)\}}{d_j^-(b_p^h) - min\{S_j^1(b_p^h) - g_j(a), 0\}} \tag{7}$$

$$C_j^+(a,b_p^h) = \frac{d_j^+(b_p^h) - min\{g_j(a) - S_j^2(b_p^h), d_j^+(b_p^h)\}}{d_j^+(b_p^h) - min\{g_j(a) - S_j^2(b_p^h), 0\}} \tag{8}$$

The second step of PROAFTN computes the partial discordance indices. The aim of determining the discordance index $D_j(a,b_p^h)$ of the criterion g_j is to apprehend the fact that such a criterion is more or less discordant with the assertion "a is indifferent to b_p^h" (Belacel, 2000). The discordance index is maximum $(D_j(a,b_p^h) = 1)$ when the criterion g_j uses its veto against this assertion aIb_p^h. It is minimum $(D_j(a,b_p^h) = 0)$ when the criterion is not in discordance with this indifference (i.e. $C_j(a,b_p^h) \notin 0$). If the criterion g_j is in discordance (i.e. $C_j(a,b_p^h) = 0$ with indifference and it does not use its veto against this indifference, we have: $0 < D_j(a,b_p^h) < 1$, which represents the intermediary zones between the non-discordance and discordance situations.

The veto thresholds $v_j^-(b_p^h)$ and $v_j^+(b_p^h)$ such as $v_j^+(b_p^h) \geq d_j^+(b_p^h)$ and $v_j^-(b_p^h) \geq d_j^-(b_p^h)$, $j = 1, ..., n$, are used to define the values from which the action a is considered as very different to prototype b_p^h for criterion g_j (Belacel, 2000).

The discordance index $(D_j(a,b_p^h)$ is represented between the values $S_j^1(b_p^h) - v_j^-(b_p^h)$ and $S_j^1(b_p^h) - d_j^-(b_p^h)$ on one hand and $S_j^2(b_p^h) + v_j^+(b_p^h)$ and $S_j^2(b_p^h) + d_j^+(b_p^h)$ on the other hand, by the linear interpolation function.

$$D_j(a, b_p^h) = max\{D_j^-(a, b_p^h), D_j^+(a, b_p^h)\}, \tag{9}$$

where,

$$D_j^-(a, b_p^h) = \frac{g_j(a) - max\{g_j(a), S_j^1(b_p^h) - d_j^-(b_p^h)\}}{d_j^-(b_p^h) - max\{S_j^1(b_p^h) - g_j(a), v_j^-(b_p^h)\}} \tag{10}$$

$$D_j^+(a, b_p^h) = \frac{g_j(a) - min\{g_j(a), S_j^2(b_p^h) + d_j^+(b_p^h)\}}{-d_j^+(b_p^h) + max\{-S_j^2(b_p^h) + g_j(a), v_j^+(b_p^h)\}} \tag{11}$$

After that, the next step calculates the fuzzy indifference relation as:

$$I(a, b_:^h) = (\sum_{j=1}^{n} w_j^h C_j(a, b_p^h)) \times (\prod_{j=1}^{n}(1 - D_j(a, b_p^h))^{w_j^h}), \tag{12}$$

where w_p^h is a positive coefficient that indicates the importance of an attribute g_j to a class C^h.

The fourth step evaluate the fuzzy membership degree $d(a, C^h)$. The membership degree is computed for each class from the set of categories C by selecting the maximal values of indifference indices from the reference alternatives of each class:

$$d(a, C^h) = max\{I(a, b_1^h), I(a, b_2^h), \ldots, I(a, b_{L_h}^h)\}, h = 1, \ldots, K. \tag{13}$$

The final step assigns the alternative to the class with the maximal membership degree:

$$a \in C^h \Leftrightarrow d(a, C^h) = max\{d(a, C^1 / l \in \{1, \ldots, K\}\} \tag{14}$$

As it can be seen, the implemented methods differ in the way they create relations between the alternatives in order to provide the classification. The PROAFTN method is based on the outranking relation while the gMCDA classifier provides a similarity relation with the application of similarity and dissimilarity thresholds. According to (I. Yevseyeva, 2007), these thresholds represent the maximal difference on the criterion value that is still small enough for two alternatives to be considered similar. In addition, it can be noted that the gMCDA classifier presents less control parameters to be adjusted (only some thresholds and criteria weights). On the other hand, the PROAFTN method encloses a veto threshold, which discriminates situations of discordance with the indifference relation.

The works of Brasil et al. (Brasil et al., 2010; Brasil, Pinheiro, Coelho & Costa, 2009a;b) demonstrated the relevance of choosing the best prototypes for both classifiers. These studies have evidenced that the methods presented above are indeed very sensitive to the choice of prototypes and that their proper choice may be instrumental for leveraging the performance levels.

3.3 ELECTRE IV

One of the complementary techniques applied cojointly with the gMCDA classifier tackles the problem of prototype selection. This technique is also based on the MCDA principles, but conversely is based on the concept of sorting of alternatives and criteria.

According to Zopounidis and Doumpos (Zopounidis & Doumpos, 2002), the indirect techniques are widely used for developing sorting models that employ the outranking concept. To apply this technique, the decision analyst specifies the parameters based on an interactive inquiry process with the decision maker. This process ensures that the decision maker preferences will be correctly captured in the model.

Differently from other similar algorithms (Keeney & Raiffa, 1993), the ELECTRE IV method (Roy & Hugonard, 1982) does not require the specification of a weight value for each criterion. Conversely, the decision analyst chooses the criterion that it wants to work with and then ELECTRE IV combines them to give birth to the outranking relations. This approach avoids the problem of trying to quantify how important a criterion is. Each criterion can be either defined as a benefit or cost criterion. When the decision analyst considers a cost criterion, the lower the criterion value, the higher its merit; the converse is true for a benefit criterion.

To employ this method to rank the alternatives of a class, the decision analyst should define only the preference and indifference thresholds for each criterion. Specifically in our MCDA approach, the ELECTRE IV method will assume the role of the indirect technique responsible for the prototype selection activity.

Basically, the ELECTRE IV method can be divided into five stages: 1) criteria selection; 2) calculus of the relative thresholds; 3) construction of weak and strong outranking relations; 4) construction of the downward and upward ranks; and 5) elicitation of the final rank.

The first step to employ the ELECTRE IV algorithm is to select the criteria that will be used during the ranking process. The second stage is the determination of the relative thresholds. This phase basically sets the relation of two alternatives under some criterion. It can be defined that two alternatives are indifferent, strictly preferred, or weakly preferred over a criterion k. After that, it is necessary to construct the weak and strong outranking relations for every pair of alternatives (Ukkusuri et al., 2007). At this point, an alternative i will either strongly or weakly outrank an alternative j based on several restrictions that compares the relative ranks and the thresholds defined (Ukkusuri et al., 2007). The next step determines the strengths, weaknesses and the qualification of each alternative, and, based on these numbers, defines the downward and upward ranks. Finally, the final rank is set using the mean of the upward and downward ranks.

3.4 Genetic algorithm

Evolutionary computation is the field of research that draws ideas from evolutionary biology in order to develop search and optimization techniques (known as evolutionary algorithms) for solving complex problems (Back et al., 1997). Most of these techniques are rooted on the neo-Darwinian theory of evolution, which states that a population of individuals, is capable of reproducing and subjected to (genetic) variation followed by selection, result along time in new populations of individuals increasingly more fit to their environment.

Genetic algorithms (GAs) comprise the class of evolutionary algorithms that uses a specific vocabulary borrowed from natural genetics (Eiben & Smith, 2003). The data structures representing the individuals (genotypes) of the population are often called chromosomes; these are one-chromosome (haploid) individuals encoding potential solutions to a problem. In standard GAs, the individuals are represented as strings of bits. Each unit of a chromosome is termed a gene, located in a certain place in the chromosome called locus. The different values a gene can assume are the alleles. The problem to be solved is captured in an objective (fitness) function that allows evaluating the adequacy of any potential solution.

As each chromosome corresponds to the encoded value of a candidate solution, it has to be decoded into an appropriate form for evaluation and is then assigned a fitness value according to the objective. For each chromosome is assigned a probability of reproduction, so that its likelihood of being selected is proportional to its fitness relative to the other chromosomes in the population. If the fitness of each chromosome is a strictly positive number to be maximized, selection is traditionally performed via an algorithm called Roulette Wheel selection (Eiben & Smith, 2003). The assigned probabilities of reproduction result in the generation of a population of chromosomes probabilistically selected from the current population. The selected chromosomes will generate offspring via the use of probabilistic genetic operators, namely, crossover (recombination of gene blocks) and mutation (perturbation through genetic variation) each one associated with a specific rate. Each new generation contains a higher proportion of the characteristics of the previous generation good members, providing a good possibility to converge to an optimal solution of the problem.

According to (Eiben & Smith, 2003), GAs have successfully been applied to a wide variety of problems, including those which are hard to be solved by other methods. In the MCDA field, their application primarily concerns the task of control parameter optimization (Brasil, 2009; Brasil, Pinheiro & Coelho, 2009; Goletsis et al., 2004; Gouvenir & Erel, 1998), the same investigated in this work.

4. Diagnosis of Alzheimer's disease

Despite the fact that the final AD diagnosis is performed by a microscopic brain tissue exam, through a biopsy or necropsy, Chaves (M.I.F. Chaves, 2000) presents evidence that it is not necessary to wait for the patient's death to know, with certainty, what is causing the symptoms and the perceived behavior.

In this context, the doctors can make a "probable" or "possible" AD diagnostic. Pinholt et al. (Pinholt et al., 1987) attests the difficult associated with the process of AD detection, wherein the authors highlight that, despite the high incidence of dementia in the elderly population, doctors fail to detect them in 21 to 72% of the cases. There is a vast number of clinical instruments that assist the clinician to obtain the diagnosis. Castro's work (A. K. Castro, 2008) summarizes some instruments as follows:

- Complete patient's and family's medical history;
- Neurological exam and neuropsychological tests;
- Review of the use of drugs;
- Physical examination;
- Psychiatric evaluation;
- Laboratorial tests like blood and urine exams;
- Image exams like: computed tomography, magnetic resonance, single photon emission computed tomography (SPECT) and positron emission tomography (PET).

Although these exams are not specific for the AD detection, they can increase its diagnosis accuracy by showing some issues related to its cognitive activity. As a neurodegenerative disease (once the brain cells are lost, they cannot be replaced), the current research challenge is to make a premature diagnose, before the cognitive functioning is impaired (K.R. Daffner and L.F.M. Scinto, 2000). In this context, Rentz e Weintraub (D.M. Rentz and S. Weintraub, 2000) stresses that the neuropsychological deficits are still the best way to detect the AD early symptoms.

It is a common sense that the AD early diagnosis can bring benefits to the patients and their families. With the constant development of drug therapies and therapeutic advances, an early treatment can delay the progress of functional decline. The families and all the stakeholders can feel the benefits as they prepare for the patient management, raising their overall quality of life (A. K. Castro, 2008).

Besides the quality of life issue, another major factor that stimulates the early diagnosis is the financial one. According to some studies of the Alzheimer's Association, the Alzheimer disease generates high costs, being one of the most expensive diseases, losing only to the cancer and cardiovasculars diseases (R. Koppel, 2002). The main reason that raises this cost is the need of a multidisciplinary treatment. Normally, the AD affects one or more cognitive areas, such as: attention, perception, memory, reasoning, sense, imagination, thinking and language. For such cases, it may be necessary treatments with psychologists, neurologists, neuropsychologists, geriatricians, psychiatrists, physiotherapists, occupational therapists, etc. Advanced cases can require the constant presence of the family and/or care providers, that are responsible for assisting the patients as they lose their abilities to interpret and express what is happening with their bodies and minds (A. K. Castro, 2008; L.P. Gwyther, 1985).

As mentioned before, this case study seeks to assist the decision maker (clinician) in the early AD diagnosis. To achieve this objective, we have manually designed a specific dataset of cases taking as reference the neuropsychological battery of CERAD standardized assessments and the Brazilian consensus of cognitive and functional evaluation. These are discussed in the following two subsections.

4.1 CERAD

The Consortium to Establish a Registry for Alzheimer's Disease (CERAD) was founded in 1986 after the Health Research Extension Act of 1985 with a specific focus on issues of diagnosis and diagnostic standardization (Fillenbaum et al., 2008). At that time, besides the fact that there had been an increasing interest over the illness, there was no uniform guideline over some issues, like diagnostic criteria, testing methods, and classifications of the disease severity, that could be followed. CERAD is a distinctive collaborative initiative to attend to this need.

CERAD has developed some standardized assessment instruments from different manifestations of Alzheimer's disease: clinical neuropsychology; neuropathology; behavior rating scale for dementia; family history interviews; and assessment of service needs. In this way, the CERAD battery improved the ability of specialists and researchers to describe and correlate clinical, neuropsychological, and neuropathologic aspects of AD.

4.2 The novel dataset

In order to provide a way to detect the presence of AD as soon as possible, we have followed the recommendations of the Scientific Department of Cognitive Neurology and

Aging of the Brazilian Academy of Neurology (Nitrini et al., 2005) while crafting our dataset of cases. This consensus specifies the recommendations over the clinical diagnosis of AD through a functional and cognitive perspective, and therefore the database was designed by following the strategy of correlating clinical and neuropsychological assessments of CERAD with recommendations provided by the Brazilian consensus.

In particular, the language evaluation exams allow for both a quantitative and qualitative diagnosis, showing the profile of the linguistic disorder (Nitrini et al., 2005). For the Brazilian consensus, the Boston Naming Test is one of the recommended tests that can be applied to break down the language aspects of a patient. This way, the first criterion (attribute) considered in the dataset relates to the amount of right answers given by each patient.

According to (Nitrini et al., 2005), the dementia diagnosis should be established in a clinical exam, documented as the Mini-Mental State Examination. To comply with the consensus, we turned this assessment into the second criterion associated with each case. This criterion reflects the sum of answers correctly assigned by each patient.

The third AD cognitive criterion designates a set of cognitive skills related to social relationships and that guarantee a proper, responsible, and effective conduct of the patient (Nitrini et al., 2005). Among the tests available in CERAD battery, we have used the Verbal Fluency exam. This test requests the patient to verbalize the highest number of animals as possible during a certain period of time. The criterion is defined by the number of items mentioned in a minute, excluding the repeated ones.

One of the main characteristics of AD is the impairment of memory. The Brazilian consensus stresses the importance of the memory evaluation and suggests the memorization of lists of words as an exam that can be applied to detect any sort of brain impairment during the early stages of the disease. This exam asks the patient to remember a ten-word list after a short period of time to evaluate the status of the short-term memory. The CERAD assessment applies three lists of ten words, so the database criterion we have devised specifies the overall number of words that were remembered by the patient.

The last criterion introduced relates to the concept of constructional ability. This CERAD assessment provides a non-verbal measure of the patient's mental health through the manipulation of geometric figures. The criterion denotes the number of elements correctly-assigned by the patient.

Besides the fact that the neuropsychological assessments available in the CERAD battery of exams were applied to more than 5,000 patients, only 119 cases could be effectively used in our experiments. This number was achieved after cross-correlating the neuropsychological and clinical assessments in order to certify whether the patient had effectively developed AD or not. By these means, the resulting dataset encompasses 5 criteria and 119 alternatives (cases).

5. An integrated approach to diagnose the Alzheimer's disease

In this section, we provide details of the experiments we have conducted so far over the database introduced previously. First, we concentrate on the prototype selection and control parameter calibration tasks conducted, respectively, by the ELECTRE IV and GA engines. The achieved results and a flavor of comparison with some state-of-the-art classifiers are presented. The gMCDA and PROAFTN classification methods were applied in order to provide the results.

Criteria	Description	+p	+q	-p	-q
C1	Boston Naming Test	0.9	0.39	-0.9	-0.39
C2	Mini-Mental State Examination	0.9	0.39	-0.9	-0.39
C3	Verbal Fluency	1.1	0.45	-1.1	-0.45
C4	Word List	1.1	0.45	-1.1	-0.45
C5	Constructional Praxis	0.9	0.35	-0.9	-0.35

Table 1. Criteria preference and indifference thresholds

The intent of this experiment is to provide a comparison of the gMCDA and PROAFTN performance levels over the same circumstances (prototypes and optimized parameters). In such regard, we have decided to compare the gMCDA and the PROAFTN classifiers assisted with the ELECTRE IV and GA engines with their performances when acting alone.

5.1 ELECTRE IV engine

The ELECTRE IV method (Roy & Hugonard, 1982) has been applied to assist in the prototype selection task through an indirect perspective. In such case, the decision analyst is responsible for providing the system with his/her preferences, which are effectively captured through the preference and indifference parameters (thresholds) associated with ELECTRE IV, so that the method can sort the alternatives.

Since the alternatives are ranked, the number of prototypes chosen while conducting the experiments was 7% of the original dataset. From that number, the prototypes were separated into their classes respecting their original distribution in the dataset. It is interesting to note that the application of the ELECTRE IV method can vary depending on the type of dataset that is under consideration. In cases where the problem presents more than two classes, the ELECTRE IV should be applied for each class separately, sorting the best alternatives of each class. This occurs because the classification problems often present conflicting criteria.

When applied to our AD dataset, as it only presents two categories,the ELECTRE IV engine needs to be applied only once to sort the patients from the most probable of not having Alzheimer to those most probable of manifesting the disease. In our experiments, we have ranked the patients from the non-AD to the AD category. For this purpose, we have established the same preference and indifference thresholds for all criteria, as they are all benefit criteria and have the same numerical ranges. For this dataset, all criteria were considered as relevant, so we have avoided discarding any attribute. Table 1 shows the preference and indifference values that were elicited for each criterion from the decision maker (clinician).

5.2 The genetic algorithm engine

According to our approach, after the best prototypes are selected by the ELECTRE IV engine, a customized GA is then employed in order to automatically estimate the gMCDA classifier's control parameters (thresholds). The GA components (Eiben & Smith, 2003) have been configured as follows: a population of 50 individuals (which initially is randomly generated) is evolved at each generation; the Roulette Wheel operator is used to select individuals to reproduce; individuals are recombined through a single-point crossover and the offspring is mutated according to a uniform distribution over the parameters' ranges; the crossover and

	1	2	3	4	5	6	7	8	9	10	Mean
gMCDA	91.66	84	83.33	95.83	91.66	95.83	87.5	95.83	91.66	85.71	90.28
Random gMCDA	58.82	56.3	64.71	58.82	55.46	58.82	67.86	67.86	67.86	70.83	62.73
PROAFTN	79.17	76	83.33	79.17	83.33	83.33	75	79.17	83.33	67.86	78.97
Random PROAFTN	70.83	74	73.75	75.42	72.92	76.67	76.25	77.92	77.92	68.57	74.42

Table 2. Performance of the classifiers when applied to the 10 test sets (results are show in percentage).

mutation rates are 80% and 15%, respectively; and the stop criterion adopted is to go through 500 generations of evolution.

To experiment with the GA, we have randomly generated 10 pairs of stratified training/test datasets from the original database, allocating 80% of the samples for training and the remaining for test. After the training phase, the best chromosome (configuration of thresholds) discovery is applied to the test data.

Classification Algorithm	Classification Rate (%)
J48	75.63%
NBTree	84.033%
OneR	82.352%
NaiveBayes	75.63%
gMCDA Classification Model	90.28%
PROAFTN Classification Model	78.97%

Table 3. Performance measures for the AD diagnosis.

5.3 Classification results

Table 2 shows the performance levels achieved by the classifiers when they had the parameters and prototypes optimized by the developed methodology. It is easily noticeable that the classifiers show a high sensitivity to the choice of prototypes and cut-off threshold values. As it was demonstrated in following works (Brasil et al., 2010; Brasil, Pinheiro, Coelho & Costa, 2009b), where the impact of the prototype selection is evidenced, it can be seen that for the AD dataset, the choice of the prototypes and control parameters seems indeed to be a key issue to be properly dealt with in order to leverage the classifiers' performance.

By contrasting the results without the application of the model with those produced by our approach in Table 2, it is possible to observe that, for some sets of prototypes, the proposed model could improve the classifiers' performance by more than 20%, taking the mean results over the 10 sets of random prototypes. Moreover, in some runs, the gMCDA classification rate could increase for as high as 33%.

Differently from the last experiment, the results produced by the gMCDA and PROAFTN classifiers can be compared here. Considering only the results produced by the model, the gMCDA classifier surpasses the PROAFTN in 90% of the executions. If we take a single execution, for example the last one (tenth), the difference comes close to 18%.

Finally, to provide a flavor of comparison with other classification algorithms, we have resorted to some well-known classification models available in the WEKA workbench (Witten & Frank, 2005). Table 3 brings the average accuracy levels achieved with each contestant model over the 10 derived datasets. The performance level achieved by the gMCDA classifier was superior to those achieved by the other models. It should be emphasized that for each of the four additional classifiers we performed some preliminary experiments in order to manually calibrate its associated control parameters. However, we can not guarantee that the sets of parameters effectively obtained were in fact the optimal ones at all. From the results discussed above, one can conclude that the ELECTRE IV and GA engines have demonstrated good potential in solving the prototype and parameter selection problems.

6. Conclusion

The Alzheimer's Disease is a global health problem that is attracting the attention of the public authorities. During the last decades, the worldwide elderly population presented a continuous growth, increasing the incidence of AD. The high costs to treat this disease and the significant deterioration in the families' quality of life have brought a new challenge to researchers and the medical community: identifying the presence of this illness when its first signs appear.

In such regard, we designed a new database that takes as reference the functional and cognitive recommendations of the Scientific Department of Cognitive Neurology and Aging of the Brazilian Academy of Neurology and the CERAD's neuropsychological battery of exams. Unlike other studies over the AD, in this case study, our purpose was to assess the performance achieved by an extended version of two MCDA classification algorithms (Belacel, 2000; Goletsis et al., 2004) while coping with the AD early diagnosis.

In this context, the employment of the ELECTRE IV algorithm revealed that the prototype selection task really exerts an important role over the MCDA classification process. Along with the ELECTRE IV, a GA engine was deployed to assist in the automatic calibration of the control parameter values (weights and thresholds) associated with both classifiers. In a general way, the devised MCDA approach achieved satisfactory levels of accuracy during the patient classification process over the conducted experiments, leveraging the performance of the classifiers and even comparing favorably against some well-known methods (Witten & Frank, 2005).

7. References

A. K. Castro (2008). Um Modelo Híbrido Aplicado ao Diagnóstico da Doença de Alzheimer, *Master thesis*, Master Program in Applied Informatics, University of Fortaleza.

Back, T., Fogel, D. & Michalewicz, Z. (1997). *Handbook of Evolutionary Algorithms*, Oxford Press.

Bana, C. A., Corte, J. M. & Vasnick, J. C. (2003). Macbeth. LSE-OR Working Paper.

Belacel, N. (2000). Multicriteria assignment method PROAFTN: Methodology and medical applications, *European Journal of Operational Research* 125: 175–183.

Braak, H. & Braak, E. (1997). Frequency of stages of Alzheimer-related lesions in different age categories, *Neurobiology of Aging* 18: 351–357.

Brasil, A. T. (2009). A novel approach based on multiple criteria decision aiding methods to cope with classification problems, *Master thesis*, Mestrado em Informática Aplicada, Universidade de Fortaleza (UNIFOR).

Brasil, A. T., Pinheiro, P. R. & Coelho, A. L. V. (2009). Towards the early diagnosis of alzheimer's disease via a multicriteria classification model, *5th Evolutionary Multi-Criterion Optimization (EMO 2009)*, Lecture Notes in Computer Science, pp. 393 – 406.

Brasil, A. T., Pinheiro, P. R. & Coelho, A. L. V. (2010). *Innovations and Advances in Computer Sciences and Engineering*, Springer Verlag, chapter The Impact of the Prototype Selection on a Multicriteria Decision Aid Classification Algorithm.

Brasil, A. T., Pinheiro, P. R., Coelho, A. L. V. & Costa, N. C. (2009a). Comparison of two prototype-based multicriteria classification methods, *IEEE Symposium on Computational Intelligence in Multicriteria Decision-Making (MCDM 2009)*, IEEE Symposium Series on Computational Intelligence 2009, Nashville, USA.

Brasil, A. T., Pinheiro, P. R., Coelho, A. L. V. & Costa, N. C. (2009b). Selecting prototypes for two multicriteria classification methods: A comparative study, *World Congress on Nature and Biologically Inspired Computing (NABIC 2009)*, Coimbatore, India.

Castro, A. K., Pinheiro, P. R. & Pinheiro, M. C. (2007a). Applying a decision making model in the early diagnosis of Alzheimer's disease, *Rough Sets and Knowledge Technology, Second International Conference, RSKT 2007*, Vol. 4481 of *Lecture Notes in Computer Science*, pp. 149–156.

Castro, A. K., Pinheiro, P. R. & Pinheiro, M. C. (2007b). A multicriteria model applied in the early diagnosis of Alzheimer's disease: A Bayesian approach, *Procs. of VI International Conference on Operational Research for Development*, pp. 9–19.

Castro, A. K., Pinheiro, P. R. & Pinheiro, M. C. (2008). A multicriteria model applied in the early diagnosis of Alzheimer's disease, *Rough Sets and Knowledge Technology, Third International Conference, RSKT 2008*, Vol. 5009 of *Lecture Notes in Computer Science*, pp. 612–619.

Celsis, P. (2000). Age-related cognitive decline, mild cognitive impairment or preclinical alzheimer's disease?, *Annals of Medicine* 32: 6–14.

Davidoff, A. D. (1986). Issues in the clinical diagnosis of alzheimer's disease, *American Journal of Alzheimer's Disease and Other Dementias* 1(1): 9–15.

D.M. Rentz and S. Weintraub (2000). *Early Diagnosis of Alzheimer's Disease*, Humana Press, chapter Neuropsychological Detection of Early Probable Alzheimer's Disease, pp. 169 – 189.

Eiben, A. E. & Smith, J. E. (2003). *Introduction to Evolutionary Computing*, Springer-Verlag.

Elias, M. F., Beiser, A., Wolf, P., Au, R., White, R. F. & D'Agostino, R. B. (2000). The preclinical phase of Alzheimer disease: A 22-year prospective study of the Framinghan cohort, *Arch Neurol* 57: 808–813.

Figueira, J., Mousseau, V. & Roy, B. (2005). ELECTRE methods, *Multiple Criteria Decision Analysis: State of the Arts Surveys* pp. 133–162.

Figueiredo, R. J. P. et al. (1995). Neural-network-based classification of cognitively normal, demented, alzheimer disease and vascular dementia from single photon emission with computed tomography image data from brain, *Medical Sciences* 92: 5530–5534.

Fillenbaum, G. G. et al. (2008). Consortium to establish a registry for Alzheimer's disease (CERAD): The first twenty years, *Alzheimer's & Dementia* 4: 96–109.

French, B. M., Dawnson, M. R. W. & Dobbs, A. R. (1997). Classification and staging of dementia of the alzheimer type: A comparison between neural networks and linear discriminant analysis, *Arch Neurol* 54(8): 1001–1009.

Goletsis, Y., Papaloukas, C., Fotiadis, D., Likas, A., & Michalis, L. (2004). Automated ischemic beat classification using genetic algorithms and multicriteria decision analysis, *IEEE Transactions on Biomedical Engineering* 51(10): 1717–1725.

Gouvenir, H. A. & Erel, E. (1998). Multicriteria inventory classification using a genetic algorithm, *European Journal of Operations Research* 105(1): 29–37.

I. Yevseyeva (2007). Solving Classification Problems with Multicriteria Decision Aiding Approaches, *Phd thesis*, Faculty of Information Technology, University of Jyväskylä.

Jacquet-Lagréze, E. & Siskos, J. (2001). Preference disaggregation: Twenty years of MCDA experience, *European Journal of Operational Research* 130: 233–245.

Kawas, C. H. et al. (2003). Visual memory predicts Alzheimer's disease more than a decade before diagnosis, *Neurology* 60(7): 1089–1093.

Keeney, R. L. & Raiffa, H. (1993). *Decisions with Multiple Objectives: Preferences and Value Trade-Offs*, Cambridge University Press.

K.R. Daffner and L.F.M. Scinto (2000). *Early Diagnosis of Alzheimer's Disease*, Humana Press, chapter Early Diagnosis of Alzheimer's Disease: An Introduction, pp. 1 – 27.

L.P. Gwyther (1985). Care of Alzheimer's patients: A manual for nursing home staff, *Technical report*, American Health Care Association.

Massaglia, M. & Ostanello, A. (1991). N-TOMIC: A decision support for multicriteria segmentation problems, *Lecture Notes in Economics and Mathematics Systems*, Vol. 356, pp. 167–174.

M.I.F. Chaves (2000). Diagnóstico Diferencial das Doenças Demenciantes, *in* O. Forlenza & P. Caramelli (eds), *Neuropsiquiatria Geriátrica*, Atheneu, pp. 81 – 104.

Mortimer, J. A. et al. (2005). Very early detection of Alzheimer neuropathology and the role of brain reserve in modifying its clinical expression, *Journal of Geriatric Psychiatry and Neurology* 18(4): 218–223.

Mousseau, V., Slowinski, R. & Zielniewicz, P. (1999). ELECTRE TRI 2.0a: Methodological guide and user's documentation, *Technical report*, Universite de Paris-Dauphine.

Nestor, P. J., Scheltens, P. & Hodges, J. R. (2004). Advances in the early detection of alzheimer's disease, *Neurodegeneration* 5: S34–S41.

Nitrini, R., Caramelli, P., Bottino, C. M., Damasceno, B. P., Brucki, S. M. & Anghinah, R. (2005). Diagnóstico de doença de Alzheimer no Brasil: Avaliação cognitiva e funcional, *Arquivos de Neuro-Psiquiatria* 63: 713–719.

Pinholt, E. M., Kroenke, K., Hanley, J. F., Kussman, M. J., Twyman, P. L. & Carpenter, J. L. (1987). Functional assessment of the elderly: A comparison of standard instruments with clinical judgment, *Arch Intern Med* 147: 484–488.

R. Koppel (2002). Alzheimer's disease: The costs to U.S. businesses in 2002, *Report*, Alzheimers Association.

Roy, B. (1996). *Multicriteria Methodology for Decision Aiding*, Kluwer Academic Publishers.

Roy, B. & Hugonard, B. (1982). Ranking of suburban line extension projects on the paris metro system by a multicriteria method, *Transportation Research* 16: 301–312.

Sandip, R. et al. (2007). Classification and prediction of clinical alzheimer's diagnosis based on plasma signaling proteins, *Nature Medicine* 13: 1359–1362.

Ukkusuri, S. V., Karoonsoontawong, A. & Kockelman, K. M. (2007). *Congestion Pricing Technologies: A Comparative Evaluation in New Transportation Research Progress*, Nova Science Publishers.

Witten, I. H. & Frank, E. (2005). *Data Mining: Practical Machine Learning Tools and Techniques*, 2 edn, Morgan Kaufmann, San Francisco.

Zaffalon, M., Wesnes, K. & Petrini, O. (2003). Reliable diagnoses of dementia by the naive credal classifier inferred from incomplete cognitive data, *Artificial Intelligence in Medicine* 29: 61–79.

Zopounidis, C. & Doumpos, M. (2002). Multicriteria classification and sorting methods: A literature review, *European Journal of Operational Research* 138(2): 229–246.

Part 5

GAs in Trading Systems

15

Portfolio Management Using Artificial Trading Systems Based on Technical Analysis

Massimiliano Kaucic
Department of Economic, Business, Mathematical and Statistical Sciences, University of Trieste, Trieste
Italy

1. Introduction

Evolutionary algorithms consist of several heuristics able to solve optimization tasks by imitating some aspects of natural evolution. In the field of computational finance, this type of procedures, combined with neural networks, swarm intelligence, fuzzy systems and machine learning has been successfully applied to a variety of problems, such as the prediction of stock price movements and the optimal allocation of funds in a portfolio.

Nowadays, there is an increasing interest among computer scientists to solve these issues concurrently by defining automatic trading strategies based on artificial expert systems, technical analysis and fundamental and economic information. The objective is to develop procedures able, from one hand, to mimic the practitioners behavior and, from the other, to beat the market. In this sense, Fernandez-Rodríguez et al. (2005) investigate the profitability of the generalized moving average trading rule for the General Index of Madrid Stock Market by optimizing parameter values with a genetic algorithm. They conclude that the optimized trading rules are superior to a risk-adjusted buy-and-hold strategy if the transaction costs are reasonable. Similarly, Papadamou & Stephanides (2007) present the GATradeTool, a parameter optimization tool based on genetic algorithms for technical trading rules. In the description of this software, they compare it with other commonly used, non-adaptive tools in terms of stability of the returns and computational costs. Results of the tests on the historical data of a UBS fund show that GATradeTool outperforms the other tools. Fernández-Blanco et al. (2008) propose to use the moving average convergence divergence technical indicator to predict stock indices by optimizing its parameters with a genetic algorithm. Experimental results for the Dow Jones Industrial Average index confirm the capability of evolutionary algorithms to improve technical indicators with respect to the classical configurations adopted by practitioners.

An alternative approach to generate technical trading systems for stock timing that combines machine learning paradigms and a variable length string multi-objective genetic algorithm is proposed in Kaucic (2010). The most informative technical indicators are selected by the genetic algorithm and combined into a unique trading signal by a learning method. A static single-position automated day trading strategy between the S&P 500 Composite Index and the 3-months Treasury Bill is analyzed in three market phases, up-trend, down-trend and sideways-movements, covering the period 2000-2006. The results indicate that the near-optimal set of rules varies among market phases but presents stable results and is able to reduce or eliminate losses in down-trend periods.

As a natural consequence of these studies, evolutionary algorithms may constitute a promising tool also for portfolio strategies involving more than two stocks. In the field of portfolio selection, Markowitz and Sharpe models are frequently used as a task for genetic algorithm optimization. For instance, the problem of finding the efficient frontier associated with the standard mean-variance portfolio is tackled by Chang et al. (2000). They extend the standard model to include cardinality and composition constraints by applying three heuristic algorithms based upon genetic algorithms, tabu search and simulated annealing. Computational results are presented for five data sets involving up to 225 assets.

Wilding (2003) proposes a hybrid procedure for portfolio management based on factor models, allowing constraints on the number of trades and securities. A genetic algorithm is responsible for selecting the best subset of securities that appears in the final solution, while a quadratic programming routine determines the utility value for that subset. Experiments show the ability of this approach to generate portfolios highly able to track an index.

The $\beta - G$ genetic portfolio algorithm proposed by Oh et al. (2006) selects stocks based on their market capitalization and optimizes their weights in terms of portfolio β's standard deviation. The performance of this procedure depends on market volatility and tends to register outstanding performance for short-term applications.

The approach I consider for portfolio management is quite different from the previous models and is based on technical analysis. In general, portfolio optimizations using technical analysis are modular procedures where a module employs a set of rules based on technical indicators in order to classify the assets in the market, while another module concentrates on generating and managing portfolio over time (for a detailed presentation of the subject, the interested reader may refer to Jasemi et al. (2011)).

An interesting application in this context is the approach developed by Korczak & Lipinski (2003) that leads to the optimization of portfolio structures by making use of artificial trading experts, previously discovered by a genetic algorithm (see Korczak & Roger (2002)), and evolutionary strategies. The approach has been tested using data from the Paris Stock Exchange. The profits obtained by this algorithm are higher than those of the buy-and-hold strategy.

Recently, Ghandar et al. (2009) describe a two-modules interacting procedure where a genetic algorithm optimizes a set of fuzzy technical trading rules according to market conditions and interacts with a portfolio strategy based on stock ranking and cardinality constraints. They introduce several performance metrics to compare their portfolios with the Australian Stock Exchange index, showing greater returns and lower volatility.

An alternative multi-modular approach has been developed by Gorgulho et al. (2011) that aims to manage a financial portfolio by using technical analysis indicators optimized by a genetic algorithm. In order to validate the solutions, authors compare the designed strategy against the market itself, the buy-and-hold and a purely random strategy, under distinct market conditions. The results are promising since the approach outperforms the competitors.

As the previous examples demonstrate, the technical module occupies, in general, a subordinate position relative to the management component. Since transaction costs, cardinality and composition constraints are of primary importance for the rebalancing purpose, the effective impact of technical signals in the development of optimal portfolios is not clear. To highlight the benefits of using technical analysis in portfolio management, I propose an alternative genetic optimization heuristic, based on an equally weighted zero investment strategy, where funds are equally divided among the stocks of a long portfolio and the stocks of a short one. Doing so, the trading signals directly influence the portfolio construction. Moreover, I implement three types of portfolio generation models according to the risk-adjusted measure considered as the objective, in order to study the relation between portfolio risk and market condition changes.

The remainder of the chapter is organized as follows. Section 2 explains in detail the proposed method, focusing on the investment strategy, the definitions of the technical indicators and the evolutionary learning algorithm adopted. Section 3 presents the experimental results and discussions. Finally, Section 4 concludes the chapter with some remarks and ideas for future improvements.

2. Trading strategy implementation

Three interacting modules compose the management system I have developed. The trading strategy is represented by the investment module, the calculation of trading signals is assigned to the technical module and an evolutionary learning component, based on Kaucic (2010), generates optimal portfolios. The core of the last module consists, in particular, of two parts:

i) a learning mechanism, that manages the information derived from the technical module;

ii) a variable length string genetic algorithm, that optimizes the portfolios according to the technical committee's sentence produced in the learning phase.

2.1 Investment module

As I mentioned in the introduction, I define the portfolio management problem in terms of a zero investment strategy (see, for example, Chincarini & Kim (2006)). According to this approach, I seek to profit from detecting perceived mispricings in individual securities. The buying and selling are concurrent events - I buy underpriced securities and simultaneously sell an offsetting amount of overpriced securities. The combination of the long and short portfolios generates the so-called long-plus-short portfolio. The excess return on this combined portfolio equals the excess return generated by the short portfolio and the interest earned on the proceeds from the short sales, increased by the excess return obtained from the long portfolio. In this sense, the ability to short, by increasing the investor's freedom to act on his/her insights, has the potential to enhance returns from active security selection. Thus, the zero investment strategy used in the portfolio management module should highlight the capabilities of technical indicators to rank assets in a stock picking perspective.

2.2 Technical module

The detection of overbought/oversold conditions and short-term changes in the relative value of stocks are tackled by applying technical analysis in order to summarize all relevant information of the past history of financial time series into short-term statistics. This approach has the advantage of obtaining up-to-date technical indicators as often as every few seconds. I adopt different types of technical indicators in order to dispose of different points of view

from which to analyze price movements and unrealized piece of news that would influence a given security in the near future. Once a signal is produced for the stocks in the market, a positive number (ID) is assigned to the corresponding parameter configuration. These IDs represent the genetic material for the next step.
The technical indicators employed are the described in the following subsections (for an exhaustive list of indicators used by practitioners, refer to Colby & Meyers (1990) and Murphy (1998)).

2.2.1 Rate of change indicator

The rate of change (ROC) indicator represents the speed at which a variable changes over a specific period of time. In this study, it is calculated as the relative difference between the current closing price P_t and the closing price n days in the past P_{t-n-1}, i.e.

$$\mathrm{ROC}(n)_t = \frac{P_t - P_{t-n-1}}{P_{t-n-1}}. \tag{1}$$

2.2.2 Relative strength index

The relative strength index (RSI) is a momentum oscillator that compares the magnitude of recent gains to the magnitude of recent losses for a given stock, in order to highlight potential short-term overbought and oversold levels. It is defined at each time t as:

$$\mathrm{RSI}(n)_t = 100 - \frac{100}{1 + \mathrm{RS}(n)} \tag{2}$$

where RS is the ratio of average gains and average losses during the last n days. It assumes values between 0 and 100. A level less than 30 indicates a buy signal, conversely, a level greater than 70 suggests a sell signal.

2.2.3 Moving average indicators

A moving average is a mean value calculated over a previous rolling period of fixed length n. I use three types of moving averages for a rolling window of length n at time t:

i) the simple moving average (SMA), defined by

$$\mathrm{SMA}(n)_t = \sum_{i=0}^{n-1} \frac{1}{n} P_{t-i}; \tag{3}$$

ii) the weighted moving average (WMA), calculated as

$$\mathrm{WMA}(n)_t = \sum_{i=0}^{n-1} \frac{n-i}{\widehat{n}} P_{t-i} \tag{4}$$

where $\widehat{n} = \sum_{j=1}^{n-1} j$;

iii) the exponential moving average (EMA), expressed by

$$\text{EMA}(n)_t = \frac{1}{n}P_t + \left(1 - \frac{1}{n}\right)\text{EMA}(n)_{t-1} \quad (5)$$

$\text{EMA}_0(n) = P_0$ and 0 is a reference date.

These moving averages constitute the building-blocks of all the technical signals I define in what follows. The idea is to use the down crossing of a shorter moving average with respect to a longer moving average as a buy signal and the crossing in the opposite direction as a sell signal.

2.2.4 Hull moving average

The Hull moving average is a smoothing signal defined by the WMA of length square root n of the difference between a WMA of length $n/2$ and a WMA of length n, i.e.

$$\text{HMA}(n)_t = \text{WMA}\left(\lfloor\sqrt{n}\rfloor\right)_t \text{of} \left(2 \times \text{WMA}\left(\left\lfloor\frac{n}{2}\right\rfloor\right)_t - \text{WMA}(n)_t\right). \quad (6)$$

HMA is more responsive to current price activity with respect to SMA, WMA and EMA while maintaining curve smoothness.

2.2.5 Variable-length moving average

The variable-length moving average (VMA), applied extensively in literature for their simplicity (see, for example, Brock et al. (1992)), is defined at time t as the difference between a n_1 days SMA (shorter) and a n_2 days SMA (longer):

$$\text{VMA}(n_1, n_2)_t = \text{SMA}(n_1)_t - \text{SMA}(n_2)_t \quad (7)$$

with $n_1 < n_2$.

2.2.6 Moving average convergence divergence

The moving average convergence divergence (MACD) is a trend follower procedure that combines two EMAs of past prices:

$$\text{MACD}(n_1, n_2)_t = \text{EMA}(n_1)_t - \text{EMA}(n_2)_t \quad (8)$$

with $n_1 < n_2$. It performs better during strong trending periods and, conversely, tends to lose money during periods of choppy trading.

I consider a variant of this indicator, according to which a trigger signal SL, expressed as a k period EMA of the MACD, is also used to obtain the MACD histogram (MACDH) indicator, defined by

$$\text{MACDH}_t = \text{MACD}_t - \text{SL}_t \quad (9)$$

that highlights variations in the spread between fast and slow signals (see Fusai & Roncoroni (2008) for a detailed description).

2.2.7 Weighted and simple moving average

The weighted and simple moving average (WSMA), proposed by Leontitsis & Pange (2004) is a twice smoothed linear combination of the difference of a n_1 WMA and a n_2 SMA and is expressed by

$$GD(n_1, n_2)_t = (1 + v)\,\mathrm{WMA}(n_1)_t - v\,\mathrm{SMA}(n_2)_t \tag{10}$$

with $n_1 < n_2$ and v is a real number used to weight the moving averages. The WSMA is obtained by applying twice the procedure used to compute GD (see Leontitsis & Pange (2004) for the exact definition).

2.2.8 On balance volume indicator

The on balance volume (OBV) represents the flow of volume in a stock and is calculated as a running cumulative total of the daily volume transactions, adding the amount of daily volume when the closing price increases, and subtracting the daily volume when the closing price decreases:

$$\mathrm{OBV}_t = \begin{cases} \mathrm{OBV}_{t-1} - \mathrm{Vol}_t, & \text{if } P_t < P_{t-1} \\ \mathrm{OBV}_{t-1}, & \text{if } P_t = P_{t-1} \\ \mathrm{OBV}_{t-1} + \mathrm{Vol}_t, & \text{if } P_t > P_{t-1} \end{cases} \tag{11}$$

where Vol_t is the volume at day t.

The signal employed for trading is obtained by comparing the OBV level with the simple moving average on the last n days of the OBV itself: an OBV greater (lesser) than the SMA indicates that the volume is on up (down) days, confirming a possible up (down) trend.

2.3 Evolutionary learning module

The portfolio selection problem can be stated as the problem of detecting the individual that produces the best risk-reward tradeoff among a set of artificial expert systems. In this context, an expert system becomes the result of the mean average of a set of technical signals, the so called plurality voting committee (PVC).

My evolutionary procedure is based on a genetic algorithm that uses an elite strategy to clone the best individual from one generation to the next. Selection is made by the stochastic universal sampling (Baker (1987)). Moreover, in order to generate portfolios consistent over time, I implement the population seeding suggested by Aranha & Iba (2007), according to which the best individual from the previous optimized population is copied in the initial population of the current optimization period.

2.3.1 Genetic encoding

My chromosome $\mathcal{S}$ would be composed of two blocks of genes. The first block uses one gene and represents the long-plus-short portfolio size. The second block represents the ensemble of technical signals. It is based on the variable length string encoding proposed in Kaucic (2010). This block uses a string of length l_{max}, fixed by the user, that represents the maximum length acceptable for an ensemble. Each gene assumes a value in the enlarged discrete alphabet $\{0, 1, \ldots, |\mathcal{S}_{all}|\}$ where each non-zero number corresponds to an ID in $\mathcal{S}_{all}$ and the zero index has been added in order to utilize the existing evolutionary operators as much as possible and corresponds to the "no rule" input. The chromosome is rearranged so that all 0's are pushed to the end. I define valid an individual when it has at least two non-zero alleles and all the included rules are different. In this manner, the genetic algorithm excludes the chromosome with all the alleles null and the ensembles with repeated signals. Subsequently, the non-zero genes of the second block are sorted in an increasing way to guarantee more diversity among population since the ensembles resulting by the PVC technique are invariant under permutations of their constituents.

2.3.2 Crossover

Uniform crossover is used to avoid the positional and distributional bias that may prevent the production of good solutions (see Reeves (2003) for a detailed discussion). A control on the composition of each offspring is included to guarantee its admissibility.

2.3.3 Mutation

An alternating mutation probability $\mu_m(g)$ that depends on the generation $g \in \{1, \ldots, G\}$, throughout a triangle wave relation, is used to provide a better balance between exploration and exploitation of the search space. The mutation operator is based on Bandyopadhyay & Pal (2007): for each position in a string, it is determined whether conventional mutation can be applied or not with probability μ_m. Otherwise, the position is set to 0 with probability μ_{m_1} and each "no signal" is set to a signal according to another mutation probability μ_{m_2}. Similar to the crossover, the string is then reordered to have the admissible form previously described.

2.3.4 Objective

My procedure applies to a general type of performance measures, grouped under the name of *reward-to-risk ratio* (refer to Rachev et al. (2008) for a detailed presentation), shortly RR. This performance measure is defined as the ratio between a reward measure of the active portfolio return and the risk of the active portfolio return:

$$RR(r_p, r_b) = \frac{\nu\left(r_p - r_b\right)}{\rho\left(r_p - r_b\right)} \tag{12}$$

where r_p denotes the return of the portfolio, r_b represents the return of the benchmark portfolio, $r_p - r_b$ is the active portfolio return, and $\nu(\cdot)$ and $\rho(\cdot)$ are a generic reward measure and a generic risk respectively. In this case r_b is the 3-month Treasury Bill. The objective is to find the portfolio with the maximum RR.

Since I base my investment solely on technical analysis and I make no hypothesis about the distributions of r_p and r_b, I can calculate $RR(r_p)$ using the available historical returns in a certain period of length T back in time. Following Kaplan (2005), let $r_t = \left(r_p - r_b\right)_t$ denote the active portfolio return at time t, $t = 1, \ldots, T$, the reward measure becomes

$$\mu\left(r_t\right) = \frac{1}{T}\sum_{t=1}^{T} r_t. \tag{13}$$

By varying the risk measure at the denominator of Equation (12), I obtain the following two RR measures:

Name	Value
Generations	300
Population size	100
Seeding size	1
Elite size	1
Crossover probability	0.5
Mutation probabilities	$\mu_m \in [0.02, 0.45]$
	$\mu_{m_1} = \mu_{m_2} = 0.95$

Table 1. Evolutionary parameters.

i) the information ratio (IR), for which the risk measure is the standard deviation of r_t, that is

$$\sigma(r_t) = \sqrt{\frac{1}{T-1}\sum_{t=1}^{T}(r_t - \mu(r_t))^2}; \tag{14}$$

ii) the Sortino Ratio (SR), for which the risk measure is the square root of the second lower partial moment of r_t, that is

$$\sigma_2^-(r_t) = \sqrt{\frac{1}{T}\sum_{t=1}^{T}\max(-r_t, 0)^2}. \tag{15}$$

A third performance measure that has become very popular among practitioners in the last years is the so-called Omega ratio, which is defined as:

$$\Omega(r_p, r_b) = \frac{\mu(r_t)}{\sigma_1^-} + 1 \tag{16}$$

where $\mu(r_t)$ comes from Equation (13) and σ_1^- represents the first lower partial moment of r_t, i.e.

$$\sigma_1^-(r_t) = \frac{1}{T}\sum_{t=1}^{T}\max(-r_t, 0). \tag{17}$$

3. Experimental results

3.1 Parameter values

In the following experiments, I used the same values for the genetic algorithm parameters, which were obtained from preliminary tests and gave acceptable convergence results. The parameter setting is listed in Table 1.

3.2 Data and experiments description

I use daily data for the Dow Jones Industrial Average (DJI) from 25 January 2006 to 19 July 2011. The data series include the highest, lowest and closing prices and the volume

Param	Value
Market	all stocks in DJI
Period	02/01/2004 – 12/10/2011
Min. size long-plus-short portfolio	4
Max. size long-plus-short portfolio	16
Objective experiment 1	Information Ratio
Objective experiment 2	Omega
Objective experiment 3	Sortino Ratio
Evaluation technique	sliding window
Training length (days)	120
Testing length (days)	60

Table 2. Experiments configuration.

of transactions. For the corresponding period I adopt the 3-month Treasury Bill rate as the risk-free rate[1].

A set of experiments is conducted to analyze whether the developed portfolio based on technical analysis suggestions and risk-adjusted measures consistently beats the index during the last 5.5 years. To this end, during the evaluation period I implement a sliding window procedure able to adapt the technical signals to the market conditions by matching the trading signal with a period in the recent past, that constitutes the training window. The resulting indicators are then applied to trading immediately after the last historical data period has expired, i.e. the testing window. A new search takes place for each new window. However, instead of starting with a completely new population, a memory is maintained of the best solution from the previous training window, that is used in the generation of the initial population for the next training window. This is achieved using the seeding operator explained in the previous pages.

The characteristics of each case-study are summarized in Table 2. It emerges that the only difference among the experiments is the risk-adjusted measure to optimize. The purpose, in fact, is to study the impact that these performance measures have on the zero investment portfolios according to changing market conditions, assuming no transaction costs.

Finally, I compare the performance of these evolved portfolios with the DJI index, which reflect the performance of the market as a whole.

3.3 Analysis of the performance

Figure 1 displays the evolution of the values attained by the three developed portfolios and the DJI index for the entire period of analysis, while Figure 2 highlights their behavior during the financial crash between 2008 and 2009. It is assumed that the initial common value is 1,000 USD at the starting date, 25 January 2006.

[1] The quotations for the DJI Index are taken from `http://www.finance.yahoo.com` and for the 3-month Treasury Bill from `http://www.federalreserve.gov/releases/h15/data.htm`

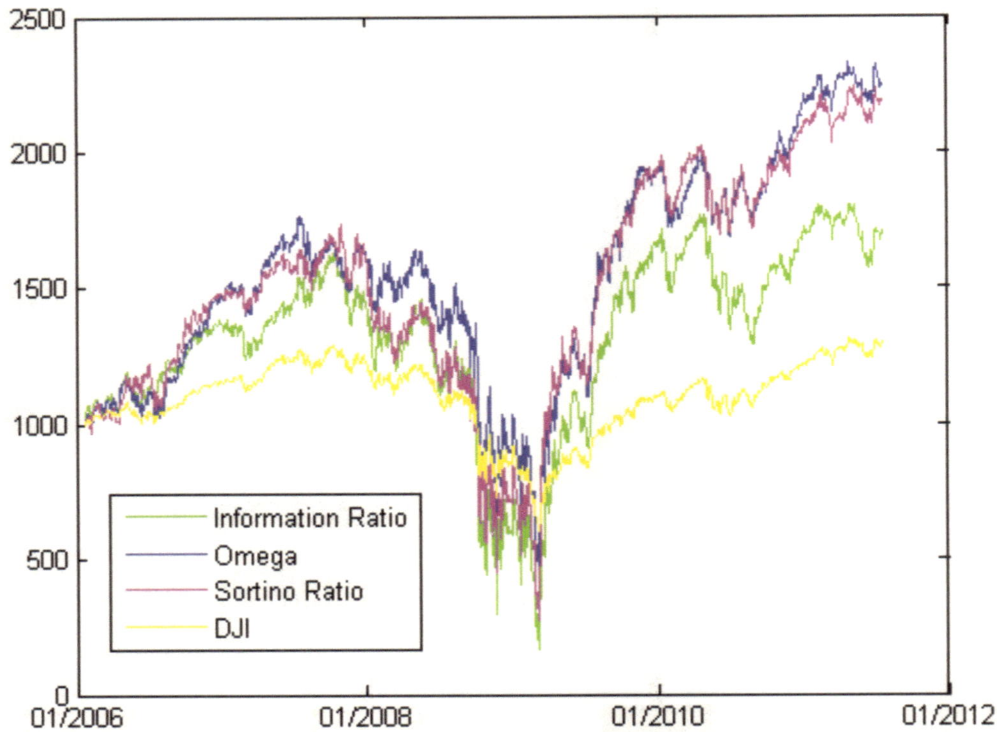

Fig. 1. Evolution of the portfolio values from 25 January 2006 to 19 July 2011 for the proposed management strategies and the DJI index. Each portfolio starts with a value of 1000 USD.

By comparing the plots, it could be observed that the optimized zero investment portfolios outperform remarkably the index during the sample testing period, except for the meltdown. However, even in that period, the Omega based portfolio is able to control the losses better than all the other competitors. After April 2009, the Sortino ratio based portfolio attains results similar to those of the Omega based portfolio. In general, the Information ratio based portfolio does not succeed in obtaining the return levels of the other two optimized portfolios.

In Table 3 I report the returns on an annualized basis and compare the realized values and the returns relative to the the 3-month Treasury Bill.

The total return represents the increase in portfolio values over the whole investment period. While the market improves slightly, with a total return of 29% and an annualized mean return of 5.5%, the Information ratio based portfolio increases by 70% with an annualized mean return of 14%. At the same time, the Sortino ratio based portfolio reaches levels of 119% and 26% respectively. The best results are attained by the Omega based portfolio, which realizes an increment of 125% and an annualized mean return of 26%. The annualized geometric mean returns, however, reveal the difficulties of all the optimized portfolios during the crisis. This is clear for the Information based portfolio, for which the geometric mean is negative (−1.35%). The portfolios I constructed present a double annualized volatility with respect to the market.

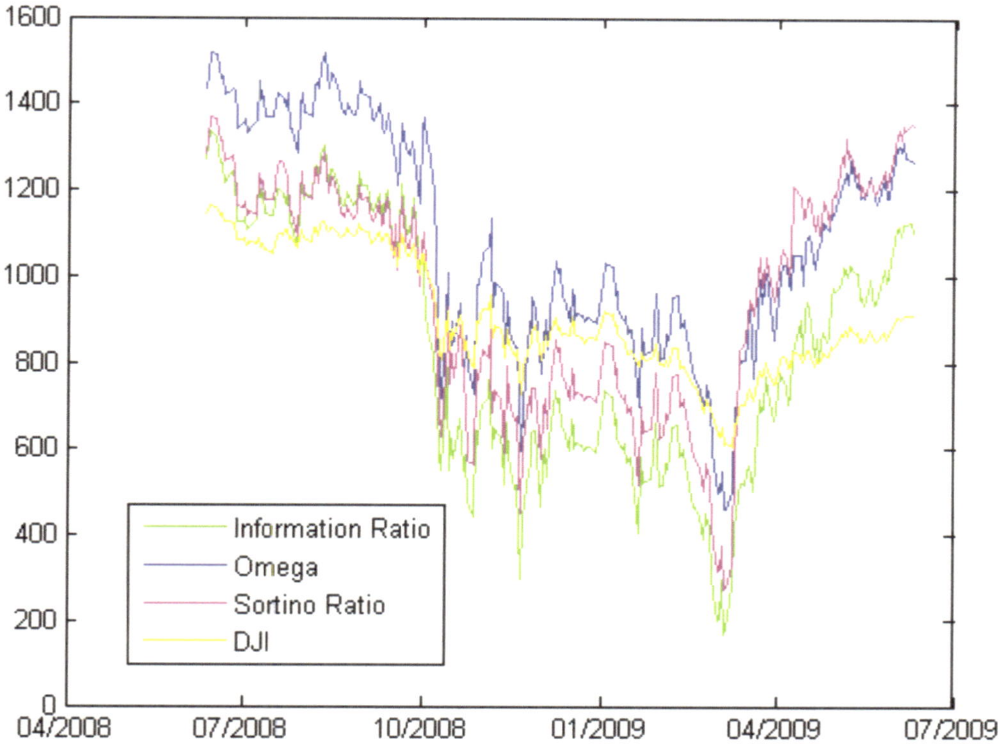

Fig. 2. Enlargement of the evolution of the portfolio values reported in Figure 1 for the period from 11 June 2008 to 9 June 2009.

The same considerations remain valid when portfolios are compared on the basis of premium returns.

Overall, from the summary statistics of the daily returns listed in Table 4 it emerges that the optimized portfolios guarantee a better return potential then the index, even if they may be more volatile. The largest loss, around -19% for all the simulated portfolios, is suffered during the crisis. In the same period the market produces a -8%. However, while the DJI returns to the pre-crisis levels only in the last weeks of the test period, the developed portfolios react faster, generating values comparable to those at the beginning of the crash after only six months.

Finally, I compare the portfolios according to the Sharpe ratio, a reward-to-variability measure that represents how much excess returns investors are awarded for each unit of volatility. It is defined as the difference between the annualized arithmetic mean fund return, $\overline{r}_p$, and the annualized arithmetic mean risk-free return, $\overline{r}_f$, divided by the annualized standard deviation $\overline{\sigma}_p$ of the fund returns:

$$\text{Sharpe}\left(r_p\right) = \frac{\overline{r}_p - \overline{r}_f}{\overline{\sigma}_p}. \tag{18}$$

Once again, the Omega based portfolio proves to be superior with respect to the other competitors.

Statistic	Information Ratio	Omega	Sortino Ratio	DJI
Realized portfolio values				
Total return (%)	70.42	124.69	119.25	29.46
Annualized arithmetic mean return (%)	13.72	25.56	24.32	5.53
Annualized geometric mean return (%)	-1.35	7.92	7.05	2.99
Annualized volatility (%)	53.30	55.30	55.03	22.06
Excess portfolio values				
Total return (%)	63.05	117.31	111.88	22.09
Annualized arithmetic mean return (%)	12.20	23.88	22.66	4.12
Annualized geometric mean return (%)	-2.67	6.47	5.62	1.62
Annualized volatility (%)	53.31	55.30	55.03	22.06

Table 3. Annualized portfolio returns: realized value and excess value above the 3-month Treasury Bill.

Statistic	Information Ratio	Omega	Sortino Ratio	DJI
Average daily return (%)	0.05	0.09	0.09	0.02
Median daily return (%)	0.15	0.15	0.08	0.06
Largest positive return (%)	24.14	28.79	28.57	11.08
Largest negative return (%)	-19.05	-19.52	-18.73	-7.87
Skewness	0.19	0.67	0.76	0.25
Kurtosis	11.37	14.40	13.77	13.03
Freq. gain $>$ 5% (%)	4.49	4.78	4.71	0.43
Freq. loss $>$ 5% (%)	5.14	5.22	5.07	0.65

Table 4. Daily portfolio return characteristics.

Measure	Information Ratio	Omega	Sortino Ratio	DJI
Sharpe ratio	0.22	0.43	0.41	0.16

Table 5. Comparisons in terms of the annualized Sharpe ratio.

4. Conclusions

In this chapter I discussed the development of artificial trading systems for portfolio optimization by using technical analysis.

From a mathematical point of view, I presented a multi-modular evolutionary heuristic capable to deal efficiently with the zero investment strategy. Optimal allocations were detected by using a trading system, structured on the basis of a pool of technical signals, in which the parameters were optimized by a variable length string genetic algorithm. In addition, the chromosome representation I adopt permitted to manage, at the same time, the parameters of the investment strategy.

From an economic point of view, I applied the developed procedure in the optimization of equity portfolios. In particular, I analyzed the efficiency of a general class of performance measures, i.e. the reward-to-risk ratios, for the generation of promising portfolios over time.

Experimental results using historical data from the Dow Jones Industrial Average index showed that the optimized portfolios tend to register outstanding performance for short-term applications. Moreover, they react faster to the market crashes, as I verified during the recent crisis between 2008 and 2009.

I plan further work to implement the transaction costs in the management phase and a more robust learning method for the definition of the technical based committee in the selection of the more informative technical signals.

5. Acknowledgements

I wish to dedicate this work to the memory of my mother, Maria Cristina, who always believed in me and whose smile supported me in the development of these ideas.

6. References

Aranha, C. & Iba, H. (2007). Modelling cost into a genetic algorithm-based portfolio optimization system by seeding and objective sharing, *IEEE Congress on Evolutionary Computation (CEC)*, pp. 196–203.

Baker, J. E. (1987). Reducing bias and inefficiency in the selection algorithm, *Proceedings of the Second International Conference on Genetic Algorithms and their Application*, pp. 14–21.

Bandyopadhyay, S. & Pal, S. K. (2007). *Classification and Learning Using Genetic Algorithms*, Springer.

Brock, W., Lakonishok, J. & LeBaron, B. (1992). Simple technical trading rules and the stochastic properties of stock returns, *The Journal of Finance* XLVII(5): 1731–1764.

Chang, T. J., Meade, N., Beasley, J. & Sharaiha, Y. (2000). Heuristics for cardinality constrained portfolio optimisation, *Computers & Operations Research* 27: 1271–1302.

Chincarini, L. B. & Kim, D. (2006). *Quantitative Equity Portfolio Management: An Active Approach to Portfolio Construction and Management*, McGraw-Hill.

Colby, W. & Meyers, T. (1990). *The Encyclopedia of Technical Market Indicators*, Dow Jones Irwin.

Fernandez-Rodríguez, F., González-Martel, C. & Sosvilla-Rivero, S. (2005). Optimizaton of technical rules by genetic algorithms: evidence from the madrid stock market, *Applied Financial Economics* (15): 773–775.

Fernández-Blanco, P., Bodas-Sagi, D. J., Soltero, F. J. & Hidalgo, J. I. (2008). Technical market indicators optimization using evolutionary algorithms, *GECCO '08*, pp. 1851–1858.

Fusai, G. & Roncoroni, A. (2008). *Implementing Models in Quantitatative Finance: Methods and Cases*, Springer.

Ghandar, A., Michalewicz, Z. & Zurbruegg, R. (2009). Return performance volatility and adaptation in an automated technical analysis approach to portfolio management, *Intelligent Systems in Acounting, Finance and Management* 16(1-2): 127–146.

Gorgulho, A., Neves, R. & Horta, N. (2011). Applying a ga kernel on optimizing technical analysis rules for stock picking and portfolio composition, *Expert Systems with Applications* 38(11): 14047–14085.

Jasemi, M., Kimiagari, A. M. & Jasemi, M. (2011). On development of technical analysis based portfolio optimization models, *Asian Journal of Industrial Engineering* pp. 1–12.

Kaplan, P. D. (2005). A unified approach to risk adjusted performance, *Quantitative research*, Morningstar, Inc., 225 West Wacker Drive, Chicago, IL.

Kaucic, M. (2010). Investment using evolutionary learning methods and technical rules, *European Journal of Operational Research* 207(3): 1717–1727.

Korczak, J. & Lipinski, P. (2003). Evolutionary approach to portfolio optimization.

Korczak, J. & Roger, P. (2002). Stoch timing using genetic algorithms, *Applied Stochastic Models in Business and Industry* (18): 121–134.

Leontitsis, A. & Pange, J. (2004). WSMA: in between weighted and simple average, 17th Annual Pan-Hellenic Conference on statistics, Leukada, Greece, pp. 519–526.

Murphy, J. (1998). *Technical Analysis of the Financial Markets*, New York Institute of Finance, New York.

Oh, K., Kim, T., Min, S. & Lee, H. (2006). Portfolio algorithm based on portfolio beta using genetic algorithm, *Expert Systems with Applications* 30(3): 527–534.

Papadamou, S. & Stephanides, G. (2007). Improving technical trading systems by using a new MATLAB-based genetic algorithm procedure, *Mathematical and Computer Modelling* (46): 189–197.

Rachev, S., Stoyanov, S. W. & Fabozzi, F. J. (2008). *Advanced Stochastic Models, Risk Assessment, and Portfolio Optimization*, The Frank J. Fabozzi series, Wiley.

Reeves, C. (2003). *Handbook of Metaheuristics*, Kluwer Academic Publishers, chapter Genetich Algoritms, pp. 55–82.

Wilding, T. (2003). *Advances in Portfolio Construction and Implementation*, Quantitative Finance Series, Butterworth-Heinemann, chapter Using genetic algorithms to construct portfolios, pp. 135–160.

16

Genetic Algorithm Application for Trading in Market toward Stable Profitable Method

Tomio Kurokawa
Aichi Institute of Technology, Japan

1. Introduction

One application of a training system, including genetic algorithm (GA), to trading in technical market is to create a good model trader using past market data so that the model trader makes good performance in unseen future market data space. It is usually easy to create a model trader to work well for in-sample data. However, it frequently happens that the created model trader makes poor performance for unseen data. This phenomenon is termed as overfitting. This chapter provides some insight into overfitting in the environment of trading in market – enormously wide spaces of in-sample, out-of-sample data and technical model trader's space – and proposes some solution coping with the problems which exist in the spaces.

2. Genetic algorithm as learning system

Learning has been considered as one of the most powerful problem solving techniques for technical market analysis or trading in market. Among many learning systems so far we have devised, genetic algorithm (GA) is considered as one of the most powerful.

Using GA as a learning system for technical market, there are three spaces (Geurts, 2005) we have to take into consideration. The first one is the past data space from which we obtain in-sample data and with which we train the market evaluation systems, say, model traders. The second one is the space of model traders. It could be a simple one—small model space to a complex model trader—large model space. The third one is the unseen future data space to which we apply the trained model trader and hopefully obtain preferable results.

All of the three spaces are so wide compared with the data we can use as past data or the data we will see in the future. As for the past data space, data for a company we can use is only an instance of the data space. We cannot have more than one instance, just one. For unseen future data, it is also true that the one we will see is just one instance, no more than that. The model trader space is possibly called as technical indicator space. The number of algorithm we can try is very limited. Computer generated ones, which are not limited, are inclined to become too particular, lacking of comprehensibility and resulting in overfitting.

3. Background literature

Overfitting has been the major problem of learning of technical market decision. Numerous researches have been done using evolutionally methods (including GA) in the literature. In some past studies, solutions were tried to be sought. Those are categorized into three areas as noted below.

First is about in-sample data selection. Wang et al. employed, in GA, the methods with which newer in-sample data were used for training by sliding the in-sample data window as the trading proceeds (Wang & Chen, 1998) . Lam et al. employed sliding (incremental and dynamic) in-sample data approach for training the system with GA and fuzzy mechanism (Lam et al., 2002). These schemes were based on the presumption that newer data might be better representing coming unseen out-of-sample data. Neely et al. used, in GP (genetic programming), a technique regarded as validation procedure, in which a selection period is placed after the training period in order to select one good program for next generation (Neely et al., 1997). Kurokawa demonstrated that trading chance was increased and at the same time overfitting was reduced by increasing number of stock names concurrently monitored (Kurokawa, 2008, 2009, 2011).

Second is related with learning itself. It is to improve the learning process so that trading rule should have good performance and avoid overfitting. Obtaining a good performance rule is concerned with many things such as learning process itself, elements of computational structure including indicators, fitness strategies, maintaining simplicity, generality and many others. In the past, Becker et al. using, in GP, reduced set of operators, set of increased indicators (elements of computational structure), and complexity penalizing strategy (fitness strategy) in the training process maintained the simplicity of the tree structure of GP-generated rule by limiting the number of nodes and the depth of the tree (simplicity) (Becker & Seshadri, 2003a, 2003b) . Simplicity plays very important roles for avoidance of overfitting because complexity is more likely to cause overfitting (Becker & Seshadri, 2003a). Lin et al. set sub-ranges for parameters of technical trading rules (fitness strategy) by GA and obtained robust results (Lin et al., 2005).

Third is to devise effective technical indicators. Technical indicators play important roles in rule making with learning, especially in evolutionary process. In the process, they are usually pre-given as essential components. For GA, indicators with computational structure are given and the parameters are optimized. For GP, though it has the ability to find good computational structure of technical rules, indicator functions such as moving averages, etc. must be given as basic component at the beginning. Eventually, some of the components play important roles in the generated rules. Such indicators were also used in GP process of the studies by Becker et al. (Becker & Seshadri, 2003a) and they showed positive results. Potvin et al. applied GP to Canadian individual stocks and reported that it did not necessarily outperform buy and & hold (B&H) approach (Potvin et al., 2004). Pavlidis et al. compared moving average based rules and GP-generated rules on money exchange rates and obtained the results that both are profitable but moving average based rule is more robust than the GP-generated one (Pavlidis, et al. 2007) . Mabu et al. included several conventional indicators in GNP (genetic network programming) and showed promising results (Mabu et al., 2007). Kurokawa tried to seek better technical indicators used in GA process (Kurokawa, 2007). More recently, Lohpetch et al. showed a method which gains fairly robust generation of trading rules which outperforms B & H (Lohpetch et al. , 2010) using GP and monthly trading.

4. Potential areas for study

Looking over a stock market, the data are very vast. Even data of a single stock name are vast when considering unseen out-of sample data of potentially numerous patterns. This makes it unreasonable to try to cope with it by learning only a small portion of past data. One or two year market data of a stock name are very small compared to unseen potentially vast out-of-sample data. Learning process is to make the target system particular. It is to adjust the system to the in-sample data. Accordingly, the target system hardly becomes general.

In order to solve the problem, some generality introducing mechanism is necessary. Possible solutions may exist in 1) in-sample data of large size and concurrent monitoring of large set of stocks in trading, 2) sophisticated but simple learning process which can make use of large set of stocks and avoidance of adjusting to the particularity of in-sample data or overfitting and 3) devising effective technical indicators.

For the first potential solution, most studies in literature about market timing by learning have been done with in-sample data of small size, that is, one or two years for a single name or an index or of several years. Small size data usually cannot have generality. Naturally it is hardly possible for any process to extract generality from data of small size. Hence in-sample data of large size are needed. Larger size data are more likely to have more generality. However, they are also difficult to handle and time consuming for processing. There are two ways of expanding in-sample data. One is with data of long period. There are, however, some limitations about the size. The other is a larger set of stock names to concurrently monitor. The latter case was examined with GA procedure using data of hundreds of stock names (Kurokawa, 2008, 2009, 2011). In this study, it is more extensively examined.

For the second potential solution, this is the area where many studies have been done in literature. In order to handle data of large size, effective learning mechanism with fast processing speed and ability avoiding overfitting becomes important. Both of sophistication with simplicity and speed are necessary at the same time. The learning should have the ability to handle the data of large size and to extract the generality. In this study, this concept was examined by introducing indirect fitness control with profit related indexes, which is supposedly essential for stable profit.

The third potential solution is concerned with technical indicator, which is directly related with data computation. It is the device by which trading signals are computed and detected. Since many market timing systems with learning employ technical indicators, developing effective indicators is essentially important. What's more, indicators are independent of learning process in the sense that they are made before learning process operates. Hence, they could bring about generality if not totally influenced by learning. Simplicity and comprehensibility could be given by human heuristics. Hence, effective indicators are of great utility. Some studies were made in this area (Kurokawa, 2007). In this study, however, a technical method (Takizawa, 1999) was used.

5. Three step experiments

This study is of three steps for trading performance improvements and its experimental demonstrations. The first one is to investigate what is overfitting and how it is related with trading performance. The second one is to demonstrate the first one by stock switching. The third one is to show some ways of seeking generality of stable and profitable trading with extensive experiments.

6. First step experiments

To examine how influential the selection of in-sample data is, three experiments using GA with the market timing indicator SP-method (Takizawa, 1999; Kurokawa, 2009) were conducted with different stock data of different sizes but of the same data period. Data from Jan. 1, 2001, to Dec. 31, 2002, were used for training and those from Jan. 1, 2003 to Dec. 31, 2004 for testing. These experiments were mainly to get information on market features, not just to find the best trading model. It did not calculate trading returns for a period but certain profit related indexes. In the experimental trading, a unit of stock was bought whenever a buy signal appeared and when the profit rate exceeded a predetermined level or stock holding went beyond a predefined number of days, the stock was sold. Trading was independent of the amount of cash held.

Another important point here is that the trading did not depend on the timing of incidentally selected buying/selling, so these results show the features of the entire stock market better. Ordinary trading simulation tends to depend on timing. Some buy decisions for some stock mean not buying other stocks – results by these decisions are dependent on timing.

Chromosome was composed of a set of parameters specifying how to run trading and was optimized in GA. They were Gene0, Gene1, Gene2, Gene3, Gene4, and Gene5 as:

1. Gene0: SP-wave rate, SP%
2. Gene1: SP-minus change rate, SP%-
3. Gene2: maximum number of days to hold bought stock
4. Gene3: minimum recovery rate to sell bought stock
5. Gene4: minimum falling speed of price
6. Gene5: maximum price level

6.1 How GA experiments were done

An ordinary fitness criterion in stock trading is conceptually simple – maximizing profit. The experiments here, however, calculate more than mere profit; they calculate the following profit-related indexes:

- Total profit (TP): the sum of all unit trade profit. "Trade" is used interchangeably here as a stock unit buy/sell pair.
- Winning count (WCT): the count of profitable trade
- Win rate (WRT): the profitable trade count divided by all trade count
- Total of profit rates (TPR): the sum of profit rates on all trades
- Average profit rate (APR): the total of profit rates divided by the number of trades.

TPR, a special index, usually not used, was to get overall market features of both quality and quantity of trading, which is why it was selected for fitness. Some quality (profit rate) must be maintained because transaction cost was ignored in the experiments.

The following represent specific definitions:

$$profit(i) = sell\_price(i) - buy\_price(i), \tag{1}$$

$$TP = \sum_{i=1}^{N} profit(i), \tag{2}$$

$$PR(i) = \frac{profit(i)}{buy\_price(i)}, \tag{3}$$

$$TPR = \sum_{i=1}^{N} PR(i), \tag{4}$$

where i is the identifier for each trade, *buy_price(i)* the stock price at the buying of trade i, *sell_price(i)* the stock price at the selling of trade i, and N total trade count. *TPR* was used as fitness to give each trade equal weight to make it independent of individual stock name's price levels. *TP* might be greatly influenced by some stocks with very high prices.

An ordinary GA was used for optimization, as shown in Fig. 1. GA parameters were crossover rate: 0.7, mutation rate: 0.1, population size: 20, number of generations: 200 and elitisms. The population size was set rather small to speed up large-scale data processing but within a generally allowable range. These specific parameters were chosen arbitrarily and involve no particular reasoning. The parameters of population size 20 and number of generations 200 were rather small, so hitting a globally optimal point is not necessarily expected. Limited optimization, however, is considered acceptable here. Experiments 1-3 are detailed below.

6.2 Data size and overfitting

6.2.1 Experiment 1-1

Ten trading simulations were done independently, one for each of ten stock names, with training done using in-sample data for each stock name, followed by testing using out-of-sample data for the same stock name. Results are shown in Table 1. WCT, TP, and TPR values in testing were much lower than those in training. Stock names No. 2, 4, 6, 7, and 8 gave no chance for trading in testing. "N/A" in Table 1 suggests that the system looked for trading signals but in vain — typical for overfitting. The model trader was so adjusted to in-sample data that it could not find a chance for out-of-sample data. The average successful trade count was 4.7 in training but only 0.7 in testing. The one single chance for Asahi Glass, for example, was not successful in testing.

Experimental results suggest that the model trader trained with a small segment of stock data could lose chances for trading. The target obtained with small in-sample data may thus not be suited to unseen data, which is assumed to be just one incident out of a potentially vast number of data patterns.

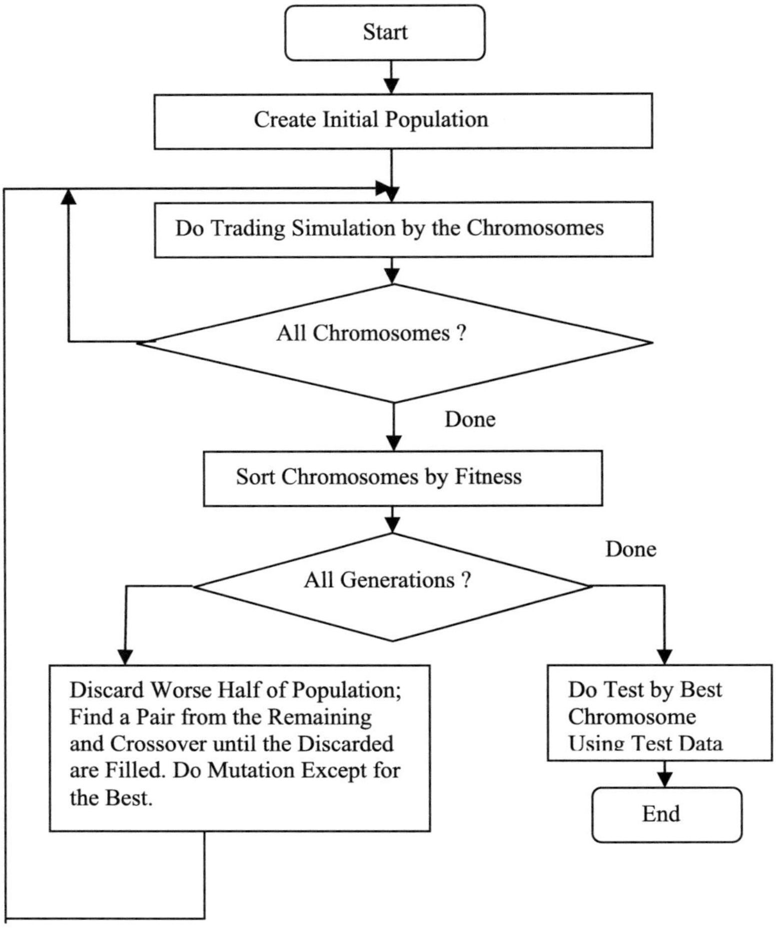

Fig. 1. GA Procedure

	Training (2001-2002)					Test (2003-2004)				
Stock Name	WCT	TP	APR	WRT	TPR	WCT	TP	APR	WRT	TPR
1 Shimizu	4	386	0.223	0.800	1.117	1	151	0.429	1.000	0.429
2 Itoham Foods	11	306	0.073	0.846	0.947	0	0	0.000	N/A	0.000
3 Oji Paper	3	456	0.316	1.000	0.948	1	84	0.180	1.000	0.180
4 Sumitomo Chemical	2	260	0.372	1.000	0.745	0	0	0.000	N/A	0.000
5 Asahi Glass	5	865	0.212	0.833	1.271	0	-20	-0.030	0.000	-0.030
6 Sumitomo Heavy Ind.	2	44	0.355	1.000	0.710	0	0	0.000	N/A	0.000
7 Toshiba	4	401	0.244	1.000	0.975	0	0	0.000	N/A	0.000
8 Matushita Electric Works	4	173	0.062	1.000	0.249	0	0	0.000	N/A	0.000
9 Sumitomo	6	788	0.147	0.750	1.174	3	159	0.100	1.000	0.299
10 Yusen	6	347	0.152	1.000	0.915	2	109	0.127	1.000	0.254
average	4.7	402.6	0.216	0.923	0.905	0.7	48.3	0.081	N/A	0.113

Table 1. Results by training using past data for one stock name for each line (10 names)

6.2.2 Experiment 1-2

Experiment 1-2 used the same stock data of those names as for Experiment 1-1. By concurrently monitoring stocks for 10 names for the in-sample period, just one trading rule was generated instead of one rule for each name. The specified fitness was TPR, the same as that for Experiment 1-1. Results are shown in Table 2. The same procedure was executed 10 times, and the averages were computed and are shown at the end of the table.

In experiments, trading opportunities appear to have been reduced in testing, apparently the result of overfitting, or losing opportunities. Overfitting, however, appears to have been reduced in these experiments. The quality of trading (APR and WRT) decreased both in training and testing from Experiment 1-1 to Experiment 1-2. Good trading opportunities in Experiment 1-2 (WCT: 37.3 in training and WCT: 13.5 in testing), however, were much improved over those in Experiment 1-1 (WCT: 4.7 in training and WCT: 0.7 in testing) and overfitting appears to have been somewhat reduced in Experiment 1-2 from the viewpoint of trading opportunities. Both APR and WRT were slightly lower in testing than in training in Experiment 1-2. APR of 0.064 and WRT of 0.743 in testing appear very good compared to the results (He et al., 2007) – return of 0.0212 for GP1, return of -0.1792 for GP2, and returns by others for Japanese stocks of the same period, though the comparisons are not direct. It may not be decisive, however, for the Japanese stock index Nikkei average, which increased about 30% during 2003 to 2004. Stocks of the ten names examined in the experiments actually had 78.5% gain as average during the period.

APR and WRT in Experiment 1-1 and 1-2 are difficult to evaluate, but given the results of "N/A" (No Trade), trading as done in Experiment 1-1 cannot be said to be advantageous.

Note that trading signals or patterns should have appeared in many places among stocks for multiple stock names.

	Training (2001-2002)					Test (2003-2004)				
Exp. No	WCT	TP	APR	WRT	TPR	WCT	TP	APR	WRT	TPR
1	23	1160	0.117	0.885	3.052	8	270	0.081	0.800	0.813
2	23	1160	0.117	0.885	3.052	8	270	0.081	0.800	0.813
3	71	1209	0.024	0.607	2.817	22	546	0.052	0.759	1.512
4	44	1298	0.060	0.830	3.186	11	173	0.038	0.733	0.576
5	46	1346	0.052	0.793	3.036	15	330	0.042	0.750	0.835
6	48	1278	0.049	0.814	2.877	16	270	0.045	0.762	0.950
7	56	1587	0.033	0.589	3.141	32	728	0.042	0.653	2.069
8	16	1304	0.112	0.667	2.681	4	208	0.075	0.444	0.673
9	23	1158	0.120	0.920	3.003	9	331	0.099	0.900	0.987
10	23	1160	0.117	0.885	3.052	10	355	0.081	0.833	0.976
average	37.3	1266.0	0.080	0.788	2.990	13.5	348.1	0.064	0.743	1.020

Table 2. Results by training simultaneously using past data for 10 stock names

6.2.3 Experiment 1-3

Experiment 1-3 used stock data of 844 stock names, from which those priced above 2,000 Yen were discarded, from Tokyo Market Division I. Experiments were done under the same condition of Experiment 1-2 except the number of stock names and the price requirement. Stocks for all names were monitored concurrently. One single trading rule for stocks of all names was generated using in-sample data instead of generating one rule for each stock name. Results are shown in Table 3. Specified fitness, TPR, was the same as that in Experiment 1-1 and 1-2.

WCT, TP, and TPR values increased greatly in both training and testing, suggesting that opportunities for trading increased in Experiment 1-3. Although not shown explicitly, it appears that there should have existed many stock names for which no trading signals appeared in the testing period. Average APR in training declined from Experiment 1-2 to Experiment 1-3 from 0.080 to 0.037, although the reason remains unclear. It may conceivably have been caused by price declines for a large number of stock names. Average APR values increased in testing from 0.064 in Experiment 1-2 to 0.071 in Experiment 1-3 and from 0.037 in training to 0.071 in testing in Experiment 1-3, possibly due to many successful signal detections in many places in the out-of-sample period.

The overall results of Experiment 1-3 seem to suggest that overfitting was reduced greatly by the concurrent monitoring of numerous stocks. Attention should therefore be paid to the results showing that differences in WCT, TP, and TPR between training and testing decreased as data size increased. As stated earlier, Experiment 1-3 also shows that signals caught by the model trader appeared in many places among stocks of multiple names, as is shown by the large WCT, TP, and TPR values in Table 3.

APR average of 7.1% and WRT average of 70.6% in testing appear to be very good compared to the study results (He et al., 2007) as shown in Experiment 1-2, though the comparisons are not direct. It also appears convincing because the number of stock names used in the experiment is large. It is not actually decisive, however, because the Nikkei Average during 2003 to 2004 rose about 30%, very large gain.

	training (2001-2002)					test (2003-2004)				
Exp. No.	WCT	TP	APR	WRT	TPR	WCT	TP	APR	WRT	TPR
1	1309	35810	0.051	0.607	109.627	799	14764	0.060	0.662	72.342
2	2696	42040	0.023	0.568	109.298	1769	35218	0.041	0.631	115.556
3	2989	45648	0.025	0.628	121.000	1948	33923	0.042	0.706	117.332
4	359	14381	0.112	0.634	63.217	21	828	0.307	0.875	7.360
5	4498	48310	0.018	0.639	126.864	2940	46511	0.034	0.726	139.323
6	1330	37274	0.050	0.608	109.137	847	16186	0.059	0.664	75.383
7	4183	45704	0.018	0.611	123.665	2742	45195	0.036	0.699	141.175
8	1859	38295	0.035	0.601	107.644	1264	26552	0.055	0.685	101.528
9	4774	45915	0.016	0.630	123.723	3170	50035	0.033	0.720	146.309
10	2912	47148	0.025	0.606	118.826	1906	34726	0.044	0.688	120.554
average	2690.9	40052.5	0.037	0.613	111.300	1740.6	30393.8	0.071	0.706	103.686

Table 3. Results by training simultaneously using past data for 844 stock names

6.3 Quantitative comparison of the results and overfitting phenomenon

Overfitting is the phenomenon in which poor performance appears for out-of-sample data despite good performance for in-sample data. We define this somewhat more formally as the ratio:

$$Overfitting = \frac{PerformanceForInSampleData}{PerformanceForOutOfSampleData} \tag{5}$$

Table 4 shows the experimental ratios. The figures in Table 4 were calculated using averages given at the bottoms of Tables 1 to 3. Note the changes in ratios during the transition in data size. TPR was used as fitness, so primary attention should be paid to the related aspects. Values in TPR row no. 3 are these ratios, which decrease as data size increases. For small-scale data, TPR performance for the in-sample was 8.01 times greater than that for the out-of-sample. For medium-scale data, it was 2.93, becoming 1.07 for large-scale data. This means that the performance difference between in-sample and out-of-sample data decreases as data size increases. This can be called reducing of overfitting by larger-scale data. Performances other than TPR showed similar trends. Take WCT, for example. Winning signals caught in the in-sample period appeared in the out-of-sample period more often for large-scale data but not for small-scale data.

Smaller ratios are seen for larger-scale data for APR and WRT also. These, however, should be regarded as accidental. The ratios smaller than 1.0 indicate that performance for out of sample data could be better than that for in-sample data, depending on the situation.

We believe that the performance difference between in-sample and out-of-sample periods should not be too big. Any big difference is usually considered caused by overfitting. If the difference is too big, the system is generally considered as not working well, possibly unstable.

Ratio: In-Sample / Out-of-Sample	One Stock Name: Small-scale Data (Experiment 1-1)	10 Stock Names: Medium-scale Data (Experiment 1-2)	844 Stock Names: Large-scale Data (Experiment 1-3)
1. WCT	4.7/0.7=6.71	37.3/13.5=2.76	2691/1741=1.55
2. TP	402.6/48.3=8.34	1266/348=3.64	40053/30394=1.32
3. TPR	0.905/0.113=8.01	2.990/1.020= 2.93	111.300/103.686=1.07
4. APR	0.216/0.081=2.67	0.080/0.064=1.25	0.037/0.071=0.52
5. WRT	N/A	0.788/0.743=1.06	0.613/0.706=0.87

Table 4. Performance comparison between in-sample and out-of-sample data and between data sizes

6.4 Other aspects of overfitting

As stated before, overfitting is the phenomenon in which poor performance appears for out-of-sample data despite good performance for in-sample data. It is usually not difficult to obtain a good model trader for in-sample data. It means that the model trader space is usually wide enough so that training system can find a good performance model trader for the sample data. Many of training systems such as genetic algorithm, neural network (NN), or genetic programming (GP) usually works well for creating a good model trader for in-sample data. NN with two or more hidden layers or GP with much flexibility of programming usually have such a wide space for model traders that it is inclined to produce a kind of nonsense trader which often makes poor performance for unseen out-of-sample data. GA is not an exception. It often produces poor performance traders for out-of-sample data. It often depends on what to optimize. In addition, the created trader with NN or GP usually does not have comprehensibility in the trading rules of the trader.

However, GA which is usually used to adjust a model trader, already structured, to the in-sample data. Owing much to the past researchers of technical analysis, GA is used to find good parameters for the model traders. The technical model traders have spaces wide enough that GA can easily adjust them for the model to work well for in-sample data. However, it is not usually easy for the created traders to work well for unseen out-of-sample data. Overfitting also often appears for GA trained model traders. This overfitting is one of the biggest problems many researchers have tried to solve for market trading. However, it is expected to be smaller for GA trained technical traders than for those by GP or NN. It is probably because the model traders' space for GA is much smaller and because their computation structure is often well organized. This is supported by the study (Pavlidis, et al. 2007).

7. Second step experiments: Switching from one stock to another with data of different sizes

It has been pointed out that large size data have more generality and therefore possibly more effectiveness than a small size data to learn. In other words, there are more generality in training and more opportunities in practical trading. However, large size data are not easy to handle. Based on the demonstrated effectiveness by the experiments with large size data (Kurokawa, 2009), simulations in this study were organized to examine the model trader of switching from one stock to another. In order to see the essence, the model was designed as simple as possible.

Two kinds of experiments were done with different stock data of different sizes for comparison. The experimental procedure was almost the same as the procedure shown by Fig. 1, which was used in the first step experiments except trading was with stock switching. They were the following two:

1. Experiment 2-1 with each single stock name (actually no stock switching), and
2. Experiment 2-2 with 10 stock names for concurrent monitoring.

But, the data periods were the same between the above two and also the same as the first step experiments. The data from 2001/1/1 to 2002/12/31 were used for training and those from 2003/1/1 to 2004/12/31 were for testing. All data were from daily data of Tokyo Stock Market Division I.

The following are how the experimental trading was done. At the start, some amount of cash, supposedly very large, was provided. For the experiment with a single stock name, whenever buy signal appeared, the stocks of the name were bought as many as possible with the available cash and when the sell condition appeared (when the profit rate became more than predetermined level or stock holding length got beyond the predefined number of days), all the stocks were sold. It is a very simple model trader with buy first and sell.

The model trader employed the same chromosome in structure and function which was used in the first step experiments. They are the genes of Gene0, Gene1, Gene2 and Gene3, Gene4, and Gene5 as previously stated. For the model with concurrently monitoring multiple stock names, more than one name could show buy timing at same time. In the case, the stock name with the smallest SP-minus change rate was chosen.

7.1 Computed indexes, fitness, and GA parameters

The first step experiments were for surveying the market – how trading signals were distributed among stocks of multiple names, how quantity and quality of trading were, etc. The second step experiments were to do more practical trading simulations taking advantage of the results of the first step experiments. The organized model trader was to do trading with stock switching among multiple stock names taking advantage to increased trading signals distributed among them and decreased overfitting. The purposes of the second step experiments are to examine how profitable the stock switching is and to compare the results with those of without stock switching.

In stock trading, an ordinary criterion for fitness is simple. It is to maximize the profit or the return. Since the purposes of this step experiments are different from the first ones, the indexes to be computed were changed from the first. The total return (*TRN*), the amount of cash at the end of the simulation divided by the initial cash at the start of the simulation, was used as fitness. Some other indexes were also computed to see how the experiments proceeded. They are the number of trades (*N*: total count of trades), win count (*WCT*: count of profitable trades), win rate (*WRT*: *WCT* divided by *N*), average return (*ARN*: total of individual return divided by the number of trades). "Trade" is used as a pair of buy and sell. The following equations are given for the specific definitions:

$$RTN(i) = \frac{sell\_price(i)}{buy\_price(i)}, \tag{6}$$

$$ARN = \frac{1}{N}\sum_{i=1}^{N} RTN(i), \tag{7}$$

$$WRT = \frac{WCT}{N}, \tag{8}$$

where i is the identifier for each trade, *buy_price(i)* is the price at the buy of trade i, *sell_price(i)* is the price at the sell of trade i and N is the total count of trades, *WCT* is the number of trades with plus profit and *TRN* is the total return, that is, the final amount of cash divided by the initial amount of cash. The actual computation was done as Equations (6) through (9).

$$TRN = \prod_{i=1}^{N} RTN(i) \tag{9}$$

As seen by Equations (6) through (9), transaction costs were ignored.

As for the optimization process, the same GA procedure and the same GA parameters were used as in the first step. They were crossover rate: 0.7; mutation rate: 0.1; population size 20; generation length 200 and elitisms. The same discussions concerning the optimization may be possible as in the first.

The population size was rather set to the small number for fast processing of large size data but within a generally allowable range. Those specific parameters were arbitrarily chosen and there is not a particular reason for them. Since the parameters of population size 20 (rather small) and generation length 200 (rather short) were also arbitrarily chosen, hitting global optimal point might not necessarily possible. The very best optimization was not supposed for this study.

7.2 Switching strategy

In the trade model of switching from one stock to another, the selection policy for next stock to buy becomes very important when more than one stock shows trading signals. There might possibly be many ways to select next stock. What is most effective is yet to be studied and is left for future study. However, a very simple but probably good method was picked up but somewhat arbitrary in this study. That is, the stock with the smallest SP-minus wave rate was selected from among the stocks showing buy timing. The very small values (minus) of SP-minus rate were supposed to show a bottom of stock price like moving average method but somewhat differently.

7.3 Experiments

The details of the two experiments were as follows.

7.3.1 Experiment 2-1

In the experiments, no switching strategy could be employed, because only one stock name was used for each simulation. Ten trading simulations were done independently, one for each of ten stock names. They are the ten used in the first step. In each simulation, training was first done by using in-sample data of each stock name, and then test was made using the out-of-sample data of the same name. The results are shown in Table 5. N-No. column shows stock name number as given previously in Table 1. As seen, the values of WCT and N in testing are much lower than those in training. On the lines with N-No. 6 and 8, there are symbols of "NA" which mean there were no opportunities for trading in the test period. These results seem showing typical overfitting. The average counts of successful trade were 5.7 in training and those in testing were only 1.7. However, the most important result, the return, TRN for the out-of-sample period was 1.207 as the average. It is not a bad result. Additionally, the win rates (WRT) also were surprisingly good, i.e., 0.921 for in-sample period and 0.811 for out-of-sample period.

At the right end of the table, start and end prices of each stock are shown as well as each return by buy and hold strategy (BHRTN). Start-P is price at the start of the out-of-sample the period and End-P is the price at the end of the period. On the bottom of BHRTN is the average of BHRTNs. It is 1.785. The average return of Experiment 2-1 is 1.207. This value

1.207 seemed good until the average return of the ten stocks turned out to be 1.785. Nikkei average during 2003 to 2004 increased about 30%. Using the start and end prices of No. 6 stock, the return of buy and hold becomes 5.69, extremely high value. The price of the stock rose up so steep in the period. Without the stock, the average BHRTN of the remaining nine is about 1.351. It is still far better than the average return of this experiment 1.207.

Experiment 2-1													
	In-Sample Period					Out-of-Sample Period							
N-No.	WCT	N	WRT	ARN	TRN	WCT	N	WRT	ARN	TRN	Start-P	End-P	BHRTN
1	5	6	0.83	1.25	3.56	2	2	1	1.41	1.99	300	514	1.71
2	8	9	0.89	1.12	2.73	1	1	1	1.02	1.02	360	520	1.44
3	5	5	1.00	1.17	2.07	1	2	0.5	1.01	1.02	517	588	1.14
4	2	2	1.00	1.37	1.88	1	1	1	1.21	1.21	478	502	1.05
5	4	6	0.67	1.18	2.46	1	1	1	1.02	1.02	759	1130	1.49
6	2	2	1.00	1.43	2.03	0	0	NA	1.00	1.00	67	381	5.69
7	5	5	1.00	1.18	2.31	1	3	0.33	0.99	0.95	385	440	1.14
8	2	2	1.00	1.16	1.34	0	0	NA	1.00	1.00	748	893	1.19
9	10	10	1.00	1.07	1.98	4	5	0.8	1.04	1.23	540	884	1.64
10	14	17	0.82	1.07	2.82	6	7	0.86	1.07	1.62	407	552	1.36
Ave.	5.7	6.4	0.921	1.199	2.318	1.7	2.2	0.811	1.079	1.207	456.1	640.4	1.785

Table 5. Performance results for Experiment 2-1

7.3.2 Experiment 2-2

In this experiment, the same data of 10 stock names of Experiment 2-1 were used. By concurrently monitoring the stocks of the 10 names for the in-sample period, just one trading rule was generated instead of one rule for each name (Generating a technical rule for each stock name and concurrently monitoring each stock with each corresponding rule in testing is possibly better, though. However, it was not examined in this study). Of course, the specified fitness was the same as that of Experiment 2-1: TRN. The results are shown in Table 6. The same experimental procedure was executed ten times. At the bottom of the table, the averages are shown. "NA" in the table suggests that the model trader looked for a trading signal but in vain. It is possibly showing overfitting. In Experiment 2-2, the trading opportunities (WCT and N) were increased in both of training and testing. Both of WRT and ARN of testing show still good values, 0.837 and 1.068. The average of the total returns (TRN) was also increased from 1.207 to 1.488 in Experiment 2-2. The average total return of 1.488 seems to be very good compared to that of Nikkei Average (Japanese representative stock index) that increased about 30% during the years 2003 to 2004. However, the average of buy and hold return of the ten stocks were about 1.785, far better than 1.488. So the result of the switching model is not surprisingly good. However, as mentioned previously, the return of 1.488 is better than the average return 1.351 which is without No. 6 stock (Sumitomo Heavy Industry) of which BHRTN is 5.69. This company did not give any opportunity of trading in the out-of-sample period of Experiment 2-1. It is probably because of too steep gain of the price. It is not clear, though, that same situation occurred in Experiment 2-2.

Experiment 2-2										
	In-Sample Period					Out-of-Sample Period				
Exp. No.	WCT	N	WRT	ARN	TRN	WCT	N	WRT	ARN	TRN
1	2	2	1.00	1.43	2.03	0	0	NA	1.00	1.00
2	10	10	1.00	1.15	3.94	4	5	0.80	1.09	1.51
3	2	2	1.00	1.43	2.03	0	0	NA	1.00	1.00
4	12	14	0.86	1.12	4.85	7	8	0.88	1.11	2.22
5	14	21	0.67	1.09	5.08	5	7	0.71	1.07	1.49
6	2	2	1.00	1.43	2.03	0	0	NA	1.00	1.00
7	10	10	1.00	1.15	4.14	5	5	1.00	1.14	1.96
8	19	22	0.86	1.10	6.95	4	6	0.67	1.05	1.34
9	8	11	0.73	1.12	3.10	5	5	1.00	1.13	1.86
10	10	10	1.00	1.15	3.94	4	5	0.80	1.09	1.50
Ave.	8.9	10	0.912	1.215	3.810	3.4	4	0.837	1.068	1.488

Table 6. Performance results for Experiment 2-2.

As seen in the table, when poor performances appeared for WCT in training (Exp. No. 1, 3, and 6), there were no trading in testing, TRN was just 1.00 in testing for all of the three. WCTs were all 2, very small, for the training of Exp. No.1, 3 and 6 in Table 6. It may be implying that in these simulations, the GA processes had fallen into local optimal points and that more optimization in training with more generations or larger population might bring about better performance for TRN in learning and testing.

7.4 Evaluation of stock switching

It is very difficult to evaluate the results of Experiment 2-2, the model trader of switching one stock to another. The average value of TRN should be considered very good, but not good enough compared with the average of buy and hold returns 1.785. However, it is true that the switching strategy brought about big improvement. That is, average return of Experiment 2-1 was 1.207, but that of Experiment 2-2 was 1.488, which is a note worthy improvement. This was brought about by switching stocks of the 10 names. Experiments with more stock names are strongly desired. It is also desired to examine how the model behaves when the market is in a down trend.

8. Third step experiments: Toward stable and profitable trading

What we have learned from the previous experiments of the two steps includes the following:

1. GA can find a good (may not a best) model trader.
2. By increasing the number of stock names, trading opportunity increases and it possibly makes overfitting less and trading profitable.
3. Stock switching is one of fairly good ways to handle multiple stock names.
4. Profitable trading might have relation with number of stock names.

The above prompted additional experiments with more stock names and the ones to seek quantity and quality of trading. The following experiments were designed:

8.1 Experiment 3-1

This experiment was done under the exactly same conditions as Experiment 2-2 except the number of stocks was increased to 50. The results are shown in Table 7. Performances were drastically improved from Experiment 2-2. The average TRN for the out-out-sample was increased from 1.488 to 2.20. Some TRNs are more than 3.0. The best is 5.77. This means the original amount became more than tripled or five times larger. This TRN was probably the result of stock switching of extremely good timing, which could hardly be expected for a small set of stock names. As we see the Exp. No. 7 in Table 7, the simultaneously obtained other indexes were also good. ARN was 1.293, which was extremely high; WRT was 1.00, perfect; WCT was 7, rather small.

One experiment (No. 6) resulted in loss, where TRN were 0.98. For this experiment ARN is 1.003, slightly profitable, though. This could happen. The results in general were very good, far better than the average return (1.49) of buy and hold for the 50 stocks. However, we don't know yet how to avoid the loss or how to pick up the one which would surely profitable or one of the best.

8.2 Experiment 3-2

Complex strategy often brings about poor results, overfitting. Even though good results are obtained for a learning period, the model traders are often inclined to pick up some particular profitable events, which would be hardly expected to happen again for an unknown future period, thus results for the unknown periods are frequently not good.

However, controlling fitness in a simple manner aiming to obtain good result may bring about good results. Since the quantity and quality are important for good profitable trading, profitable trading is considered to depend on the frequency of good quality trading. Since those two are considered to be essentially important in both periods of learning and testing, say in any situation, controlling quantity and quality of trading could create a good model trader. With this idea, we made the fitness of the GA to be Equation (10), which is composed of the following indexes. The similar idea was tried (Kurokawa, 2005). The indexes are the total return (TRN), the number of successful trading (WCT), the rate of profitable trading against the number of total trading (WRT) and the average return (ARN), all of which are essential factors for good quality trading. We consider those indexes are essentially related with profit (TRN) and consistently important in any situation. Another point of view for those indexes is the fitness has to be balanced among those indexes. Accordingly, the following index was tried for the fitness to control the experiment (Experiment 3-2).

$$fitness = TRN * WCT * WRT * ARN \tag{10}$$

The results are shown in Table 8. The average return (TRN) was improved from 2.20 to 2.32. One (No. 29) out of 30 experiments resulted in loss. The average successful number of trading (WCT) increased from 17.8 to 59.4. This is a sort of big change. The average return (ARN) changed from 1.059 to 1.008. This is also a significant change. The average winning rate (WRT) changed from 0.69 to 0.58, which is considered a slight change. The phenomena are understood as

1. The frequency of the trading increased significantly.
2. The individual trading profit rate decreased significantly.
3. The success rate decline was a little.

The above means that the obtained model trader would do frequent trading with each small profit. However, it is questionable if it is profitable after trading cost with such a low profit rate.

By the way, the company codes of the 50 stocks are as:

1515, 1803, 1812, 1928, 2002, 2503, 2897, 3402, 3407, 3861, 4005, 4183, 4452, 4502, 4519, 5001, 5333, 5401, 5405, 5706, 5802, 6113, 6301, 6448, 6702, 6753, 6902, 6991, 7011, 7203, 7733, 7735, 7912, 8001, 8015, 8031, 8233, 8332, 8355, 8604, 8801, 9007, 9064, 9101, 9104, 9301, 9302, 9501, 9502, 9719. As the codes suggest, the stocks are from almost all industries. All are from Tokyo Market of division I. The buy and hold rate for all the 50 stocks for the two year period 2003 to 2004 is 1.49. So the results of the above methods are said to be very good compared with B&H.

8.3 Experiment 3-3

In this experiment, simulation data period was shifted two years ahead. The learning period was from 2003 to 2004; the test period was 2005 to 2006. No other conditions were changed from Experiment 3-2. The results are shown in Table 9. The average return (TRN) was changed from 2.32 to 1.52, large decline, which is still considered to be good. This means performance could fluctuate somewhat extensively. No experiment out of the 30 was in loss. The average successful number of trading (WCT) changed from 59.4 to 48.8, not a drastic change. The average return (ARN) changed from 1.008 to 1.007, not significant. The average winning rate (WRT) changed from 0.58 to 0.63, which is also not significant. As a whole, trading characteristics were unchanged, though the total return shows a seemingly big change. By the way, the average B&H profit rate for the 50 stocks was 1.70, which is far better than the average performance of the experiment.

8.4 Experiment 3-4

With the results of Experiment 3-3, a question arose what would happen for Experiment 2-2 if the data period was changed. This experiment was for that. With the data period advanced two years with the previous 10 stock names and the fitness be just the TRN, unchanged, the experiments were done. The results were shown in Table 10. Seven out of 10 experiments had no trading for testing period. This is considered as that overfitting occurred or evolutions were immature. Any way the performance was very poor. TRN was just 1.09 compared with B&H was 1.63.

8.5 Experiment 3-5

This experiment was conducted with the fitness changed from Experiment 3-4, no other change. Fitness employed was Equation (10). The results are shown in Table 11.

The average TRN was 1.35 improved from 1.09; that for WCT was 16.5 from 2.2; that for WRT 0.70 from 0.87; and ARN 1.019 from 1.023. In general, the performances were similar to those of Experiment 3-3. This model trader is characterized as the sort of Experiment 3-3, frequent trading with each small profit.TRN was 1.35, which was still below B&H (1.63).

Experiment 3-1 50-Stocks Fitness=TRN										
	In-Sample(2001-2002)					Out-of-Sample(2003-2004)				
Exp.No.	WCT	N	WRT	ARN	TRN	WCT	N	WRT	ARN	TRN
1	7	8	0.88	1.167	3.18	5	7	0.71	1.057	1.35
2	5	9	0.56	1.129	2.55	5	8	0.63	1.085	1.78
3	10	14	0.71	1.115	4.04	8	14	0.57	1.083	2.57
4	59	97	0.61	1.016	4.12	49	95	0.52	1.008	1.99
5	25	40	0.63	1.028	2.47	20	39	0.51	1.012	1.43
6	25	45	0.56	1.026	2.76	24	45	0.53	1.003	0.98
7	6	7	0.86	1.215	3.57	7	7	1.00	1.293	5.77
8	6	7	0.86	1.222	3.78	6	7	0.86	1.248	4.12
9	9	14	0.64	1.115	3.74	10	14	0.71	1.079	2.55
10	33	36	0.92	1.047	5.06	24	27	0.89	1.040	2.72
11	43	64	0.67	1.032	6.54	31	58	0.53	1.010	1.63
12	7	8	0.88	1.167	3.18	5	7	0.71	1.057	1.35
13	7	9	0.78	1.165	3.23	5	7	0.71	1.100	1.83
14	42	45	0.93	1.038	5.08	16	19	0.84	1.018	1.37
15	8	11	0.73	1.128	3.62	6	10	0.60	1.081	2.05
16	20	24	0.83	1.083	6.15	11	19	0.58	1.010	1.12
17	21	30	0.70	1.054	4.30	18	30	0.60	1.040	2.90
18	18	24	0.75	1.076	5.27	15	18	0.83	1.072	3.22
19	29	45	0.64	1.039	4.85	26	45	0.58	1.017	1.94
20	7	7	1.00	1.204	3.57	5	7	0.71	1.123	1.93
21	14	16	0.88	1.074	3.03	12	15	0.80	1.057	2.23
22	28	45	0.62	1.033	3.67	27	45	0.60	1.014	1.67
23	25	32	0.78	1.049	4.25	17	24	0.71	1.023	1.57
24	34	60	0.57	1.026	3.99	33	61	0.54	1.003	1.14
25	30	32	0.94	1.049	4.50	27	29	0.93	1.049	3.80
26	61	97	0.63	1.017	4.63	49	86	0.57	1.012	2.39
27	28	31	0.90	1.051	4.30	16	19	0.84	1.039	2.00
28	23	37	0.62	1.032	2.83	23	35	0.66	1.020	1.80
29	29	45	0.64	1.038	4.50	25	45	0.56	1.016	1.84
30	8	12	0.67	1.120	3.41	8	11	0.73	1.110	2.92
Ave.	22.2	31.7	0.75	1.085	4.00	17.8	28.4	0.69	1.059	2.20
						B&H Ave. Return Rate				1.49

Table 7. Performance results for Experiment 3-1.

Experiment 3-2 50-Stocks Fitness=TRN*WCT*WRT*ARN										
	In-Sample (2001-2002)					Out-of-Sample(2003-2004)				
Exp. No.	WCT	N	WRT	ARN	TRN	WCT	N	WRT	ARN	TRN
1	83	129	0.64	1.011	3.83	69	118	0.59	1.010	3.09
2	88	124	0.71	1.014	5.14	70	116	0.60	1.011	3.22
3	78	116	0.67	1.015	5.26	60	109	0.55	1.006	1.78
4	68	119	0.57	1.012	3.52	63	115	0.55	1.005	1.70
5	78	114	0.68	1.016	5.73	64	104	0.62	1.012	3.11
6	43	64	0.67	1.032	6.54	31	58	0.53	1.010	1.63
7	74	113	0.66	1.014	4.54	70	105	0.67	1.017	5.18
8	78	120	0.65	1.014	4.96	70	109	0.64	1.013	3.66
9	75	119	0.63	1.012	3.65	63	114	0.55	1.006	1.77
10	59	73	0.81	1.019	3.54	39	55	0.71	1.013	1.83
11	72	128	0.56	1.011	3.60	65	126	0.52	1.003	1.32
12	69	101	0.68	1.014	3.80	57	92	0.62	1.012	2.69
13	71	115	0.62	1.012	3.24	48	107	0.45	1.001	1.00
14	88	123	0.72	1.014	4.81	68	112	0.61	1.012	3.33
15	64	102	0.63	1.013	3.44	53	99	0.54	1.009	2.18
16	63	102	0.62	1.016	4.52	63	98	0.64	1.016	4.12
17	63	104	0.61	1.015	3.98	56	101	0.55	1.010	2.49
18	75	119	0.63	1.013	3.92	64	115	0.56	1.006	1.81
19	55	98	0.56	1.012	2.72	52	98	0.53	1.003	1.21
20	69	101	0.68	1.014	3.80	57	92	0.62	1.012	2.69
21	71	116	0.61	1.012	3.47	52	109	0.48	1.004	1.35
22	78	116	0.67	1.015	5.26	60	109	0.55	1.006	1.78
23	73	128	0.57	1.011	3.57	66	126	0.52	1.003	1.36
24	79	132	0.60	1.012	4.13	81	118	0.69	1.011	3.50
25	73	128	0.57	1.011	3.77	65	126	0.52	1.003	1.30
26	76	120	0.63	1.013	4.08	62	114	0.54	1.005	1.68
27	88	124	0.71	1.014	5.14	69	115	0.60	1.011	3.22
28	59	73	0.81	1.019	3.42	37	56	0.66	1.010	1.62
29	42	82	0.51	1.014	2.59	39	82	0.48	0.997	0.69
30	88	124	0.71	1.014	5.14	70	116	0.60	1.011	3.22
Ave.	71.3	110.9	0.65	1.014	4.17	59.4	103.8	0.58	1.008	2.32
						B&H Ave. Return Rate				1.49

Table 8. Performance results for Experiment 3-2.

Experiment 3-3 50-Stocks Fitness=TRN*WCT*WRT*ARN										
	In-Sample (2003-2004)					Out-of-Sample (2005-2006)				
Exp. No.	WCT	N	WRT	ARN	TRN	WCT	N	WRT	ARN	TRN
1	80	128	0.63	1.018	8.21	58	109	0.53	1.005	1.67
2	75	107	0.70	1.018	6.12	49	85	0.58	1.006	1.62
3	86	135	0.64	1.015	6.84	73	125	0.58	1.006	1.89
4	85	135	0.63	1.015	6.74	73	129	0.57	1.002	1.29
5	63	78	0.81	1.023	5.35	41	63	0.65	1.002	1.06
6	77	108	0.71	1.019	6.76	44	75	0.59	1.006	1.47
7	87	134	0.65	1.015	6.45	77	127	0.61	1.003	1.46
8	82	127	0.65	1.018	8.61	59	110	0.54	1.004	1.44
9	83	135	0.64	1.015	6.84	75	126	0.60	1.005	1.79
10	73	110	0.71	1.014	4.18	63	101	0.62	1.006	1.65
11	40	41	0.98	1.036	4.28	20	24	0.83	1.004	1.03
12	83	136	0.63	1.015	6.90	73	126	0.58	1.005	1.75
13	61	69	0.88	1.028	6.45	35	45	0.78	1.007	1.29
14	43	70	0.69	1.024	4.44	42	70	0.60	1.016	2.73
15	30	32	0.94	1.051	4.65	21	27	0.78	1.018	1.52
16	46	49	0.94	1.031	4.42	34	40	0.85	1.016	1.83
17	86	134	0.64	1.015	6.84	74	128	0.58	1.003	1.43
18	75	107	0.70	1.018	6.12	48	85	0.57	1.005	1.51
19	71	106	0.67	1.020	7.45	17	29	0.59	1.013	1.42
20	68	99	0.69	1.021	7.31	17	28	0.61	1.013	1.42
21	46	68	0.68	1.028	5.66	10	20	0.50	1.001	1.00
22	86	135	0.64	1.015	6.76	71	129	0.55	1.002	1.16
23	87	134	0.65	1.014	5.97	76	127	0.60	1.003	1.42
24	77	108	0.71	1.019	6.76	44	75	0.59	1.006	1.47
25	86	136	0.63	1.015	6.90	77	126	0.61	1.006	2.01
26	56	79	0.71	1.020	4.43	41	69	0.59	1.003	1.17
27	61	69	0.88	1.028	6.45	32	43	0.74	1.005	1.19
28	42	44	0.96	1.036	4.55	23	27	0.85	1.022	1.73
29	76	117	0.65	1.016	6.06	22	37	0.60	1.010	1.41
30	86	135	0.64	1.015	6.84	75	125	0.60	1.006	1.93
Ave.	70.4	102.2	0.72	1.021	6.18	48.8	81.0	0.63	1.007	1.52
						B&H Ave.Return Rate				1.70

Table 9. Performance results for Experiment 3-3.

Experiment 3-4 10-Stocks Fitness=TRN										
	In-Sample (2003-2004)					Out-of-Sample (2005-2006)				
Exp. No.	WCT	N	WRT	ARN	TRN	WCT	N	WRT	ARN	TRN
1	11	14	0.79	1.162	7.44	0	0	NA	1.000	1.00
2	15	19	0.79	1.127	8.81	0	0	NA	1.000	1.00
3	7	7	1.00	1.339	7.28	0	0	NA	1.000	1.00
4	9	10	0.90	1.230	7.31	0	0	NA	1.000	1.00
5	6	6	1.00	1.382	6.87	0	0	NA	1.000	1.00
6	9	9	1.00	1.274	8.35	0	0	NA	1.000	1.00
7	20	26	0.77	1.087	7.77	15	25	0.60	1.000	0.95
8	9	9	1.00	1.274	8.35	0	0	NA	1.000	1.00
9	13	15	0.87	1.149	7.49	2	2	1.00	1.111	1.23
10	20	26	0.77	1.091	7.99	5	5	1.00	1.116	1.71
Ave.	11.9	14.1	0.89	1.212	7.77	2.2	3.2	0.87	1.023	1.09
						B&H Ave. Return Rate				1.63

Table 10. Performance results for Experiment 3-4.

Experiment 3-5 10-Stocks Fitness=TRN*WCT*WRT*ARN										
	In-Sample (2003-2004)					Out-of-Sample (2005-2006)				
Exp. No.	WCT	N	WRT	ARN	TRN	WCT	N	WRT	ARN	TRN
1	41	43	0.95	1.031	3.73	28	33	0.85	1.017	1.68
2	33	33	1.00	1.040	3.62	0	0	NA	1.000	1.00
3	68	95	0.72	1.015	4.03	5	7	0.71	1.019	1.14
4	24	28	0.86	1.077	6.74	4	5	0.80	1.105	1.63
5	29	43	0.67	1.038	4.29	21	40	0.53	1.012	1.49
6	41	43	0.95	1.031	3.73	31	35	0.89	1.018	1.82
7	26	32	0.81	1.049	4.41	15	28	0.54	1.016	1.50
8	59	67	0.88	1.023	4.42	23	34	0.68	1.005	1.15
9	14	16	0.88	1.147	8.48	0	0	NA	1.000	1.00
10	51	68	0.75	1.017	2.86	38	59	0.64	1.002	1.05
Ave.	38.6	46.8	0.85	1.047	4.63	16.5	24.1	0.70	1.019	1.35
						B&H Ave. Return Rate				1.63

Table 11. Performance results for Experiment 3-5.

8.6 Discussions for third step experiments

There are three points to discuss for this section. First point is that some model traders demonstrated extremely good performances. This happened for a somewhat large group of stock names, 50. The results so far shown are good from a general point view as well. However, it does not mean we can always get such good results. Nonetheless, it demonstrated that some model traders exist which could bring about extremely good results maybe depending on the situations and timing. Therefore we should keep investigating what kinds of stock groups are profitable.

Second is that the same GA process works differently depending on the time period. One time, it works extremely well; on another time it works very poorly. We like to seek what would cause such differences. This may be significant because some solutions may exist behind the difference.

Third is a special point of the second. It is related with what is essentially important for good model traders for both of training period and testing one, say in any situation. It is probably true that there is not such a consistent general matter. However, the two experiments Experiment 3-2 and Experiment 3-4 demonstrated that the fitness of Equation (10) brought the change to the trading quantity and quality as well as the TRN increase. That is, the winning number of trading increased and the individual trading profit rate declined. This suggests that it may be possible to control the quantity and quality of trading by the fitness and that there is also a possibility of profit related general matters around those indexes. It is worth investigating those indexes further. We hope there is even only a bit of essential generality around them.

9. Discussions for what to seek

Much difficulty comes from the facts that the spaces of in-sample and out-of-sample data are so wide that cause and effect relations are hard to find. In addition, there may exist many factors which do not appear in data. The space widths, the ever-changing market conditions and often contradicting data of the market are considered to be major causes of overfitting and instability.

What we need is a stable good performance model trader with generality. It is, however, true that we can find a good trader for in-sample data. We want the created trader will work well again for unseen out-of-sample data with good probability. What we like to seek is the factors, which are extracted for the in-sample data, which play important roles for the out-of-sample data, too. Those factors should play important roles for out-of-sample data thus reducing overfitting. One of the important points is that frequently repeated events for in-sample data would happen again, hopefully repeatedly and frequently for unseen out-of-sample data.

In our social world, events which happened many time for a period are expected to happen many times again for other period, too. Stock market events are not exceptions. So it is considered important to find a model trader that can catch the profitable and frequent trading events.

In the above sense, the factors of Equation (10) are considered important. The equation for the fitness affected significantly the quantity and quality of trading. Those of profit related indexes are considered consistently important for both of in-sample and out-of-sample periods and in any situation, should play important roles for organizing a good stable model trader even if it may depends on random processes. Including those indexes, we should keep seeking indexes which are of more consistent, general and profit bringing matters.

10. Conclusion

The following are concluded:

1. Overfitting is defined somewhat formally as Equation (5).
2. Trading opportunity increased by increasing data size. This decreased overfitting. Some experiments verified it numerically.
3. Trading chances appear in many places among stock names.
4. Stock switching demonstrated good results.
5. Increased number for stock names demonstrated some extremely good results.
   Some model traders with switching from one stock to another showed the big performance improvement in experiments.
6. The same GA process which worked well in some situations does not necessarily work well for other situations.
7. Generally acceptable profit related matters which work well consistently in any situations should be sought.
8. Equation (10) for fitness demonstrated the potential ability to create a stable profitable model trader, and experiments suggests that equation and the related indexes have some potential to control quantity and quality of trading.

11. References

Becker, L. A. & Seshadri, M. (2003a). Comprehensibility and Overfitting Avoidance in GENETIC PROGRAMMING, *Worcester Polytechnic Institute, Computer Science Technical Report WPI-CS-TR-03-09*, Retrieved from http://www.cs.wpi.edu/Resources/techreports.html?/

Becker, L. A. & Seshadri, M. (2003b). GP-Evolved Technical Trading Rules can Outperform Buy and Hold, *Worcester Polytechnic Institute, Computer Science technical Report WPI-CS-TR-03-16*, Retrieved from http://www.cs.wpi.edu/Resources/techreports.html?/

Geurts, P. (2005). Bias vs Variance Decomposition for Regression and Classification In: *The Data Mining and Knowledge Discovery Handbook*, Maimon, O. & Rokach, L. (Eds.), pp.749-763, Springer, ISBN-10: 0-387-24435-2

He, H.; Chen, J.; Jin, H. & Chen, S. H. (2007). Trading Strategies Based on K-means Clustering and Regression Models, In *Computational Intelligence in Economics and Finance, Vol. II*, Chen, S. H. ; Wang, P. P. & Kuo, T. W. (Eds.), pp.123-134, Springer

Kurokawa, T. (2005). Evolutionary Stock Trading Method by Effective Catching of Market Recovery Reaction, *The Proceedings of the 6th International Symposium on Advanced Intelligent Systems*, pp.806-811, Yeosu, Korea

Kurokawa, T. (2007). Evolutionary Method to Optimize Composite Indicator for Market Timing, *The Proceedings of the 8th International Symposium on Advanced Intelligent Systems*, pp.264-269

Kurokawa, T. (2008). On Overfitting of Technical Market Timing with Evolutionary Process—Effects of In-Sample Data Selection, *The Proceedings of the 9th APIEMS-2008*, pp.451-458, Bali, Indonesia

Kurokawa, T. (2009). Learning and Technical Market—Effects of In-Sample Data Selection, *Journal of Advanced Computational Intelligence and Intelligent Informatics*, Vol.13, No. 6, pp.726-730, ISSN 1343-0130

Kurokawa, T. (2011). Stock Trading with Genetic Algorithm-Switching from One Stock to Another, *Journal of Communication and Computer*, Vol.8, No.2, pp.143-149, ISSN 1548-7709

Lam, S. S. ; Lam, K. P. & Ng, H. S. (2002). Genetic Fuzzy Expert Trading System for NASDAQ Stock Market Timing, In: *Genetic Algorithms and Genetic Programming in Computational Finance*, Chen, S. H., (Ed.), pp.197-217, Kluwer Academic Publishers, ISBN 0-7923-7601-3, Massachusetts, USA

Lin, L. ; Cao, L. & Zhang, C. (2005). Genetic Algorithms for Robust Optimization in Financial Applications, *Proceedings of the Fourth IASTED International Conference of Computational Intelligence*, pp.387-391

Lohpetch, D. & Corne, D. (2010). Outperforming Buy and Hold with Evolved Technical Trading: Daily, Weekly and Monthly Trading In: *Application of Evolutionary Computation 2010 Proceeding, Part II*, Chio, C. D. et al. (Eds.) , pp. 171-181, Springer-Verlag, Berlin Heidelberg, ISBN-10: 3-642-12241-8

Mabu, S. ; Hirasawa, K. & Furuzuki, T. (2007). Trading Rules on Stock Markets Using Genetic Network Programming with Reinforcement Learning and Importance Index, *Transaction of IEE Japan C*, Vol.127, No. 7, pp.1061-1067

Neely, C. ; Weller, P. & Ditmar, R. (1997). Is Technical Analysis In The Foreign Exchange Market Profitable? --- A Genetic Programming Approach, *Journal of Financial and Quantitative Analysis*, Vol.32, No.4, pp405-427

Pavlidis, N. G. ; Pavlidis, E. G. ; Epitropakis, M. G. ; Plagianakos, V. P. & Vrahatis, M. N. (2007). Computational Intelligence Algorithms for Risk-Adjusted Trading Strategies, *IEEE Congress on Evolutionary Computation (CEC)*, pp.540-547, ISBN 978-1-4244-1339-3

Potvin, J. Y.; Soriano, P. & Vallee, M. (2004). Generating Trading Rules On The Stock Markets With Genetic Programming, *Computers & Operations Research*, Vol. 31, pp.1033-1047

Takizawa, T. (1999). *SP-Wave Method*, Pan-Rolling Publishing, Tokyo, Japan

Wang, J. & Chen, S. (1998). Evolutionary Stock Trading Decision Support System Using Sliding Window, *Proceedings of the IEEE Conference on Evolutionary Computation*, pp.253-258